CW00530811

STRIKING BACK

STRIKING BACK

The End of Peace in Cyberspace
– And How to Restore It

Lucas Kello

YALE UNIVERSITY PRESS
NEW HAVEN AND LONDON

Copyright © 2022 Lucas Kello

All rights reserved. This book may not be reproduced in whole or in part, in any form (beyond that copying permitted by Sections 107 and 108 of the U.S. Copyright Law and except by reviewers for the public press) without written permission from the publishers.

For information about this and other Yale University Press publications, please contact:
U.S. Office: sales.press@yale.edu   yalebooks.com
Europe Office: sales@yaleup.co.uk   yalebooks.co.uk

Set in Adobe Garamond Pro by IDSUK (DataConnection) Ltd
Printed in Great Britain by TJ Books, Padstow, Cornwall

Library of Congress Control Number: 2022939727

ISBN 978-0-300-24668-1

A catalogue record for this book is available from the British Library.

10 9 8 7 6 5 4 3 2 1

CONTENTS

INTRODUCTION
The Evolving Menace of Technological Aggression

1972: PRELUDE TO OUR TIMES

Markus Wolf, the Stasi's chief of foreign activities, needed one thing to execute his plot: a viable target for bribery and blackmail among West Germany's politicians. It was the spring of 1972, a turning point in Cold War relations. Willy Brandt's election as chancellor three years earlier had produced a relaxation of tensions in Europe under the mantle of *Ostpolitik*. Brandt's signature foreign policy delivered notable spoils to the Communist bloc: a non-aggression treaty fixing the location of contested borders in Eastern Europe, formal recognition of Poland, commercial ties that could fuel economic growth, and a cross-border transit agreement. A calmer and stabler continent on which to pursue greater integration and arms reduction was in the offing. Gone were the decades of intense standoff, not least over the troubled status of West Berlin.[1]

Wolf and his political masters worried, however. Spoilers in the Bundestag threatened to ruin the mood of conciliation and deny Communists their prizes. Chief among them was Bundestag opposition leader Rainer Barzel of the Christian Democratic Union. Sensing an opportunity to replace Brandt as chancellor, Barzel prompted a parliamentary vote of no confidence in the government. He opposed Brandt's economic opening and diplomatic rapprochement with the East. Communists throughout Europe looked on with concern. The cherished *Ostpolitik* was in peril of parliamentary derailment.

And so began "Protect Brandt Week," an information campaign headed by Wolf under Moscow's instructions. The aim of the operation was to infiltrate the political firmament in Bonn and save Brandt – or rather, his policy – by disrupting the confidence vote. The very future of East–West relations was at stake.

Wolf found his target in Leo Wagner. The Bavarian Bundestag member from the Christian Social Union hardly fit the code name "Lion" that was given by his Stasi handlers. Wagner's recruitment by the Stasi played out over several years. Operatives of Department X of the Main Directorate for Reconnaissance (HVA), which was responsible for information campaigns, had long monitored him. His intelligence profile noted: "Catholic, married, two children" – a picture of moral probity that did not accord with the secret reality of his nocturnal excursions. Among Stasi spies, he had the reputation of an unreliable debtor and an alcoholic scoundrel. Rumors had it that in a single night he spent thousands of deutschmarks on women and drinks. And yet he enjoyed high esteem among party officials. Fellow lawmakers did not foresee his path to personal and financial ruin. East German intelligence officials were more perceptive. "We tried to recruit Leo Wagner because he was so open to attack, especially for financial reasons," recalled former Stasi agent Horst Kopp.[2] This tale of political drama features no protagonists, only antagonists.

The hook was ready to be dangled. Wagner had made first contact with the Stasi in the mid-1960s when he met Georg Fleissman, a Bavarian journalist and recruiter on Wolf's team. Fleissman now showered the libertine Lion with money to fund his extravagances. "He just wanted to receive the money and maintain his lifestyle," explained Kopp.[3] Finding himself in a position where refusal to cooperate seemed impossible because it would expose his depravities to the public, Wagner almost immediately acceded to Fleissman's request to abstain in the Bundestag vote.[4]

The vote that decided Brandt's political fate on April 27, 1972, was tight. Merely two abstentions, Wagner's and Julius Steiner's, among Brandt's political opponents, ensured his and his foreign policy's survival (Stasi agents, it later emerged, had also bribed Steiner, another lost soul). The voting outcome was celebrated not only in the Chancellery but also in the Stasi headquarters on Ruschestrasse and in the Kremlin.

CYBERSPACE AND THREATS TO DEMOCRATIC INTEGRITY

Nothing in the Wagner episode stands out in the context of the current cyber revolution. Its main elements are familiar to us today: intense geopolitical rivalry between the Kremlin and the West; a fractured political scene within democracies; some Western politicians hewing a closer line towards the adversary without grasping its opportunistic maneuvers; and naïve party figures assuming rather than questioning the integrity of their personal communications and the secrecy of their private lives. The Wagner episode seems like a rehearsal for our own times. And like foreign electoral interference today, the Communist bloc's intervention in West German domestic politics had more global than domestic implications.

In short, the principles and objectives of Russian information warfare remain largely the same today as in the Cold War. But its scope and methods have changed dramatically. In relation to contemporary threats against democratic systems, the episode of 1972 is as much an analogy as it is a disanalogy; we can derive relevant insights from it while also identifying differences.

In Wagner's time, before the era of the "social" Internet, foreign interference in Western domestic politics played out in a limited arena. The list of viable targets was small. Relevant information with which to ensnare them was difficult and costly to acquire. A successful intrusion required as sordid and feeble a character as Wagner operating at the heart of the democratic polity. Aided by misinformation traveling the radio waves and, more laboriously, the print media, Communist agents could achieve greater public effect than if their activities remained strictly private, as a form of blackmail. But still their information campaigns were typically circumscribed within a small locality or region. True, Department X often supplemented its campaigns with publicly diffused disinformation – for instance, the joint KGB–Stasi Operation INFEKTION that ran between 1983 and 1987 and which falsely attributed the origins of the HIV virus to a bioweapons research lab in Maryland.[5] But generally, the private information space was a more potent operational realm than the public information space.

The explosive expansion of cyberspace and especially the Internet during the last two decades has radically altered this situation. Today, an aspiring intruder into democratic politics has at his disposal nearly the entire political class among which to select possible targets of compromise. For who is the politician who has never shared imprudences in an email or snapped indecencies on a mobile phone which are then accessible by sophisticated foreign hackers?

Hacking is only the latter stage of the problem; its essential precondition is the digitization of vast aspects of both public and private life that were never before captured in electronic form.

The hacking activities of Russian military agents during the 2016 U.S. presidential election reveal the magnitude of the contemporary problem. In July 2016, two candidates faced each other in the race to represent the Democratic Party against Republican Party nominee Donald Trump in the presidential vote in November of that year. Bernie Sanders, the senator and former congressman representing Vermont who had until recently eschewed party affiliations, was the maverick option. He had disdained, often publicly, much of the Democratic Party's established figures and policies. His opponent for the nomination was Hillary Clinton. As the former secretary of state under President Barack Obama and the wife of ex-President Bill Clinton, she was the conventional candidate. Sanders was a figure of revolutionary disruption within the party; Clinton was one of continuity. The former secretly worried many Democratic Party stalwarts for his promise to remake the party's image; the latter represented a force of stability who promised invigoration through constancy.

Therein lay the problem: although the party chiefs were meant to exercise strict neutrality in the candidate's selection, many Sanders supporters suspected that the leadership secretly favored Clinton. WikiLeaks' release of private email messages obtained by hackers from the GRU – the intelligence unit of the Russian military's general staff – three days before the Democratic Convention, a time designed to cause maximum political discord within the party, gave proof to the lie of impartiality. The leaks revealed that party chairwoman Debbie Wasserman Schultz and other senior party figures in fact did favor Clinton. Public confirmation of the prejudice against Sanders instigated a crisis of legitimacy within the party among his voters. When Clinton was nominated, a fierce insurrection erupted within the party that may have cost Clinton enough Democratic votes in crucial swing states to deny her victory against Trump in November – a plausible if unprovable scenario.[6]

The GRU's hack was remarkable for its brazenness and sophistication. Although innovative, the operation was neither new nor isolated. It fit a larger program of activity of using computer information as a tool to influence human minds and as a weapon to disrupt machine functions – both with the aim of sowing discord and division within the polity in order to weaken U.S. foreign policy resolve and influence abroad. Information warfare in the cyber era had come of age.

THE WEST'S PUNISHMENT PROBLEM

The current cyber revolution brings forth new problems of security strategy. One in particular bedevils Western nations: the punishment problem. Repeatedly, other nations use cyberspace to assail their political and economic interests.[7] Repeatedly, Western leaders warn about the gravity of such actions. The White House depicted the Sony Pictures hack in 2014 as a "serious national security matter."[8] National Security Advisor John Bolton described Russia's public release of hacked email records of the Democratic Party during the 2016 U.S. presidential election as "an act of war against our constitutional structures."[9] The head of Britain's MI6 intelligence agency warned that the manipulation of social media by foreign powers during the "Brexit" referendum presented "a fundamental threat to our [nation's] sovereignty," adding: "They should be a concern to all those who share democratic values."[10] French President Emmanuel Macron decried Russian hackers' release of private emails belonging to his campaign staffers in 2017 as an attempt at "democratic destabilization" during a presidential election.[11] Amid the Covid-19 pandemic, European Commission President Ursula von der Leyen chastised China for intruding upon European public health infrastructures, warning that such behavior "cannot be tolerated."[12]

And yet repeatedly, Western nations failed – with few exceptions – to punish the offenders in order to deter them. Obama promised firm penalties against North Korea; only weak economic sanctions followed. In 2016, he publicly rebuked Russia for the Democratic Party hack, but merely expelled some Russian diplomats and issued some narrowly targeted financial sanctions. "The punishment did not fit the crime," lamented former U.S. ambassador to Russia Michael McFaul. "Russia violated our sovereignty, meddling in one of our most sacred acts as a democracy – electing our president. The Kremlin should have paid a much higher price for that attack. And U.S. policymakers now – both in the White House and Congress – should consider new actions to deter future Russian interventions."[13] Another Obama Administration official similarly criticized his government's response: "It is the hardest thing about my entire time in government to defend. I feel like we sort of choked."[14] Macron's foreign policy advisor warned that France had "a doctrine of retaliation when it comes to Russian cyberattacks," adding ominously: "We are ready to retaliate to cyber-attacks not just in kind but with any other conventional measure."[15] Yet, no punishment ensued for the intervention in the election. French authorities did not even attempt to intimidate the hackers by revealing their identities, which over time could help to build reputations of behavior through signaling and learning procedures.[16] So far, the European Union has not levied any penalties for China's health system intrusions. Riven by internal division, the Union remains largely quiescent against foreign cyber threats, sanctioning, for example, just a small number of individuals and organizations for incidents as significant as Operation Cloud Hopper, a multi-year Chinese espionage campaign targeting private corporations on six continents.[17] Meanwhile, some EU member states continue to source vital infrastructure components from Huawei and other Chinese companies despite warnings of compromised security.[18]

In the highly classified cyber domain, where states often operate covertly – whether because divulging an operation's existence can reveal the vulnerabilities it exploits in the adversary's systems or because the attacking nation does not want to attract political and diplomatic attention to its actions – it is possible that some punishments are publicly unobservable. Researchers, however, must formulate their analysis on the basis of available evidence; if they entertain a conjecture, they must extrapolate from evidence in relevant incidents. A considerable number of years has now transpired since Western nations began to experience strategic cyberattacks by other states or their non-state sympathizers.[19] Has any new evidence emerged showing sterner responses than previously seen? So far, no. No new information has revealed major punishments for the actions against Sony Pictures, U.S. and French demo-cratic institutions, and other strategic incidents. Until such evidence emerges, analysts must assume that governments have not secretly punished cyber activity more firmly than has been observed. At any rate, secret punishment would complicate third-party deterrence: it weakens the message of retaliation to other aspiring attackers. A former senior British government official questioned the thesis of covert punishment in cyberspace: "Very often, nothing is said about a response – not because it was classified, but because nothing actually happened."[20]

In short, the West suffers from a problem of *under-proportionate response*: it fails to punish cyber intrusions sufficiently to convince adversaries that the retaliatory costs outweigh the gains.

Officials are aware of this problem. About the threat posed by Russia and China, U.S. Director of National Intelligence Daniel Coats asserted: "These states are using cyber operations as a low-cost tool of statecraft, and we assess that they will work to use cyber operations to achieve strategic objectives unless they face clear repercussions for their cyber operations."[21] Governments have not let these acts go entirely without a response. Foreign culprits have been indicted, targeted sanctions have flowed, disabling preemptive measures have struck – for example, during the U.S. mid-term elections in 2018, Cyber Command disrupted the Russian Internet Research Agency's network connection.[22] Some leaders see the necessity for a united stance that maintains the sinews of strength, but they lament its absence. "I think Western nations, quite naturally, are not interested in seeing any sort of escalation," mused Estonian defense minister Sven Mikser in 2014. "But when dealing with any sort of regime like that of Mr Putin's, weakness is more provocative than strength. It is very important that the West is . . . strong and united. That is the best way to deter Russia."[23]

Yet, the responses have not significantly diminished the intensity of offensive actions. Aggressors are often named but rarely shamed, sternly rebuked but only meekly punished, harassed but largely undeterred.

The apparent success of deterrence against true acts of cyberwar is a notable achievement, especially in light of naïve warnings of a "Cyber 9/11" or a "Cyber Pearl Harbor."[24] But below the threshold of war, adversaries have not been rebuffed forcefully enough to prevent further ordeals. In July 2019, Microsoft reported that Russian and North Korean actors had conducted political hacking activities against presidential campaign targets in the United States. Three months later, the company warned that state-backed Iranian hackers were targeting the email accounts of almost three thousand U.S. government officials, presidential campaign officers, and journalists. U.S. officials considered striking Iran's computer infrastructure in retaliation; evidence for such an action actually having taken place does not exist.[25] Even after suffering a slew of financial sanctions and criminal indictments between 2016 and 2020, Russian state hackers continued to penetrate the most prized U.S. governmental systems.

In one major incident, the "SolarWinds" intrusion, authorities suspected the presence of Russian hackers in thousands of computers in more than a dozen federal departments and agencies. Microsoft president Brad Smith described the incident as "the largest and most sophisticated [cyber]attack the world has ever seen."[26] Joe Biden used the opportunity of his first phone call as president with Vladimir Putin to protest the intrusions. Even so, prominent former officials and analysts warned about the danger of spiraling conflict from the United States hitting back too hard, or even at all.[27] A series of targeted sanctions issued by the Biden Administration in 2021 partly sought to impose costs on Russia for the intrusion.[28] They achieved no notable deterrent effect. One year after the discovery of this sweeping intrusion operation, the culprits remained highly active. They continued to refine their tradecraft to sustain a persistent presence within compromised systems.[29] The failure to carry out dissuasive repercussions in the cyber domain endures as a sore point for Western policymakers.

Why and how this situation arose, and what to do about it, is the subject of this book, which argues that the prevailing Western strategy for cyber-conflict reduction has failed spectacularly.

THE CHANGING TIDES OF MODERN CONFLICT

Western responses to offensive cyber operations have emphasized the centrality of existing international law and norms in regulating state conduct. Officials perceive the legal framework as a tool to introduce predictability and reduce risk in an unruly domain of conflict.[30] Let us call this approach *cyber legalism* for its attachment to the appurtenances of the international legal system.[31] The current legal and normative framework is not adequate for the purpose that many policymakers and analysts ascribe to it,[32] because it does not provide sufficient grounds to credibly respond to invasive actions falling short of war.

Nor can the framework be easily reformed owing to fundamental differences in legal interpretation among large nations. Legal scholars have made much progress in evaluating the application of legal and ethical standards of proportionality and discrimination to cyber conflict.[33] There remain, however, glaring gaps in thinking and practice, especially on the question of the relationship between legal doctrine and strategic doctrine – how a particular interpretation of the former constrains the latter's development.

What is required instead is a pragmatic benchmark of cyber response that focuses not on building an ideal world among norm-abiding rivals, but on achieving *results*: the successful prevention of future hostile actions, not merely above the war threshold, where deterrence is working, but also below it, where current policy routinely fails to prevent harm against democratic institutions and economic infrastructures. The existing legal system does not supply a framework on which to build norms and design policy that satisfies such a benchmark.

The solution to contemporary security problems, therefore, must be found not primarily in current law and norms, but in the refinement of doctrine: figuring out how to respond to activity – in order to deter its recurrence – that international legal traditions and security strategy do not ordinarily recognize as punishable.

The main source of Western policy paralysis is a doctrinal failure to grasp the changing tides of modern conflict. Traditionally, war has been the principal force of change in international affairs. The First World War consumed three historical empires – Tsarist Russia, Imperial Germany, and Austria-Hungary – out of whose remains emerged the twentieth century's two transforming ideologies, Communism and Fascism. The Second World War crushed the European great powers that had dominated world politics for centuries, enabling the emergence of two non-European superpowers in the mid-twentieth century, the United States and the Soviet Union.[34]

The era since the late twentieth century has been different. The relevance of war to historical transformation has diminished. War no longer alters history as it did in the past. War today often plays an essentially conservative function: it preserves the existing international order more than undermining it – as in the First Iraq War (to correct the transgression of Saddam Hussein's invasion of

Kuwait) or NATO's air campaign against Libya (to stop Muammar Gaddafi's violent suppression of civilian protestors).

Relative to the rich history of warfighting in the last century, a distinctive feature of conflict in the current century is the silencing of guns among large nations. Their leaders grasp that even a minor armed confrontation among them is almost inconceivable because its consequences would be economically and politically ruinous.

True, some world leaders behave as if the choice to use arms in an epochal war still existed. Leaders in Moscow and Pyongyang threaten to annihilate their foreign enemies with thermonuclear weapons. The regime in Russia has deployed its military to settle territorial disputes along its geographic periphery. Think of the incursion into Georgia in 2008, the annexation of Crimea in 2014, or the ruthless invasion of Ukraine in 2022 – classic land grabs befitting the era of tank warfare and aerial combat that marred much of international politics in the twentieth century. And in some regions, such as the Middle East, civil war and armed intervention endure as a blight of diplomacy.[35] If anything, however, the tragedy and brutalities of war in Ukraine remind us of just how ruinous a direct war involving Russia or China and the United States or Britain would be economically and in human terms. Large nations – especially nuclear powers – threaten war primarily to avoid it. This situation does not guarantee the avoidance of war; unwanted and accidental war can still occur with possibly catastrophic results. Rather, it means that the main geopolitical competitors seek to resolve their quarrels primarily in other planes of conflict. Even as the risk and costs of war on the periphery of relations among large nations increase, the prospect of a millenarian clash among them remains low. That is how to interpret Putin's allusion to nuclear annihilation at the start of the Ukraine war in February 2022: he rattled the atom in order not to have to use it.[36]

Less war does not mean more peaceful means of rivalry, however; these too have waned in relevance. All of the cyber incidents described above share a defining characteristic: their cumulative effects inflicted greater political, social, and economic damage than even some isolated acts of conventional war, yet their non-violent nature placed them below war's legal and institutional definition. It is important to realize, though, that these incidents also violated the definition of peace: a state of restrained rivalry (if not comity) and respect for sovereignty in which nations are largely free to manage their internal political and economic affairs without decisive foreign intervention – a situation that statesmen normally aspire to achieve for their nation in the midst of international anarchy.

Not long ago, some analysts optimistically celebrated the emergence of an era of "cyber peace" marked by tolerable acts of minor aggression.[37] It is true that non-violent cyber actions present states with potential alternatives to real war, such as the use of the "Stuxnet" worm instead of conventional airstrikes to destroy nuclear enrichment centrifuges at the Natanz nuclear facility in Iran. Others, however, enable more damaging forms of conflict below that threshold: for example, the disruption of a small country's financial infrastructure or a large nation's democratic election remotely and surreptitiously, which would be difficult to achieve with arms of war. The statements of leaders cited above reveal that they do not want to tolerate such acts of aggression, which they nevertheless struggle to punish. The absence of major war among geopolitical opponents cannot obscure the fact that we live in a period of intense technological rivalry – one that Western nations are currently losing.

Western strategic thinking fails to address a central truth: much of modern interstate rivalry fits neither the destructive criteria of war nor the acceptable boundaries of peace. Rather, it is *unpeace*, or mid-spectrum rivalry, which is more damaging than traditional peacetime activity (such as financial sanctions or criminal indictments), but not physically violent like war.[38] Although states have conducted sabotage, assassinations, special operations, and covert action throughout history, unpeace is different because direct forms of violence do not occur, nor are they threatened.

Unpeace has limits. Even the most potent computer code cannot conquer territory. And while it might coerce state behavior, it cannot do so easily. Rather, its main strategic utility is another: to debilitate adversaries from within. Strategic cyber activity primarily seeks not to alter adversaries' behavior – although that is possible – but to weaken it by degrading their political institutions, social cohesion, and economic infrastructures. The central premise of the method is that the dilution of policy can deliver some of the strategic gains of reversing it, while avoiding the serious penalties that the use of force and overt coercion can elicit. To coerce a large nation bent on pursuing its policy entails

11

an enormous contest of wills; it requires the mobilization of many resources and risks grave outcomes. Conflict methods below the war line can avoid them. In the realm of unpeace, more relevant than altering policy is weakening it and its makers. There is also the matter of *absolute* harm: even if cyber activity does not alter or weaken policy, it can still cause political and economic harm on a scale that affects national security.

One often hears – correctly – about the absence so far of war in cyberspace. A less obvious but equally important point concerns the loss of peace. The period since the Second World War that political scientist Steven Pinker labelled the "long peace" between large powers is, more accurately, a long absence of epochal war among them.[39] But in the current circumstances of incessant technological conflict among the large powers, the absence of war no longer means the prevalence of peace. Unpeace has become a more relevant force of change in international politics than war itself. Nations can use cyberspace to achieve some of the political and strategic objectives of war: interfering with another nation's governmental institutions, disrupting its economy or financial system, seizing its military and financial assets, crippling its public administration and communications infrastructure, disrupting its civilian power supply, and so on – all without firing a single shot.[40] The lack of deterring penalties betrays not tolerance of aggression but a failure to devise a response strategy commensurate with the legal and doctrinal peculiarities of technological unpeace.

Cyberspace is an intelligence-rich domain. For this reason, some thinkers have fallen into the temptation of analogizing cyber activity with the logic of espionage.[41] Important differences exist in the activity's scale (think of NotPetya's disruption of global shipping),[42] remoteness (imagine foreign agents infiltrating a nation's vital infrastructure without actually being physically present), and variety of threat actors (consider the vast universe of state and non-state players with possibly unknown motives and aims who participate in some large cyber operations).

But there is more. Cyberspace is altering the aims and methods of espionage. In the traditional logic of espionage, stolen information generally loses its value the more it is shared or publicly disclosed. Although much espionage in cyberspace seeks to remain in the shadows (as in the SolarWinds and

Microsoft Exchange hacks),[43] increasingly it willingly comes to light. No longer content with merely using stolen secrets quietly, adversaries now more frequently seize information in order to reveal it publicly, such as in "kompromat" (or hack-and-leak) operations.[44] And that is the point: to release stolen information publicly in order to cause political or social disruption. In relation to conventional intelligence gathering, then, some forms of cyber espionage represent a difference in kind and not in degree. Rather than being shaped by the traditional logic of intelligence gathering, developments in cyberspace have altered it.

It was not always so. Computers have existed since the 1940s, a few years after the English mathematician Alan Turing conceived of them. For decades, they enhanced the functions of military weapons systems (such as naval guns), the operations of private businesses (such as accounting), and the access to election data (such as voter registration records). Yet, problems of computer security did not emerge until the late 1980s – almost two decades after the launch of the Internet's first iteration, ARPANET. Since the infamous "Morris Worm" caused a partitioning of the Internet in 1988, threats to computers and networks have rapidly grown. In 1995, a daring hacker named Kevin Poulsen infiltrated the phone network in Los Angeles to ensure that he was the 102nd caller in a local radio contest offering a Porsche 944 S2 (Poulsen won the car and a short prison sentence). In 2002, criminals targeted all thirteen Domain Name System root servers with torrents of data, prompting the Internet's brief interruption. Humorous as such incidents might seem today, they were all criminal affairs – matters for prosecutors and defense lawyers to address, rather than concerns of diplomats and national defense officials.

In brief, cyberspace during most of its long existence was in a state of peace – meaning that it was not a domain of strategic action and nefarious state activity. Mainly criminals threatened its operations. Governments were broadly able to exercise sovereign control over their internal information space. With few exceptions, such as in the "Moonlight Maze" intrusion by Russian hackers in 1996 or the "Titan Rain" infiltration by Chinese operatives in 2003,[45] cyberspace was not a realm of national security significance. That situation changed dramatically in the early 2000s with the advent of nation-state hacking against financial and governmental systems. Vast quarters of the virtual realm have become arenas of geopolitical contention. Vanished is the peaceful era when "hacking" denoted not state threats against orderly elections and the integrity of government, but sportive antics among a niche of specialists unconcerned with interstate dealings.

Yet, the rigid thinking about war and peace prevails in Western capitals. Officials to be sure increasingly recognize the reality of unpeace without, however, sufficiently adapting to it. As U.S. Cyber Command noted: "Adversaries continuously operate against us below the threshold of armed conflict. In this 'new normal,' our adversaries are extending their influence without resorting to physical aggression. They provoke and intimidate our citizens and enterprises without fear of legal or military consequences."[46]

Recognizing the problem of unpeace, however, is not the same as addressing it adequately. The unfinished – possibly unbegun – task is to develop *spectral* rather than binary security doctrines and more versatile methods. The refinement of doctrine to guide strategic action in the new genus of conflict remains primitive, even if its legal and normative enterprise is robust, because the West is so behind in doctrinal ingenuity. Because security policy still operates mainly within the bounds of the war–peace binary, yet much of security competition is increasingly neither one nor the other, this policy approach produces seriously flawed results.

Western understandings of modern conflict either prioritize the language of war or fuse the opposite notions of war and peace into a single, convoluted phenomenon. The vague term "hybrid war" that mars much doctrinal writing illustrates this flawed conception. The term ordinarily denotes the combination of war and non-violent means of conflict, often by a mix of state actors and private citizens acting with or without their government's direction, such as in the cyberattacks against the National Bank of Georgia in August 2008 during the country's military invasion by Russia.[47] It offers little analytical value; the existence of conventional acts of war situates the scenario, legally and politically, within the framework of armed attack. If, however, the term denotes actions that are not traditionally warlike, then it merely emphasizes what we already knew: the activity was not violent, in which case the term hybrid war is misleading.

Slogans of "Warfare during Peacetime" that are popular among Western politicians are similarly flawed. The 2016 Republican Party Platform declared:

"Russia and China see cyber operations as a part of a warfare strategy during peacetime."[48] This is a splendid fallacy: war and peace are definitionally exclusive. Such utterances hold intuitive appeal because the activity in question is neither warlike nor peaceful – but nor, logically, can it be both at once. Other examples of conceptual acrobatics are "next-generation warfare" and "non-linear warfare," terms for information operations that are popular among Russian military thinkers. They, too, are misleading – perhaps purposefully so. This activity appeals to Russian strategists precisely *because* its non-violent consequences fall short of war, even as it often surpasses the tolerable limits of peacetime competition. Analytically, the blurring of the concepts of war and peace is sloppy; policy-wise, it is a formula for disaster.

More specifically, this book exposes the failure of Western strategy to address three major challenges lying at the forefront of current debates about national security. One is defensive: the failure to protect against foreign intrusion in or damage to domestic information spaces while preserving democratic values of freedom and openness. Autocratic nations such as Russia and China are able to manage their information spaces centrally with heavy-handed surveillance and censorship measures that confer advantages in information security. They are contrary to liberal democratic values, however. Instead, Western governments must preserve openness while developing effective defenses against pervasive and continually changing information threats. They must do so, moreover, in conjunction with private technology firms, such as Facebook and Twitter, that are not subject to the centralized controls in which Russian and Chinese technology companies operate. Different to autocratic regimes, democratic governments cannot reasonably expect that multinational firms will obey a single political authority.

A second, graver policy error concerns the punishment problem. Because Western nations consistently fail to penalize offensive acts decisively, these acts continue unabated. Because security thinking privileges the legal and diplomatic conventions of traditional war, it struggles to deal with actions – no matter how damaging – that fall below its recognizable threshold of violence. The book proposes guidelines to orient the application of a superior strategy for countering technological threats that exist largely outside of the rigid confines of the legal system – a strategy rooted in the new concept of *punctuated deterrence*. Rather than penalizing traditional warlike actions, this approach can help to deter offensive tactics that are neither warlike nor peaceful. The book proposes solutions to contemporary technological aggression by exploring the conceivable application of punctuated deterrence in empirical contexts. It considers this defensive strategy's efficacy relative to classical deterrence techniques. The strategy of punctuated deterrence departs radically from the current punishment regime; it seeks to transform the psychological basis of adversaries' offensive calculations by focusing on responses to the cumulative effects of incessant cyber activity. The analysis also explores the use of innovative technological tools – such as Estonia's "data embassies" project – to address the widening defensive gap of cyberspace. Such defensive measures can enhance deterrence by denying adversaries the expectation of gains from cyberattacks. Key public figures feature prominently in these accounts. The book's discussion of current policy problems and suggestions for novel responses draw on new data generated in interviews with senior policy officials in the United States and Europe.[49]

A third shortcoming concerns not defensive losses but offensive gains: Western nations have been less adept than their main adversaries at devising principles of strategic competition in the technological realm. Here, again, is a splendid irony: the United States and Britain probably possess the most potent offensive computer code; their native technological bases are the best in the world. Furthermore, the United States still enjoys a preponderance of power in the conventional realm of conflict, beyond the cyber domain. Yet, material primacy has not yielded strategic accomplishment. As Russia and China rise to the top of the pantheon of nations, often challenging the institutions and values of the existing international order, the opportunities for the dominant players to exercise their power for strategic gain diminish. Although this book does not emphasize the adoption of the strategic offense, it is important to recognize the implications of a situation in which mainly autocratic nations seize it while their democratic victims eschew it.

Against this backdrop of Western policy failures, Russia and China have become the masters of the modern methods of technological conflict. In particular, Russia's intrepid actions reveal the superiority of its strategic cyber doctrine in an era of unpeace. Strategists in Moscow and Beijing grasp two essential truths better than their Western counterparts: first, in the twenty-first century, disruptive cyber methods can achieve some of the strategic effects of the destruction of war as well as new ones; and second, so long as their physical effects do not rise to the level of war, the action will largely go unpunished. U.S. Senator John McCain articulated the essence of the problem in 2017: "We don't have a policy and we don't have a strategy" for dealing with Russian cyber activity, adding: "it is the one aspect of our confrontation where I believe our adversaries are ahead of us."[50]

Technology lies at the heart of the story in these pages. Computers and information networks have exponentially expanded the interconnections among states' financial and economic systems, thereby increasing the possible cascading costs of war. Because of new inventions, the conceivable economic and social costs of direct armed conflict among large and especially nuclear powers have never been higher. New technology has helped to sustain a rational, if sometimes uneasy, state of rivalry among nations bent on avoiding their own destruction. But the state of peace has been largely lost. Technological change has enabled enduring harmful action, though mostly short of physical destruction. The same global network of computer infrastructures that helps to prevent war by elevating its costs also enables new forms of strategic harm without actually waging it.

To summarize a central argument of the book: the rise of challenger states in the international system has intensified the security competition among large nations, as geopolitical flashpoints in Europe and Asia-Pacific illustrate. The main contenders strive to avoid direct war among themselves while seeking new technological means of inflicting strategic pain short of it. The risk of war at the periphery of relations among large powers (think of Russia and Ukraine, China and Taiwan, or the United States and Iran) and the risk of unpeace in direct dealings among them rise concurrently – precisely because they wish to reduce the chances of an epochal military clash. Western nations' renunciation of unpeace, by failing to develop new doctrine appropriate to it, will place the international order at the mercy of the players most eager to defy it.

Much of the book's focus is on cyber conflict. But it is not the only concern. The analysis also considers the development of technologies such as data embassies, or backup government servers residing on foreign soil, which can affect

17

national security in ways that far transcend cybersecurity. New technological means of resilience and redundancy can provide advantages in the protection of governmental services and the polity's integrity against foreign manipulation.

A major theme of this work, then, is technological revolution, a historically recurring problem that has manifested throughout history, for example, from the advent of submarine warfare in the First World War to the emergence of mechanized warfare in the Second and the proliferation of nuclear weapons in the Cold War era. Contemporary observers can derive lessons and insights from past experience to resolve current technological disruptions. Here, history provides guideposts for the present and the future. It reveals the roots of present policy failures in dealing with weaponized code, intelligent bots, drones, and other new inventions. In addition, it offers lessons on how policymakers can overcome the persistent failure to reduce technological conflict rather than continuing to rely on outmoded theories of war and deterrence that allow it to intensify.

In sum, the book explores the changing character of international rivalry in new technological arenas; the persistent failure of Western security planners to adapt their strategies and policies to unprecedented threats; the superior defensive mechanism of punctuated deterrence to prevent, mitigate, and punish aggression in its new forms; and the development of technological resilience in case deterrence continues to fail. More than merely offering a diagnosis of policy failures, the work presents methods and recommendations on how the West can win the cyber revolution in strategic affairs and restore peace to core compartments of cyberspace.

PLAN OF THE BOOK

The remainder of the book is organized into ten chapters. Chapter 1 explores the problem of technological revolution in historical context. It reviews the plight of practitioners who must devise security policy against urgent threats under conditions of technological uncertainty and the consequent strategic blunders that can ensue. In particular, the chapter examines the rise of submarine warfare, strategic bombing, and mechanized warfare in the first half of the twentieth century. The cases reveal an important lesson: in the midst of a technological revolution in strategic affairs, the failure to interpret the meaning of the new technology correctly can be enormous. More important than developing potent weapons is the design of superior doctrine to guide their use. In this regard, the current cyber revolution presents an irony: the nations most adept at technological innovation, the United States and Britain, are behind the times in grasping its security implications.

Chapter 2 deals with the follies of cyber legalism. It argues that the prevailing legal and normative framework is inadequate to the task that Western diplomacy ascribes to it in reducing cyber conflict. Because the framework privileges the physical world over the virtual world, because it prioritizes war rather than sub-threshold conflict, it fails to provide clear restraints against offensive cyber activity, which so far transpires entirely below the war threshold. Many observers decry Russia's and China's apparent breaches of international law and norms; in reality, what they should lament is the legal system, which fails to prohibit actions that in fact do not clearly breach the law or defy the thin normative consensus.

Chapter 3 examines the concept and problem of revisionism in international relations. It analyzes how challenger states seek to subvert the international order rather than upholding it. One cannot grasp Russia's and China's strategic maneuvers in cyberspace without first understanding this important point. Accordingly, the chapter draws from my conceptual framework on technological revolution developed elsewhere to orient the task of evaluating varieties of foreign policy activism historically and today.[51]

The analysis in Chapters 4 and 5 applies the revolution framework to the study, respectively, of Russia's and China's activist foreign policy today. It argues that these countries' maneuvers in cyberspace seek to subvert the liberal international order – an objective that is lost on observers who focus mainly on considerations of physical security and economic wealth. The countries have developed strategic doctrines commensurate with the technological and ideological elements of modern conflict; they emphasize the informational rather than the material plane of contention. Virtual weapons are at the core of this conception of rivalry and its methods.

Chapter 6 returns to problems of Western policy by examining the failed quest for stable deterrence in cyberspace. Attachment to the rigidities of the legal system and its prioritization of traditional war hinders the search. The recently launched U.S. concept of "persistent engagement" represents an important doctrinal advance; but it suffers limitations that call forth new approaches emphasizing more robust punishment. What is required beyond defending forward is a policy of *punishing backward*: a willingness to respond to bold security threats with one's own boldness – that is, a commitment to strike back to restore peace in some quarters of cyberspace.

Chapter 7 explores an alternative conflict prevention approach, punctuated deterrence, which addresses flaws in Western strategic doctrine. The analysis presents principles of action for a stabler and more credible deterrence posture against cyber actions: the accretional principle and the principles of virtual integrity, issue linkage, and declaratory credibility.

Chapter 8 examines NATO's ongoing adaptation to cyber threats. It also illustrates how the principles of punctuated deterrence could be applied within the alliance's framework. Collective punctuation, it argues, could deliver better results in conflict prevention than a unilateral approach.

Chapter 9 examines the Estonian government's data embassies initiative. These foreign-based backup servers seek to protect the continuity of the digital state in the midst of a national emergency, such as a major cyberattack (possibly worse than the incident in 2007) or a military invasion (as Estonia experienced in June 1940 and Ukraine suffered in February 2022). The initiative has the potential to redress some of the offense–defense imbalance that prevails in cyberspace. As a result, it can shore up the presently weak mechanism of deterrence by denial, which works by diminishing the effectiveness of adversaries' weapons.

Chapter 10 summarizes the book's main arguments and presents policy conclusions for practitioners who recognize the flaws of current policy approaches while striving to achieve more effective methods of conflict reduction.

1
TECHNOLOGICAL REVOLUTION IN HISTORICAL PERSPECTIVE
Lessons for Our Times

ELEMENTS OF STRATEGY

The roots of Western security failures lie in strategy: in the irrelevance of policy dogmas to new forms of technological conflict. To grasp the nature and extent of the problem we must ask: What is strategy? At the risk of oversimplification, it has three main elements: axioms about the realm of possible behavior; assumptions about adversaries' motives and objectives in the plane of contention; and principles of action that relate these assumptions to each other and to one's own objectives and resources. In the adaptation of strategy to the cyber revolution, problems abound in all three elements.

The first set of problems concerns prevailing understandings of the world as shaped and constrained by science. What forms of behavior are possible (even if one has not seen it all) and how does technology both expand and limit the scope of action? Crucially, this domain of strategy encompasses not only observed but also plausible behavior. More important than inventing resources that enable new forms of strategic action is devising axioms that enable one to identify and foresee them before the opponents – and thus prepare for the growing scope of conceivable rivalry.

Problems exist, second, in assumptions about the nature of the opponents, chiefly Russia and China, but also other capable subversive players, such as North Korea and Iran, and, increasingly, private culprits who operate below the structures of the state system but whose actions sometimes affect interests within it. What motivations and grievances drive them, to what ends, and what capabilities do they possess especially in relation to one's own? And about ourselves we must ask: What are we willing to risk and what for? As Chapter 2 will discuss, the main thrust of Western policy efforts to prevent technological

aggression seeks to co-opt autocratic opponents into a liberal legal and normative framework – more imagined than real – not recognizing that they interpret the framework differently, as a guide to pursue activist foreign policies
which seek to subvert the international order to serve their own ends.

Third are problems involving the synthesis of these various elements: how
to relate new technological possibilities for action, the adversaries' intentions,
and one's own resources to the pursuit of valid goals without committing or
risking too much. This collection of understandings is organized – sometimes
formally, other times only implicitly, but always influentially – into *doctrine*,
the guidebook of principles and goals that orients policymakers' pursuit of
interests amid the uncertainties of international politics. Doctrine has more
than one form. It can be declaratory – what policymakers want their actions to
look like – or operational – how actors actually behave.[1] Or, in the words of
J. David Singer, a state's "official or articulated ideology" can differ from its
"operative ideology."[2] As Chapter 6 will argue, while new doctrines such as the
U.S. notion of persistent engagement address some flaws of previous policy,
they also amplify them owing to misguided assumptions about the realm of
action and its players.

Whatever the content of one's doctrine, its strength has both an absolute
and especially a relative quality. For one thing, we can assess the merits of
doctrine based on its accuracy in deciphering a new technology's effects on the
horizon of strategic maneuver and in interpreting the adversaries' exploitation
of that widening horizon. These two tasks are strictly analytical; they are right
or wrong regardless of how one operates. Another measure of success involves
one's own efforts: the adjustment of policy dogmas into a new political or scientific reality; and their translation into deployable instruments of power and
influence. Among the hardest challenges of doctrinal development is to avoid
the intellectual reflex of merely applying unrefined notions to the circumstances
of a revolutionary situation. All of these exercises in doctrinal development
have an absolute quality: it is possible to measure their degree of success regardless of other players' experiences.

The more important question to ask in doctrinal adaptation is relational:
Does one's doctrine contain superior principles for offensive and defensive
action and are one's instruments of power more effective than the adversaries'

– in short, does one see the new horizon for action better and is one better equipped to maneuver within it? Good strategic doctrine is nothing if it is not superior to the understandings of the opponents against which it is applied.

The race to adapt security strategy to the contemporary technological revolution is being won in Eastern capitals. Adversaries of the West – especially Russia – have been far more adept at designing a framework of concepts and principles attuned to the new possibilities of technological conflict. The West has a problem not with technology itself, at whose creation and refinement it excels, but with the *interpretation* of its security implications. In other words, the main shortcoming of Western policy does not involve the design of new weapons or technical measures to protect vital assets against them; rather, it is rooted in misguided conceptions of the new boundaries of modern conflict.

The problem in short is primarily not of machine engineering but of human analysis. The central challenge of strategy today is to construct principles for a growing spectrum of action that remains largely unexplored by Western minds. Much of the problem inheres in the absence of an organized system of thinking about forms of conflict that transpire below the threshold of armed conflict – that is, outside the realm in which Western superiority, both doctrinal and material, is nearly unquestionable. The United States and Britain do not enjoy a hundred years of experience in the weaponization of information, a method of strategic competition that Russia has been refining – now with new technological tools at its disposal – since the Bolshevik seizure of power in 1917.

And yet the West's experience of technological revolution in the last century is rich, encompassing inventions no less profound in their implications for the nature of conflict than the airplane, the tank, or that fantastical weapon, the nuclear bomb, which transformed conflict mainly by eradicating it among the weapon's possessors. These revolutions grew out of Western scientific ingenuity and engineering prowess. From them we can derive lessons and insights for the resolution of problems arising from today's cyber revolution.

This chapter examines the problem of technological revolution in security affairs: the appearance of a new class of weapon whose use in the international system is difficult to model and regulate even among supposedly rational players (a presumption that enjoys a wide appeal among political scientists).[3] To set the stage for further study in later chapters, the analysis begins by describing the gap between technological capacity and strategic learning in the cyber revolution. It then examines previous cases of technological revolution to derive lessons and insights that can help to close the gap. The first case is modern submarine warfare: a poor grasp of this new technology of conflict caused the obsolescence – almost overnight – of core tenets of naval strategy, which was based on the preponderance of surface vessels, during the opening stages of the First World War. Second is the emergence of strategic bombing in the period between the two world wars. Early experience showed that Stanley Baldwin's maxim of bomber superiority was correct – until the deployment of a countervailing invention, radar, redressed the offense–defense imbalance. Third is mechanized warfare in the same period. Germany's superior doctrine enabled it swiftly to defeat France, then regarded as the world's preeminent military power. Before 1940, French commanders had largely ignored the tank's strategic significance.

The analysis below is not an attempt to rewrite the history of the follies of technological interpretation. It is instead a historical exercise to guide the design of more effective security policy in our own time. What attitudes failed and which ones succeeded? What does this body of experience teach us about the relationship between technological revolution and strategy in conditions of geopolitical flux?

CYBER POWER AND STRATEGY: THE PLIGHT OF THE WESTERN TITANS

A central irony of the cyber revolution is that Western ingenuity created the technologies which enabled the security threats bedeviling security planners. An English mathematician, Alan Turing, conceived of computers in 1936.[4] One year later, a team of American engineers from IBM and researchers at Harvard University first built one, the Mark I, providing naval gunners advantages in the battlefields of the Second World War.[5] Private firms based in San Francisco and London such as Google's DeepMind lead today's race to bestow on the machines an artificial intelligence.[6] These and other corporations, including IBM and Google, lead the quest for the world's first universal quantum computer as well as efforts to expand the Internet of Things into all quarters of the home and office setting.[7]

Defense industries have translated these accomplishments into great offensive capacity. Although the size of national cyber arsenals is difficult to determine because governments tightly classify them and because intangible computer code presents few physical signatures to detect its existence, the empirical record suggests a rough ordering of national offensive strength. Western nations dominate it. The United States mounted, in partnership with Israel, the most spectacular cyberattack to date, the "Olympic Games" operation that in 2009 destroyed almost one thousand uranium enrichment centrifuges at the nuclear facility in Natanz, Iran.[8] Other powerful weapons drew from stolen U.S. resources. The notorious WannaCry ransomware that struck computers around the world in March 2017 propagated via an advanced exploit, "EternalBlue," that the North Korean culprits had adopted after it was leaked from the U.S. National Security Agency's arsenal by a hacker group called the Shadow Brokers.[9]

Atop the pantheon of cyber powers stands alongside the United States its close ally Britain. The country operates the world's oldest electronic spying agency, Government Communications Headquarters (GCHQ), which since its creation in 1919 has been at the forefront of electronic espionage.[10] No longer just a passive generator of signals intelligence, the agency today harvests data that it uses to conduct offensive operations in foreign networks – for example, the disruption of Islamic State's online propaganda and recruitment activity as well as the destruction of the group's network equipment in Syria in 2018.[11] "In the past, you could characterize what we did as producing pieces of paper which we handed to government who could take action," explained GCHQ's historian Tony Comer. "Now we are the ones actually taking the action."[12]

Together or alone, the United States and Britain would likely win an all-out cyberwar against other nations – if by winning we mean destroying more computer assets than the adversaries. A recent national ranking of cyber capacity, notable for its creative methodology, which considers not just capabilities but also intent, ranks the United States above China and Russia; Britain ranks between them.[13] Another recent study puts Britain first and the United States second.[14] So vast are the technical ability and financial resources of the two large Western partners, so pervasive are the vulnerabilities of computer software and hardware – even the best-designed products – that one can easily imagine greater material devastation than the Stuxnet worm caused. But let us not diminish the worm's demonstrative importance: it proved to doubters (if any existed) that information organized and stored in the form of electrons can harm the physical world, in this case by manipulating the industrial controller that governed the behavior of IR-1 uranium enrichment centrifuges. The absence so far of graver destruction or fatalities via cyberspace is likelier the result of successful deterrence (on which more in Chapter 6) than it is the consequence of limits in technological capacity. Despite their intangibility (the activation of a virtual payload causes no explosion), virtual weapons can achieve astonishing disruptive and destructive effects, ranging from the interruption of central bank operations and voting machines to the destruction of power grids and nuclear turbines.

On many fronts, then, it is Western ingenuity that has expanded the limits of technological ability in the current era. The observation applies not just to offensive arms but also to technological ability broadly. A recent report identified the United States, Britain, Australia, Germany, Canada, and France as the most advanced nations in the digital arena across a number of fields, including technology infrastructure and the regulatory framework.[15] Four of those nations (the English-speaking ones) formally collaborate on electronic espionage within the "Five Eyes" community,[16] the world's oldest and most advanced intelligence club, which in the late twentieth century operated a global surveillance program ("ECHELON") that collected vast amounts of corporate, civilian, and governmental data across the world, including the personal information of German Chancellor Angela Merkel and Iranian Supreme Leader Ali Khamenei.[17]

And yet the essential task of molding security strategy to new inventions is being won in Eastern capitals. Let us ask a question that will unsettle policymakers in Washington and London: Who is the world master at seizing prized industrial and military secrets via cyberspace? How easily one is tempted to answer: the governments of the United States and Britain, the nations that dominate the league tables and which carried out pervasive mass surveillance programs across the globe. Events, however, suggest a different master: the government of China, a nation in which the Internet fails to penetrate almost half of the population and almost one in twenty adults cannot read printed words, let alone electronic zeros and ones.[18] Yet, China has been able to conduct industrial espionage on a scale that no country in the world rivals.[19]

And now more rattling: What nation is the chief disturber of domestic political order via online information spaces? Here, again, one must suppress the temptation to think of the two leading material powers – the nation that invented the Internet in 1969 and gave it its widest economic expression in the 1990s, and the nation that launched electronic espionage more than a century ago in the midst of a world war. Both the United States and Britain are familiar to students of European and Asian history as avid exporters of their domestic political creed of liberalism; and yet the two countries are not the chief ideological agents on the global Internet. This distinction belongs to the government of Russia, a country that shares with the dominant players a penchant for the spreading of political beliefs (see Chapters 3 and 4) but whose population obtains, by a vast margin, news and information about the world primarily from television rather than online and where almost one third of residents do not use social media – the very instrument that feeds the state engine of foreign political disruption.[20]

Starkest of all is the situation of North Korea. A combination of scientific backwardness and offensive boldness is a cause almost for embarrassment for the rogue nation's more technologically advanced yet strategically lagging Western opponents. What technological base does this revolutionary state – the *bête noire* of cyberspace – enjoy? There is almost no native scientific foundation to speak of. The Internet penetrates society but thinly, mainly among the political elites, rarely among common citizens who live their lives in almost total ignorance of the marvels of modern computing. There is no meaningful hardware or software industry beyond the tightly controlled industry of code weaponization. And yet the country's elite military hacking unit, most notably the Lazarus Group, continuously harasses Western opponents and their allies, for instance, by destroying three-fourths of computers and servers at the California-based entertainment company Sony Pictures in December 2014, by disabling computer systems in British hospitals with the WannaCry ransomware in March 2017, and by hacking into cryptoasset exchanges in South Korea.[21]

The league tables of cyber power, in sum, display a glaring discrepancy between, on the one hand, raw offensive capacity, which large Western nations possess abundantly, and, on the other, strategic conception, in which adversaries outrank them. Never before in the history of technological development, perhaps, have the masters of invention lagged so far behind the later adopters in adapting strategy to it. The nations that field the most potent arsenals, the ones that are also most adept at harnessing the social and economic gains of cyberspace, have fallen to the wayside in the race to design principles of offense and defense.

The West's predicament, though ironic, is not unprecedented. Societies that create a revolutionary technology are not always the first or most adept at mastering its strategic implications. For the tendency of new technologies of conflict is to outgrow the purposes set by its creators.

The problem has two main roots. One concerns the structure of the Western scientific enterprise: it customarily separates "basic" and "applied" research in a linear fashion. The original exponent of this approach in the United States was Vannevar Bush. As head of the U.S. Office of Scientific Research and Development during the Second World War – a period of spectacular scientific industry – he argued that applied innovations follow linearly from basic research. But the separation of basic and applied research is facile. Contra Bush's view, critics pointed out that the two kinds of research are, or should be forced to become, closely entwined.[22] The assumption of a linear relationship is flawed. Science often advances in an integrative and parallel, rather than a sequential, manner. New basic understandings of the natural world can enable new practical inventions. Equally, social and political imaginations can inspire the development of these understandings and their attendant technology in the first place.

Consider the case of nuclear technology. Advances in basic research in physics preceding the Second World War – Wilhelm Röntgen's discovery of X-rays, Henri Becquerel's encounter with radioactivity, Albert Einstein's completion of relativity theory, etc. – opened up a field of knowledge that later enabled humans to manipulate atoms for applied purposes. Einstein's theory of special relativity was particularly important. It showed that mass was but a super-concentrated form of energy which could be extracted. Forty years later, the strategic imperatives of the world war, in particular the necessity of defeating Japan in a single blow that would avoid a lengthy and costly invasion, prompted the U.S. government to apply Einstein's insights to the development of fission bombs that Washington unleashed on Hiroshima and Nagasaki. As Einstein warned in a letter to President Franklin D. Roosevelt in 1939: "[T]he element uranium may be turned into a new and important source of energy in the immediate future . . . This new phenomenon would also lead to the construction of bombs, and it is conceivable – though much less certain – that extremely powerful bombs of a new type may thus be constructed."[23] Here, physicists' theoretical ingenuity pre-dated decisionmakers' imperatives to apply them in practice. But that is not the end of the story. From the study of the atom's awesome powers there emerged new scientific understandings – and further applications – in the fields of physics (how heavier elements form out of lighter ones), medical research (the use of radiotherapy in cancer treatment), earth sciences (the effects of radiocarbon on the atmosphere and oceanic movements), and astrophysics (the confirmation of stellar nucleosynthesis and the birth of gamma-ray and infrared astronomy). As Neil deGrasse Tyson and Avis Lang put it: "Many significant advances in our understanding of the cosmos are by-products of government investment in the apparatus of warfare, and many innovative instruments of destruction are by-products of advances in astrophysics."[24] The bifurcated approach of Western scientific research impedes the advancement of an integrative approach in which real-world uses of technology inspire its development, even as new applications pave the way for improved understandings.

A second challenge inheres in the nature of modern technology itself: it is rarely stable, often advancing faster than the designers – however ingenious – grasp its implications. The problem also concerns the nature of the technology's possessors: players other than the creators acquire it whose motives and goals differ and whose guiding concepts might be superior.

While searching for a solution to the problems of technological revolution, different actors will impose upon it their own conception. Technologists may define technical responses that neglect the technology's policy and strategy dimensions. Let us solve computer security threats with intricate anti-malware devices! Strategic thinkers operating outside the technical realm may succumb to the reverse tendency, a belief that the problems of technological transformation afford a purely human response. "Increase research budgets," "threaten to shoot first" become recipes for overcoming a failure to grasp the rudiments of a complex technical reality. What, email is hackable? "I haven't worried about an email being hacked, since I've never sent one," remarked Senator Lindsey Graham of South Carolina in the midst of Russia's hacking operation into the Democratic Party email records in 2016. "I'm, like, ahead of my time."[25] In the context of grave concerns about the privacy of digital communications, Graham's quip must have seemed an ideal answer to computer security threats – except that it implies the wholesale renunciation, impractical in our times, of mobile phones and computers.

Decisionmakers with responsibility for security policy know that technology defines the material bounds of action in conflict and crisis. But they also like to stress the enormous powers of the will, as if it were a pill that could overcome practical limits to human conduct and could cure the deficiencies of the world. Policymaking is, after all, a celebration of the power of individuals over history; in new technology they seek not evidence of constraints but a new freedom of action. World affairs in short can be controlled so long as objectives are defined clearly and technological means to them are selected prudently.

Reality is often exactly the reverse. For officials ordinarily lack the time to ruminate over strategic puzzles or to master the arcana of the technology which gave them rise. The pressures of office in the midst of a crisis – technologically induced or not – demand action, sometimes *any* action. The actions might violate both the technologist's concern for technical detail and the strategic thinker's regard for human psychology. Recalling his transition in January 1969 from Harvard professor – a life that elevates quiet reflection about the world almost to a vice – to President Richard Nixon's national security advisor – a profession that abhors passive rumination – Henry Kissinger reflected on this problem: "The convictions that leaders have before reaching high office are the intellectual capital they will consume as long as they continue in office. There is little time for leaders to reflect."[26] The academician's challenge, by contrast, is the opposite: how to craft theories and concepts about a world whose complex events and personalities often exist beyond easy understanding. Kissinger, the protagonist of world crises, realized that in the midst of pressures for immediate and decisive action under conditions of uncertainty that pervade in the halls of power, there would be little recourse to the reflections of the deep-thinking professor. Whatever assumptions the policymaker has about the state of the world have to rely on intellectual capital that cannot accrue free from the demands of the very events they ponder.

The result, neither inevitable nor easily escapable, of this situation is strategic blunder in face of new technological realities. The problem recurs historically. Take almost any disaster in the history of warfare during the last century and you will find behind it some bad theory of what at the time was a new invention. Three stand out: the failure of British naval strategists in 1914 to grasp the obsolescence of their vast surface fleet in seas where undetectable German submarines roamed; the inability, initially, of British air defenders in 1940 to understand how to reverse Stanley Baldwin's dictum that "the bomber will always get through," which the German Luftwaffe had proved in Guernica in 1937, and the failure, later, of German aviation planners to comprehend radar's air-defense implications;[27] and the adaptation of *Blitzkrieg* to the new possibilities of mechanized warfare in 1940. Let us explore these examples in detail.

SUBMARINE WARFARE AND THE SILENCING OF THE ROYAL NAVY

On February 10, 1906, enthusiastic crowds and journalists from around the globe cheered King Edward VII at Portsmouth Harbor as he christened the HMS *Dreadnought*. British naval commanders celebrated the gargantuan ship as "the most deadly fighting machine ever launched in the history of the world,"[28] or in the words of the former First Sea Lord, Admiral Lord West: "a most devastating weapon of war, the most powerful thing in the world."[29] The castle of steel featured ten 12-inch guns that could blast four-foot shells packed with half a ton of explosives across ten nautical miles. It expressed a transformation in naval arms not just for its size and awesome firepower but also for its wiring: it was the first vessel to transmit firing commands electrically rather than mechanically.

It was also among the least used items in Britain's vast naval arsenal during the First World War. What follows is the story of how an awesome weapon became a spectacle of strategic derision.

The *Dreadnought* was the latest addition to the Royal Navy's already magnificent fleet, which by 1914 comprised millions of tons of mainly surface hardware, including thirty-three battleships (four of them dreadnoughts with another six under construction), more than two hundred cruisers (ten of them battlecruisers), and two hundred destroyers. It was easily the mightiest naval force in world history up to that point. As the fleet's most cherished vessel, the *Dreadnought* expressed the truisms of naval doctrine at the turn of the twentieth century: the superiority of large surface ships, the effectiveness of clustered offensives, and the primacy of direct engagements among naval forces at sea.[30]

The beast of the sea's transforming potential was in fact illusory. Rather than heralding a new era of naval battle rooted in the surface-vessel supremacy, it encapsulated outmoded military dogma – or so British naval commanders discovered during the early stages of the First World War.

As the Royal Navy set off to fight the Imperial German Navy in September 1914, a new invention erupted onto the battlefield, the U-boat. By virtue of its slim design and submersible capacity, enemy vessels struggled to detect the U-boat's presence in the waters. Even if they could detect the sleek tubular objects, few existing armaments could be brought to bear upon them.[31]

The moment of shock came on September 22 as three armored cruisers – the HMS *Aboukir*, *Hogue*, and *Cressy* – set out to patrol the English Channel. It was a potent force. Each ship displaced 12,000 tons, brandished 9.2-inch guns, and carried a complement of several hundred sailors. And on that day they all perished at the hands of a single enemy vessel, the U-9. Reflecting the doctrinal fashion of the time, the War Orders of July 28 had warned of attacks by German destroyers, not submarines. The *Aboukir* was the first to suffer the U-9's torpedo attack, which struck its starboard side. Because no enemy vessel had been sighted, Captain J.E. Drummond concluded that his ship had struck a mine. The *Hogue* and *Cressy* approached to assist their immobile cousin, whose engines had flooded. Upon resurfacing, the German skipper Otto Weddigen immediately ordered a fresh attack. Both British ships spotted the enemy vessel, fired their guns at her but, like a sea ghost, she quickly disappeared below the waterline unscathed. The *Hogue* capsized within ten minutes. The *Cressy* listed to starboard and capsized before sinking about thirty minutes later.[32]

In the aftermath of this and ensuing naval fiascoes,[33] the question began to ring in Royal Navy command posts from the Barents Sea to the Straits of Otranto: What good is it to be able to blast enemy targets several times past the visible horizon if they appeared suddenly at a distance of just a few hundred meters, only to disappear within minutes of firing torpedoes that could sink a capital ship with a single blow?

Despite the shocking events of September, the main potential of submarine warfare lay elsewhere, in commerce warfare, whose principles and techniques the Germans perfected in 1915.[34] Even the Germans, for all their foresight about the submarine's strategic significance, at first failed to grasp this new potential. In the first six months of the war, U-boats sank just ten merchant ships. They did so at their skippers' own initiative rather than on the orders of superiors applying received doctrine.

To a contemporary, the earlier sinking of the three Royal Navy cruisers would probably have elicited more shock and seemed more important than the attack on the merchants. Recall the presumed primacy of direct naval engagements. Commerce warfare at the time suffered the constraints of the "prize rule," an oddity of international law that required submarine commanders to surface and scuttle merchant vessels after allowing their crews to abandon ship. Realizing that this was no way to win a war against the world's preeminent naval power, an island nation for whom the enveloping sea was as much a protective moat as a lifeline of essential economic supplies, German naval commanders decided to flout the prize rule.[35]

And so a new genus of conflict was born: unrestricted submarine warfare against merchant fleets, whose main objective was to eliminate Britain economically as much as militarily before the United States entered the war. The German U-boats wandered far from their North Sea port. They trained much of their firepower on the Mediterranean, where they caused enormous shipping losses. By early 1917, German U-boats sank a monthly average of 614,000 tons of British shipping – worse even than the losses suffered in the next world war.[36] Gone were the verities of centuries of naval dogma. Small submersible vessels acting alone could inflict substantial losses on large capital ships and commercial targets.

It fell upon Admiral of the Fleet John Jellicoe to reflect upon the revolution that was unfolding beneath the sea "from week to week." In an aptly named book, *The Crisis of the Naval War*, he explained that the chief dilemma involved the balance of offensive and defensive moves: whether more shipping losses could be avoided by deploying surface vessels to hunt U-boats or by deploying the assets to protect merchants. About the submarine hunt Jellicoe made an astonishing admission: "There was always great doubt [in the Royal Navy] whether any particular offensive operation undertaken by small craft would produce any result, particularly as the numbers necessary for success were not available."[37] Whereas the enemy science of unrestricted submarine warfare had quickly achieved its zenith, the science of anti-submarine warfare was but rudimentary. An observer who believes, from the safety of posterity, that the moment of danger is an opportune time for doctrinal experimentation must recall Kissinger's somber maxim: in a crisis there is little time for leaders to reflect, to which Jellicoe gave proof: "[T]he situation was so serious in the spring of 1917 that we could not carry out experiments involving grave risk of considerably increased losses."[38]

Against the discomforts of the unknown the desperate British naval commanders invoked the comforts of the known. They redeveloped the muscular destroyers into submarine hunters, beginning with a fleet of six destroyers armed with depth charges, the only technological remedy to the submarine but which was in limited supply.[39] The hardy old sea master Jellicoe lamented "the length of time required to produce the vessels and the weapons . . . to employ in the anti-submarine war."[40]

In the end, no new countermeasures defeated the German U-boats. Instead, the commerce warfare campaign failed because of the availability of vast fleets of neutral merchants which no degree of ruthlessness emanating from below the waterline could sink or sequester in port. The submarine menace was defeated not by the number of U-boats sunk but by the number of merchant vessels that made it past their hunting nets.[41]

In the history of the development of submarine warfare until that time one finds real ironies. It had been France, not Germany, that had led the world in submarine fleet size up until 1914. It was naval shipyards in Britain that had constructed most of the submersibles. Germany, by contrast, was slower to integrate them into its fleet. Before 1906, it had no U-boats. And yet the real innovations in naval technologies occurred not in Toulon and Paris, or in

Portsmouth and London, but in Heligoland and Berlin. Germany achieved advantages by producing fewer ship designs, which economized training and battlefield maintenance costs, and, as we saw, by launching commerce warfare, which not only contravened international law but also challenged the dogmas of allied naval strategy.

What became of the celebrated HMS *Dreadnought*? In an ironic twist that expressed rare good fortune rather than changing naval realities, the castle of steel's only significant contribution to the war was the ramming and sinking of U-29 near the Pentland Firth in Scotland in March 1915. The submarine's skipper Weddigen had previously captained U-9, which in the previous year had sunk the three cruisers. The pride and fury of the Royal Navy had no further notable engagements in the war. It missed the Battle of Jutland because of refitting, never fired its guns again, and was sold for scrap in 1919.

THE BOMBER GOT THROUGH

To observers of the terror unfolding in the Spanish city of Guernica on April 26, 1937, the allegory of the Apocalypse acquired a worldly expression. Except that it was not falling stars or burning mountains displaced by a divine being that scorched the Earth below, but squadrons of Heinkel 51 fighter planes sent forth by the Fascist dictators in Berlin and Rome. Having invented the technique of "carpet bombing" in Oviedo earlier in the Spanish Civil War, Nazi Germany's Condor Legion now turned to the experimentation of new aerial terror tactics. Cattle ablaze in white phosphorus ran down the streets in a frenzy. Entire families were buried in rubble. Almost one-third of the city's population perished.[42] Never before in the history of warfare had the terrors of industrial war been unleashed directly into the heart of an urban population from the skies – so swiftly, so easily, and so unexpectedly.[43] For the first time, the images of charred urban skylines and entirely razed neighborhoods (the unmissable flat patches of land amid molten surroundings) erupted into the human consciousness.

The Condor Legion's combat report (*Gefechtsbericht*) stated that the air raid's purpose was to block the passage of withdrawing Republican forces. The Spanish Nationalist account was even more devious. General Francisco Franco's representatives blamed the city's destruction on a scorched-earth maneuver by the withdrawing defenders – a fiction backed up by his allies in the Catholic Church.[44]

But as the Luftwaffe Colonel Wolfram von Richthofen attested in his war diaries, everything pointed to a trial of the new methods of aerial terrorism.[45] The indiscriminate bombing was a test to spread fear and horror among the civilian population. In the words of British war reporter George L. Steer who was at the scene, "The raid on Guernica is unparalleled in military history. Guernica was not a military objective. A factory producing war material lay outside the town and was untouched. The object of the bombardment was seemingly the demoralization of the civil population and the destruction of the cradle of the Basque race."[46] None other than Luftwaffe chief Hermann Göring exposed the lie of German and Nationalist accounts of the episode: "[The attack] was an opportunity to test under fire whether the material had been adequately developed" – a test, that is, of new tactics under realistic conditions. Not just the bombing of Guernica but also Germany's broader military involvement in the civil war was a testing ground for a larger future war. "Two years of combat experience are more useful than 10 years of peacetime training," mused a German general.[47]

German military planners were not the only ones deriving lessons from Guernica. Others elsewhere also watched for clues about evolving trends in warfare.

One observer more prescient even than many Germans was former British prime minister Stanley Baldwin. His astuteness in grasping the transforming effects of strategic bombers, a new technology of conflict developed during the interwar period, had preceded the Guernica bombing. In a speech in 1932, he warned his colleagues in the House of Commons: "It is well . . . for the man in the street to realize that there is no power on earth that can protect him from being bombed, whatever people may tell him. *The bomber will always get through.*"[48]

With the sharpness of an expert tactician, Baldwin enumerated the reasons behind his maxim. Imagine any large town you like, he said, whether in Britain or on the Continent that was reachable from an enemy airfield. The town's and its suburbs' defense would require the division of the airspace into sectors. Consider that enemy bombers will fly from an altitude of at least 20,000 feet.

Now do the math: you will have defense sectors the size of tens or hundreds of cubic miles! But there is more: the sectors are often covered in cloud and fog, which complicates the task of intercepting the enemy with fighter planes (for another of this seer-politician's maxims was, "The only defense is offense"). The resulting situation of offense superiority was not the only cause of concern, he continued. Worse were the lessons of the history of technological revolution. The only means of avoiding catastrophe was by way of complete disarmament ("abolishing flying"), but that was impossible. "We have never known mankind to go back on a new invention," he concluded ominously. "It might be a good thing for this world, as I heard some of the most distinguished men in the air service say, if men had never learned to fly."[49]

The Luftwaffe's scorching of Guernica gave initial proof to Baldwin's maxim about offense superiority in the era of strategic bombers. But the largely undefended Basque city was no formidable test of the maxim. More convincing proof came in 1940 in the "Battle of Britain." In the interim, strategic bombing technology had improved. The fitting of bombers with multiple engines and the development of night raiding tactics further widened the defensive gap. Some military analysts such as the Italian general Giulio Douhet stretched Baldwin's maxim to its logical limit, predicting that the side which destroys the enemy's industrial capacity from the air first would win future wars completely.[50]

The Battle of Britain began on July 10, 1940 with an attack by almost two hundred German bombers on British shipping convoys in the English Channel and on a dockyard in South Wales. The battle did not start well for the air defenders, whose lack of ingenuity gave Baldwin's truism a self-fulfilling quality. Germany's intense and incessant bombing campaign steadily struck industrial targets and population centers in England, Wales, and Scotland until October.

An inherent flaw of Baldwin's maxim was its absoluteness: of course, the bomber would sometimes *not* get through owing to machine malfunctions, adverse weather conditions, pilot error, and the occasional defeat by defenders flying technically advanced Spitfire fighter planes in a dogged effort to protect the homeland. But the maxim's central insight of offense superiority was in the main accurate. The bombers indeed mostly did get through. The hardest day for the Luftwaffe was on August 18, not because its bombers were shot down, but because the Germans sought to wipe out the Royal Air Force by attacking its airfields. By taking the fight directly to the defenders, the German planes temporarily nullified their basis for superiority. The defenders were able to fill the many cubic miles of "sectors" more quickly than when the raiders hit targets further afield.

The most important defensive refinement was found in a countervailing technology: radar. Developed secretly for military purposes by a number of countries before the war, radar was not deployed decisively on the battlefield until the Battle of Britain. There, its contribution to the war's outcome was perhaps greatest. Adoption of radar in Britain was not a straight and easy path. Prime Minister Winston Churchill's chief scientific advisor, the German-born Oxford professor Frederick Lindemann, was so skeptical of radar's utility that he obstructed its development.[51] Air Chief Marshal Hugh Dowding, however, was deeply impressed from the beginning. Armed with insights gained from his previous service as head of the RAF's research arm, he pressed for the creation of an intricate array of fifty radar stations – the so-called Dowding system – stretching from northern Scotland (which was visited by German planes originating in Norway) to Wales. At its narrowest stretch, the array was only twenty-one miles wide. It enabled the air defenders to locate enemy planes as far away as one hundred miles. As a result, the time window for bomber interception widened significantly. So, too, the interception rate grew. Whereas in the early stages of the Battle of Britain the rate of interception of enemy planes had been about 30 percent, by the end of the battle it rose to between 90 and 100 percent.[52]

The story of radar's adoption in the battlefield presents its own ironies. Although German scientists had pioneered much of radar's underlying technology, their country's military planners failed to grasp its strategic implications. By contrast, by perceiving radar's significance, British military planners were able to develop – at a critical point in the war – a countervailing technology that redressed the offense–defense imbalance in the air domain. The pathway of strategic adaptation was not all technological, however. It also involved Dowding's masterful understanding of how to integrate radar into human systems effectively. His intricate air defense shield – comprising a comprehensive array of reporting stations, operation rooms, a command center, and intercepting pilots operating at a high state of readiness – ensured that the bomber would no longer get through without difficulty.

MECHANIZED WARFARE: MIGHTY FRANCE FALLS

Ask anyone today what country enjoyed a global reputation as the world's mightiest military power on the eve of the Second World War and few people would guess the correct answer, France. That this answer seems implausible reflects both a conceit of posterity: Nazi Germany's rapid conquest of Europe makes it appear as the military master of the time, when in fact the German army still lacked the material resources to pursue Continental conquest; and a peculiarity: although France emerged on the victors' side of the war, in 1940 it had fallen swiftly to the invaders. The German army, widely regarded as unprepared for a major onslaught westwards, defeated the world's preeminent military power in just six weeks. Images of German troops marching down the Champs-Élysées in June 1940 gave an ironic twist to perceptions of French martial greatness. The defeat was much swifter than defense planners anywhere had considered plausible except in Berlin (although doubters existed there too). Few observers, in fact, considered it at all possible.

We know *today* that France was not fit for battle with Germany, but this truth was not broadly realized at the time. So powerful was the conceit of French predominance that it survived the domestic turbulences that afflicted the country in the period immediately after the First World War.

Political turmoil and financial disarray in France, especially a severe monetary crisis between 1924 and 1928, impeded the growth of military spending. There was no significant rearmament effort; for much of the interwar period, the French military relied mainly on arms acquired in the previous war. Instead of manufacturing arms on an industrial scale like Germany, France dialed back preparations for a future war. Munitions stores diminished and became outdated. In 1919, the government reduced the length of conscription service to one-and-a-half years; ten years later to one year. The barracks gradually emptied.

Meanwhile, the colossal menace across the Rhine river grew. Upon ascending to power in Berlin in January 1933, Hitler rapidly expanded and modernized Germany's armed forces, at first covertly but later openly. In 1936, the aggrieved loser of the First World War completed a massive rearmament program that produced a formidable land army of 700,000 men (of whom 260,000 were professional soldiers), 1,500 aircraft, and numerous mechanized divisions. The country's relative demographic situation was militarily favorable. Sixty-six million Germans could produce a far larger number of soldiers than could forty-one million Frenchmen.[53] Gone were the days of military emasculation that the Treaty of Versailles imposed upon Germany, which had included prohibitions against the acquisition of offensive arms and the construction of garrisons in the Rhineland as well as the imposition of a demilitarized zone bordering France (which in 1923 French soldiers assertively occupied to force reparations payments).

The tardy realization of Germany's military revival reversed French and European attitudes towards the necessity for military preparations. France restructured its military formations. It spent lavishly in the construction of defensive fortifications, erecting the magnificent but obsolescent Maginot Line that stretched the vast distance from the Rhine to the Moselle rivers. A scramble to acquire offensive arms ensued.

And yet, amazingly, in the minds of many contemporaries the conceit of French martial greatness endured even after Hitler's meteoric rise to power. For all the rapacity of his incursions in Central and Eastern Europe – Germany's absorption of Austria and Czechoslovakia in 1938 – a French general remarked that his country was "assured of being able to provide its troops with an armament equal in quality to that of the Germans."[54] Despite demographic and armaments asymmetry, there was some material basis to the idea of French preeminence. Together with its British ally, France possessed a larger number of tanks than Germany, whose panzers were by some accounts technically inferior to allied tanks. As late as October 1938, an American military observer remarked that French military power sufficed to defeat Germany. Little did he imagine, when he called for French arms to rescue (even without British support) Czechoslovakia from Hitler's clutches, that Europe's designated rescuer would itself soon succumb to the dictator in Berlin.[55]

If, by 1940, France and its allies were in some respects materially superior to Germany, why did Germany defeat them so quickly? The answer is compelling even if it risks oversimplification: because of the opponent's superior conception of mechanized warfare, at the time a largely untested form of conflict. Material superiority over Germany did not compensate sufficiently for the failure to answer satisfactorily the vital questions of strategy (voiced by a French general) that vexed allied military commanders: "How are tanks to be allotted? Shall they be distributed among the [infantry] units or is it preferable to keep them among the general reserves of the armies or groups of armies?"[56]

The relationship between technological revolution and strategy thus lies at the heart of the story of France's stunning defeat. Like many other strategic blunders before and after it, behind this one was a bad theory of an emerging weapon – the tank.

Here come the ironies. Tanks had made their appearance in the battlefield on French soil at the Battle of the Somme in 1916. Britain's Royal Tank Regiment – the world's first mechanized unit – sent several dozen of the new contraptions into battle. Only a small number penetrated the German lines. The clumsy instruments experienced difficulties navigating the rough trench terrain. They could not push through trees or cross wide rivers. They moved slowly. An infantryman walking briskly could outpace them. Although their fortified steel carcasses could stop bullets and some shrapnel, a direct mortar hit was normally fatal. The interior air exposed the crew to noxious carbon monoxide fumes. Temperatures could reach fifty degrees Celsius. Crewmembers collapsing from exhaustion had little room for rest because the petrol engine located at the center occupied most of the inner space. The noise of the engine and tracks more than stifled cogent conversation; it rendered the occupants' wireless transmitters useless.[57] Few tanks were used again in the First World War.

By the 1930s, therefore, although the tank's existence was not new, the *theory* of its strategic utility remained largely undeveloped. The tank's inauspicious record during the last war framed French and British strategic planners' mechanized warfare doctrine. They drew the wrong lessons. They dismissed the "engines of destruction" as a strategic irrelevance.[58] Lord Kitchener, Britain's strategic super-planner, dismissed the tank as a "pretty mechanical toy." That even the leaders of the nation that had pioneered the technology misinterpreted its implications for strategy gives proof to the irony – true as we saw of the current cyber age – that the initiators of technological revolution often fall behind in the task of studying its lessons.

Not all allied thinkers fell behind. It is remarkable that, in 1936, an obscure colonel by the name of Charles de Gaulle predicted the tank's strategic significance; not in the least notable that superiors ignored his unorthodox teachings at the Center for Higher Military Studies.[59] For in an epoch of change the swings of technology do not always reveal themselves readily to the scrutiny of contemporaries. What to some observers seems like valid foresight to others appears like false conjecture. Inferences of a new reality become subsumed by prejudices forged in an another era. So it was in France when the tank encountered the cult of defense forged in trench warfare during a war whose battle lines moved but slowly, with vast armies fighting to win – only quickly to lose – a few meters of worthless soil.

In contrast to French theorists' defensive mantra, German military commanders devised a doctrine of *Blitzkrieg* premised on the vitalness of offensive speed and surprise. The possibilities of mechanized warfare were at the heart of this doctrinal development. Commander of Germany's 5th Panzer Army Hasso Eccard von Manteuffel marveled at the French interpretive blunder. Although the allies possessed more, and technically superior, tanks, their defensive posture prescribed the weapons' dispersion rather than their concentration in rapid offensive thrusts. True to the doctrine, of the eighty German divisions that defeated France, eleven were motorized.

The mindset in Paris on May 5, 1940 – the eve of Germany's invasion of Western Europe – illustrates the old thinking's inadequacy. As German forces poured into the Low Countries, the French cabinet in a desperate meeting focused on operations two thousand miles away in Norway. To their credit, some ministers sought to replace the army's chief commander General Maurice Gamelin, a man wedded to static defensive dogma who had proudly overseen completion of the obsolescent Maginot Line which Hitler's forces expertly circumvented by moving through Belgium. But Gamelin was the man of Prime Minister Édouard Daladier, who threatened to resign if Gamelin was replaced. Defense Minister Paul Reynaud threatened the same if an espouser of bolder doctrine did not replace him.[60] None of this political controversy in the end mattered: the realization of doctrinal inadequacies roiling the French cabinet came several years too late. The appearance on their soil of a new method of warfare that contravened French military doctrine evicted the officials from office and indeed the country, many of them soon fleeing to Britain and other friendly nations.

The ironies do not end there. The German generals did not want a war with France and Britain, preferring instead the seemingly simpler conquests to the

East. They disingenuously presented Hitler with mediocre invasion plans of Western Europe that replicated the follies of a war of attrition. General Erich von Manstein punctured the subterfuge. He presented Hitler with a rapid invasion plan built on achieving surprise with planes and tanks, the very embodiment of *Blitzkrieg*. "Speed of response to the unexpected was a hallmark of German military leadership," noted historian Max Hastings.[61]

The French defenders, meanwhile, remained prisoners of their own dogma. As diversionary German forces swooped through the Low Countries, Allied reconnaissance reported long lines of panzers concentrating on the German side of the Ardennes Forest. Gamelin foolishly passed up the opportunity to bomb this bottleneck of exposed enemy armor.

On May 15, German forces crossed the Meuse into France, which the defenders had regarded as unpassable by tanks. So swift was the German advance that French reinforcements struggled to catch up behind their own lines.[62] Marshal Philippe Pétain warned the government about the loss of strategic cohesion among the defending forces. Reports quickly circulated in Paris of German forces ravaging the suburbs of Amiens seventy miles away. The next day Boulogne, Arras, and other towns in the direction of the English Channel fell. French and Belgian forces in the northeast were cut off from the bulk of the defenders to the south and west. Approximately one million Nazi troops roamed the country mostly unimpeded. No one in Paris knew how far the mechanized invaders had advanced towards the capital. By then, newly appointed military commander General Weygand had lost confidence in the correctness of defensive dogma. Only the determination to win remained – but without a set of viable principles to express it.

On June 14, 1940, Hitler paraded his triumphant troops down the Champs-Élysées. A remark by French general André Beaufre captured the mood in Paris and much of the world: "[The] few weeks' campaign, which led to a defeat so total and so sudden, was from first to last an endless surprise exposing our inability to cope with the enemy's torrential advance or to find any way to answer it."[63]

Mighty France's rapid defeat in face of "the new irresistible weapons" offers lessons for current and future generations of strategic thinkers grappling with the uncertain implications of technological revolution. The case reveals errors in the three main elements of strategy. First were mistakes in interpreting the horizon of technological possibility. French military commanders (much like their British counterparts) failed to grasp the tank's strategic significance. They flattered themselves with two misconceptions: the superiority of defensive warfare that had won them the last world war and which would now win them the second; and the new invention's inadequacy for use in offensive thrusts. Wedded to expired dogmas they clung to the notion that the cherished Maginot Line would arrest the transforming contraptions' advance. As Reynaud solemnly observed, "The truth is that our conception of warfare has run counter to a new conception." Divisions of tanks were "the basis of this conception." In May 1940, a French defender searching through his doctrinal playbook for prescriptions on how to deal with a rapid tank thrust – never before seen in history – would have failed to find them. He might have done as countless others in his place did: flee.

A second set of errors concerned the adversary's revolutionary designs for the new technology. After the victory in 1918, French leaders set themselves the task of shaping European politics according to a conception of national purposes that kept the former adversary in a state of permanent servility. For reasons that will be left to students of sociology, they did not fully realize that the new regime in Berlin had revolutionary aims on the battlefield and on the world scene. Nazi Germany's mastery of the principles of mechanized warfare in the late 1930s illustrates an important point: more important than the question of how technology enables new forms of conflict is how it empowers players seeking to use it to subvert the international order.

Third was the most complex problem of all: how to relate strategy to the adversary's objectives and to one's own resources. Here, too, the failures were spectacular. Although French leaders held a vision of international predominance, they combined it with the thinking of a second-rate power. Slow in grasping the nature of the menace across the Rhine, they failed to equip their military with the principles necessary to win a war that, to more prescient minds, seemed inevitable and different to all others before it. That a flawed conceit of national greatness and an obsolete defensive dogma which failed to address the sensational technological advances of an existential foe combined to produce a dazzling military blunder can be grasped more readily by us than by officials in Paris in the spring of 1940. Such is the tragedy – always harsh but never inevitable – of the failure to adapt security strategy to technological inventions.

2
CYBER LEGALISM
The Limits of Law and Norms

A FLAWED APPROACH

Western attempts to curtail cyber conflict have focused on the preferred methods of Western diplomacy: the fostering of laws and norms of international conduct. Adherents of the doctrine of cyber legalism stress the importance of existing international institutions to prevent hostile actions. They emphasize the value of forums, such as the United Nations Group of Governmental Experts (UNGGE) or the Open-Ended Working Group, which explore how legal conventions such as the UN Charter principles apply to the regulation of cyber conduct (a central point of contention among participating nations). They stress the reasonableness of their preferred norms, as if the transgressors in Moscow or Pyongyang had failed for all these years to grasp their self-evident validity.[1]

The existing legal framework reinforces the traditional war–peace binary that underpins Western strategic doctrine. As former general counsel to U.S. Cyber Command Gary Corn observed: "International law comes down on the side of Clausewitz. It draws some fairly bright lines. The distinction between armed conflict and non-armed conflict is stark, because once you cross that Rubicon, you are able to kill based solely on a person's status, not his or her immediate conduct."[2] But cyber conflict often occurs along a spectrum between the poles of war and peace. Thus, the legal order in which Western officials search for solutions to the challenge of cyber conflict prevention in fact impedes them. The binary thinking that underpins the legal framework (Give us war or give us peace for anything in between we struggle to interpret!) hinders the refinement of doctrine for a new era of conflict. It offers no, or few, clear benchmarks to guide the response to technological acts of unpeace.

Western policy in brief demands of the existing legal order more than it can presently give. From the clash of legal interpretation and doctrine on the one side and the new realities of conflict on the other emerges a posture of inaction or weak action that is characteristic of policymaking in times of technological revolution. As Corn aptly put it: "What the ambiguities of the gray zone do is create decision delay and often paralysis because of uncertainty in the legal interpretation of actions."[3]

This argument does not deny the important advances in global cooperation over technical aspects of the Internet – even on the backdrop of a contest of governance models. The open model championed by Western nations and early Internet pioneers (such as Vint Cerf) seeks to preserve nearly unfettered information exchange, that is, away from the prying eyes and censoring arm of the government. A competing closed model (or models, if one considers differences among Russian, Chinese, and other authoritarian "intranets")[4] implements stringent information controls and surveillance. Yet, despite the clash of models, which increasingly plays out in nations and regions (think of Africa) not yet wedded to one or the other approach, cooperation at the technical level (e.g. over Ipv6 deployment) has been successful. Functionally speaking, the Internet remains a largely interoperable realm. Indeed, possibly it is too interoperable: the ease of information exchange between machines (especially in the open Internet) facilitates the acts of unpeace that mar cyberspace. In sum, although interstate cooperation over cyber conflict remains poor, cooperation over technical Internet matters below the radar of diplomacy has seen relative success.[5]

The United States is among the chief proponents of cyber legalism. In 2010, not one year after the establishment of U.S. Cyber Command, its first commander General Keith Alexander affirmed before the Senate during his confirmation hearing: "[Department of Defense] operations are conducted consistent with international law principles in regard to what is a threat or use of force in terms of hostile intent and hostile act."[6] As if a vow of obedience to international law was a prerequisite of the job, Alexander invoked UN Charter principles – especially the principle of self-defense – as guiding lights of policy. Similarly, Defense Secretary Chuck Hagel stated in 2014 that his country "will maintain an approach of restraint to any cyber operations outside of U.S.

government networks."[7] General Paul Nakasone, Alexander's current successor, and senior advisor Michael Sulmeyer reaffirmed: "[U.S.] cyber forces abide by widely accepted principles of international law, and when they take direct action, they narrowly tailor the effect," emphasizing the laws of war. "[O]ur actions must also remain consistent with the law of armed conflict and other important international norms."[8] This policy course follows the direction set by the first U.S. International Strategy for Cyberspace, which expressed a commitment to build a "global consensus" around norms of conduct drawing from existing international law.[9] Constructing the consensus was the chief task of Christopher Painter, the first U.S. Coordinator for Cyber Issues, who assiduously pursued his remit in "a new era of foreign policy" within multilateral forums.[10] Diplomats have strived for consensus particularly within the UNGGE, a vehicle of norm construction (or more often norm contestation) drawing from existing international law, whose efforts the United States initially underplayed but today champions.[11]

Recent U.S. policy changes that adopt a more assertive posture nevertheless seek to respect (or be seen to respect) the rigid adherence to law. The new U.S. policy of persistent engagement paves the way for more intrusions in adversaries' home networks – for example, searching through or disabling foreign computers to impede offensive moves. It is a refinement of the older notion of "active defense," whose defining characteristic was out-of-perimeter activity.[12] But as a manifestation of the doctrine of "Defending Forward," the policy operates within the broad realm of self-defense. It manifestly does not prescribe offensive action for deterrence purposes. Rather, it seeks "to disrupt and degrade the capabilities our adversaries use to conduct attacks" – that is, to undermine the attack by imposing costs on attackers but not to penalize them.[13]

Allies and close partners of the United States also espouse the mantra of cyber legalism. In 2018, the French government assembled an international group of public officials as well as representatives from private industry and civil society to promote an "open, secure, stable, accessible, and peaceful cyberspace." The resulting "Paris Call" stated: "We reaffirm that international law, together with the voluntary norms of responsible State behavior during peacetime and associated confidence and capacity-building measures developed within the United Nations, is the foundation for international peace and security in cyberspace"[14] – a fine attestation of the tenets of the legalistic approach. In 2019, Britain endorsed a commitment to "law, norms, and confidence building in cyberspace."[15] Echoing Painter's mission, the British national cyber strategy emphasized the aim of building a "global alliance" promoting the respect of international law in cyberspace.[16] European Union officials have toed a similar line. Drawing from their union's record of pacifying a continent where for centuries the resort to war was an accepted device of statecraft and the quest for domination its occasional aim, EU officials pride themselves on Europe's status as a "normative power" that can uphold the international (or at least regional) order and resolve interstate quarrels peacefully.[17] In 2019, EU foreign policy chief Federica Mogherini expressed the Union's aspiration of becoming "a forward-looking cyber player," for which policymakers devised a "toolbox" of measures, including punitive economic sanctions, to strengthen "the rules-based order in cyberspace, including the application of international law and the adherence of norms of responsible state behaviour."[18] NATO, too, has chimed in. Responding to malicious intrusions targeting public health infra-structure during the Covid-19 pandemic, for example, the alliance's governing council declared: "We all stand to benefit from a rules-based, predictable, open, free, and secure cyberspace."[19]

Cyber legalism, in sum, is not an emerging or debated approach within Western policy circles; it is the central thrust of the strategy of conflict reduction. It represents an expansive normative program, one in which, at least implicitly, the familiar corpus of principles, rules, and norms that were developed to constrain war in other domains of conflict should also apply, in some as yet undefined and contested but sorely needed way, to constrain damaging actions below its threshold.

IS LEGAL TALK JUST CHEAP TALK?

Cynics may see in these pronouncements a subterfuge of large nations and the organizations they control to cloak power politics in the legitimacy of international law. After all, soon after affirming in the Senate a commitment to legal constraints, Alexander presided over the most destructive cyberattack on record, the "Olympic Games" operation that destroyed approximately one thousand uranium enrichment centrifuges in Iran, an act that some observers have regarded as an illegal use of force.[20] Or else, large adversaries may perceive cyber legalism as a tool of Western "normative imperialism," an attempt to impose a liberal vision of international affairs in a poorly defined realm of action that offers dominant players many imperialistic spoils.[21]

The former cynical view resonates with the "cheap talk" theory of international rhetoric in which leaders use moral language as a ruse to deflect the attention of domestic or foreign publics from the coercive pursuit of material interests, which could violate the very standards of behavior that the leaders invoked (hence the talk's "cheapness").[22] The theory helps to explain Western rhetoric in other domains of conflict. In 2003, George W. Bush referred to legal provisions of the UN Security Council requiring Saddam Hussein to dismantle weapons of mass destruction and Tony Blair invoked the self-defense principle to protect his country against their implied threat, while, on the ideological plane, both leaders appealed to ideals of democracy expansion – all in order to secure payoffs of cooperation and avoid costs of dissensus with other states, including democratic partners whose security and economic interests did not align with the two leaders' planned invasion of Iraq. The rhetoric of legal obligations and democratic virtues reflected the true views of many American and British people (if not also of Bush and Blair). Moral imperatives, however, did not drive the military adventure or its subsequent resistance by much of the international community. More important were considerations of material interests and regional power.[23]

Despite its success in other conflict domains, the cheap talk model does not go far in accounting for Western attitudes in the cyber domain. Adherence to law and norms is not merely a verbal device of rational actors pursuing their preferences in situations of multiple equilibria. Weighing the option of punitive cyber strikes against North Korean computers in the aftermath of the Sony Pictures hack, former director of national intelligence James Clapper faced the anxieties of legal advisors (because the attacks could have crossed other countries' networks). "The lawyers went nuts," he revealed, "so we didn't do anything on the cyber front. We ended up sanctioning a bunch of North Korean generals."[24] "Everything we did at U.S. Cyber Command was subject to legal commitments," affirmed Corn. "I saw this in practice multiple times. International law plays the tempering role that it ought to play. Responses to cyberattacks have to remain calibrated so that they don't infringe upon international law."[25]

One might expect former senior officials to hew to law and norms. But their apparent self-restraint attests to their commitment's sincerity, especially because it seemed sometimes to override security concerns. Some states pursue cyber legalism as an end in itself. For how else to explain the high material costs of obedience to legal ideals that adversaries repeatedly flout? In open adherence to international law, the United States has shown restraint in the destructive use of cyberweapons even when tactical or strategic considerations supported it. In 2003, the Bush Administration decided not to attack the financial system of Saddam Hussein's Iraq in the leadup to that country's invasion.[26] In 2011, Obama reportedly eschewed the use of destructive cyberattacks against the communications infrastructure of Muammar Gaddafi's Libya in the leadup to NATO's airstrikes against the country.[27] In the few known instances in which the United States and its allies carried out destructive cyberattacks, their purpose was largely conservative: to support the international order by imposing costs on defiers against it, such as the targeting of the Natanz nuclear facility to degrade Iran's suspected nuclear weapons program or the disruption of Islamic State's communications infrastructure to curtail the terrorist group's online publicity efforts.[28] The legal restraints in these and other cases seem to have involved considerations of both *jus ad bellum*, the question of whether sufficient cause exists to justify an act of aggression (the condition of necessity), and *jus in bello*, whether the action's effects are legal regardless of its justness or not (e.g. the requirements of proportionality and distinction).

And what of Stuxnet, was it a breach of international law? The answer hinges partly on whether the operation's effects amounted to a use of force. Let us concede to the cheap talkers that it met this criterion. Even so, the operation stands out as restrained when compared to the common actions of the large norm transgressors. It was finely customized to disrupt only the machine complex at the Natanz facility. Although it infected computer systems in many countries, its payload affected only this one. Compare Stuxnet with the Russian NotPetya malware, which disrupted infrastructure and affected economic interests in a cascade of industries and countries. And then there is Stuxnet's purpose: to arrest the suspected development of nuclear weapons by a nation prohibited by treaty from obtaining them, whose authorities occasionally obstructed the inspectors of the International Atomic Energy Agency and had expressed a hostile attitude towards the operation's co-authors, the United States and Israel, thereby possibly providing grounds for offensive action under the principle of anticipatory self-defense. Most important, the virtual, non-lethal method of attack meant that it was far less destructive than the alternative on the table – an airstrike – which the Israeli government reportedly preferred.[29] Overall, what stands out about the Stuxnet operation is not that it was the closest example of the use of force in the cyber domain, but that despite its potency it manifested offensive restraint by its narrow targeting and by its replacement of an armed attack.

The motivations of Western nations' vocal commitment to international law are both domestic and international. They are domestic insofar as they reflect the imperative of elected officials to cultivate the perception among their public that they abide by law and norms. Infraction of international agreements and defiance of established ethical standards do not constitute conduct that a liberal democratic public will commonly excuse except in circumstances of "extreme emergency," such as Churchill's decision to scorch with fire Dresden and other German cities during the Second World War.[30] The point holds even if one accepts that democratic governments will deceive their own citizens about the legality of foreign policy conduct. Consider the Nixon Administration's concealment of the bombing of Cambodia during the Vietnam War, an action whose legality was broadly challenged and which invoked impassioned rebukes even among the president's supporters. The motivation behind law adherence (or its perception) is also international: to violate law and norms blatantly is to undermine the coherence of all law in a jungle of sovereign states whose tendencies for violence and chaos officials want to tame with an arsenal of rules, norms, and institutions to enforce them.

Cyber legalism in brief represents a true, if often tested, commitment of the United States and other Western nations to uphold the restraints of international law and norms as they might apply in the realm of unpeace. Cyber activity's vague status within the law and its possibly norm-violating nature (from a Western perspective) explain why these nations protest acts of unpeace directed against them while they themselves rarely carry them out. It is possible that Western nations conduct more damaging cyberattacks than the empirical record reveals. But that is not likely, because acts of unpeace by definition produce social, political, or economic harm that can be difficult to conceal from public scrutiny.

Adherence to law (or one's perception of it) limits the design and application of strategic doctrine. Whatever dimension of doctrine one considers, declaratory or operational, it must conform with the values of the organized society – even if the crudities of anarchic politics mean that law often exists in a state of tension with power and interests. As Samuel Huntington explained in relation to U.S. defense policy: "Inevitably, the Administration must legitimate its action by invoking general values which command broad support."[31] What may seem like policymakers' insignificant attention to the semantics and phraseology of law is a means to secure the legitimacy and endorsement of policy. That does not always mean that lawfulness supersedes security or negates the use of disciplined coercion to achieve it. Rather, the pining for rules and norms and the flashes of raw power are two aspects of the same doctrinal ethos; they cannot be separated into distinct paradigms. Even the warrior is moved by a cause that (by his lights) benefits the world. Even the worldliest diplomat is tempted to brandish the sword to realize a harmonious ideal. It was said of John Foster Dulles that he flashed the Bible in one hand and the nuclear bomb in the other. The parody of the quip applies as much to the statesman as to his whole nation's style of statecraft. As an ideational enterprise, cyber legalism is inward-looking. A liberal vision of international affairs underpins it. It reflects the basic necessity of a national psychology that judges itself and the world according to intentions more than actions or capabilities. As Nakasone and Sulmeyer tellingly put it: "[W]e are protecting U.S. interests from cyber threats and staying true to the nation's core values."[32]

TWO UNIVERSALISMS IN A FRAGMENTED WORLD

Having reviewed the roots of cyber legalism, let us delve into its workings and limitations more closely. It is a universal doctrine in two key respects.

One is its presumption of *universal acceptance*: international law and norms appeal to all members of the international community; where transgression occurs, it is more the result of misperception or the distortions of dictators than of inconsistent values among peoples. To be sure, ambiguity and disagreement exist between states regarding the precise interpretation of law and norms in given contexts.[33] "There is no international consensus on a precise definition of a use of force, in or out of cyberspace," remarked Alexander. "Consequently, individual nations may assert different definitions, and may apply different thresholds for what constitutes a use of force. Thus, whether in the cyber or any other domain, there is always potential disagreement among nations concerning what may amount to a threat or use of force."[34] But individual states' assertion of their own interpretation of legalities does not erode the supposed deeper consensus on broad principles of interstate conduct. For cyber legalism is not just inward-looking; it also looks *outward* by universalizing the expectation that peoples of other nations – no matter the ruthlessness of their regimes – will also wish to inhabit the imagined liberal utopia. Therefrom stems an important basis for self-restraint within the perspective: the desire to sustain at least the perception of abidance of laws (which officials expansively construe) in an effort, internationally, to civilize a jungle marred by dizzying instability and, domestically, to legitimate policy in an emerging realm of conflict.[35]

A second key feature of cyber legalism is the presumption of *universal applicability*: the existing legal framework suffices to restrain conflict in the new (some say revolutionary) arena of cyberspace. Thus, there is no need to create legal principles. Rather, one must figure out how to apply old principles in new contexts. The United States' position is that the law governing armed conflict "should regulate the use of cyber tools in hostilities, just as it does other tools."[36] The presumption is also conveyed by Mogherini's commitment to "the existing consensus" on international law, a consensus supposedly embodied in multilateral reports of the UNGGE or the Open-Ended Working Group.[37] NATO too reiterated "that international law applies in cyberspace and must be respected,"[38] betraying a frustration, easily detectable in alliance officials' regular protests against Russian actions, that adversaries neither respect nor apply the law.[39]

Are these two universalistic tendencies accurate? Despite protestations that Russia, China, and other nations routinely violate international law and norms in cyberspace – for example, Obama's claim that the Democratic National

Convention (DNC) hack breached "established international norms of behavior"[40] or Stoltenberg's condemnation of Russia's "blatant attempts to undermine international law and institutions"[41] – the notion of universal acceptance is in a sense accurate. Let us not forget that Russia and China publicly accepted the non-binding recommendations of the 2015 UNGGE report affirming that international law applies to cyberspace.[42] As permanent Security Council members, they participated in all rounds of UNGGE discussion. Indeed, the Russian government was the first to propose, in the late 1990s, the creation of a multilateral forum for the clarification of norms of offensive cyber conduct. Putin has publicly avowed his country's commitment to international law. In 2013, he promoted "the preparation and adoption by the United Nations member states of international legal instruments regulating the application of the principles and rules of international humanitarian law in the use of ICTs."[43] A Russian representative at the United Nations similarly affirmed in 2020 that "the existing universally recognized norms and principles of international law fixed in the UN Charter are fully and unconditionally applicable to the sphere of information and communication technologies."[44] None of this is to argue that Russia, a challenger state against the international order, obeys international law for reasons other than the national interest. It is merely to point out that in the view of geopolitical adversaries, established law and norms apply to cyber actions but in a way that does not offer the clear constraints that Western leaders ascribe to them. Rather, the framework applies in the sense that it does not clearly limit acts of unpeace.

The heat of the argument about the law of cyber conflict, therefore, obscures the fact that the main contenders agree on a fundamental point: they all support the application of existing international law to the cyber domain, if for opposite reasons – one side because it wants to use the framework to limit unpeace, the other because the framework enables more than limits it.

The notion of universal applicability is more problematic. Nations differ on the question of the legal framework's relevance to cyber conflict. The Western view might find credence in rulings of the International Court of Justice (ICJ), although it requires interpretive stretching. In 1996, the Court stated that the UN Charter provisions defining prohibitions on the use of force, the right of self-defense, and the Security Council's competence to authorize uses of force "apply to any use of force, regardless of the weapons employed." That is, the principles of *jus ad bellum* that define acceptable grounds for the use of weapons among states apply to the regulation of cyberweapons. The court voiced a similar view in relation to *jus in bello* by noting that international humanitarian law applies to new "means and methods" of warfare. This interpretation draws further support from Article 36 of the Additional Protocol I to the Geneva Convention, which requires a review of new means of warfare.[45] Western references to the applicability of international humanitarian law and the law of armed conflict to cyberspace, then, imply a stretching of the logic of the ICJ's rulings to forms of conflict less than war.

The empirical record paints another picture, however. The existence of the punishment problem betrays the weakness of the notion of universal applicability. The persistent failure of Western nations to punish activity that their leaders regard as gravely damaging to national security suggests that they struggle to situate the activity within the existing legal universe. The vast corpus of international law and norms regulating interstate rivalry, ranging from the UN Charter principles and the law of armed conflict to regional security arrangements such as NATO, centers on the two benchmarks of armed attack: a clearly defined notion denoting significant destruction of physical property and loss of life; and the use of force, a more ambiguous notion that implies physical harm if not necessarily armed attack. This framework does not commonly recognize the right of nations to carry out reprisals outside of situations of armed conflict. Yet, no cyber action so far has clearly met the criteria of armed attack. As we saw, it is disputable whether Stuxnet was a use of force; even if it was, the incident remains an outlier event. Tellingly, even the operation's Iranian victims played down its consequences, as expressed by President Mahmoud Ahmadinejad in 2010: "[The attackers] succeeded in creating problems for a limited number of our centrifuges with the software they had installed in electronic parts."[46]

And yet a growing number of cyber actions have abused the customary limits of strategic competition in peacetime. It is by now familiar to point out that cyber conflict occurs below the threshold of war. The main interpretive value of the notion of unpeace is to emphasize the possibly more important but less recognized point that much of it also transpires *above* the threshold of peace. For this reason, the term unpeace is analytically more useful than the alternative label "non-war"; it emphasizes the difficulties of figuring out how to respond to non-war offensive action with peacetime devices of international law that do not pack a sufficiently strong punitive punch.

Although not explicitly defined by treaty, statesmen and scholars alike have regarded the notion of peace to mean the absence of acts of war or gross human rights violations (which do not always occur in wartime). This treatment is implied in the language of UN documents referring, for example, to the goal of "restor[ing] peace following the outbreak of armed conflict, and to promote lasting peace in societies emerging from wars."[47] Similarly, the diplomacy of preventive disarmament focuses on the preservation of peace by reducing small arms in conflict-prone regions; on peacekeeping in the demobilization of troops and the maintenance of ceasefires; and on peacebuilding to establish the social, economic, and institutional conditions that prevent a recurrence of civil war. The UN Security Council resolution specifying the purposes and tasks of the Peacebuilding Commission explicitly references "post-conflict" scenarios that, by their nature, entail ruinous physical violence and loss of life.[48] These peace-oriented activities are diverse and sometimes only vaguely defined, but they share a central feature: the absence, prevention, or eradication of physical violence.

Political thinkers have supplied a similarly binary understanding of war and peace. Thomas Hobbes famously and darkly described life in the anarchic jungle as a "state of war" – of "war of all against all" – not because war is incessant but because it can at any time break out. Hobbes wrote primarily about life in the domestic state of nature; he was less concerned about the international jungle. But some international relations thinkers (particularly realists such as Hans Morgenthau and Stanley Hoffmann) have applied his concepts to make sense of international relations.[49] In a Hobbesian conception of international anarchy, peace is a state in which actors expect and prepare for future war. Relations among coexisting states constantly alternate between a situation in which war is "on" and one in which it is "off."

The absence of violence is not the only defining element of peace. Equally important for our purposes is the notion of peace implied in Hedley Bull's idea of an "international society" (which has affinities with classical realism in international relations theory) in which sovereign states bound by common basic values seek not merely to limit war, especially a generalized war (such as the two world wars) that threatens an implosion of the states system, but also to keep interstate rivalries within acceptable boundaries so that the units' sovereignty and security are preserved even if no war occurs.[50]

Also notable is the unforgettable definition of cyber peace provided by the International Telecommunication Union: "a universal order of cyberspace" that features a "wholesome state of tranquillity, the absence of disorder or disturbance and violence."[51] Ambitious for its allusion to a stable political order among states, the notion is loftier than historical developments have allowed. But it is useful for analysis because it points to a fundamental condition of peace, namely, the existence of regularized interactions among players such that, even in the absence of a World Leviathan to punish deviators, they can achieve stable expectations of behavior in a competition for security that is tolerable because its aims are limited and its means are familiar.

Whatever benchmark one uses – the absence of interstate violence and even rivalry or the commitment to contain them within acceptable bounds – it is clear that peace, like war, occurs in degrees. There is at one end of the peace sub-spectrum the shadow of always possible and sometimes impending war described by Hobbes, in which peace is but a precarious opportunity to prepare the nation for the call to arms against one's neighbors. At the other end is lasting comity: a state of affairs – rare in the system of anarchy – in which not merely violence but even the prospect of it are absent, a civilized quarter of the jungle where thoughts of war among nations do not arise because it is *unthinkable*. Consider today's integrated Europe, a zone of peace as permanent as can occur (short of the "graveyard" peace of all-out nuclear war) in international relations, where nations share a single currency, where physical borders are mostly imaginary, and where nations sustain armies not to conquer or defeat each other (the bane of European international relations before 1945) but to address threats outside the pacific union.

The existing legal and normative framework captures much of peacetime cyber activity, but chiefly within the narrowly conscribed realm of domestic law (see Table 1). Financial fraud or the theft of money via the Internet, such as North Korea's hacking of cryptoasset exchanges,[52] are normally proscribed by the domestic penal code of the victim nation. National authorities struggle to prosecute the culprits if they reside in a foreign jurisdiction, however, but at least the applicability of law – some law – is clear.

The framework applies most neatly in the realm of war. The absence of cyberwar in the presence of arms to carry it out reveals a rare strength of the international legal order: there has been no cyberwar because it is the easiest form of conflict to address. A scheming attacker knows that it would almost certainly elicit a response commensurate with conventional war. Cyberwar, then, is a realm of conflict in which international law and deterrence doctrine neatly align – hence its absence so far.

When does a cyber action entail a sufficient cause to invoke a belligerent reprisal? The question is important because the absence of cyberwar does not signify the impotence of modern weapons. Scenario modeling suggests that cyberattacks could inflict severe physical damage on vital infrastructure and thereby produce human deaths. Conceivable examples are easy to find: a cyberattack that kills people by disrupting a city's power supply or by derailing a passenger train; or one that creates an "existential" danger by disabling a nation's nuclear arsenal.[53] These scenarios would implicate the UN Charter principles of a use of force or even an armed attack. Harder (and still unre-solved almost ten years after Jack Goldsmith and Eric Posner posed it) is the question of when a cyberattack that slowly degrades the functionality of a critical infrastructure amounts to a use of force or war.[54]

Less clear is the case of unpeace: harmful action whose magnitude does not rise to the level of war, and whose instruments therefore do not apply, even as it breaches the acceptable bounds of peacetime competition, whose punitive options thus will fall short of a satisfactory response. Cyber espionage in the form of kompromat operations is perhaps hardest of all to address because the legal framework says almost nothing about espionage. Acts of unpeace create problems of legal interpretation for nations such as the United States that apply a "traditionally high threshold for response to adversary activity."[55] When it comes to deciphering an appropriate response, individuals with responsi-bility to shape it have few clear guideposts to orient them. In the words of Sony Pictures CEO Michael Lynton: "There is no playbook,"[56] an insight that applies as much to government decisionmakers as to industry executives.

Table 1. Legal Categories of Hostile Cyber Activity

Peace	Unpeace	Armed Attack / Use of Force
Examples:	Examples:	Examples:
• Standalone cyber espionage or reconnaissance • Bulk data collection of foreign targets • Cryptoasset exchange hacking • Financial fraud	• Large-scale infiltration and surveillance of government networks (e.g. SolarWinds) • Indiscriminate industrial disruption (e.g. NotPetya) • Disruption of public health services (e.g. WannaCry) • Systemwide computer malfunction (e.g. Shamoon) • Financial system manipulation (e.g. Bangladesh Central Bank heist) • Information operations during national elections or referenda • Power grid disruption (e.g. Ukraine 2015) • Physical infrastructure destruction (e.g. Stuxnet) • Large-scale industrial espionage (e.g. Aurora operation) • National-scale economic convulsion (e.g. Estonia 2007)	• Fatal cyberattack against hospital systems • Fatal cyberattack against transport systems • Disruption of tactical operations in wartime (e.g. Georgia 2008)
Applicable legal instruments: • 2004 Budapest Convention • Domestic penal code	Applicable legal instruments: • Domestic penal code (e.g. U.S. indictment of People's Liberation Army officers) • Countermeasures (possibly applicable, if a breach of international law can be established) • "There is no playbook" (Michael Lynton, Sony Pictures CEO)	Applicable legal instruments: • Law of Armed Conflict • UN Charter (e.g. Articles 51 and 2(4)) • Regional security organizations (e.g. NATO)

International law allows the use of countermeasures – unilateral actions adopted by one state in response to another's actions – but only if the victim can establish that the other side breached international law (such as the principles of sovereignty or non-intervention). But, as we saw, it is often contestable whether such a violation has occurred through cyberspace. But even when countermeasures are allowed because a breach can be established, international law tightly constrains them. Countermeasures require prior notification, thereby potentially diminishing their tactical effectiveness; they cannot be used against non-state actors, limiting their application against proxy agents that often play an important tactical role in cyber conflict; they cannot be applied collectively among allies, reducing the compounding effects of a coordinated response; and they cannot be used to deter future aggression (merely to curtail, or seek reparations for, an ongoing wrongful action).[57] Countermeasures are an un-proactive, non-punitive, state-oriented, uncoordinated form of adversary denial. The result is a situation in which international law limits the victim's response more tightly than the attacker's initial move.

Cyber legalism, in sum, constrains Western behavior in two ways: first, because of uncertainties about where and how existing law applies (though apply it must!) to cyber actions that are neither war nor peace; second, because of officials' desire to sustain at least the perception of law abidance through self-restraint in the global enterprise of norm creation.

The approach suffers severe limitations. The liberal view on which it draws fails to grasp an essential truth about the world it seeks to shape: the anarchical states system does not tolerate noble adherence to law – obeyance of rules for its own sake. What good is it to live according to the precepts of an ideal society if one's neighbors are intransigent villains? To accept the constraints of international law while others flaunt it is to pay the costs of adversaries' imaginative exploitations. There is in the legalistic paradigm a self-propelling righteousness: the greater the adherence to law among nations, the greater the costs of neglecting it – hence the necessity, ultimately, for universalism. But it embodies also a dilemma: if nations stray from the rules they themselves espouse – even as a temporary interruption in the imagined order – because others break them, then the norm proponents damage their own ideal enterprise. The inward project of norm enactment and its attendant self-restraints are a precursor to the outward-facing project of norm expansion.

This dilemma seems insoluble under present conditions. Cyber legalism implies a universality that the realities of international politics do not allow but without which the approach cannot succeed. To assert that nations must adhere perfectly to legal and normative obligations implies that nations want or can be persuaded to do so. But the end of legal infringements by sovereign states is neither historically possible nor philosophically desirable.[58] For this scenario requires a perfection in the design of law that cannot be implied and the presence of an impartial enforcer which the anarchical states system cannot guarantee. Nations, especially large ones, disagree – sometimes fundamentally – about the legal vagaries of cyber conflict. Adherents of cyber legalism assume that international law limits actions above *and* below (to a point) the level of war and use of force. Adversaries' persistent violation of the poorly defined lower boundaries suggests that, in their view, legal constraints apply mainly (possibly only) above the war threshold. They constrain unpeace only weakly; it goes unpunished mainly because it is *unpunishable*.

Gaps in the applicability of international law to cyber conflict mean that much of the effort to tighten institutional constraints falls into the realm of *lex ferenda*, or future law. The curtailment of intensifying aggression, however, cannot wait for a future that might never arise. Until and unless the legal system is equipped with instruments to limit technological acts of unpeace, policymakers must find a solution to problems of cyber conflict prevention elsewhere – in the realm of strategies to deter aggression by rational means (on which more in Chapter 7).

THE NECESSITY FOR NEW STRATEGY

The highest aspiration of politics in an anarchic system is not peace but order. For the preservation of sovereign rights under anarchic conditions sometimes requires the force of arms. A peace that is eternal risks calling forth a tyranny that is universal. But whereas the international system can endure outbreaks of limited war, and even some generalized war, it cannot thrive for long in the absence of stable patterns of relations – hence the necessity to establish them in the presence of a destabilizing technology. In this regard, the international cyber domain is not just an unpeaceful but also a *pre*-anarchic environment: it lacks stable expectations of behavior among sovereign contenders. Policymakers and analysts have yet to develop the institutional conditions of orderliness that make security competition in other conflict domains largely bearable because it is regularized and because clear rules and expectations of behavior guide the rivals.[59]

For all the assertions that international law can regulate cyber conflict, dissonances among states reveal the failure of the legal and normative framework to curtail it. To Western nations, the framework is relevant because it constrains behavior. It allows them to chart a course towards an imagined orderly universe they want to inhabit even as they still lay down its institutional foundations. To adversaries such as Russia and China, the legal framework is relevant for the opposite reason: it offers few clear limits on a large and expanding range of unpeaceful rivalry that the autocrats carry out to pursue their interests. To Western officials, international law is a map out of the chaotic jungle towards a more restrained society. To the autocrats, it is a very different kind of map: it reveals roads inside rather than out of the jungle; it guides movements within a primitive society of only thinly shared ideals and few punishments for violating them.

Therefrom stems a major contradiction in Western cyber strategy: it is both too lenient, because it fails to deter actions that law and norms, after all, do not clearly limit, and too strict, because a narrow interpretation of the rules curtails its own scope for strategic maneuver. It passes up opportunities to seize strategic gains even as it struggles to check adversaries' pursuit of them.

Incessant breaches of the peace in the absence of war betray the failure of dominant Western policy to address the problem. Existing policy approaches that prioritize a framework of law that does not apply neatly and universal norms that do not yet exist – and which one cannot unilaterally wish into existence – reveal the extent to which the problem of cyber conflict prevention is chiefly doctrinal rather than institutional. Institutional solutions possibly lie in wait. But until the legal system is upgraded, unless a new normative consensus emerges, an approach that prioritizes law and norms will feed, rather than solve, the problem of recurring conflict.

3
CHALLENGER STATES
Revisionism in the International System

THE WESTERN LIBERAL ORDER UNDER THREAT

A resurgent Russia and a rising China present the foremost threats to the Western liberal order, both domestically and internationally. For they are no ordinary world powers. Their foreign policies pursue revisionist aims; they strive to alter the international system more than preserve it. This aspiration embodies ideological as much as material goals. Russia and China seek not only security and wealth – a universal concern of nations – but also a particular view of their leading place in the world. Still lamenting the dissolution of their empire in the late twentieth century, leaders in Moscow aspire to reclaim Russia's former status atop the pantheon of nations.[1] Resenting the inglorious treatment by the European colonialists in previous centuries, but recalling that their vast nation was once Heaven's trustee on earth, the leadership in Beijing seeks to assert China's global role as a model for other nations to follow.

In both nations, but for different reasons, repulsion towards liberal democracy feeds the sense of geopolitical grievance. Their challenge operates by eroding the dominant liberal states' political and social cohesion from within; that is, by seeking to weaken Western nations' foreign policy resolve and fracture the alliance systems that emerged in Asia-Pacific and in Europe after 1945, or at least to curtail their expansion towards the motherlands' frontiers. For if democracy's eastward march was the fire that consumed the Soviet empire and which threatens the legitimacy of the autocratic behemoths, then the rollback of political liberalism at home and its repulsion in the near abroad is a vehicle for the assertion of new centers of global power. Although contemporary Russia has eschewed the dogmas of Soviet Communism in favor of market openness, and while nominally Communist China has embraced open-market innovation, albeit heavily influenced by the state, the political philosophy underpinning capitalism – liberalism – remains an object of suspicion and derision in Moscow and Beijing.

Champions of the ideology of liberal democracy like to regard their creed as universally valid.[2] That two of the most powerful nations in the world (and many others) reject it betrays a different reality: there is no, and there never has been a truly universal "rules-based international order." The prevalence of rules over raw power, and the triumph of consensus over coercion – a remarkable historical achievement – does not extend beyond the zones of internal peace that encompass the community of liberal democracies. The community's deprecation of the role of force and its failure to master lesser forms of conflict misses their importance in the struggles that mar interstate dealings beyond its own borders. Far from being unique, Russia's invasion of Ukraine has shades of 1956 and 1968. Were China to invade Taiwan, as some analysts increasingly fear,[3] it would mark a return to the historical mean of regional wars (think of Korea or Vietnam) rather than a deviation away from it. Similarly, the convergence of cyberspace and geopolitics in relations among large nations is no longer an emergent trend; it is defining. Future historians (the good ones) will ask how Russia's bold intrusions upon Western elections or China's pervasive insertions into prized infrastructure foreshadowed things to come.

In short, when Western leaders decry the autocrats' violation of the rules-based international order what they really lament is its absence. Recall an important point from Chapter 1 popularized by British political thinkers: an international society exists but thinly (on which more below). Beyond the common goal of avoiding a millenarian war that risks consuming the states system itself, the large nations share few objectives and diverge fundamentally in political values.[4] Hence the intensity of global contests for power: many grievances fuel it, but few shared goals override them. Because the liberal rules and institutions that Western nations designed after 1945 cannot curtail the quest for power to supersede them, the universality of liberal institutions remains more aspiration than accomplishment. Because Western nations dominate the international order, but because their dominance no longer equates to preeminence, they and their aspiring partners (such as Ukraine and Taiwan) are the targets of the challenger states' activist foreign policies.

Only by understanding the true nature and origins of the foreign policy activism behind Russian and Chinese strategic cyber activity can Western and democratic nations improve the efficacy of their attempts to curtail it. To this end, this chapter examines the historical phenomenon of revisionism in international relations. It provides a conceptual framework to guide the task of identifying and evaluating the revisionist aspects of the challengers' foreign policies. The framework will guide the analysis, in later chapters, of Russia's and China's use of cyberspace for transforming ends. Although the framework is applicable to any challenger state, the historical discussion below focuses on Russia because of its preeminent role in geopolitics during the last century.[5]

REVISIONISM IN THE INTERNATIONAL SYSTEM: A FRAMEWORK

An important step in analyzing the challenger states is to define a benchmark of revisionism against which to evaluate the degree of their foreign policy activism. International relations theory supplies useful concepts to guide this task.

For political scientists, the international system is an ideal type. It often assumes two basic sets of assumptions. One concerns the players in the system: a broad consensus that states (often only large ones) are the principal and irreducible actors; other actors, domestic and international, exist but are subordinate to the states. This view identifies the actors that possess independent authority to act and whose actions most directly influence their security and welfare. Other factors, such as the actors' goals and relative capabilities, especially military power and industrial capacity, reside within the parameters of a given system. Second are assumptions about the existence of an "international society"[6] whose main defining feature is a set of basic values and goals, chief of which are state survival and the preservation of order, and acceptable means of pursuing them – especially the avoidance of a general war.[7] The existence of society means that nations commonly accept the right to protect their own interests, even if in certain instances the clash involves an outbreak of limited war – always violent and sometimes devastating, but never to an extent that destroys the system's sovereignty of units. The system's societal element defines limits of conduct within which states pursue their clashing interests. The body of international law and norms, which includes the law of armed conflict (see Chapter 2), helps to guide this process. States know that the international jungle is anarchic; they seek solutions to problems of cooperation by establishing governance rules and institutions without their domestic concomitant, the centralized state.

This concept of international society allows us to identify two broad types of foreign policy activism. The most extreme form is *first-order revisionism*, which involves an attempt to alter the international system's organizing tenets.[8] It seeks to destroy the system's constitutional structure by reordering the hierarchy of units within it. Examples abound in history. Among the most prominent are the plans for world conquest of Napoleonic France or Nazi Germany. Both nations sought to crush the European states system by fusing its sovereign states into a single political entity under the domination of Paris or Berlin.

A less extreme but still significant form of international activism, *second-order revisionism*, affects the system's ideological building blocks: the shared values, norms, and customs. It arises when a state or a group of states reject this basic political framework. It may involve outright rejection of common goals (consider North Korea's repeated attempts to disrupt East Asian international affairs) or the accepted methods for achieving them (recall Saddam Hussein's illegal annexation of Kuwait in 1990). Whatever its ideological content, second-order revisionism differs from first-order revisionism in one crucial way: it leaves state sovereignty – the system's main organizing principle – untouched. That is, it seeks to alter the character of international society without reordering the "balance of players" within it.[9]

This basic framework suggests an important point about the relationship between foreign policy revisionism and war: revisionism does not by definition entail a country's pursuit of violent conquest or even the resort to armed force. For war might be an accepted form of international conduct within the existing order in which a challenger state arises. True, two of the most extreme revisionist powers, Napoleonic France and Nazi Germany, were among the most violent nations in history. Millions of people were lost to each of their armies. But revisionism is defined more by the variation between, on the one side, the revolutionary power's values and goals and, on the other, the international system's defining customs. The methods of foreign policy can matter in identifying a revolutionary foreign policy, but only when they are so repulsive or shocking that they violate the fundamental rules that underpin accepted standards of conduct.

This point should not be construed as a theoretical assertion about the influence of rules and norms on state conduct.[10] It is merely to indicate that the analytical task of identifying a revisionist power requires an evaluation of that country's behavior in relation to the standards of conduct which prevail in a given international order. States do not always obey the traditional body of rules; they routinely destroy them. Consider Saddam Hussein's use of chemical weapons against Kurdish people in Iraq in 1988 or Bashar al-Assad's use of similar weapons against his fellow Syrians in 2011. The international community regarded both actions as repulsive to the customs of statecraft. Both crimes were punished but to different extents. In 2010, the High Criminal Court of Iraq, which at the time was under U.S. military occupation, condemned and executed the Iraqi official who ordered the Halabja chemical attack. President Barack Obama's infamous promise to punish the al-Assad regime for its attack did not materialize. His successor Donald Trump launched damaging but limited airstrikes against regime targets. Al-Assad and his adherents remained in power in Damascus. When considering such transgressions (and responses to them), the analyst's central task is to determine the extent to which they represent a mere interruption in the moral fabric of international society versus a determined program to redraw it.

Revisionism in brief has a relational, not an absolute, dimension; it says nothing about the character of the international order that the rebel power wishes to revise or the methods which it applies. The system may be a Hobbesian world of frequent war among nations, as in the Europe of Napoleon or Hitler, or a Kantian realm of permanent peace as in today's European Union. What matters is the presence of a power that is large enough to challenge the established order and which defies its shared conventions of behavior. In sum, the presence or absence of revisionism in a nation's foreign policy depends on the nature of its goals and methods in relation to the dominant international customs of the time. Does the challenger state enact those customs or does it seek to subvert them? To lay the ground for analysis in later chapters, let us now ask this question of historical Russian foreign policy.

RUSSIAN REVISIONISM: HISTORY AND TRENDS

The armies of the Tsars subjugated small neighboring peoples. Soviet agents of revolution plotted violent uprisings in pursuit of world Communism. Vladimir Putin's Russia invaded Georgia and Ukraine, sent an army into Syria, disrupted presidential elections via cyberspace in the United States in 2016 and in France in 2017, and interfered in other democratic processes such as the Brexit referendum in Britain and the vote determining the new name of the country of North Macedonia – an aspiring entrant of the NATO alliance. Some of this behavior manifested a defiance of the international order and possibly a desire to alter it. Some of it, however, was conservative; it reflected, rather than challenged, prevailing customs.

How do the two benchmarks of revisionism laid out above apply to Russian foreign policy? The answer varies across regimes and eras. To different Russias we must apply the rules and customs of their respective times.[11]

Let us begin with the era of the tsars. War was an acceptable feature of foreign policy; in fact, it was the *ultima ratio* of state survival, a concern that bedeviled nations small and large.[12] In Europe, the period of the seventeenth and eighteenth centuries was rife with wars of conquest carried out by the world's first professional armies. The period witnessed more than twenty years of almost uninterrupted war between 1792 and 1815. So common was war, in fact, that it gave rise to the first systematic condemnation of war by the French physiocrats and adherents of Adam Smith.[13]

The Russian regime of the period enacted these foreign policy fashions. During Peter I's reign, a Russian army sought to expel the Crimean Tatars and their masters, the Ottomans, from the Azov fortress, a key strategic outpost that threatened Russia's access to the Black Sea.[14] A few years later, undeterred by the war's spectacular failure, the daring young tsar launched one of the grandest military campaigns in European history, the Great Northern War, which featured two decades of battles in which Russian armies seized the Swedish dominions of modern-day Finland, Estonia, and Ingria.[15] An excursion in the final years of the great tsar's life to expand Russia's influence in the Caspian Sea and Caucasus, a region that Ottoman forces increasingly penetrated, produced a war with Shah Tahmasp II of Persia. In all of Peter I's military adventures, hundreds of thousands of lives perished.

Viewed through the lens of today's political customs, Peter I's expansionist aims and extremely violent methods might appear reprehensible. Scenarios of a military invasion of Northern and Eastern Europe by Putin's army are more than just conceivable; they have played out in Georgia and Ukraine (more on this in Chapter 4). But their plausibility at a similar scale of destruction and death is lower today than in the intensely bellicose era of the tsars. Political speculators, some more creative than clever, have presented invasion scenarios involving, for instance, Russia's absorption of a small NATO nation or a nuclear attack against the alliance.[16] Such moves would seem almost universally repulsive to the basic values of the current international order, however.

Let it be stated again: in historical analysis one cannot impose one's own values upon eras long past. Because revisionism is relational, it must be evaluated on the standards of the subjects' times – not ours. For all the annihilation and destruction wrought by tsarist military endeavors, none evinced a revolutionary ambition by the standards of their age. While Russia expanded in its near abroad, Western European nations battled each other and thrust their armies across the oceans into the Americas, Africa, and Asia.[17] Rather than decry Peter I's spoils, some states joined in them. Prussia annexed parts of Swedish Pomerania. The Electorate of Hanover seized Bremen-Verden. Wars of expansion were a going concern in international affairs; absorption of weaker nations, a common practice.

Some thinkers – not least the Soviet agents of Marx and Engels, who excelled at applying their own political project's prejudices to the telling of history – have seen in the tsarist expansions an aspiration to world dominion,[18] an aim that would have been revolutionary even in their own context. Close scrutiny reveals the flaws of this view, however.[19] If anything, the Russia of Alexander I, for example, was a victim of a campaign of world conquest – Napoleon's. He and his successor Nicholas I served as stewards of the Concert of Europe arrangement that (largely) preserved peace in Europe following Napoleon's defeat. By their own lights, then, the tsars' foreign policy would not have been revisionist in either the first or the second sense. It evinced instead a quintessentially conservative character.

Soviet foreign policy presents a different case: it embodied a limited revisionism. Here, we must distinguish the theory and the practice of the Communist worldview. The dogma behind Marx's and Engels's ideal of international revolution that motivated much of Soviet foreign policy was revolutionary in the first order. A state basing its foreign policy ambitions faithfully on this ideal would have pursued the dissolution of sovereign states into a unitary global community organized on the basis of a stateless proletariat.

Yet, the state's disappearance did not figure prominently in the revolutionary designs of the early Bolsheviks. In fact, Lenin's pursuit of revolution violated the German prophets' final vision. He, and later Stalin, affirmed the necessity of an intermediary stage, "the dictatorship of the proletariat," in which the state's influence on economic, military, political, and private life was supreme. As an end point of Soviet political reconstruction, the stateless society was more imaginable than achievable.[20] Vested political and bureaucratic interests ensured that in the Soviet revolutionary context, the intermediary stage in fact became permanent, and so the professed world revolution (that is, a revolution involving first-order revisionism) acquired a statist quality.

The Soviet Union's pursuit of world revolution was revisionist only in the second, *ideological* sense. It entailed a forceful campaign to refashion, often by force of arms, the composition not of the states system itself but of certain individual members: the Baltics in 1940 (and again in 1944), Hungary in 1956, Czechoslovakia in 1968, Afghanistan in 1979, and so on.

The quintessence of this approach was Stalin's foreign policy, which sought to redraw the nations that it conquered, or which fell under its tutelage, in the figure of its own domestic image – economic and political centralization and subservience to the dictator in Moscow. The approach represented a direct challenge to the notion of pluralism that characterized the classical states system, the idea that the society of states is only thinly formed, because the basic common goals shared among them do not paint a universal political identity. By contrast, Stalin's quest for world revolution sought to mold a global community of purpose defined by conformity to Marxist maxims and fealty to its paramount leader. Ideological and material commitments were often indistinguishable. Membership in the Cominform during the 1940s and 50s was an act of ideological observance at least as much as it was an expression of foreign policy subservience. The ejection of Yugoslavia from the Communist camp in 1948 occurred not because of Tito's deviance from Marxism (he was a true Communist) but for refusing to obey Soviet dictates.[21]

What emerges from this brief review of the history of Russian foreign policy are varieties of conservatism and revolutionism. We found in the history of tsarist foreign policy, with its penchant for grand wars of conquest, a form of interstate conduct that today would seem repulsive to the basic political framework of international relations but which in fact conformed with the customs of the time. The Soviet Union's behavior on the world scene, by contrast, was less revolutionary than what the theoreticians of world Communism professed. It sought to refashion not the international system's constitution, but its defining values and their espousal by members of the Communist bloc. Let us now turn to a discussion of the role of technological revolution in the Soviet Union's foreign policy activism.

TECHNOLOGY AND REVISIONISM: THE SOVIET EXPERIENCE

Champions of the Soviet political system celebrated it as a centralized mechanism that enabled the concentration of national resources for scientific advancement. Critics denounced it for the stagnation of bureaucratic inertia, for inefficiencies in industrial production, and for unimaginativeness in the application of new technologies beyond the military realm. These two perspectives were actually not far from each other; they involved two sides of the same relationship between coinciding revolutions – the ideological and the technological.

On the one side of this relationship was a record of extraordinary achievement. In the field of space exploration, the Soviet Union launched the first orbital satellite, Sputnik, in 1957 and the first human, Yuri Gagarin, into space in 1961. In the nuclear realm, it was the second nation to assemble an atomic bomb, in 1949, and the first – building on the successes of the space program

71

– to fit a hydrogen bomb into an intercontinental ballistic missile, in 1959. These achievements enabled the Soviet Union to enshrine its physical survival within the logic of "mutual assured destruction," while also achieving the global prestige of scientific prowess. Although the crushing of popular revolt in Hungary in 1956 besmirched the Soviet reputation (including among Communist adherents who puzzled over their proletarian brethren's repudiation of the loving Socialist state), it was perhaps at its highest point in this period of great scientific accomplishment than at any other time during the Cold War.

Coinciding with the fortieth anniversary of the Bolshevik Revolution, the Sputnik launch in particular was a cause for great festivity. The top leaders from sixty-four Communist parties gathered in Moscow (Marshal Tito excepted: the heretic of the Communist bloc prudently sensed trouble) to celebrate both earthly and heavenly achievements. For Socialism had not just caught up with, but also surpassed, the engineering ability of the great capitalist rivals.[22] The conceit that science and technology could thrive only within the freedoms afforded by the open market was thus seemingly defeated; they thrived in the skies above even as the terrestrial aspirations of world revolution faltered. As if to reinforce the unison between material advances and ideological fervor, the leaders gathered in Moscow announced the creation of a new journal to provide ideological orientation to their global movement. The occasion climaxed with the declaration of the Soviet Union as the leading nation of the Communist bloc – a suggestion put forth ironically by Mao, who looked up to the Soviets for their scientific leap even as he sought for his nation parity with them.[23]

But feats of science and engineering were not the only achievements. At least equally important were innovations in military strategy that fed off the scientific enterprise – the intangible leaps of the analytical mind. It is a testament to the ingenuity of Soviet military thinkers that they often mastered the theory of technological revolution before acquiring its material rudiments. In the 1970s, a fundamental change in the nature of conflict seemed in the offing. The integration of telecommunications and automated decision functions into military weapons systems and the emergence of unmanned flying objects, some Soviet thinkers mused, promised to transform the depth and speed of future conflict. Not merely the operational aspects of conflict would change, but also its strategic ends and possibilities.

The writings of military theoreticians such as Marshal Nikolai Vasilyevich Ogarkov, Chief of the General Staff between 1977 and 1984, display the thoughts of minds that grasped the unfolding changes in conflict before they had fully materialized. The emerging technologies would enable a "qualitative leap" in the future battlefield that would allow opponents to "see and strike deep" into enemy territory, observed Ogarkov. "The sharply increased range of conventional weapons makes it possible immediately to extend active combat operations not just to the border regions, but to the whole country's territory, which was not possible in past wars."[24] The reflection was astounding for its perspicacity in grasping novel linkages among new technology, the limits of warfighting, and the attendant requirements on military preparations. He drew conclusions about automated conflict and drone warfare before automation and drones hit the battlefield. Such depth of perception thrived in some Soviet military circles despite the distorting incursions of ideology. It endured the imprecations against theories of war not wedded to dialectical materialism. At times it even superseded dogma, as in Ogarkov's daring redefinition of war as a "sociopolitical phenomenon,"[25] which departed from Lenin's overtly material reading of Clausewitz.[26] As former chairman of the Joint Chiefs of Staff David Jones noted during the SALT II negotiations with Ogarkov, "[the Soviets] could get to the specifics without all the dialectical rhetoric,"[27] which marred much of the exchange among the superpowers' political representatives.

On the other side of the relationship between Communist ideology and technological revolution were the retardations associated with delays in modernization. Most notable was the Soviet Union's inability in the Cold War's latter stages to foster a vibrant computer industry at a time when the Western adversaries reaped from it many economic and social rewards.

In the American system of nearly unbridled entrepreneurship, the ARPANET network that emerged in 1969 as a resource-sharing tool among esoteric scientific communities developed, in just two-and-a-half decades, into an immensely popular information-sharing tool owing to the explosive adoption of email and the World Wide Web. By contrast, the Soviet system sought to impose centralized control upon the nascent information space. Although some intrepid planners saw computer networks as a tool of decentralization and reform of decayed government institutions, this view – so offensive to Marxist sensibilities! – did not prevail. Government agencies succeeded in appropriating from citizens the primary role in the integration of computers into society. What emerged in contrast to the open and global Internet, which Putin later denounced as a "CIA project," was an archipelago of closed data repositories subordinated to the interests of state bureaucracies.[28] Even prominent espousers of computers hewed to orthodoxy. Editor-in-chief of *Pravda* (the mouthpiece of the Communist Party's Central Committee) Viktor Afanasyev warned that the technicians supervising their use must always be under close Party scrutiny.[29]

Behind the Soviet shortcomings in the field of computing one finds the pernicious effects of ideology. Communist luminaries denounced computers as "capitalist tools." Among them, for example, was Boris Agapov, the science editor of *Literaturnaya Gazeta*. Writing in May 1950, he criticized American society's enchantment with "thinking machines" and scoffed at its "sweet dream" of a future society populated by enslaved robots. The unspoken but important assumption here was that computer programing could be manipulated to reflect Marxist-Leninist tenets. What of the use of large amounts of information to support economic and financial analysis? Nonsense – an addiction to data no different than the sick American patient's "love for patented pills!"[30] Within these ideologically tinged circles, muses of the emerging information age such as Norbert Wiener – the conceiver of the field of cybernetics – became subjects of ridicule among their Soviet counterparts. This attitude fed the backwardness of Soviet computing ability. Technologists focused more on denouncing the threat posed by capitalist machines than on creating ones that could pursue Soviet security and defense objectives.

4
RUSSIA AND NEW TECHNOLOGICAL THREATS TO DEMOCRACY

RUSSIAN REVISIONISM UNDER PUTIN

Guiding Putin's foreign policy activism is a strategic doctrine that is peculiar to modern Russia. As we saw in the preceding chapter, historical Russian attempts to alter the international order were marked by extreme violence – the assassination of foreign government officials, military invasion and occupation of other nations, tyrannical suppression of captive peoples, and so on. Conventional military superiority was a central tenet of Soviet revolutionary strivings on the world scene. Unable to close the conventional forces gap, the United States and its allies nullified it by casting a shadow of assured nuclear destruction over the relationship with Moscow. Epochal wars of conquest receded to scenarios that no serious military planner could aspire enacting. And yet the Soviet Union's four million soldiers, vast airpower, and formidable naval fleet betrayed that it remained resolute about fighting them – a contradiction that ultimately bankrupted it.[1]

The shock of the Soviet Union's demise made explicit what had long been implicit: even a conventional military showdown with the Western alliance was impossible to win and should not be fought. In the aftermath of the momentous events of the late 1980s and the internal dislocations of the 1990s, there emerged for the modern tsar a practical question: What place for war in the strategic doctrine of a regime for whom the Soviet debacle was, in the words of Vladimir Vladimirovich, "the greatest geopolitical catastrophe" of the twentieth century?[2]

For all its harkening back to past martial glories, contemporary Russia's strategic doctrine refutes the Soviet tenet of military preeminence. Brutal but often limited, revolutionary but not radical, the doctrine eschews war as an instrument of international reform in direct dealings with the United States, Britain, and other large nations. A clear expression of this posture is Russia's embrace of the nuclear deterrent – a sign of weakness more than of strength. In 1993, the country formally reversed its no-first-use nuclear policy; it reserves the option to incinerate enemies whose conventional forces threaten the country's survival (or more honestly, the regime's).[3] But rather than signaling a tolerance for nuclear war, or any war, with Western powers, Russia's nuclear rhetoric seeks to *control* the process of escalation towards it.[4] Although Russia has implied a willingness to use tactical nuclear arms against non-nuclear nations (think of Ukraine), nothing suggests that the threshold of nuclear attack against other nuclear powers has dropped.[5]

To be sure, the choice of arms remains firmly on the geopolitical table. But it applies mainly in dealings with smaller powers that Russia strives to subjugate – especially nations such as Ukraine, Georgia, and Moldova that rejected the proffered subservience in search of democracy and comity with the West. Some observers have lamented that Russia's invasion of Ukraine in February 2022 with almost 200,000 troops signaled a return to the doctrine of military primacy. It did not. The supreme blunder of that military adventure, tragic as it is for Ukrainians, and perilous as it might become for Putin if it stirs unrest at home, encrusts the dangers of a doctrine wedded to conventional war precepts. There is an irony such as war often produces: Putin invaded Ukraine partly to arrest NATO's further expansion; in fact, its likely consequence is that the alliance will gain Northern Europe's two militarily neutral states, Finland and Sweden.[6] Putin has preserved the status quo (so far) in Ukraine while altering it, against his favor, in Russia's northwestern flank. Former Estonian President Toomas Hendrik Ilves predicted: "The Baltic Sea will essentially become a NATO lake," thereby realizing a recurring fear of Soviet and Russian leaders during the last seven decades.[7]

At any rate, Russia's military campaigns in Ukraine and Georgia were no quest for world or even European domination. And the more that such land grabs falter, the less likely they will become one. Perhaps the only conceivable scenario of an intentional military clash with the United States and NATO is one where the Kremlin views war – even a war risking atomic annihilation – as the final option to preserve the regime against imminent collapse. And perhaps that is the main lesson of the vacillations of 1991: to not risk fighting a war is to risk losing more than just it. But that dire scenario is at the extreme low end of the scope of probability. Putin rattled the atom against other nuclear powers to prevent its use against them (non-nuclear Ukraine remains a plausible target). Much like President Joe Biden warned about the certainty of "World War 3"[8] if Russia attacked NATO to help prevent it, Putin warned Western nations of consequences "never encountered in your history"[9] in order to avoid inflicting them.

Rather than focus on decisive military contests – the centerpiece of Soviet and Western military thinking – Russian strategic doctrine has emphasized the ideological and psychological aspects of conflict. But while it departs from Soviet dogmas it also builds upon them. In the early 1960s, Soviet military theory began to outgrow the Clausewitzian paradigm of interstate violence of which Lenin had been a faithful student. Military luminaries such as Svyatoslav Kozlov, Andrei Grechko, and Nikolai Ogarkov widened the concept of war beyond violent means to encompass economic, diplomatic, psychological, and ideological means of struggle.[10] That the term "war" survived this doctrinal transformation as a common label (e.g. "next-generation war" and "non-linear war") is possibly more deceit than conceit. It is precisely because the newer means of rivalry are non-violent that they are so appealing to Russian strategists.

The information space thereby became a central arena of contention. Russia's spectral conception of conflict has sought new creative opportunities for strategic action in it. As Katarzyna Zysk observed, "Russian theories of war and warfare have never been one-dimensional."[11] Opportunistic and shrewd, the doctrine seizes chances to fan discontent in the heart of democratic opponents' open and often divided societies while repulsing the intrusion of alien liberal values into the country. For all the terror of the pulverization of Chechnya in the 1990s by Russian forces or their present brutalities against Ukraine, for all the military swagger that appears at the Victory Day Parade on Red Square every year on May 9, it is not Russia's hydrogen bombs or its one million troops that most plausibly menace the West, but rather the pernicious information that it hurtles across cyberspace.

Today, beyond flashpoints such as Ukraine, the chief instrument of Russian revisionism abroad is not armed force but virtual weapons, whether computer code to disrupt vital machine functions or online information, often false (or true but misleading), to sway human minds. Russian revisionism pursues *information supremacy* at home and within its defined region of national interest. To be sure, control by territorial conquest in the style of Peter the Great or Stalin remains an option. But it is highly risky, for it confronts the limits, and exposes the failures, of conventional military reforms (which have suffered from bureaucratism and rampant corruption).[12] Especially in security competitions with the militarily superior Western powers, the choice method of rivalry is cunning maneuvers within their exposed information spaces.

Viewed in its totality, Russian strategic doctrine seems more motley than unitary, less planned than adaptive. Against one set of opponents and in some limited scenarios apply the most vicious means of war. To other, more powerful foes go the subtler means of technological unpeace. And perhaps that is the product of a particular strategic vision rather than a sign of its absence. Much as the internal division and competition among Russia's security services can produce operational vigor,[13] so too the disharmony of their methods can be a source of strength in a world where technology constantly alters them.

Only by understanding the true nature and origins of the foreign policy activism behind Russian strategic moves in cyberspace can Western nations improve the efficacy of their responses to them. The framework developed in the preceding chapter helps to guide this understanding. It identifies Putin's Russia as a second-order revisionist power in the international system. The country seeks to export its political values and disturb the polity of foreign adversaries, without confronting them directly, even as it seeks limited territorial aims within its near abroad. Putin's drive to conquer Ukraine, although it could spiral into a wider conflict, does not seem like a millenarian war. Rather, the invasion seeks to redraw – in the image of the Kremlin – the political makeup of a large East Slavic nation that dared to adopt democracy while seeking closer Western ties. The military adventure caused a shock in the moral firmament of the liberal international order; it has not redrawn the configuration of world or even European power.

This chapter examines Russia's use of cyberspace for revisionist ends in the international system and the West's failure, so far, to counter it effectively. The scope of the analysis covers Russian cyber operations in a broad sense that includes the disruption of computer infrastructure, data theft, and social media information campaigns – a newer threat that Western cyber doctrine has not normally prioritized.[14] The analysis explores the adaptation of Russian revisionism to the new possibilities of cyberspace. Later chapters will sketch out alternative policy courses to counter it.

The chapter argues that virtual weapons confer a crucial advantage to Russia's foreign policy activism. They enable it to compete strategically in the reconstruction of a Russian sphere of influence in Europe and beyond without firing any guns, thereby avoiding serious reprisal – possibly even a military clash – for actions that the governments of the victim nations regard as intolerably harmful to their national interests.[15] The main strategic utility of Russian cyber activity is not conquest (how could it be?) or even interstate coercion. Instead, it is to weaken adversaries' foreign policy resolve by maneuvering deeply within their home terrain. Contrast Russia's ruinous war in Ukraine with its cyber operations during the U.S. presidential election in 2016. One strengthened the bonds among political factions in the United States and the West, while the other fractured them.

Russia's bold cyber posture manifests a *risk paradox*: the desire to limit the risk of a direct military clash with large nations increases the willingness to accept the risk of conflict short of war. As discussed in Chapter 2, because the consequences of technological unpeace defy classification within familiar categories of war and peaceful rivalry, they go largely unpunished. Therein lies the technique's main attractiveness: it affords Russia a means to pursue national security interests and to subvert the liberal international order in a manner that bypasses its institutional and legal constraints. The limitations of the legal system – its many holes and rigid categories amid expanding zones of unpeace – are, from the Russian strategic perspective, a weakness to exploit.

PUTIN'S RUSSIA: IDEOLOGICAL ORIGINS AND GEOPOLITICAL GRIEVANCES

Is contemporary Russia a revisionist power? There is abiding controversy among scholars regarding the nature and objectives of Putin's foreign policy. A central line of contention concerns the relationship between law and power:

Does Russia accept the existing international legal order, even if the country seeks to alter some of its customs, or does it try to undermine – even destroy – some of its defining features?

Two broad views on the question exist. One affirms the primacy of law over power in the conduct of Russian foreign policy; the other places power above law.[16] Both perspectives accept the importance of law and power; the debate revolves around which consideration prevails in the halls of the Kremlin when events force them to clash.

Western diplomacy, we saw, has betrayed a strong preference for the legalistic view. It regards the world through the same lens as its practitioners regard themselves. It believes that if only other states, too, abided by the dictates of a just world, then lasting peace, stability, and prosperity in the international jungle could be achieved. The lens through which officials regard the outside world is shaped by their own experiences. Did not Japan and Germany rejoin the community of respectable nations following the travesties of the Second World War by adopting the liberal creed that the occupying armies of the triumphant democracies fought to uphold? One finds here a replication in a larger sense of the liberal worldview that underpin the dogmas of cyber legalism: a tendency to perceive the world as it ought to be, more than as it truly is.

A similar hope lived in many Western capitals in relation to the Soviet Union's main successor state. Observers often assumed that, insofar as Russia challenged the international order, it did so from a position of accepting its basic elements. Occasionally, Russia rubbed against, or even transgressed, the limits of acceptable state behavior in cyberspace – which, after all, are broad and sometimes vague – but never decisively and always remaining within its main confines.

Frustrations over Russia's malicious cyber activities did little to dispel the presumption that Russia is more a partner in, than a competitor for, security, less a challenger state against the international order than its joint custodian. President Donald Trump praised Putin as a partner with whom he could strike a deal on matters as complex as the territorial status of Ukraine (having once called Putin a "genius" for his invasion of the country). Following a summit with Vladimir Putin in Geneva in June 2021, President Joe Biden affirmed that Putin takes "very seriously" his "significant responsibility for global stability."

Even as Biden announced the preparation of penalties for Russia's political hacking activities, he explained that the United States "could have gone further" but chose not to do so in the interest of fostering "a stable, predictable relationship."[17] And so kicked off "a strategic stability dialogue to pursue cooperation" with a major geopolitical competitor and determined defier of the international order. Mirroring Biden's move, later in the same month, French President Emmanuel Macron and German Chancellor Angela Merkel called for closer engagement in the European Union's dealings with Russia and a "reset" of their relations.[18] Merkel's successor Olaf Scholz went further. While accusing Russia of violating norms against the forceful moving of borders in Europe, he called for "a new Ostpolitik" premised on the notion of a "common security" architecture – a veiled plea to treat Russia as a security partner rather than a competitor.[19]

In brief, much of the Western approach to Russian aggression has exhibited the hallmarks of a confused and contradictory foreign policy: castigation for repeated violations of the law and norms combined with the assumption that the transgressor is more a partner meriting attempts at cooperation than a foe to be resisted. The more Russia challenged the European and international security system which the United States and its democratic partners have dominated during the last three decades, the more they sought to draw the opponent closer towards the norms and institutions it repudiates. Traces of this perspective have endured even the atrocities in Ukraine. It enjoys a special appeal among Western illiberal figures, such as French opposition leader Marine Le Pen, who vowed to restore close ties with Russia,[20] and Hungarian Prime Minister Viktor Orbán, who after winning reelection in March 2022 received Putin's celebratory phone call.[21]

The expansion of war in Ukraine exposed the hollowness of this legalistic orientation. The view misunderstood the true objectives of Russian foreign policy, whose practitioners, in fact, reject the legalism underpinning the current order even while professing to embrace it. Not everyone missed them. Former U.S. ambassador to Estonia James Melville grasped the nature of the problem: "Russia and its corrupt, authoritarian government are a threat to the rules-based order and the fundamental values and interests of the United States and its allies."[22]

Adherents of the prevailing view of cyber legalism hope that law and norms will restrain Russia because they broadly reflect the rules-based order that Western nations erected after 1945. But as we began to discuss in Chapter 2, when Moscow invokes the legal rulebook, it is to serve Russian national interests – not to enter into a closer orbit within the imagined liberal universe. Russia's obsession (shared with China) with defending the sanctity of national sovereignty against foreign military intervention feeds the Western liberal conceit.[23] Putin's castigation of the West for its interventions in Kosovo in 1999 and in Libya in 2011, often expressed in strict normative language, and ignoring for a moment Russia's military adventures in Georgia and Ukraine, nourished the impression that geopolitical disputes afford purely legal solutions and that power ceases where definable laws begin.

Were they alive today, Lenin and Stalin would recognize two activist elements of Putin's foreign policy. One is the desire to refashion Western (or Western-leaning) nations in the image of Russian political values, which are marked by illiberalism – a centralized political structure oriented to the figure of one powerful leader, suppression of freedoms of political organization and expression, co-optation of private sector elements in the interest of the state, and a general disdain for liberal social mores.

Orienting this political orientation is a central premise: the Russia–West divide involves a grand contest of conceptions about the nature of the domestic and international political order. This is no quest for world revolution (as in Soviet times) or for control of a buffer zone on the eastern Baltic shore among nations who accept each other's right to pursue expansion wherever their armies can reach (as in the epoch of the tsars). It is, instead, a contest for political and social dominion within contested cultural and regional areas. The central arenas of contention are the areas closest to Russia that have adopted Western political institutions – for instance, Estonia, Latvia, Lithuania, and North Macedonia – or which seek to adopt them – Ukraine, Georgia, Moldova, Montenegro, Serbia, and other countries. Crucially, the contest also plays out within the domestic information spaces of the large adversary nations – especially the United States and Britain, occasionally France, and increasingly also Germany.

Some experts believe that Russia's crusading illiberalism reaffirms the pluralism of the states system, a diverse political house that harbors ruthless regimes such as North Korea's, which devotes its economy to the industries of war and repression, alongside doves such as Costa Rica, a nation so pacifist in its worldview that it abolished its army.[24]

That view goes too far. When contrasted against Kim Jong-un or Carlos Alvarado Quesada, even the Putin whose tanks charged toward Kyiv seems like a moderate among political extremes. But whereas the dictator in Pyongyang perceives his nation as largely an outsider in the international order, whose rules and customs he openly defies, the Kremlin's foreign policy seeks not to withdraw from the family of nations but rather to influence its core values so that they more closely reflect Russia's perspective and interests. That this aim contravenes the supposed universalism of the liberal creed is a reason for pressing forward with the program of change rather than for pause. Russia does not seek strategic stability; it strives for strategic reform, for which carefully manufactured instability is to be pursued with determination.

To grasp the ideological underpinnings of modern Russian revisionism, we must turn to the failure of democratization in Russia and its concomitant advance in erstwhile Communist nations after 1989. As the Cold War ended, Soviet President Mikhail Gorbachev foresaw a bridging of the ideological rift. He held a grand vision for the future of Europe in which military competition among the Cold War rivals would dissipate within economic and social integration. Commercial goods and cultural ideas would flow more freely from Dublin to Vladivostok. The arms race would end. Later, during Boris Yeltsin's presidency, the vision acquired an important new feature: the democratization of Russia itself, a historical enterprise never before attempted to which Moscow attached an expectation of major financial assistance – debt servicing, a fund to stabilize the ruble exchange rate, and infrastructural investments. Also implicit (some Russians say explicit) in the project was a commitment by NATO not to expand eastward.[25]

None of these conditions materialized. U.S. Presidents George H.W. Bush and Bill Clinton ignored pleas (including from their own advisors)[26] to deliver a financial aid package to Russia. The Western military alliance grew in two explosive bursts: first in 1999, welcoming Poland, the Czech Republic, and Hungary; and again in 2004, absorbing seven nations, including the former Soviet captives Estonia, Latvia, and Lithuania.

This is not the place to debate the rightness or wrongness of the West's Russia policy after the Cold War. We focus instead on its consequences. The policy's chief effect on Russia's emerging new paramount leader was clear: Putin perceived the dual expansion of democracy and alliance membership as contrary to his nation's core security interests. He asked a stunned crowd at the Munich Conference on Security Policy in 2007: "What happened to the assurances our Western partners made after the dissolution of the Warsaw Pact? Where are those declarations today? No one even remembers them. But I will allow myself to remind this audience what was said. I would like to quote the speech of NATO Secretary General Mr Wörner in Brussels on May 17, 1990. He said at the time that: 'the fact that we are ready not to place a NATO army outside of German territory gives the Soviet Union a firm security guarantee.' Where are these guarantees?"[27] Ever the geopolitical griever, Putin neglected to note the main reason behind the absence of such a guarantee: that the nations which Russia had recently subjugated did not trust its own guarantee to them.

Chief among Russian foreign policy objectives is ensuring that nations such as Ukraine or Georgia which are of central strategic importance to Moscow, but less so to the West, remain outside of its liberal fold. Ukraine is of special importance. Viewed from the Kremlin, the prospect of its absorption into NATO's military architecture and the European Union's single market was no imaginary danger drawn on an archaic map. It would threaten Russia's vital national interests by reducing its ability to station troops in a geopolitical chokepoint at the mouth of the Black Sea (through which Russian military power is projected and hydrocarbon exports flow), reduce Russia's access to important markets for goods and labor (in peacetime, the Ukraine–Russia corridor is the world's second-largest migration route), and deprive Russia of a crucial member state of the Eurasian customs union that Putin plans to erect (even if the majority of Ukrainians prefer EU accession).[28] More fundamentally, it would blow a hole into the edifice of illiberalism at the historical heart of Kievan Rus, the first of the ancient Rus territories from which modern Russia emerged.[29] To allow a brethren people (whose distinct identity Putin openly rejected) to adopt false foreign values was to risk their seeping back into the modern motherland. Remember what Gorbachev's political opening did to the old empire! The true threat posed by the Western community is not its armies and sanctions, but its values and institutions; they imperil not national security but the current regime's survival. Putin's foreign minister Sergei Lavrov justified Russia's grab at empire in Ukraine as a "process of freeing the world from the West's neocolonial oppression"[30] (international politics does produce its ironies!)

At this point a puzzled observer might ask: If a primary goal of the Putin regime is to preserve itself, why then take the struggle for change beyond nearby contested lands and into the middle of Western societies?

The answer lies as much in the character of the regime as in the character of Western liberalism: it is inherently expansionist. At the core of the liberal worldview is the perception that democratic government is the highest form of political organization available to modern humans, that its principles of free political expression are sacrosanct, that the electoral selection and accountability of leaders is a vital source of strength, and that these ideals are valid universally – a view that Samuel Huntington derided as a "liberal conceit."[31] An almost messianic zeal to expand the reach of their political system underpins much of liberal democracies' foreign policies in the current era.[32] To deprive poor foreign souls suffering abuses of autocracy the righteous fruits of freedom was unconscionable.

The Putin regime grasps liberalism's expansionist nature: to multiply democrats means to topple or at least weaken autocrats. Western intervention in Kosovo in 1999 or in Libya in 2011, for example, have fueled the perception in Moscow that the West, too, pursues a reformist agenda abroad.[33] "Against whom is this expansion intended?" he admonished his Western counterparts in Munich, referring less to NATO's weapons than to its values.[34] Putin's assumption of a fusion of democratic and military expansion was sound. Adoption of political and economic liberalism was a formal precondition of NATO accession. In Brussels, ideological and political reform were indistinguishable from military reform. As Russia's 2014 military doctrine soundly observed, NATO's deployment of military forces in "states contiguous with the Russian Federation and its allies" has the effect of "exerting political and military pressure on the Russian Federation."[35]

In brief, the central dramas of the current Russia–West rivalry are primarily ideological more than material. They involve a contest of opposing political systems as much as a clash of raw power and material interests, even if Putin and the *siloviki* who design Russian security policy regard economic and military might as vital ingredients of international status and influence in the grand global contest. But because of Russia's relative material weakness, it has focused on the ideological and psychological elements of conflict.[36]

Against this backdrop, Russian revisionism today seeks to prevent the entrenchment of liberal democratic values and institutions within Russia itself. Every autocrat knows that there is no plausible scenario of political liberalization within which his regime can survive. The Russian government pursues a number of strategies to avoid this danger. It constantly harasses members of domestic pro-democracy organizations with fines and imprisonment. It severely curtails financial and organizational support of such groups by foreign entities. For Putin's regime, the preservation of autocracy at home is no less an existential matter than the preservation of the nation's territorial integrity. If, in the Soviet days, Moscow worried about Western political pressures producing a revolt in its satellites, today it worries more about a revolt at home.

In its ideological underpinnings, today's rivalry is similar to the Cold War.[37] Both sides espouse competing political values. But the current rivalry is different in a crucial respect. Gone is the Russian belief – so central in Soviet political dogma – that its domestic political system would prevail universally. Russian foreign policy thinking has shed its own universalistic Marxist conceits (whether liberal democracies have shed theirs remains questionable). Political expansion today is mainly preemptive rather than predative; it strives to forestall the intrusion of foreign values within Russia; it is by nature defensive, oriented to securing the regime, rather than offensive, seeking it glories. But if Russian revisionism in the first decade or so after 1991 sought to stem the advance of liberalism, today it seeks its rollback *away* from national frontiers. In the logic of political contestation, preemptive defense entails proactive offense.

There is a second element of activism in Putin's foreign policy that the old Communists would recognize: the acceptance that international political change cannot come at the cost of a military showdown with other large nations. The existence of an overarching political contest that spans Europe and the Atlantic – though no longer, as in the Cold War, the entire globe – does not refute the notion of a thin international community whose members accept mutual restraints, especially on the use of armed force among them. It merely assumes that the anarchical society is only primitively developed. Thus, despite the existence of a civilizational clash and occasional outbreaks of vicious war against former satellites such as Ukraine, the violence that occurs does not directly pit the armies of the two sides against each other, much less does it risk the eruption of a millenarian war in the style of the Second World War or a nuclear conflict.

The question of war presents a fundamental difference between Western and Russian strategic doctrine. Western doctrine is *binary* on this point: it emphasizes and distinguishes between the methods of physical destruction in wartime and of diplomacy and law in peacetime. The international legal system codifies the neat separation between the two conditions of international life. The definition of war is the absence of peace; one has peace because there is no war. Lost in the binary segmentation is the realm of unpeace, or mid-spectrum rivalry lying below the physically destructive threshold of interstate violence but whose harmful effects far surpass the familiar and often tolerable level of peacetime competition.

Russian doctrine, by contrast, is *spectral*: it eschews the war–peace binary in preference for the middle methods. It strives to circumvent the legal system's restrictions by carrying out harmful actions that its conventions do not neatly capture. As the poisoning of a former KGB officer with a banned nerve agent in a sleepy English city in 2018 showed, even a minute act of violence on Western soil can attract serious diplomatic ire and financial sanctions. If the Salisbury poisoning was a test of the limits of toleration of Russian malfeasance within Western territory, then the message to the transgressor was clear: the fatal targeting of defectors, a common and accepted practice during the Cold War, is potential cause for major penalties.

To be sure, Putin's government has not neglected the importance of military might, particularly in the conduct of its relations with satellite states such as Ukraine and Georgia (on which more below). The road of embarrassing military blunders that ran from the First Chechen War in the mid-1990s to the sinking of the Kursk nuclear submarine in 2000 to the excursion into Georgia in 2008 and yet again into Chechnya in the early 2000s, and which risks repeating in Ukraine, taught Russian officials lessons about the necessity for the modernization of the country's armed forces. In the 2010s, the Russian military budget soared, nuclear weapons were deployed, naval ships were fitted with highly maneuverable cruise missiles (the Kalibr), the air force acquired more than one thousand new aircraft (including the country's most advanced fighter jet, the SU-35S) while land forces obtained mechanized units with advanced thermal optics (such as the T-72B3 tank), and the infantry forces came to rely less on conscripts than a professionalized and slimmed-down army that includes some of the most capable special forces units in the world.[38]

But military action abroad risks inviting serious penalties from other states. The use of virtual weapons can avoid them. Because the consequences of Russian actions in cyberspace, though harmful, defy classification within familiar categories of war and peaceful rivalry, they go largely unpunished. Therein lies the approach's main attractiveness: it affords Russia a means to subvert the international order while bypassing its defined institutional defenses.

In sum, Russian foreign policy is revisionist not just because of its ideological aims but also for the character of its preferred methods. Despite Western perceptions that the military incursions in Ukraine and Georgia violated basic international rules governing the use of force, Russia's security posture is not revisionist in a fundamental way: it seeks to avoid a generalized war. Moscow explicitly rules out a direct military conflict with the West. The central arena of foreign policy activism in Russia's relations with Western nations lies elsewhere, primarily in cyberspace – a technological realm that is altering the very nature of force and conflict in the international system.

TECHNOLOGY AND MODERN RUSSIAN REVISIONISM

Virtual weapons offer contemporary Russian revisionism a powerful alternative to traditional war. It can use them to influence the international order while avoiding the risks of military contests that it cannot win. An intense record of Russian foreign policy activity illustrates this point. In spring 2007, Russian political activists crashed Estonia's financial infrastructure in the midst of social disturbance among the country's Russian ethnic minority. In 2016, Russian bots and trolls conducted information campaigns via social media platforms, fanning political discord in Britain during the Brexit referendum.

Later that year, Russian military hackers exposed secret emails from senior Democratic Party officials in the United States, miring the presidential election between Donald Trump and Hillary Clinton in a controversy that endures to this day. The intrusive and disruptive activity continues incessantly. Worse, it intensifies as opportunities to grapple with opponents on their home turf expand amid growing political fissures.

Consider the American election context. In defiance of his own intelligence community's universal assessment, Trump insisted that Russian and other foreign agents neither intruded upon the 2016 election nor operated during his reelection bid. His FBI director disagreed and in April 2019 warned that Russian information operators sought to meddle in the upcoming 2020 election and thereby presented "a significant counterintelligence threat." They had already sought to influence the Congressional elections in 2018.[39] Secretary of Homeland Security Kirstjen Nielsen raised similar alarms. Her department's Cybersecurity and Infrastructure Security Agency established a "24/7 virtual war room" accessible by election officials throughout the country who feared that foreign actors had infiltrated their states' voting infrastructure or information spaces. In a dazzling spectacle of domestic discord, senior security officials were at public odds with their political master, sometimes concluding that it was prudent for their political survival not to raise the alarm with him.

However harmful to the political and economic interests of the targeted nations, Russian cyber actions were not warlike. They did not produce significant physical destruction or loss of life. But they were not peaceful either. The politically and economically disruptive effects transgressed the recognizable bounds of a peaceful rivalry. The actions in cyberspace did not represent ordinary foreign policy conduct; they were overtly subversive, surprising, and largely beyond the scope for punishment by way of the legal rulebook. Therein, as we saw, lies a vital point: the defining revisionist element of Russia's foreign policy activism is not a willingness to resort to armed force – a readiness that even the system's dominant members occasionally display – but rather the circumvention of the system's legal boundaries by operating below them.

Russia's use of virtual weapons represents an adaptation of the country's deep-rooted information warfare doctrine to the new possibilities of computer technology. Offensive cyber activity is new; the doctrine of information warfare that gave it rise is not. The doctrine originated in political and social necessities following the Bolsheviks' seizure of power in 1917. The fledgling new government harnessed information as a weapon in its quest to cement power. The Russian population was a prime target of these efforts, much as Russians today are a prime target of intense Internet surveillance and censorship within the SORM system (see Chapter 7).[40] To suppress the domestic opposition, the authorities flooded their society with self-assuring falsities. Later, Stalin organized large purges based on trials featuring fabricated evidence.[41]

With power secured at home, the battle over information spaces spread far beyond the Soviet Union's borders. It spanned the globe as a core element of Soviet efforts to alter the internal political institutions or foreign policies of other nations.[42] Information warfare offered a distinct attraction to the agents of revolution: it enabled them to engage in strategic competition with Western opponents outside of the realm of conventional war. Information warriors could achieve strategic results by affecting the views of open societies abroad.

Putin's regime has fused cyberspace into information warfare doctrine. The main element of the revised theory is the so-called Gerasimov doctrine. Mark Galeotti has questioned the appropriateness of the label; after all, it hinges on a single speech from 2013.[43] But whatever label (if any) one wants to apply, the doctrine embodies recognizable assumptions and principles. "The very 'rules of war' (*pravila voiny*) have changed significantly," affirmed the doctrine's namesake. The "methods of conflict" – "non-linear war" or "next-generation war" – now involve "the broad use of political, economic, informational, humanitarian, and other non-military measures."[44] The lines between war and peace have become blurred. The central arena of modern conflict is not the conventional battlefield but the battle over control of the minds of machines and humans. In this regard, a core assumption of the doctrine is the notion of a global information war between Russia and Western nations. Some observers who view Russia as the chief culprit of information warfare will miss an important element of Moscow's worldview: the perception that Russia, not the West, is on the receiving end of information (or "values") warfare, as evidenced by repeated foreign interventions in the country's domestic political affairs.[45]

Although the doctrine invokes the language of war, its main methods are not warlike. As a starting axiom, Gerasimov recognized that Russia cannot win a conventional military contest with large Western nations. A direct military clash with the West is folly. Rather, the doctrine prescribes the technological methods of unpeace: influence campaigns via social media, cyberattacks against infrastructure, kompromat operations to damage political opponents' reputations, and so forth.[46] The new technological means "will not alter the essence of future wars," remarked two prominent military analysts, Sergei G. Chekinov and Sergei A. Bogdanov.[47] And that was the point, for they also affirmed what the champions of conquest in Ukraine later forgot: "[N]ot only the role of military capabilities have been diminishing, but . . . these are no longer any good for achieving relevant objectives."[48] Instead of conquering foreign foes, rather than coercing them, Russia could seek to weaken the policies it feared by undermining the domestic resolve behind them.

The doctrine was put into action in the cyberattacks against Estonia. Media falsities helped to fuel social disorder in the capital city Tallinn. Torrents of Internet data expanded the disturbances to vital machines in the economy and society. Social disorder in the polity combined with the disruption of financial and commercial activity in cyberspace in an attempt to weaken the cohesion and resolve of the government (specifically, regarding the removal of a Soviet war memorial from the center of Tallinn). Another prominent manifestation of the doctrine occurred, as we saw, during the 2016 U.S. presidential election, which involved the release by Russian state hackers of email records belonging to the Democratic Party leadership.[49] Meanwhile, torrents of social media postings fanned discord over contentious political and social issues. The combined operation masterfully fused techniques affecting the minds of computers with those influencing the minds of humans.

In the doctrinal playbook of Russian revisionism, the inanimate realm of machines and the animate realm of humans are a unitary plane of contention. Virtual space has acquired an equal, if not greater, significance than physical space. The concern of Western military doctrine is to win war; Russia's is mainly to circumvent it while violating the peace.

Some observers have framed Russian cyber activity as a continuation of espionage on a new plane. They apply the logic of intelligence competition to analyze the theft of industrial and military secrets (at which the Chinese People's Liberation Army (PLA) excels) or the manipulation of information online and the destruction of machine functions (a special area of competence of Russian state hackers).[50] We saw in the Introduction that this view is misguided; it overlooks two very important facts. One is the sheer scale of espionage activity in cyberspace. To be sure, it includes intelligence gathering for traditional purposes, such as industrial and military espionage. But even when the goal of a cyber operation lacks political intent, the virtual theft of information is on a scale that far surpasses what is possible with conventional espionage techniques. But then there are the political and strategic aims of espionage. While China excels in the industry of intelligence theft, Russia is adept in the use of stolen 0s and 1s for subversive ends. Burrowing oneself deeply with code into the apparatus of government or a private organization can afford means of access not only to secret information, but also to vital machine functions. Espionage is a precursor to customized destructive attack. Not so the disruptive cyberattacks and the manipulative information campaigns, because their driving aims are ideological. Treating Russian actions as a new manifestation of old espionage risks weak policy action against them.

Let us recall from Chapter 1 a vital question of doctrine: every strategic actor must ask how much it is willing to risk to achieve its goals. Russia is willing to risk a lot – far more, at least, than many of its Western adversaries. Yet, despite the recklessness of war in Ukraine, Russia remains firmly averse to the risk of a direct military clash with them. Instead, it has preferred to seek strategic gains within cyberspace. The result is the aforementioned paradox: Russia seeks to reduce the risk of war with its geopolitical foes in the physical world, which in turn increases its risk appetite for adventure in the virtual world.[51] Moscow seems to grasp the danger that the two sides of the paradox might nullify each other. If the cyber activity is serious enough, then it could escalate into a real war – hence why it has ceased (so far) at the boundary of war.

RUSSIAN CODE: VARIETIES OF METHOD

The shock of Russia's subversive activity in cyberspace is all the greater if we consider its wide range of methods. It is important to grasp their diversity, even if one must treat them as elements of a uniform campaign of strategic competition (see Chapter 7). For it is precisely the diversification of the opponent's capabilities, targets, and actions that affords it such great possibilities for strategic maneuver.

The question confronts Western security planners: How far is Putin's regime willing to go in its use of unpeaceful technologies to pursue Russian national interests and to upset the liberal international order? The question is important: recall from Chapter 2 that grasping the adversary's intentions and capabilities is a central component of strategic doctrine. The record of cyber incidents – subtle or explosive, disruptive or destructive – over the last fifteen years offers important clues in answering it.

Russian offensive activity in cyberspace is of two broad kinds. One involves the use of computer code as a *weapon of destruction*. Among the defining features of the current cyber revolution is a fundamental change in the role of information in strategic competition. Information existing in the traditional analog form (i.e. in print, photography, or telephony) cannot inflict direct harm upon the material world. For all the enormity of history's great information heists, it would have been impossible for the thieves to use the secrets destructively. Consider Robert Hanssen's delivery to the Soviets of thousands of classified files about secret agents and U.S. nuclear weapons technologies. Alone, the secrets could not harm the exposed moles or the opponent's missile systems. Achieving these effects required human intervention. The stolen information had a different value: it allowed the Soviets to uncover double agents within their ranks and to design a more robust response mechanism against U.S. nuclear attack.[52] In other words, although analog information can be an important source of power, it cannot become force by itself.

By contrast, computer code can cause direct harm upon the material world. Information that was once stored on paper or tapes can now be used in the form of 0s and 1s (which constitute all computer code)[53] to destroy or disrupt the operations of machines and other physical objects. The mechanism of action involves a complex causal chain that ties the manipulation of intermediary objects (think of the industrial controller at a nuclear enrichment facility or the traffic signaling system in a railway network) with adverse effects on the machines that it governs (uranium enrichment centrifuges or high-speed trains) and with possibly further adverse effects on humans whose wellbeing relies on the compromised machines' proper functioning (plant operators or train passengers). Thus, there is a crucial difference today between the use of information *as power* to degrade the effectiveness of an opponent's security strategy – an idea that the classical military theorist Carl von Clausewitz contemplated – and the use of information *as force* to harm the other side's physical assets – a defining novelty of the cyber revolution.[54]

Examples of Russian actors' use of destructive code abound. Take the cyber-attacks against the Ukrainian energy sector. On a freezing afternoon in late December 2015 in the western Ukrainian region of Ivano-Frankivsk, approxi-mately 230,000 people suffered a power outage. Countless homes and busi-nesses went dark. The problem originated in the control system of the regional power plant. The facility's operators noticed that the mouse cursor on one of the industrial controller's screens had acquired a life of its own, dancing around and refusing to respond to the human operators' prompts. An unknown hacker had seized control. Frantically but helplessly, the operators observed the hacker disable the circuit breaker in a substation: thousands of residents had just lost power. Within minutes, about thirty other substations were disabled. In addi-tion, the hackers turned off two more power distribution centers and backup generators.[55] Here, for the world to witness (particularly incautious skeptics who had quipped that squirrels threatened energy supplies more than weap-onized code),[56] was the first confirmed case of a major power disruption caused by a cyberattack.

The U.S. government and Ukraine's intelligence service attributed the operation to "Sandworm," a highly capable group of Russian state hackers.[57] Indeed, the attack sequence was not of the kind one might expect from a private-citizen hacker. It bore the hallmarks of a state-level operator: an ability to surreptitiously penetrate the control system of a vital civilian infrastructure by exploiting human weaknesses in a "spear-phishing" campaign (involving a variant of the "BlackEnergy" malware suite); undetected residency within the machine complex (for how long one cannot even guess); tailoring of the malware payload (including the use of a "KillDisk" wiper to override the master boot record of the operator stations) to the specifications of the targeted machine, which required intimate knowledge of its labyrinthine architecture of industrial controllers, workstations, and power distribution centers as well as the location of key files within them; and, to top it off, a run-of-the-mill distributed denial-of-service attack (of Russian IP provenance) against customer call centers to impede the public's attempts to contact their energy provider.[58] Any one of these attack elements, except the last one, which was technically unsophisticated, could have merited the commendation of security analysts; together, they were ingenious.[59]

A second category of offensive action involves the use of cyberspace as a *weapon of political disruption.*[60] Here, we can observe various activities. One concerns the use of malware against the computer infrastructure of democratic elections. Malicious code could be used to hamper access to, or corrupt the data in, voter registration systems; or it could interfere with the collection, transmission, or tallying of electronic votes. Either action would affect the voting tally and possibly the election outcome.

In July 2019, the U.S. Senate Intelligence Committee concluded that Russian state hackers targeted election systems in all fifty states as part of "an unprecedented level of activity against state election infrastructure." In at least one state, Illinois, the intruders "were in a position to delete or change voter data."[61] Evidence of attempts to penetrate Illinois's election systems first emerged a few months before the 2016 presidential election, when monitors discovered anomalous network traffic flowing out of the voter registry website. The investigators concluded that the intruders had exfiltrated voter data. Although no evidence emerged regarding the corruption of voter registry data or vote tabulations on November 3, the Committee's insights into such possible scenarios was by its own admission limited.[62]

In another (unidentified) state, election officials shut down the voter registration system for more than a week following the discovery in workstations connected to election infrastructure of a criminal hacker associated with a Russian server.[63] There is irony in this story: the Russian government petitioned by diplomatic channels to send observers to polling stations! Little could election officials have known at the time, although the most prescient among them might have suspected it, that Russian state actors were already residing within some compartments of the country's fragmented election infrastructure.

Much of the Senate report (possibly its most sensitive and explosive details) was redacted. From its published findings one cannot derive an accurate sense of the investigators' level of confidence in the conclusion that foreign intruders did not alter voter registration records or vote tallies. But the technical vulnerabilities that render such effects possible, and by some accounts not difficult for a large state actor to achieve, have been extensively analyzed. A particular object of concern are vulnerabilities in the software and hardware components supplied by private companies – for example, the voter roll management software provided by VR Systems to election officials in Florida, which federal officials believe Russian hackers breached.[64] In 2018, the U.S. Senate Intelligence Committee concluded that they "scanned databases for vulnerabilities, attempted intrusions, and in a small number of cases successfully penetrated a voter registration database" in an attempt to undermine the election. "[T]hese cyber actors were in a position to, at a minimum, alter or delete voter registration data," the report stated.[65] As J. Alex Halderman warned: "If Russia or other attackers can break into a state's election management system, they can spread malicious software to voting machines throughout that jurisdiction, and potentially change all of the digital records."[66] The fragmentation of the U.S. election system across fifty-one jurisdictions, each with its own voter registries and vote tabulation systems, increases the work factor of aspiring election hackers. But it does not confer much security in the election outcome's integrity, because closely contested U.S. presidential elections are sometimes decided in a small number of hotly contested states or even districts.

Yet, intruders need not alter the voter registry or alter the actual vote count to disrupt the democratic process. Merely the *knowledge* of their presence within the election machinery, or the understanding that they have the *capacity* to compromise its functions and alter its data, could erode the vote's legitimacy – especially among losing candidates and their supporters.

That was the possible aim of the Russian hackers in 2016 according to investigating officials.[67] The election unfolded in a political environment polarized even by the standards of American presidential elections. For the first time in more than twenty years, majorities in both the Republican and Democratic Parties expressed "very unfavorable" views of the opposing party. The revulsion consisted not only of frustration but also of fear and anger. Nor was the negative sentiment merely about parties and institutions; it also had a personal element.[68] Consider, also, that Trump refused to promise to accept the election's legitimacy if it did not put him in the White House.[69] American intelligence officials imputed a similar intent to degrade public confidence in election legitimacy during Russia's cyber activity at the time of the 2018 mid-term elections.[70]

The aftermath of Trump's defeat in the 2020 presidential election is instructive. Armies of the former president's unbending supporters seized upon computer vulnerabilities to substantiate the false argument (popular among them) that technical chicaneries helped to override his landslide election victory. Trump's lawyer Sidney Powell claimed in court, more creatively than cleverly, that the vote-counting machines and software produced by Smartmatic and Dominion that were used in key states were compromised in Venezuela – Russia's chief economic and security partner in the Americas.[71] Congressman Louie Gohmert of Texas claimed, falsely, that the Spanish company Scytl, which provided election support in several states, colluded with rogue U.S. intelligence operatives to corrupt voting data on servers based in Germany.[72] The confabulation was perhaps greatest in Jeffrey Clark, a former assistant attorney general, who claimed that China had altered votes in Dominion machines by exploiting vulnerabilities in "smart" thermostats.[73] None of this is to say that disaffected political agitators can seize upon innate computer weaknesses and nefarious foreign activity to undermine the foundations of a large and vibrant democracy. But their claims (plausible or specious) can aggravate political divisions that further fracture the polity.

Another politically disruptive activity involves kompromat, or the release of sensitive hacked information belonging to political candidates, campaigns, or party officials at a time that is calculated to cause maximum disturbance within the political system.[74] Because this method involves data theft, it often relies on malicious computer code or hacking techniques, but rather than targeting the election machinery and data themselves, it goes after the information of individuals and institutions. The implosion within the Democratic Party in 2016 caused by WikiLeaks' revelation of the email records of party officials seized by Russian military operatives showed the possible impact of kompromat operations. Plausibly, but not demonstrably (historical counterfactuals cannot be proven), Hillary Clinton would have won the election had Bernie Sanders's many supporters not been incensed by the leaked emails, which showed that the party leadership secretly favored Clinton as their candidate.

Yet, another form of political disruption transpires through the social web in the form of information warfare. The method is opportunistic: its primary aim is not to create new divisions within the adversary's polity but to aggravate already flaring ones. Pro-Kremlin agitators on platforms such as Twitter and Facebook aim to fan political and social divisions during elections or public crises (such as the Covid-19 pandemic). Their objective is to diminish the polity's internal cohesiveness by eroding public trust in the integrity of democratic institutions and election processes, distracting the attention and sapping the energy of government officials, or shaping public sentiment in favor of Moscow.[75] For example, the U.S. Senate Intelligence Committee concluded that Russian operatives such as the Internet Research Agency used "social media to wage an information warfare campaign designed to spread disinformation and societal division in the United States" during the 2016 election.[76]

Various cyber techniques, then, can damage the perceived legitimacy of free elections. Some involve the manipulation of infrastructure: hacking of machines that register voters (e.g. to corrupt data that prevents a defined demographic group from casting votes), machines that record votes (where voting is performed in electronic booths), and machines that count them (in jurisdictions that accept paper ballots).[77] Remember: an adversary need not succeed in altering voter records or vote tallies to undermine the election's legitimacy; merely the knowledge that the relevant machines have been penetrated by foreign or unknown actors suffices to achieve this aim, especially in electoral contexts where the losing party challenges the outcome. Think of Trump's allegations of large-scale voter fraud, including the use of supposedly compromised vote-counting machines, during the 2020 U.S. presidential election.[78] Another pathway of disruption affects the minds not of machines but of humans: information campaigns via social media or web postings that seek to sow confusion or division about the legitimacy of political candidates or the voting outcome by disseminating either false information or truthful information that is presented in a misleading manner.

Fueling further concern is the variety of threat actors, which include state clients: criminal elements who wield ransomware and other potent hacking tools. In May 2021, they carried out the largest cyberattack against U.S. infrastructure when their ransomware hit the facilities of Colonial Pipeline. The attack forced the suspension of half of fuel supplies in the East Coast.[79] Swept up with a patriotic fervor in the midst of war, there is no telling what their response will be and whether the Kremlin can (or will even want to) control it.[80] Then there are the state actors. Forensic evidence shows that Russian intruders have burrowed themselves deeply within key U.S. systems.[81] The intelligence community's 2022 Annual Threat Assessment cautioned that Russia was honing its ability to target underwater cables and industrial control systems.[82] Reports of Russian GRU hackers penetrating the electrical grid are commonplace. In March 2022, for example, the U.S. government indicted four Russian operatives for installing backdoors and launching the "Triton" malware within energy facilities, including at a foreign oil refinery. The skillful hackers penetrated or targeted systems in more than 135 countries. "Russian state-sponsored hackers pose a serious and persistent threat to critical infrastructure both in the United States and around the world," warned U.S. Deputy Attorney General Lisa O. Monaco.[83] But perhaps the clearest indication of the growing risk of breakdowns in cyberspace was President Biden's public warning – as tanks rolled deeply into Ukrainian territory – that the West should expect them.[84]

Strategic cyber activity targeting democratic societies departs from the traditional logic of political subversion. Subversion is traditionally covert: it involves the use of agents, information, money, and other assets to maneuver within an adversary's political space clandestinely.[85] Think of Russia's planting of operatives in the Western political scene or its secret financing of right-wing parties in Western Europe. Insofar as these efforts become publicly known – as in the revelation in 2013 that Marine Le Pen's French political party borrowed millions of euros from a Russian bank – they typically lose effectiveness.[86] Political disruption of the nation's virtual integrity by information operations, however, is different. It often works *overtly* for demonstration effect. The penetration of vital infrastructure follows a similar logic. But here, the covert phase ordinarily lasts longer, because the target machines are generally harder to penetrate than the public information space. But the effects of the demonstration phase can nevertheless be consequential for the political world if they coincide with its events.

In sum, artful cyber disrupters customarily cover their tracks long enough to overcome a target's technical defenses, while, thereafter, operating openly to manifest their intrusion abilities and strategic prowess. And that is the whole point: to reveal to the affected party its weakness and to the world its unreliability as a security partner. Their activity is tactically covert (to facilitate intrusion) while strategically overt (to instigate public spectacles of weakness within the affected polity or community of nations).

FORGOTTEN MAXIMS? CYBERSPACE AND WAR IN UKRAINE

Against the backdrop of Russia's revisionist ambitions described earlier, the maneuvers within Ukrainian cyberspace become understandable. Putin's military campaign of conquest, however, might seem puzzling. How do we make sense of it in light of Russian strategic doctrine?

The answer must begin with the political scene in Ukraine: in early 2014 it turned decisively against Moscow. Before Ukraine suffered any major cyberattacks, the country was plunged into political crisis as a popular uprising toppled its Russophile president Viktor Yanukovych. With the deposed president in exile (more forced than self-imposed) in Moscow and with the new leader Oleksandr Turchynov (a close associate of the firebrand reformist Yuliya Timoshenko) seeking to revive the previous administration's integrationist policies towards the West, the country seemed poised to peel itself away from the historical Russian orbit. A striking move by the former master derailed the country's westward drift: in February 2014, Russian military forces, in the guise of ununiformed "militias," invaded and annexed the Crimean Peninsula, which housed Russia's mighty Black Sea Fleet comprising dozens of cruisers, frigates, corvettes, submarines, and other naval assets (Russia had annexed the peninsula once before, in 1783).

Tellingly, it was the push towards an association agreement with the European Union, a political and economic club, rather than a move towards NATO – a more common objection – that prompted Yanukovych's reorientation towards Moscow in defiance of the popular will a few months earlier. Here was proof that, in the eyes of the former captor, Ukraine's absorption into the West's political and economic structures could trigger the revisionist impulse – even if integration into NATO seemed remote.

But there is more. To seize Crimea was to prevent Russia's eventual loss to the West of a prized military and strategic asset it had controlled for centuries. Arresting the bigger loss of Ukraine itself, the second-largest European country by size after Russia, required a continuous campaign of internal splintering. For if institutional reform and political cohesion were the necessary preconditions for EU and NATO accession, then institutional stagnation and political fragmentation were its obstacles. Therein lay the probable objective, and desired effect, of the cyber operations: to weaken the Ukrainian public's confidence in their country's public infrastructure and political institutions as well as to sow further doubt in the minds of officials about the nation's integrity in face of external – possibly existential – peril.

In short, if Ukraine could not be prized away from Western clutches, then it would be wrecked – preferably through cyberspace alone, but if necessary also on the battlefield. As the head of the Ukrainian national security and defense council put it in January 2022: "The No. 1 task of Russia is the shattering of the internal situation of our country. And today, unfortunately, they are doing this successfully," for which he voiced his government's remedy: "Our task is to do our jobs in a calm and balanced environment"[87] – an unenviable task when your nation's vital infrastructures are infested with unknown weaponized code and bands of partisan fighters (some of them foreigners) roam freely within one of your most heavily industrialized regions (the Donbas).

Cyber activity alone, however, could not deliver Ukraine to Moscow's clutches. At best, it could help to impede the country's integration into the Western community. Let it be stated once and again: intangible computer code cannot seize territory and it can coerce only with difficulty. Instead, its main strategic use is to weaken adversaries internally – that is, to dilute and eviscerate the opponent's policy rather than reverse it, thereby achieving some of the strategic effects of conquest and coercion while avoiding its risks.

The seizure of Crimea, the armed insurrection in the Donbas, and the stabs deeper into Ukraine show that Russia is willing to apply military force to subjugate smaller nations on its periphery seeking assimilation into the Western community. But Russia has had to pay enormous military and economic costs for its campaign of conquest. Russian strategists forgot their own maxims: avoid military adventures that risk drawing in the Western giants or their resources into the struggle; focus on the methods of unpeace which can circumvent the severest penalties of the legal system; dominate the virtual and informational, not the territorial and martial worlds.

Cyber activity, in sum, offers advantages over the use of military force. It enables Russia to degrade the political institutions and economic infrastructures of former captive states that lean westward, thereby diminishing their value and interest to the West; to weaken the political base of the Western nations themselves in an attempt to debilitate their foreign policy assertiveness in areas that matter to the Kremlin; and to penetrate their institutions and infrastructures so deeply that the prospect of a breakdown of modern society looms large in the minds of officials contemplating intrusions into Russia or its areas of interest.

There is a sameness in Russia's interventions in nations that aspire to break away, or have recently broken away, from its political and diplomatic clutches, which reveals a strong preference for the use of virtual weapons over troops and tanks. As we noted in Chapter 2, Russian cyber strikes against targets in Western and Western-aligned nations, including countless raids into Ukrainian cyberspace, have elicited only a weak reaction or none at all – even when an operation's cascading effects swept widely through computer systems around the globe. The "NotPetya" incident illustrates the point. Unleashed onto targets in Ukraine on the eve of the country's Constitution Day in June 2017, the ransomware virus – an ingenious creation of the technical minds of Russia's Sandworm – rapidly spread and caused enormous commercial damage to numerous Western companies. Although 80 percent of targets were located in Ukraine, including computers and servers in the National Bank, the rest were spread out globally. Among the affected companies was the Danish shipping giant Maersk, which at the time moved 20 percent of the world's shipping volume and which shut down its networks to address the infection. Other affected companies were FedEx, which experienced a loss of $400 million, and the French construction firm Saint-Gobain, which suffered damages of $384 million. The White House estimated that NotPetya inflicted total damages worth $10 billion in 2017.[88]

The American, British, and Australian governments replied to Russia's brazen action with stern warnings of "international consequences."[89] But, as in the aftermath of other similar incidents, the penalties were narrow. The United States sanctioned multiple individuals and entities, a penalty that the subjects might have perceived as a badge of merit no less honorable than the Medal for Courage or the Medal of Suvorov.[90] The "scorched earth" maneuvers in cyberspace have so far allowed Russia to evade the international legal system's clearest restrictions on interstate conduct and, with it, the severest penalties for violations of sovereignty.

By contrast, the territorial intrusions into Ukraine invoked a much sterner reaction. Following the annexation of Crimea, the European Union embargoed the export of arms, dual-use technologies, and oil industry equipment to Russia. Canada imposed bans on Russia's energy and financial industries. The United States restricted Russian banks' access to the U.S. debt markets. Even greater penalties flowed from Western states and their partners (including Japan and South Korea) following Russia's expansion of the war in 2022. Some of the sanctions were broad spectrum; they went beyond the targeted financial penalties that the U.S. Treasury Department has applied to cyber culprits. They far surpass, too, the scope and effects of Britain's diplomatic and financial penalties in response to the GRU's poisoning operation (with the banned chemical agent novichok) against its former agent Sergei Skripal in Salisbury in 2018. The war sanctions regime was particularly potent because it has included an extraordinary freeze on central bank assets and the expulsion of some of Russia's largest banks from the global interbank payments system, SWIFT.[91] The country thereby became the most heavily sanctioned nation in the world, even more so than North Korea.[92] In addition, hundreds of multinational and mostly Western companies have exited the Russian market. The ruble has undergone dramatic price drops not seen since the 1998 financial crisis, which has inflicted economic pain on the general Russian population. The net result of these economic dislocations is a forecasted drop of 15 percent in Russian gross domestic product in 2022 – a decline that would reduce the national economy to its size in 2007 at current prices.[93]

In the Russian strategic concept, cyberspace is a central plane of geopolitical contention. Strategists contemplating the disasters of war might seek to restore their preference for the non-violent methods of unpeace.[94] The more limited Russia's gains on the Ukrainian and other battlefields, and the higher the costs of war beyond them, the likelier it is that Russia will return to the maxims of old. Like other geopolitical flashpoints (think of Iran's suspected nuclear weapons program), war in Ukraine portends breakdowns in cyberspace in Russia and in the nations that sanctioned it or armed Ukraine.[95]

5
CHINA AND CYBERSPACE
The Rising Technological Hegemon

VIRTUAL WEAPONS AND CHINESE REVISIONISM

China's rise is transforming the structure of world power. But the implications of this ascent are not only material: it is also creating a ripple within the political firmament of international relations. President Xi Jinping's aspirations to national greatness and the Communist Party's autocratic character challenge not only Western military and economic power but also the values that underpin the world's governing institutions. Vanished is the era when the United States and its partners could shape the security and economic affairs of the Asia-Pacific region without serious challenge from within it. Gone is the certainty – if ever it existed – that democratic liberalism will triumph over all other political creeds.[1]

Alongside the political revolution of a power transition is the strategic revolution of cyberspace. For the first time since the Industrial Revolution, when Britain harnessed the power of factories and the steam engine to achieve hegemony, China's upward climb within the international hierarchy coincides with rapid technological disruption. Not only is the distribution of power in the states system shifting, but also its very nature is changing. True, the concomitant political and technological revolutions do not rely on each other; each would have occurred in the other's absence. But their tracks converge in important points; thus, they cannot be analyzed in isolation.

To a considerable extent, then, addressing the challenge of China's rise relies on an accurate understanding of new technology's implications for security and its place within the Chinese strategic concept. One cannot grasp the political and moral transformations without also mastering the technological. To accept that the distribution of power is changing, while affirming that the character of force and conflict remains the same, is to risk falling further behind in the doctrinal race that Western and democratic nations are already losing.

This chapter explores China's integration of cyberspace into an activist foreign policy that challenges the U.S.-led regional and, increasingly, international order. The analysis examines two important ongoing evolutions in China's cyber efforts. One involves the configuration of cyberspace – the country's transition from a consumer of foreign innovations to a native technology creator that enables it to export its political values abroad. A second change involves China's offensive cyber posture. The country no longer focuses only on defensive concerns such as the arcane quarrels of Internet governance or the organization of domestic information security, or on passively offensive activity such as cyber espionage. Rather, China operates in cyberspace increasingly like Russia: to meddle in the internal affairs of democratic nations and to erode confidence in the integrity of their vital infrastructures.

The chapter argues that the growing convergence of geopolitics and cyberspace affords China new methods to undermine the regional and international order without resorting to war with all its attendant risks. As we discussed in the Introduction, the technologies of unpeace are expanding the realm of conflict between the extremes of violent war and peaceful rivalry. Instead, the war–peace binary has morphed into a spectrum of security competition offering a broad menu of non-violent, but potent, options to contenders who correctly interpret the technology's strategic implications and are able to derive from its peculiar characteristics superior principles of action.

Recall the main lesson in Chapter 1 from the history of technological revolution: the adaptation of human minds to machines is more important in the assertion of national power than the perfection of the machines themselves. Here, again, as in the case of Germany's challenge to French preeminence during the 1930s and 40s or a fallen Russia's resurgence in the present era, the Chinese challenge to America's global hegemony rests less on technological prowess than on doctrinal ingenuity. China has excelled in the exercise of doctrinal refinement. It has developed new modes of strategic competition that have allowed it to undermine Western power and its supporting institutions without resorting to the violent methods of war and thereby avoiding its repercussions. Like Russia, China deftly maneuvers within cyberspace to challenge the established liberal order by circumventing the legal system's traditional constraints on interstate rivalry. The Asian behemoth has succeeded in exploiting the rigidities of the institutions that Western nations rely on to defend the system that they dominate but which hinders the development of spectral doctrine. Although technological and doctrinal innovations in cyberspace alone will not define the outcome of the epochal power transition, they will increasingly shape the character and reach of a future *Pax Sinica*.

The argument comes in two parts. The first concerns China's drive to global preeminence: it expresses a particular view of China's place in the world rooted in the country's millennial history as a gigantic but mainly isolated regional power, a perception of greatness that today is imbued with the ideological strivings of Marx and Mao, which have not shed their pretensions of universalism. The second part involves the sources of power and influence: China has sought to harness cyberspace for strategic gain, first by using the spoils of stolen Western technology – the country has been the world master of cyber theft – to build up a native technology industry; and more recently by proactively exploiting the openness of foreign information spaces and economic infrastructure for political ends. A fundamental evolution in the character of the Chinese cyber threat is presently under way: it no longer primarily concerns the quiet theft of information assets; it increasingly involves the use of cyberspace for ideological and politically disruptive purposes.

XI'S CHINA: HISTORICAL EXCEPTIONALNESS TINGED WITH REVOLUTION

A preliminary step in the analysis of China's cyber posture is to ask: Does the leadership in Beijing pursue a revisionist foreign policy?[2] Answering this question will help us grasp how China has integrated cyberspace into its strategic concept, with important security implications for Western security interests.

A similar question appeared in previous power transitions. Observing the growing mass of German power in 1907, British Foreign Secretary Eyre Crowe famously wondered whether officials in Berlin pursued a "vague and undefined scheme" or an organized plan of "Teutonic expansion."[3] International relations theorists have asked a deeper tangled question: are the workings of the states system automatic or contrived? As Crowe intimated, large powers do not require a foreign policy scheme to carry out their mutual dealings; they can transpire organically as if by a natural order of things. Writing nearly two-and-a-half thousand years ago, Athenian historian Thucydides foreshadowed this view. He observed that the will to power in human nature came together with the distrust inherent in anarchic dealings to produce an epochal clash among the dominant state Athens and its main challenger Sparta – even though both sides wished to avoid it.[4] In the eighteenth century, Genevan philosopher Jean-Jacques Rousseau wrote that the mechanics of great power politics played out automatically; the conscious endeavor of statespersons was not necessary to operate a machine that contained within itself the logic of a naturally programed behavior. There is some truth in this view: strangers encountering each other in "the state of nature" would know instinctively whether to fight or to flee. But as we saw in Chapter 1, the questions of *whether* to fight *or* to flee and for what *aims* and with which *means* – the substance of strategic doctrine – present gaps for analysts to examine and decisionmakers to fill.

Skeptics of the existence of a Chinese grand strategy believe that officials have not filled the gaps coherently. They argue that China lacks a strategic vision to guide its growing influence within the international jungle.[5] Among these doubters are prominent Chinese scholars such as Wang Jisi who lamented: "There is no strategy that we could come up with by racking our brains that would be able to cover all the aspects of our national interests."[6] Yet, it is misguided to think that China does not pursue clearly defined goals according to a choate strategy; it has announced them plainly and pursues them evidently.[7] Central among them is to displace American hegemony – with its liberal institutions and supporting alliances – as the chief provider of international order. This posture rests on China's particular view of its place in the world, deriving from the country's history as an immense nation that flourished in conditions of total or near isolation for more than two thousand years.

In other words, China's foreign policy behavior is not driven merely by material interests and the structural constraints of the distribution of power – Rousseau's natural mechanics. Guiding it is a peculiar strategic culture that interacts with those mechanics to produce policy approaches. It is not necessary here to review at length what volumes of scholarship have already discussed.[8] A brief review of Chinese strategic culture will suffice.

Chinese rulers, beginning with Zhou in the eleventh century B.C., regarded their vast realm as the center of human civilization. The leaders of nearby barbarians were not blessed like the "Son of Heaven" who ruled the Chinese lands. China's historical name, "the middle kingdom," which draws from the country's native name, *Zhongguo*, reflects the sense of exceptionalness. It conveys an identity of national greatness in conditions of global isolation – a combination of qualities that no Russian tsar or German Kaiser could ever presume or aspire to achieve. In the Chinese conception, the homeland was the main stage for commercial exchange, political intrigue, and war. China's last imperial dynasty, the Great Qing, did not consider it necessary to operate a foreign ministry, for were internal imperial matters not the center of earthly affairs?[9] Rather, the state resorted to a variety of agencies to conduct its commercial and other largely inconsequential dealings with the inferior foreigners, who in the presence of the emperor prostrated themselves in the *kowtow* ritual (as ordained by a Ministry of Rituals) regardless of their official status back home.

Vast but isolated China viewed itself differently than the European great powers perceived themselves. Even the mightiest nations in European history understood themselves to be objects within a constellation of states vying for influence. For centuries, they struggled for mastery over the Continent. Yet, no conqueror after the Roman emperors ever achieved it (despite attempts by Charlemagne, Napoleon, Wilhelm II, and Hitler). By contrast, struggles for power involving China were mainly internal. For two thousand years, China was united under a single imperial rule. Or when disunity and rebellion occurred, they did so largely free from decisive foreign meddling.[10] Until the inglorious intrusions of European colonial powers in the early nineteenth century, no external actor disturbed the domestic battles for supremacy within the empire. Were it not for the arrival of European explorers in the early nine-teenth century, imperial authorities would not have believed that advanced civilizations could flourish elsewhere or that their militaries could penetrate deeply within Heaven's earthly quarters.[11] Theirs had been a China-*only*, rather than a China-centric, view.

In short, within the European political order in which Russia and other large powers emerged, the nations were components of a system whose customs they learned even when vying to dominate it. No component was ever superior to the whole; it was a system *among* nations. The Chinese political setting was different: it was a system *within* a nation. European great powers liked to imagine themselves as the center of the world's political system; for Chinese leaders, the nation *was* the system.

The deep historical perception of national greatness endured beyond the intrusions of European colonialism that carved out the empire. It survived the period of humiliations – a blip against the millennial record of divine exaltation – as well as the vicious Civil War and the takeover of power by Mao Zedong's Communists in October 1949. What today we call in English the People's Republic of China in Mandarin betrays the historical identity of grandeur – *Zhonghua renmin gongheguo*, or "the middle glorious people's republican country." Sensitivity to historical indignities was one side of the national conscience; it fueled the other side: aspiration to greatness. Flustered by the prostrations to the Soviets during the 1950s, Mao declared: "Ours will never again be an insulted nation. We have stood up."[12]

After the ruling elite's adoption of Communist ideology in 1949, the enterprise of national greatness acquired a peculiar revolutionary zeal.[13] Embodying the tenets of Marxian materialism, for the first time in its history the country undertook a massive scientific advance. Soviet support (some might say tutelage) aided this task. China's scientific drive became a companion piece to the Soviet Union's aspirations to world revolution. But then, between 1966 to 1976, came the Cultural Revolution. Tragic and abhorrent are the words that come to mind when contemplating that period. For a while, it was safer to be red than an expert. Schools and universities mostly closed down (a sure sign that agrarian zealots ruled the land).[14] The staff of entire research institutes were marched off to the countryside to relearn Marxist dicta in the purifying company of menacing peasants. Riots, famine, political assassinations, mass purges, and bureaucratic indecision paralyzed the fledgling scientific enterprise. Many more than a hundred intellectual flowers died or failed to bloom.

Following the end of upheaval and Mao's death, Hua Guofeng proposed four modernization efforts in 1978. Party slogans shed their exhortations for cultural destruction and their penchant for elite feuding. "Shed the Four Olds" and "Smash the Gang of Four" gave way to "Reform and Opening Up." Building on a very low base, Deng Xiaoping (who had ousted Hua, showing that old customs die hard) set in train a process of economic opening and technological rejuvenation. By 1997, Party speeches were extoling the virtues of wealth, strength, and democracy – but only the first two were the object of real ambition. Under Jiang Zemin, the self-anointed priest of China's cyber revolution, and his successor Hu Jintao, the country began to leap forward technologically (we will return to this topic below).

Amid this turmoil and despite the occasional menace of the Soviet shadow, Chinese leaders viewed themselves as the only legitimate interpreters of Marx's dogma. The pretension gained strength following the Soviet Union's demise in the late twentieth century. Today, it endures in Chinese preachments about the reform of socialism in places such as Vietnam or Cuba.[15] Tellingly, China's Communist theoreticians sometimes issue pronouncements on their implications for the future of the movement, much as Soviet luminaries enlightened (often with a blast rather than a beacon) other nations' paths to Communist orthodoxy during much of the Cold War. Some of the learners have paid close attention. In 1979, in the midst of Sino-Soviet tensions, Fidel Castro derided Deng as "a caricature of Hitler."[16] By 1993, however, he had miraculously discovered and read all of Deng's published works (an arduous task even for a ravenous reader) and praised the virtues of China's "socialist market economy."[17]

Therein lies a central element of the contemporary Chinese worldview: the presumption of the superiority of China's centralized political system over the openness of Western liberal democracy. Viewed from the Great Hall of the People in Beijing, the Soviet empire's fall marked not "the end of history" but the start of a new era of reformed socialism and political centralization guided by the shining light of the Chinese example of Eastern autocracy.

The modern Chinese worldview has deep roots in the philosophy of Confucius that emerged in the sixth century B.C. Its defining precepts reflect the tendencies of Xi's regime: a reverence for social order, a commitment to the preservation of the community's cohesion, the attendant prostration of the individual citizen to political authority, the subservience of private interests to the enterprise of national rejuvenation. Since becoming paramount leader in 2012, Xi has cemented the political centralization process. An account of a government meeting in 2021 recorded that officials at all levels of government are expected to show "absolute loyalty to the core, resolutely defend the core, closely and constantly follow the core."[18] Long past were the days of open defiance and violent factionalism that marred political life under Mao.

Absent from this worldview is adherence to the maxims of John Locke or Machiavelli that so marked the development of Western political philosophy – a reverse subservience of government to private interests and the preservation (even the fanning) of political division to achieve one's ends. Missing from the Chinese political creed is Locke's essential questioning of governmental authority or Edmund Burke's ineradicable contestation among political factions which (to a point) give democracy its vitality. The conditions that Western thinkers established for the citizens' overthrow of the government would seem abhorrent to Chinese philosophers for whom the "state of nature" was not war and violence, not flight and individual preservation, but a state of harmony between the ruler and his subjects. The righteousness that Locke's imagined citizens demanded of their government was a quality that Confucius's students naturally assumed of their ruler. Mock though we might modern Chinese laws against "picking quarrels and provoking trouble"[19] – a charge commonly levied against domestic democracy advocates – they reflect the hierarchical orientation of Chinese political culture, which exalts the community and its centralized authority over individuals and their freedoms.[20] "Strength through diversity" is not a phrase that one encounters in the repertoire of Chinese revolutionary rhetoric. And the song popularized during the Japanese invasions in the 1930s, "Unity Is Strength," is too polite. A more accurate slogan for the modern mantra of centralized and forced assimilation might be, "Sameness Under the Ruler."

Yet, Western liberalism and Chinese centralism share a basic common feature: presumptive universalism. China's political orientation manifests a tendency to redraw first the regional, and then the international, order according to precepts of hierarchy and cohesive community that place the modern successors of the "divine sons" at the center of international power and influence.

The perceived supremacy of the Communist Party's creed and its manifestation in an activist foreign policy that increasingly reaches beyond East Asia is what marks China as a revisionist power. Remember, the chief defining characteristic of revisionism in international affairs is a nation's desire to refashion the system's institutions and the identity of its members in the image of its own values. The tendencies of Chinese foreign policy reflect not only a desire for security and wealth, but also an ideological drive. In the words of Xi Jinping: "China would become a global leader in terms of composite national strength and international influence," through which the country would strive to create "a new type of international relations and build a community with a shared future for mankind."[21]

Grasping the maxim that power without institutions is not lasting, China has begun to make important strides in erecting regional and international institutions that fit its political vision and serve its interests. Chief among them is the recently established Asian Infrastructure Investment Bank. We can hazard, without much risk, an opinion about its aims: not merely to foster economic and social development in Asia-Pacific, but also to increase China's power and influence in its economic affairs and governance – much like the United States has used its influence over the International Monetary Fund and the World Bank as a levers of national power to propagate free-market practices that served its interests.[22] So, too, in the security and defense realm: in April, Xi proposed the creation of a "Global Security Initiative." If China's territorial assertions (backed up by military threats) over Taiwan and in contested regional waters are anything to go by, then the initiative risks recreating – in China's own image – the very things that Xi decried when announcing it: "hegemonism, power politics and bloc confrontations."[23]

And let us not for a moment neglect the digital realm. Announced by Foreign Minister Wang Yi in September 2020, China's "Global Data Security Initiative" aimed at "contributing Chinese wisdom to international rules-making" on information security and infrastructure protection.[24] Chinese political values permeate the initiative. Its focus on data sovereignty and data-localization practices, for example, reflect Beijing's fixation with the maximization of state control over domestic information flows, which seeks to curtail the flow of democratic values and Western political influences. Scratch a Chinese "global" initiative and you will find a deeper aspiration to Chinese hegemony.

As in other historical brands of universalism, one finds here the self-assurance of the revolutionary actor: the sense that the global expansion of one's own political creed is foreordained by its inherent superiority over other systems. Much as the superiority of Britain's market capitalism enabled it to displace Spanish hegemony, so too the cohesiveness of China's political system will enable it to draw the curtain on the era of American predominance.

But Chinese foreign policy is not only about ideology; it embodies also a drive for material power and influence. Under Xi's rule, the regime's priorities have steadily shifted from implementing the abstract Confucian principles of "virtuous rule" to the worldly quest for "wealth and power."[25] Revived by the scholar Wei Yuan amid the turmoil of foreign interventions during the nineteenth century, the transition from a concern for internal virtue to a quest for external power reflects a truism derived from the humiliations of Yuan's era: What good is it to embody virtue in political affairs if one lacks the instruments to implement and protect it against the intrusions of lesser foreign beliefs?

The notion of National Rejuvenation, a core theme of Xi's regime, captures the vision and the opportunity to realize it. As Xi put it in 2018: "The world today is undergoing great changes unseen in a century, and the realization of the rejuvenation of the Chinese nation is at a critical period. . ."[26] The sense of historical grievance motivating the great leap upwards is never far from the mouthpiece of the government. "By 2050, two centuries after the Opium Wars plunged the 'Middle Kingdom' into a period of hurt and shame [i.e. after Britain and France defeated the technologically inferior Qing forces], China is set to regain its might and reascend to the top of the world," affirmed an observer in the state-run news outlet Xinhua during the 19th Party Congress in 2017.[27]

The quest for world power begins close to home: with the construction of an Asian "Community of Common Destiny." In this community, China lies at the center of a network of economic dependence while the system of military alliances tied to the United States is systematically dismantled. Economic enmeshment is thus at the core of the challenger state's method. It emerges not naturally but by the design of Chinese diplomacy, the principles of which Xi and other leading officials laid out in July 2013 at the aptly named meeting

"Let the Sense of the Community of Common Destiny Take Deep Root in Neighboring Countries." Building on the "diplomatic political guidelines" drawn up at the 18th Party Congress, this important forum affirmed that building the community required "actions that will win us support and friendship" in the region – for example, investment packages and other economic inducements.[28] A related pathway to the assertion of foreign power involves the establishment of an alternative system of global finance, one that would enable China and its partners to circumvent the levers of power through which Western nations dominate the world's monetary and financial architecture – institutions such as the International Monetary Fund, the G7, and the inter-bank global payments system, SWIFT. For example, profiting from the turmoil following the 2008 financial crisis, China encouraged the use of the renminbi in international trade by signing currency swap agreements that would allow it to settle trade in its native currency.[29]

Rejuvenation is not all economics. Military aggrandizement is another crucial pathway. Military texts since 1989 reveal a shift in focus towards conflict with the United States. Contemplating the end of the bipolar order, and observing the show of American military might against Saddam Hussein's Iraq in the Gulf War, China's top military official Liu Huaqing in 1993 drew lessons about the necessity for the modernization of his country's armed forces. Sharpening the lesson, a rising policymaker warned that U.S. military strikes with superior technology could have the effect of isolating and blockading China, which could disintegrate through internal disorders by democratizing the country. In these comments one finds a splendid combination of military prowess and immured ideology: the necessity to sharpen the sword in order to protect the nation's cohesion against foreign political values.[30] And in them one hears, too, echoes from the Kremlin: Look what political and economic opening under Gorbachev did to the mighty Soviet Union!

Yet, a military clash with the incumbent hegemon is neither foreordained nor desired. Among the most prominent themes of Chinese security policy is the notion of "a peaceful rise," which Hu Jintao's government formalized into policy at the beginning of the twenty-first century. The slogan seeks to reassure worried neighbors that China's ascendance will not threaten regional peace or international stability; in fact, they stood to benefit from China's growth and development.[31]

Wars of conquest and expansion, therefore, are not a centerpiece of Chinese security strategy, except in the resolution of matters affecting the nation's geographic integrity, principally Taiwan, or in settling localized territorial disputes with vastly smaller states such as the Philippines or Vietnam. The crushing of dissent in Tiananmen Square in 1989 and in Hong Kong in 2020 suggests that belligerent threats against Taiwan – the "renegade province" harboring the successors of Mao's nationalist enemies, the Kuomintang – are not all bluster.[32]

For all the prowess of the rapidly expanding PLA, for all its credible menace to democratic Taiwan and other Western-aligned nations in the region, Chinese officials prefer to avoid a major military confrontation that their armies might not win (supposing that, by some miracle, it is even possible to "win" a war among nuclear powers). The logic behind the preference is unassailable: Why pay the possibly suicidal price of an epochal clash in the Pacific when one can achieve some strategic effects within the virtual realm?

Therein lies an important feature of China's strategy of geopolitical displacement: the avoidance of a military showdown with the United States and its allies.[33] Accordingly, the techniques of unpeace are a prominent item in Beijing's foreign policy toolbox. By contrast, as we saw, the war–peace binary dominates Western security thinking. As popularized by English philosopher Thomas Hobbes, the doctrine regards international affairs as a "state of war," not because war always occurs but because it can break out at any time. Chinese philosophy offers a different take: strategic competition entails seizing gains while avoiding war. In the Western conception, international politics alternates between *periods* of war and peace; the state of war switches on and off in accordance with the play and counterplay of the will of states. In the Chinese view, it involves struggles between the *conditions* of war and peace, a yawning gulf that offers new possibilities for strategic action. In the words of philosopher Sun Tzu, "To subdue the enemy without fighting is the acme of skill." An important doctrinal text, *Science of Military Strategy*, teaches that "Non-War Military Activities" are "an important strategic means" to secure Chinese national interests abroad, because they avoid the direct military confrontation that pervades Western thinking.[34]

Although a war of displacement between China and the United States is neither impossible nor inconceivable, and while China's rise makes it more likely, that does not mean that China desires one. Such a desire would have to assume that the war – nuclear as it might well be – was winnable. History affords no case study of a hegemonic displacement under the shadow of nuclear devastation. That shadow increases the likelihood that any such war would be epochal rather than limited; it presents the antagonists more dangers than opportunities.

In sum, following China's rude awakening from a splendidly grand isolation, the modern successors of the Sons of Heaven were thrust into an international system that they had not known existed. Infused with a millennial vision of national grandeur that became tinged with a Communist revolutionary zeal, yet cognizant of the realities (and brutalities) of power politics, the succession of leaders from Mao to Xi have sought to develop means of asserting their vision of world order by circumventing the rigid rules and brittle institutions of the liberal system of international relations. In the nineteenth and twentieth centuries, force of arms taught reluctant Chinese rulers the syntax of power politics.[35] Having learned the rulebook, they have begun to expand its grammar to fields of action that confound Western thinking. Where the use of military force risks devastation, China turns to the technologies of unpeace to tip the geopolitical scales. It uses cyberspace to pursue foreign policy ambitions "as part of an epochal geopolitical shift,"[36] while avoiding the "Thucydides Trap" that plunged Athens and Sparta into a ruinous battle.[37] Here again, as in the Russian case, one finds the risk paradox: the desire to limit the risk of a military catastrophe among large and nuclear powers increases the willingness to run risks of destabilization below the war line.

A GROWING TECHNOLOGICAL ASSERTIVENESS

China's posture in cyberspace is changing notably. It is evolving from an inward orientation focusing on domestic imperatives of information security and technological advance to an outwardly assertive ambition involving the disruption of foreign information spaces and infrastructures.[38]

Initially, the focus of China's cyber policy attention was on domestic information security and Internet governance. A vast apparatus of information controls tightly surveils and censors Chinese users' online habits. Western

Internet platforms such as Gmail, Facebook, WhatsApp, LinkedIn, and Yahoo were either banned by Beijing or the companies voluntarily exited the Chinese market owing to regulatory hostility. China has also sought stronger control of global Internet standards, specifically by attempting to push the International Telecommunication Union into a more restrictive model suiting Chinese preferences. In effect, Beijing has strived to remake large swaths of the Internet to fit "its own image" of an autocratic society. During this period, insofar as China operated abroad, it was mainly to influence Internet governance standards and to quietly seize industrial and intellectual secrets – not to infiltrate and disrupt strategic infrastructures or to interfere in foreign political systems.[39] To achieve preeminence over the Internet, China would have to dominate what Joseph Nye called "the global regime complex," the loosely coupled set of regimes governing the rules, norms, and technical standards of global information exchange. China (alongside Russia) has supported a restrictive normative structure that transfers more powers of information control to the state.[40] The regime complex's overlapping and fragmentary nature all but ensures that no single country could ever dominate it.

China's inward orientation has been morphing into a more ambitious and daring cyber posture. No longer absorbed with insulating its populace from tainted foreign beliefs, moving beyond the goal of invigorating the native technology industry, Xi's regime increasingly seeks to harness its inventive powers for external activism. The new foreign assertiveness is embodied in Xi's ambition to turn China into a "cyber superpower" on the international scene. The original domestic mission of shoring up cyber sovereignty has expanded into an outward program of geopolitical activity. China increasingly carries out foreign information operations to disrupt or influence the political affairs of other nations – for example, in India during the "Doklam" border dispute of 2017,[41] in Taiwan via Twitter during the Covid-19 outbreak,[42] and in the Philippines via Facebook in 2020.[43] All three information campaigns played out in the context of territorial and sovereignty disputes between China and the affected nations.

On other occasions, the targets of intrusion were leaders of Western countries. Facing a reelection campaign in 2019, Australian Prime Minister Scott Morrison turned to WeChat, a popular social media platform among

Chinese-Australians, to reach them. Morrison had followed a hard line of opposition to Beijing's growing assertiveness in Oceania. Suddenly, his account with almost 80,000 subscribers was frozen; neither he nor his staff could access it. The account and its data were now under the control of the Chinese company.[44] Even the opposition leader Anthony Albanese, who in other circumstances might have relished his adversary's silencing, repudiated it. "We cannot allow a foreign authoritarian government to interfere in our democracy and set the terms of public debate in Australia,"[45] he seethed.

Among the more traditional threats, Chinese strategic espionage remains a major concern. Although, in 2015, Xi formally agreed with President Barack Obama to curtail it,[46] cyber theft has continued unabated.[47] The incidents are far too many to list. Some stand out for their scale and brazenness.

The Aurora operation that began in 2009 exploited zero-day flaws (vulnerabilities that are not known to defenders) in the Internet Explorer browser to target the servers of companies such as Google, Adobe, Northrop Grumman, and Morgan Stanley. According to computer security experts, its aim was to steal and possibly modify the source code (in the words of Dmitri Alperovitch, the "crown jewels") of American defense contractors and technology companies.[48] In April 2015, Chinese state hackers struck again. Breaking into the servers of the Office of Personnel Management, they seized the personnel files of more than 20 million U.S. government employees. In July 2020, ahead of negotiations on the Catholic Church's activities in China, hackers entered the Vatican's computers, infiltrating the Apostolic Library's invaluable intellectual treasures and intercepting communications between the Church and its diocese in Hong Kong.[49] That same year, investigators uncovered a large-scale espionage campaign that seized more than 320 gigabytes of secret data from a defense contractor, an energy consortium, medical researchers, and human rights activists in Australia.[50] In the midst of the Covid-19 pandemic in 2020, the highly capable threat actor APT41 disrupted the systems of British social care providers; computer viruses and other tools hindered efforts to defeat the real virus. Hackers based in Wuhan – the city that gave the world the pandemic – also targeted various European health infrastructures.[51] But the most spectacular intrusion, perhaps, was the penetration of the Microsoft Exchange Servers uncovered in January 2021. "Hafnium," a hacking group closely tied to Beijing, exploited four zero-days (itself a remarkable technical feat) to install a backdoor into a network of an estimated 250,000 machines, including at 30,000 organizations in the United States and 7,000 in Britain. So sweeping and indiscriminate was the operation that one analyst dubbed its approach "pillage everything."[52]

We cannot know for sure, though perhaps one day we will learn, the full purposes of China's strategic cyber theft. Among the conceivable scenarios, one stands out darkly. The vastness and diversity of data that Chinese hackers have amassed (and which can be aggregated) about officials and citizens in democratic societies suggests that they know us better than we know ourselves. In principle, the superior depth of knowledge – call it the "base understanding" of society – confers advantages in the design of tactics to maneuver within open information spaces: for example, identifying viable targets of kompromat operations exposing election candidates' secrets or indiscretions. Compounding the threat is the data's utility in the design of artificially intelligent agents. Computer algorithms work on the basis of parameter assumptions (which are coded into them) about humans and the world. They also rely on contextual data (which they are fed or capture) about the environments, and their people, in which the algorithms operate. The data underpinning one's base under-standing of societies, therefore, are the sinews of strength in the emerging field of AI technology – an area where China has invested massive resources and where knowing more means being able to manipulate and harm more.[53]

But there is more. U.S. defense planners have warned about the growing potency of China's offensive cyber arsenal. For example, it is now capable of disrupting national fuel supplies for weeks. They also warned about the possi-bility of "demonstration strikes … against select military, political, and economic targets with clear awing effects" to shape the outcome of a future diplomatic or military crisis.[54] Reflecting the gravity of this threat assessment, the deputy chief of U.S. Cyber Command singled out China as "the number one threat" and "number one priority" of his country's cyber forces.[55]

However reckless China's intrusions, however potent its penetrative code, it has not decisively coerced other states or influenced their election outcomes. But recall an important point from Chapter 1 about the strategic importance of cyber activity: more relevant than the capacity to coerce behavior is the ability to weaken it. Coercion among large states risks the consequences of a direct confrontation. Weakening policy can achieve strategic effect while avoiding them. And then there is the question of the absolute harm: even if cyber activity does not alter or weaken policy, it can still affect national and economic security in a way that political leaders will want to avoid.

Against this backdrop, concerns about regional and global cyber conflict involving China have grown. Amid ongoing territorial and diplomatic disputes, officials in Japan, South Korea, Singapore, and Taiwan have warned of the growing threat of Chinese information operations that seek to weaken their countries' social and political cohesion.[56] A spokesperson for President Tsai Ing-wen of Taiwan – the main target of Chinese disinformation abroad[57] – stated that the country was "on the front lines of cyber warfare, with hackers trying . . . to create dissent in Taiwan society."[58] Australia's Foreign Minister Marise Payne has accused Beijing of spreading disinformation that "contributes to a climate of fear and division."[59] In June 2021, NATO leaders issued a communiqué warning about China's "systemic challenges to the rules-based international order," underscoring "cyber, hybrid, and other asymmetric threats, including disinformation campaigns" and "the malicious use of ever-more sophisticated emerging and disruptive technologies."[60]

A diverse collection of Chinese actors toil away in the enterprise of foreign information warfare. They include operatives within the Communist Party (e.g. the Propaganda Department and International Liaison Department), the national executive (in particular, the Ministry of State Security), and the army (e.g. the Strategic Support Force and its specialized information unit – "Base 311" – located in Fuzhou). This burgeoning community also includes a motley of client actors within the technology, media, and other relevant industries.[61]

Consider more closely the case of Taiwan. A military invasion of the island nation of twenty-three million inhabitants would incur enormous costs for China. Security accords with the United States would likely lead to the activation of military support from American fighter jets and regional carrier strike groups, which could repel the invaders until the arrival of more U.S. assets. A storm of potent cyberattacks from the PLA could soften Taiwan's defensive glacis and deliver the invaders tactical advantages. Taiwan's Ministry of Defense recognized the danger, noting that cyberattacks could strike "national critical infrastructures and C2 [command and control] systems to cause turbulence and chaos in its society and decimate the internal security kept by the military and law enforcement organs of the nation and its government functions." According to a local expert, it would amount to a form of virtual "decapitation" of the Taiwanese government.[62] But even if the invaders made it into the country, Taiwan's military reserve force of more than one-and-half million citizen soldiers would threaten to draw them into a protracted guerrilla war in the island's cities and mountainous terrain. By contrast, standalone cyber activity offers Beijing options to weaken Taiwan's political system without resorting to armed force. True, intangible computer code cannot capture and retain geographic soil. But the PLA's highly active "Internet armies" can operate to inflame domestic differences on divisive policy matters, most notably the question of Taipei's potential declaration of independence – a hotly contentious diplomatic issue. Past disinformation campaigns have targeted politicians such as President Tsai, celebrities, and journalists who have supported the independence line.[63] China could not succeed in capturing Taiwan via cyberspace. Cyber activity might not even coerce Taiwan to alter its foreign policy. But the domain offers non-violent means to prevent the island nation's formal severance and to impose costs for closer political and military relations with the Western community while avoiding the risks and penalties of a war of conquest.

At the center of the expanding geopolitical contest of cyberspace is the integrity of global supply chains in vital technology sectors such as chips and semiconductors. They are used in everything from cars to personal computers to mobile phones and already face a world supply shortage.[64] The sector is dominated by Western-aligned nations in the region such as Taiwan and Japan. One Taiwanese company alone, TSMC, accounts for half of the world's chip market.[65] The United States hosts the largest global workforce in the design of semiconductors.[66] China has long sought to catch up with its technological competitors but remains behind.[67] As the geopolitical competition in Asia-Pacific intensifies, China has new incentives to interfere in the parts of the global supply chain that are located in the region's democratic countries.[68]

Other supply chain risks involve the export of Chinese software and hardware components for 5G and personal computers, which security analysts have warned could be compromised with design vulnerabilities and "sleeper" malware. In 2015, for instance, the FBI announced that Chinese agents concealed an extra chip loaded with "backdoors" in a computer manufacturer's servers. They also compromised the motherboards of Lenovo machines.[69] In 2021, Chinese state hackers exploited zero-day vulnerabilities to insert backdoors in the Microsoft Exchange email server – an operation that affected more than a quarter-million servers worldwide, including systems in medical research institutes, universities, think tanks, law offices, defense contractors, and government bodies (such as the Norwegian parliament).[70]

As the industrialized world prepares to adopt 5G infrastructure, security concerns about Huawei have intensified. The company is a major provider of hardware and software components for the Internet's next generation. It also has deep roots within China's security establishment. The company's founder, Ren Zhengfei, is a retired colonel in the PLA. Governments from India to Britain and the United States as well as their partners within the "Five Eyes" intelligence-sharing community have banned the use of Huawei products in government systems out of concern that they could be compromised. "Hackers find and exploit existing cyber vulnerabilities," warned a report from the U.S.–China Economic and Security Review Commission in 2016. "A nation-state that takes the long view, such as China, may also seek openings in the supply chain to implant vulnerabilities that can be exploited later. Were Huawei or ZTE to succeed in entering the U.S. telecommunications market, for example, their opportunities for supply chain manipulation could be significant."[71]

The important question here is not: Is Huawei a nefarious actor? In fact, the company has repeatedly denied any complicity in Chinese hacking.[72] That might not, and need not, be demonstrated. Rather, if Western countries allow Huawei to build their 5G and other vital infrastructure, and in a future diplomatic or military crisis Chinese authorities pressure Huawei to facilitate access to the systems it designed, then what future risks does the adoption of Huawei's products invite?

Recent experience bears out the fear. Consider again the Doklam border crisis. Four months after the crisis, Chinese hackers disrupted the services of a large power company in Mumbai. Hospitals in the midst of the Covid-19 pandemic switched to power generators. The stock exchange stopped trading. Trains stopped running. Forensic reports reveal that the flow of Chinese malware into the affected power grid's control systems spiked during the border spat.[73]

No available primary data has revealed the hackers' objective. We can infer it from China's broader infrastructure hacking activity. The aim is not to facilitate territorial conquest or to destroy infrastructure in the midst of a real war. Infrastructure hacking, to be sure, can support such aims. Instead, the aim is likelier to be to weaken the adversaries' foreign policy resolve by eroding expectation that its society's basic functions will operate in an orderly manner. Moreover, in a future regional war, China could exploit weaknesses in infrastructure by activating sleeper threats within it to deter the United States and its allies from entering the fight or to control its escalation.

At the core of China's sense of global supremacy is a superior relationship between technology and politics: the belief that China's rise will displace American hegemony because centralized management of the inventive process is better suited to the conversion of new industries to strategic advantage. China is no longer primarily a stealer and replicator of foreign technology. It has become a technological powerhouse in its own right. As the native technologies diffuse more widely across the world, the opportunities for China to spread its political values and project its power into the distant heart of foreign societies will continue to grow.

Increasingly, China's cyber activity resembles the impositions of Russian doctrine more than the blandishments of a "peaceful rise."[74] Recall the avoidance of war through lesser forms of conflict no longer guarantees peace. More and more, Chinese thinking merges the philosophy of Machiavelli with the tenets of Sun Tzu – a mix of fearsomeness and guile, coercion and persuasion, rivalry and conflict short of war that have become the hallmarks of Chinese foreign policy activism.

6
THE DIMENSIONS OF CURRENT STRATEGY
To Deter or Not to Deter?

THE PRICE OF LAWFULNESS

Western nations consistently fail to penalize offensive cyber acts decisively within the current legal and doctrinal framework. As a result, these acts continue unabated. Adversaries have not been rebuffed forcefully enough to dissuade further ordeals. Where is the deterring power of past criminal indictments and targeted financial sanctions? Why has persistent engagement – now in its third year of implementation – failed to disarm, disorient, or lure foreign culprits away from prized targets? Drawing from a liberal reading of international affairs that events refute, the early cyber norm abiders are condemned to pay the price of transgressors' exploitative maneuvers. The state of unpeace afflicting Western interests intensifies. The more that optimistic observers herald a coming era of cyber peace,[1] and the louder the prognostications that offensive activity will subside,[2] the more it grows in number, scope, and severity.

The attempt to develop more effective deterrence is hindered by the very legal system that makes it necessary. Old modes of thinking about security and conflict, which we discussed in Chapter 2, are at the root of Western failures to resolve the problem of cyber conflict prevention. Because policymakers privilege the legal and diplomatic conventions of traditional war, they struggle to deal with actions – no matter how politically or economically damaging – that fall below its recognizable threshold of violence. For the international rulebook prioritizes acts of aggression that involve overt physical destruction and loss of life; or else a non-destructive but physical violation of national territory so serious that it merits the label of a use of force.[3]

An incident in the summer of 2019 illustrates the problem. When, in June 2019, Iranian-backed Houthi rebels launched a drone strike that destroyed Saudi Aramco's oil infrastructure in Saudi Arabia, the United States responded with a cyberattack disabling missile launchers in Iran. Concerning the drone strike, U.S. Secretary of State Mike Pompeo remarked: "There were no Americans killed in this attack but any time you have an act of war of this nature, there's a risk of that."[4] At around the same time, Microsoft reported that Russian and North Korean actors were conducting political hacking activities against presidential campaign officials in the United States. Three months later, the company warned that state-backed Iranian hackers had been targeting the email accounts of almost three thousand U.S. government officials, presidential campaign officers, and journalists.[5] U.S. officials considered striking the adversaries' computer infrastructure in retaliation.[6] Evidence of punishment having taken place does not exist; only minor tactical operations to protect the networks can be observed. U.S. Cyber Command's chief General Paul Nakasone framed the response strictly in terms of denial: "We have obviously looked to impede what [foreign adversaries are] trying to do. I look at it more as, are we imposing a degree of cost that's making it more difficult to do their operations?"[7]

What emerges is a paradoxical picture of the place of cyber activity in strategic doctrine and of its weight on the scales of international law. Cyber activity can be serious enough to use in meting out punishment for an armed attack, but by itself it is insufficiently grave to call forth severe penalties. In other words, Western strategic planners have begun to figure out *when* and *how* to use cyber activity as an instrument of security policy, including in situations of war, while continuing to grapple with the reverse side of the puzzle – how to penalize to *prevent* it.

The manifestation of this problem in policy practice is the subject of this chapter. Chapter 2 analyzed the legal and normative roots of the cyber punishment problem. This chapter explores its expressions in policy and strategy. The analysis will elaborate upon the earlier diagnosis: that failure to prevent cyber conflict has occurred because the prescribed punishment has not been robust enough to suppress activity that respects the boundaries of war but breaches the tolerable limits of peaceful rivalry.

THE SEARCH FOR A STABLE DETERRENT

From a historical standpoint, the challenge of designing new strategy to prevent cyber conflict is recent. In fact, it is "new" if we consider that the body of directly relevant experience available to guide the effort is thin even if the underlying technologies are decades old. To be exact, the challenge is only fifteen years old. Before cyberattacks paralyzed Estonia's financial system in the spring of 2007, the cyber application of deterrence strategy did not feature prominently in national security agendas. Few security planners pondered them. Cyber threats were largely conscribed to the realm of technical experts preoccupied with mundane criminal activities such as financial theft. The Estonian events altered that mindset; thereafter, cyber threats cast an ominous shadow over the world's political, economic, and social scene.

Western security planners, particularly in the two security and defense behemoths, the United States and Britain, quickly caught on to the gravity of cyber threats. The picture that emerged over the next decade or so was mixed. On the one hand, the old alarmists' prophesies of a calamitous cyberattack proved erroneous. It became clear that a true cyberwar producing destructive effects and fatalities equivalent to an armed attack was likely to occur only within a conventional war – in which case conundrums involving the legal system would largely disappear. On the other hand, skeptics' dismissals of threats below the war threshold appeared naïve. To election officials tasked with protecting the integrity of the apparatus of democracy – the vote-counting machines susceptible to malware manipulation, the voter registration systems vulnerable to forced data corruption, the electorate's information space poisoned by deception and falsities, etc. – the assertion heard in some quarters that deterrence was working where it should work (i.e. above the war threshold) but failing where it did not matter (below it) would have seemed facile.[8]

Despite the improbability of cyberwar, the specter of technological aggression loomed menacingly. Military threat assessments, bureaucracy, budgets, and doctrine strived to adapt to the new realities. In the years after the Estonian events and the establishment of a military cyber command, the U.S. government formally ranked cyber threats as the top strategic threat facing the nation. In 2008, just one year after the Estonian crisis, the U.S. Department of Defense had suffered a major breach of its classified computer networks. William Lynn, the Pentagon's number two official, recalled the event with trepidation: "It was a network administrator's worst fear: a rogue program operating silently, poised to deliver operational plans into the hands of an unknown adversary."[9] Britain followed suit. In 2010, the country's new national security strategy categorized cyber threats as "Tier One," making them equal in priority to a terrorist attack involving weapons of mass destruction and more important than the threat of conventional war posed by other states. In other words, technological aggression below the war line was a greater concern than interstate war.

For better or for worse, security strategy had to be adapted to the novel assumption that avoiding military clashes with large opponents was no longer sufficient to securing a stable peace. Vital security interests and the nation's political integrity could be affected by forms of conflict less than war. The nature of interstate rivalry had changed.

This new reality motivated the search for an effective strategy to deter adversaries in cyberspace. A senior British official in the security services framed the challenge for his country as follows: "The key focus of GCHQ [Britain's signals intelligence agency] and the government is, How do you raise the costs of attack for the attacker?" adding, astutely: "This is not a technical question; it's one of strategy and policy."[10]

The content of deterrence strategy soon crystallized. The first Obama Administration expressed a willingness to deter harmful cyber activity by two main methods: punishment, which promises penalties for attacks, and denial, which works by diminishing the effectiveness of the opponent's arms. In 2011, the U.S. Department of Defense pledged ominous but vague reprisal for "certain hostile acts conducted through cyberspace," which could elicit "actions under the commitments we have with our military treaty partners."[11] In other words, the U.S. government was implicitly willing to trade attacks with computer code for attacks with conventional arms. In 2015, the White House set forth a vision to create "strong defenses" and "resilient systems that recover quickly from attacks" alongside punitive measures that "inflict penalties and costs against adversaries that choose to conduct cyber attacks."[12]

Growing recognition that in cyberspace the offense enjoyed wide advantages over the defense, and that this situation would likely endure because of "structural reasons" in the operational environment, produced a shift in emphasis from denial to punishment. Lynn's assessment is instructive: "[T]he U.S. government's ability to defend its networks always lags behind its adversaries' ability to exploit U.S. networks' weaknesses."[13] While not abandoning efforts to deny enemies their gains, punishment became the preferred posture. As a Pentagon report put it: "[S]hould the 'deny objectives' element of deterrence not prove adequate, DoD maintains, and is further developing, the ability to respond militarily in cyberspace and other domains."[14] Similarly, appearing before the Senate Armed Services Committee in 2014 for confirmation as the Commander of U.S. Cyber Command, Vice Admiral Mike Rogers attested to both the punishment problem and the necessity for sterner action. "I believe the U.S. may be considered an easier mark because our own processes and criteria lead the adversary to believe, rightly or wrongly, that we do not have the will to respond in a timely and proportionate manner, even when attribution is available," he said, going on to affirm the need "to impose costs on the adversary" for operating offensively within domestic networks.[15]

For all its assertions of disrupting previous presidents' policies, including in the realm of foreign and defense policy, the Trump Administration continued to toe the line of deterrence set forth by its predecessors. The 2018 National Cyber Strategy reaffirmed the by-now familiar mantra of punishment, "the imposition of costs through cyber and non-cyber means" to deter adversaries.[16] Another strategy paper declared, more assertively and ominously, a readiness "to employ the full range of military capabilities in response"[17] – a reminder that the promise of penalties extended well beyond the realm of electrons. It was by now a clear matter of declaratory national defense policy: a failure to prevent hostile action in cyberspace could invoke a stern punishment in other domains.

The semantics of the cyber strategy that emerged in the period between 2018 and 2020 were familiar to students of the nuclear era (some of them astute observers of the cyber revolution such as Joseph Nye and Robert Jervis),[18] the era from which deterrence doctrine had emerged: resilience, redundancy, denial, penalties, "increase the costs of the attacker," "stop all attacks." One has the sense that the gestalt of the nuclear revolution that so dominated strategic thinking in the last century had carried over into an era in which its maxims might not, in fact, apply.[19]

IMPLEMENTING DETERRENCE: THE ELUSIVE GOAL

Few decisionmakers denied the necessity for punishment. Former cybersecurity policy coordinator at the U.S. National Security Council Rob Joyce affirmed: "We have to impose costs in a visible way to start deterrence."[20] To these echoes of the necessity for greater punishment are attached the laments of not doing enough, as evinced by Chris Painter, Obama's top cyber diplomat: "I don't think we've been particularly good at imposing costs on state adversaries when they do something unacceptable. It's been too easy for adversaries to say 'There is not a big cost to this.' If we don't actually impose costs – and I get [that] it is not easy to do that – then they just do it again."[21] So fixated with the "cost imposition" was the strategic community that the phrase appears more than two dozen times in the report of the Congressional Cyber Solarium Commission tasked with performing an extensive reevaluation of strategy.[22]

Yet, no one seemed willing to implement the mantra of penalties decisively. The weakness of observable punishment practices bears out the vacuity of assertions of a robust response. Punishment has been of two general kinds: targeted economic and financial sanctions and criminal indictments. A review of their use by the United States will show their inadequacy relative to the scale of the harm that they seek to punish and deter.

Western governments have levied economic and financial sanctions against foreign perpetrators. The United States, in particular, is in a privileged position to impose sanctions, because their enforcement involves the use of national levers of power, such as denying the sanctioned parties access to the financial infrastructure that routes the payment flows of the U.S. dollar, the world's largest reserve currency.[23] Sanctions are thus a powerful instrument in the United States' strategic arsenal. Here, we must distinguish between, on the one hand, *broad-spectrum sanctions* affecting the economy or industry of a nation, or a large government entity within it, and, on the other, *narrow-spectrum sanctions* affecting the financial interests of individuals or small entities. Broad-spectrum sanctions pack a larger punitive punch than narrow-spectrum sanctions inconveniencing individual operatives. Moreover, sanctioned individuals and companies often receive compensation from their parent government, whereas governments seeking a protective shield against broad-spectrum sanctions must secure the support of foreign collaborators – a more difficult task involving the intricacies of diplomacy and the national interests of sovereign nations.

Despite their generally higher potency, broad-spectrum sanctions have been much less common than narrow-spectrum sanctions. One rare exception was the Obama Administration's response to North Korea's hack of Sony Pictures' computers in December 2014. The Lazarus Group used weaponized code to destroy about three-fourths of the computers and servers at the California-based entertainment company. The group also divulged the contents of stolen email records, causing reputational damage to the company and its leadership. One top executive resigned in embarrassment following the revelation that her emails contained racial innuendoes of Obama (she had breached the cardinal rule of email security: write every message as if it will become public). Observers decried the attack for its potential self-censoring effects on the American film industry. President Obama himself publicly lamented the company's initial decision to suspend the release of *The Interview*, a film satirizing the Supreme Leader in Pyongyang that had motivated the attack.[24]

In the cyberattack's aftermath, the White House issued an Executive Order authorizing the Treasury Department to restrict access to the U.S. financial system and U.S. persons by three entities controlled by the Kim regime – the Reconnaissance General Bureau, North Korea's preeminent intelligence organization; the Korea Mining Development Trading Corporation, the country's primary arms dealer; and the Korea Tangun Trading Corporation, which procured commodities and technologies from abroad to feed the regime's defense research program. The order also sanctioned ten individuals, including central government officials and diplomats with ties to Russia, Africa, and the Middle East.[25]

Although the sanctions affected named individuals and entities, they were not narrow, because the scope of their effects far transcended the interests of the named targets. More than just punishing North Korean citizens or government departments – although such punishment was also intended – the sanctions sought to disrupt the regime's arms procurement and defense research activities, thereby damaging its interests in those important areas of national security. Washington's explanation of the sanctions' purpose revealed their broad intent: "to hold North Korea accountable for its destabilizing, destructive and repressive actions, particularly its efforts to undermine U.S. cybersecurity and intimidate U.S. businesses and artists exercising their right of freedom of speech."[26]

Narrow-spectrum sanctions have been far more common. They have been a favored instrument of U.S. action against Russian political hackers. Consider the case of the DNC hack during the 2016 presidential election – an action, recall, that Trump's former national security advisor John Bolton misguidedly, but tellingly, repudiated as an "act of war" against American constitutional democracy. Three features of the response stand out, all for their tentativeness in hurting Russian strategic interests. One notable characteristic is their slowness. Although an earlier package of penalties (which included diplomatic expulsions) came in December 2016,[27] the stronger package materialized only in early 2018 – almost two years after the hack occurred – and involved targeted sanctions (plus indictments).[28] Another feature was the sanctions' highly customized scope. The financial penalties targeted five entities and nineteen individuals with ties to the government, notably the Internet Research Agency (IRA), an obscure organization whose social media trolls lined up outside 55 Ulitsa Savushkina in Saint Petersburg every morning during the election season to replace the moonlighters inside. The IRA's thousands of social media ads reached millions of people, charged the Treasury Department. The organization also conducted political rallies and opened financial accounts with stolen identities in the leadup to the elections. The purpose and effect of the activity was "to underm[ine] and interfer[e] with election processes and institutions."[29] Other sanctioned entities were even more obscure: a consultancy firm and a catering company that provided financial assistance to the IRA. Among the named individuals were the IRA's general director, Mikhail Ivanovich Bystrov, and analyst Vadim Vladimirovich Podkopaev, who translated and curated U.S.-focused content.

The sanctions also affected two Russian security organs, the Federal Security Service (FSB) and the Main Intelligence Directorate (GRU), and their operatives. The FSB, Russia's foreign intelligence agency, was charged with targeting the computers and information of U.S. government officials, including White House personnel and U.S. diplomats. The GRU, Russia's main military intelligence outfit, had a more direct involvement in the DNC affair, having hacked into the email accounts of top Democratic Party figures. Both entities, the sanctions order noted in a probably unintentional admission of deterrence failure, had been previously penalized.

The second wave of targeted sanctions – also weak in their punitive punch – hit Russian offenders in June 2018. Five entities and three individuals, again operating in shadowy circumstances where a connection with government organs was suspected but not affirmed, were selected for punishment. The targets had allegedly provided "material and technological" support to the FSB in a number of actions, most notably NotPetya.[30] Although the sophisticated attack was probably designed to affect computers in Ukraine, it also disrupted operations at the Danish shipping giant Maersk. For a period of two weeks, the activities of the company that operated 20 percent of global shipping cargo were largely paralyzed. And while the NotPetya code was sophisticated, exploiting vulnerabilities in tax-filing software obtained from the secretive NSA hacking group "EternalBlue," its poor customization meant that it produced two kinds of collateral effects: direct harm to untargeted machines that were infected because of the malware's self-propagating tendency; and economic effects that cascaded beyond the affected machines.[31] So poor, in fact, was the malware's customization that it affected machines belonging to large Russian companies such as Rosneft – a case of blowback, whereby a cyberattack harms interests back home.[32] Other similar uses of targeted financial penalties involved sanctions against a diversity of culprits: fifteen GRU members for computer activities involving electoral interference and the World Anti-Doping Agency (December 2018);[33] a financier and other Russian actors who allegedly attempted to influence the 2018 mid-term elections (September 2019);[34] Evil Corp, a Russian-based criminal organization (with putative ties to the Russian government) which was behind the "Dridex" malware and which infected machines in hundreds of financial institutions in dozens of countries, causing more than $100 million in financial losses (December 2019);[35] two Russian nationals for carrying out a phishing campaign in 2017 and 2018, affecting cryptoasset users who lost $18.2 million (September 2020);[36] the Central Scientific Research Institute of Chemistry and Mathematics, a government-controlled body responsible for crafting the highly customized "Triton" malware that manipulated industrial safety controls at a petrochemical facility (October 2020);[37] three state-linked cyber groups (Lazarus Group, BlueNoroff, and Andariel) in North Korea for their actions against vital infrastructure (September 2019);[38] Iran's Islamic Revolutionary Guard Corps's Quds Force and an obscure front company, Bayan Rasaneh Gostar Institute, for their covert media efforts to amplify political divisions in the United States during the country's 2020 presidential election (October 2020);[39] and two Chinese nationals who laundered cryptoassets stolen by the Lazarus Group (March 2020).[40]

The list of U.S. punishments of foreign cyber activity via narrow-spectrum sanctions is long and will certainly grow longer. The punished parties in these and other cases include government officials and agents as well as private citizens acting independently or in collusion with them in Russia, Iran, North Korea, and China. The punished actions encompass a range of activities such as social media information campaigns to fan political division, attempts to penetrate election infrastructure, disruption of industrial facilities, assistance with the creation of state malware, financial system disruption, and cryptoasset theft.

Thus, the record of targeted sanctions exhibits little consistency. They have been applied to punish both state and private actors for activities as diverse as strategic-level action (e.g. interference in a presidential election) and low-level criminal action (e.g. property theft). The scale of harm of the punished actions was large, yet the narrow penalties applied were unremarkable. Although the frequent use of narrow-spectrum sanctions demonstrates the U.S. government's commitment to publicly penalize individuals and organizations involved in nefarious cyber activities, the measures did not affect the broader economic interests of the nations that harbored the sanctioned parties.

Criminal indictments are another common tool of the punishers. These, too, are weak forms of punishment – if, indeed, they punish at all. Indictments of cyber criminals have been highly public affairs, as they often must be: the culprits reside in a foreign jurisdiction, often under the protection of their parent government. The prospect of arraignment before a judge in the indicting nation is extremely slim. Why, then, the public fanfare? After all, the more public the indictment, the more chance the purported criminals will have to evade the arm of the law. The indictments' highly public nature reveals a choice made by the sanctioning government. Assuming that the indicted parties will likely never set foot on its soil, accepting, further, that their parent government is unlikely to extradite them for involvement in offensive activity that the government may itself have directed, the sanctioning authorities opt instead to name and shame the attackers.[41]

Examples of criminal indictments for participation in cyber operations against Western interests abound. One notable U.S. case was the indictment of five Chinese military hackers on espionage charges in 2014. The named defendants, all of them officers of the notorious Unit 61398 of the PLA's Third Department, were alleged to have conspired to infiltrate the machines and steal the data of six U.S. citizens. In some cases, the intruders seized trade secrets that were directly beneficial to competing Chinese companies; in others, the hackers stole sensitive internal communications providing insight into competitors' commercial strategies. U.S. Attorney General Eric Holder voiced the mantra of punishment with a prosecutorial air: "The range of trade secrets and other sensitive business information stolen in this case is significant and demands an aggressive response ... This Administration will not tolerate actions by any nation that seeks to illegally sabotage American companies and undermine the integrity of fair competition in the operation of the free market." Assistant Attorney General for National Security John Carlin added a further admonition: "Cyber theft is real theft and we will hold state sponsored cyber thieves accountable as we would any other transnational criminal organization that steals our goods and breaks our laws."[42]

In these words there is more pathos than boldness. For the officials behind the indictment must have known of the near impossibility of arraigning the suspects. They must have also grasped that indictments could even elevate the suspects' reputation in the murky world of secret state agents and sophisticated criminals for whom the evasion of irked authorities is often a source of pride and honor – not shame. Why, then, issue the indictments? One can only speculate about the motives and objectives. By publicly attributing the attackers, the indictments unlock prosecutorial and investigative action that can disrupt malicious activity. They can also help to build norms of conduct and convince their parent governments to crack down on proxy actors within their jurisdictions.[43]

To the most intractable challenges of national security and international order, therefore, Western officials have applied the instruments of peaceful sanctions. They have mainly targeted individuals and entities – some of them private, others state-linked – rather than the regimes that participated, supported, or tolerated the offensive activity. They have also applied the levers of domestic criminal law, which have proven largely symbolic because they are incapable of reaching offenders who enjoy the protections of adversarial governments in whose jurisdictions the culprits reside. To prosecute the named Russians, Chinese, and other foreigners, the U.S. government would have to haul them before a judge on national soil, or else await their possible entry into the country as tourists or on business – a highly unlikely scenario owing to the indictments' publication.

The main forms of punishment – broad-spectrum sanctions, narrow-spectrum sanctions, and criminal indictments – qualify as acts of peacetime rivalry under international law no matter the degree or kind of their effects. The mismatch between the scale of the punished attacks and the scale of the punishment becomes clear: Western nations have tended to respond to technological aggression with penalties befitting peacetime competition, not acts of unpeace. What is in fact a concern of national security strategy and interstate diplomacy is treated effectively as a matter of domestic law and order. Securing the integrity of the democratic process against foreign intrusion and arresting "the greatest transfer of wealth in history,"[44] as Keith Alexander described the economic consequences of Chinese cyber espionage, requires sterner and more credible deterring measures (more on this in Chapter 7).

Another possible form of punishment is in kind – cyberattack in response to cyberattack. Some analysts have endorsed such a response as the most proportionate.[45] It has three main advantages. One is that it enables the large Western powers to engage punitively with an opponent in a realm in which they enjoy superior offensive capacity. Recall that the United States and Britain are at the top of the league of offensive cyber power; their ability to inflict material costs on adversaries is higher than theirs. Second, a response in kind avoids the legal and normative pitfalls of cross-domain deterrence. Despite their peaceful status, broad-spectrum sanctions could inadvertently escalate the conflict to a level of intensity that the punishing state wants to avoid. Because of the paucity of experience dealing with cyber conflict, there are no clearly agreed "conversion tables" to guide the effort of translating the victim's costs of hostility in cyberspace into proportionate and legitimate costs of punishment.

A third advantage concerns the war in Ukraine: reaction to Russia's invasion has reduced the options to apply sanctions against it for cyber activity. As we saw in Chapter 4, Russia is now one of the most heavily sanctioned countries in the world. With the sanctions toolbox emptying out, and the aversion to direct military measures prevailing, a viable pathway to affect Russian calculations in cyberspace might be found in offensive actions within it.

The punishment of code with code suffers important limitations, however. One concerns the potential for direct or indirect blowback. As we discussed above, the damaging effects of a cyberattack can cascade beyond the machines, individuals, organization, or national economy that it intended to hit. Another problem involves international law: as we saw in Chapter 2, it severely constrains a defender's scope of maneuver in the use of cyber countermeasures – an important limitation affecting strict law abiders respecting the self-restraints of cyber legalism.

The biggest obstacle to the quest for stable deterrence in cyberspace concerns yet another problem: the "stability–instability" paradox.[46] The sterner the punishment that one promises to levy for a hostile action, the greater the potential for a spiraling conflict following a failure to deter. Policymakers have expressed the concern of cascading conflict poignantly. They have struggled to situate the declaration of punishment within a "golden zone," in which the retaliatory response is strong enough to deter future attack but not so strong that it accelerates the conflict or aggravates it if deterrence fails. Former director of national intelligence James Clapper's words on this problem merit a detailed citation:

[R]eciprocity and collateral damage in cyberspace are very difficult to control. NSA and Cyber Command . . . had tremendous capabilities, and we felt it was reasonable – but not certain – that if we did decide to attack someone, we would affect only the systems we specifically targeted. But no one else in the world could reasonably be that confident about their abilities, and the infrastructure of the Internet was largely independent of international boundaries. So if we attacked someone in cyberspace and they returned fire,

> Cyber Command and even DOD and the [Intelligence Community] might have some level of protection and defense, but the New York Stock Exchange or telecommunications in Eastern Europe or a power grid in Central America might well be taken offline. No one could predict the unintended consequences and potential damage such an assault might cause.[47]

In other words, Western policymakers are trapped in a "double escalation" vise: striking back for a major cyber action risks escalating the conflict; not striking back or striking back weakly (current policy practice) is itself escalatory, because it conveys unreadiness or unwillingness to reduce the adversary's net gains in the attack. The situation seemingly presents a "damned if I do, damned if I don't" conundrum.

Following Russia's brazen intervention in the 2016 presidential election, recognition of the failures inherent in prevailing deterrence strategy grew within policy circles. Security planners began to awaken to the adversary's superior use of cyberspace as an arena in which to pursue strategic interests below the threshold of war, that is, in the realm of unpeace. The 2018 *Command Vision for U.S. Cyber Command* poignantly articulated this vital realization. "Adversaries continuously operate against us below the threshold of armed conflict," it observed. "In this 'new normal,' our adversaries are extending their influence without resorting to physical aggression. They provoke and intimidate our citizens and enterprises without fear of legal or military consequences." There followed a recognition of the self-imposed limitations of cyber legalism and the underlying liberal vision that it seeks to advance: "[Adversaries] understand the constraints under which the United States chooses to operate in cyberspace, including our traditionally high threshold for response to adversary activity. They use this insight to exploit our dependencies and vulnerabilities in cyberspace and use our systems, processes, and values against us to weaken our democratic institutions and gain economic, diplomatic, and military advantages."[48] Or in the words of the characteristically blunt U.S. Senator John McCain:

> What seems clear is that our adversaries have reached a common conclusion: that the reward for attacking America in cyberspace outweighs the risk. For years, cyber attacks on our Nation have been met with indecision

and inaction. Our Nation has no policy and thus no strategy for cyber deterrence. This appearance of weakness has been provocative to our adversaries who have attacked us again and again with growing severity. Unless we demonstrate that the costs of attacking the United States outweigh the perceived benefits, these cyber attacks will only grow.[49]

One could not ask officials for a more faithful recognition of the failures of current deterrence strategy than this statement.

ACTIVE DEFENSE COMES OF AGE

What was to be done about the failures of strategy? The shortcomings of attempts to adapt deterrence to the peculiarities of virtual weapons have led some observers to question the wisdom of deterrence as a viable approach to cyber conflict reduction. Some analysts have declared it unfixable. A new concept emerged to supplant it: persistent engagement.[50]

Persistent engagement represents a major advance in the development of U.S. cyber doctrine. In its first decade, Cyber Command focused on perimeter defense, a reactive approach that failed to sufficiently deny sophisticated intrusions.[51] Persistent engagement is bolder: it seeks to bolster denial by debilitating opponents' actions: that is, to address the problem of incessant conflict by grappling with adversaries relentlessly – not to deter them, but to degrade their offensive capacity by taking the fight to them. It is important to realize that persistent engagement eschews punishment as a policy option; it seeks to bury, not rescue, the sick patient of deterrence.

Developed by Pentagon security planners under the Trump Administration, the policy approach clashed with the administration's isolationist and non-interventionist tendencies. The approach embodied the opposite perspective: a willingness and a prescription for constant grappling with opponents on turfs beyond one's own. Its starting assumption was that the cyber domain is "an environment of constant contact." Consequently, threats and risks are permanent; there can be no such thing as a cessation of hostilities.

There flowed from this recognition an important conclusion: the objective of deterring all major cyber actions – a goal ported over from the nuclear era that has defined much of deterrence thinking – was futile. Rather than deter attacks, adherents of the new concept sought to reverse the net deficit in the strategic balance of cyber interactions. Accordingly, the policy's parent framework – Defending Forward – expressly entails an out-of-perimeter aspect.[52] Some thinkers regard persistent engagement as a novel approach. But in at least this important regard, it revives and gives substance to the old notion of "active defense," which emerged in 2011 and whose central characteristic was activity within enemy or neutral networks for defensive purposes. As the Pentagon put it, active defense "operates at network speed by using sensors, software, and intelligence to detect and stop malicious activity before it can affect DoD networks and systems."[53] The new policy approach, therefore, paves the way for more intrusions in adversaries' home networks – for example, searching through or disabling foreign computers to impede offensive moves. As a manifestation of the doctrine of Defending Forward, the policy, at least putatively, operates within the realm of self-defense. It manifestly does not prescribe offensive action for punishment or strategic gain. It seeks "to disrupt and degrade the capabilities our adversaries use to conduct attacks"[54] – that is, to undermine the attack by impeding the attacker but not to penalize it.

Although the authors of persistent engagement like to argue that deterrence is unsalvageable, what they really mean is that sterner punishment is not viable. Theirs is essentially a more proactive and muscular form of deterrence by denial. It reflects Joyce's prescription for stronger defensive action: "We have to go out and try and make those operations less successful and harder to do."[55] And while the policy adopts a more assertive posture, it nevertheless seeks to respect the rigid interpretation of law and norms which, as we saw in Chapter 2, tightly constrains defensively oriented behavior transpiring in foreign terrain.

Cyber Command's response to Russian attempts to tamper with the 2018 U.S. mid-term elections demonstrates the policy's defensive and forward-operating nature. Between the options of punishment to deter (the old declared approach) and reactive perimeter defense (the old approach in practice) lay the middle option of defensively engaging with the opponent abroad. Following the new course, Cyber Command created a "Russian Small Group" to monitor Russian activity, coordinated with the FBI to disrupt the moves of foreign trolls and bots on social media, and sent personnel on a "hunt-forward" mission to search for Russian malware on foreign networks. Similar efforts sought to protect the integrity of the 2020 U.S. presidential election.[56] In October 2019, Cyber Command sent a hunt-forward mission to Podgorica to investigate a possible Russian intrusion into the Montenegrin government's computers. "[T]he team saw an opportunity to improve American cyber defenses ahead of the 2020 election," explained Nakasone and Sulmeyer.[57]

Proponents celebrate persistent engagement as a proactive approach that seizes the initiative from adversaries.[58] And proactive it is: adversaries must constantly be wondering where Cyber Command's highly capable teams will appear next on their turf. Wherever the presence is felt, adversaries will expend resources to eradicate the intruders. Consequently, less capacity will be available to carry out offensive action against America and allied targets.

But proactiveness is not the same as initiative. The net effect of persistent engagement in fact might be a *loss* of initiative because it directs national resources to areas in which adversaries already operate, transit, or plan to target. Although the policy's actions are proactive insofar as they deploy resources outside of the home terrain, they are reactive in a larger strategic sense. The defensive and non-punitive posture behind persistent engagement potentially dooms the policy to improvise a response according to the other side's planned or actual moves. It seizes initiative at a micro level by tailoring a creative response abroad, while at a macro level it follows the initiative determined by the adversary's actual or planned moves. As a policy of constant grappling, persistent engagement potentially suffers the same cardinal folly as Cold War containment policy: it commits national resources to a contest of unknown scope, duration, and intensity. Whatever the final scale of the security competition, it guarantees that the engagement will be continuous to a degree defined by the opponent's designs, but it will endure to a point set by one's own finite resources. Persistent engagement invites persistent costs; it risks consuming resources blankly.

7

PUNCTUATED DETERRENCE
How to Strike Back

PUNISHING BACKWARD

Western cyber strategy has focused on the most intractable aspect of conflict prevention: fostering rules and norms of responsible state behavior. Upholding ideals that the main geopolitical opponents reject requires nations to stake their national security and the integrity of their democratic institutions on a legal rulebook that leads back into the international jungle more easily than it points to an exit. As we saw in Chapter 2, the cyber legalism doctrine leaves few options for dealing with opponents who deliberately breach and weaken a normative framework that neither reflects their values nor serves their interests. Future generations of lawyers and diplomats might one day craft adequate rules and norms to stop the incessant technological aggression.[1] In their absence, however, the prevailing doctrine will not provide a satisfactory basis for conflict reduction.

A security policy looking towards future norms should, therefore, have as a cardinal element a program to prevent conflict in the interim – or indefinitely, in case the ideal consensus does not emerge. The interim solution must be found within a consequentialist logic of action, one that appeals to opponents' considerations of material interests through punishment rather than to a sense of appropriateness through norms.

Despite promising a consequentialist program, Western policymakers have shrunk from implementing it – almost as if the imposition of costs to deter future ordeals would instigate them, or because of a lack of clarity about the nature of punishment for the limitation of conflict in an uncertain domain. But we saw in Chapter 2 that one-sided norm construction is hopeless: it cedes the strategic advantage to the norm defiers who, from the failure to punish, conclude that their transgressions will bear few costs of response. Norm consensus and self-restraint would be excellent solutions to the problem of recurring conflict if only they had a chance of succeeding. The problem lies not in their desirability – they are legitimate aims – but in the consequences of their failure. The more assiduously Western nations seek consensus on norms by which they constrain themselves but which adversaries flout, the greater the costs of the failure. By framing conflict as a legal and normative problem, cyber legalism might in fact aggravate it.

A program of punishment, by contrast, seeks *calculated deterrence*: to convince adversaries that the material gains of aggression are smaller than its combined operational costs and retaliatory penalties. Deterring attack through punishment is the reverse of reducing conflict by pleading that it should not occur or by disarming the contenders through diplomacy. For it signals the absence of normative consensus and calls for the use of the weapons that one seeks to lock up.

A consequentialist approach has the main advantage of being immediately executable. It does not require the lengthy mechanism of socialization implied by legal reform and global norm construction. Such a mechanism faces significant time-consuming obstacles, beginning with the question of norm definition – about which nations already disagree and on which much interpretive work remains to be done, even if there is consensus on starting principles – and followed by norm internalization, a complex and lengthy process, even when nations agree on which norms to institutionalize.[2] Conjuring a logic of consequences does not require abandoning the normative enterprise; one can still construct norms for a future world. And that is the point: to exact penalties *ex ante* for the violation of rules that one seeks to institutionalize *ex post*. Nor must calculated punishment contradict the norms that one seeks to build. Recall that the question is how to *prevent* acts of unpeace by carrying out, or threatening to carry out, a commensurate response, not when to conduct it for offensive purposes (a question for separate analysis).

But why seek to deter in the first place? After all, as we saw in Chapter 6, the limitations of deterrence in the cyber domain are well documented. They include difficulties of attributing the identity and location of the attacker; the tendency (borrowed from the nuclear era) of seeking to deter all attacks ("total deterrence"); and the absence of a clear benchmark for evaluating the punishment threshold of attacks that, singly, might not merit a response because they do not meet the recognizable criteria of armed attack or sovereignty violation.[3]

The last problem is the most acute. The power to harm national security interests has never been so far divorced from brute force. Whereas nuclear weapons – the main source of technological revolution in the twentieth century – allowed power to catch up to force, the cyber revolution – the great revolution of our times – has spun the relationship in the opposite direction. A deterrence dogma that emerged on the basis of an obsessive quest to prevent the use of brute force (the brutest of all) is devalued by the growth of intangible weapons that can inflict harm without ever having to exit the virtual minds of machines.

The central challenge, then, is to devise a rational approach of conflict prevention that addresses the expansion of lower forms of aggression. This chapter develops such an approach, *punctuated deterrence*. It seeks to address the follies of cyber legalism, and the gaps in the legal system that mar it, while correcting the internal flaws of both classical deterrence and persistent engagement.

Persistent engagement, as we saw in Chapter 6, works by grappling with opponents so consistently that they are forced to divert their offensive resources away from targeting the high-value assets of others and towards defending their own. In this respect, the policy approach has a proactive element: it takes the fight to the other side's computer terrain. There is no reason, despite its defensive mantra, to limit the application strictly to defensive purposes. Practitioners could also apply it as a prism through which to derive principles of strategic competition beyond the goals of network defense – that is, as a policy of *attacking forward*. But that is not the current conception. Instead, it is a mainly reactive policy that commits unknown national resources to wherever the opponent brings the fight or is preparing it.

Punctuated deterrence departs radically from the classical regime of deterrence by punishment, which prescribes responses to single incidents. The strategy seeks to transform the psychological basis of opponents' calculations by punishing a *series* of actions and their *cumulative* effects (more on this below).[4] Moreover, it gives the victims the option to retaliate wherever and whenever fits their interests and capacities.

Crucially, the penalties are not persistent; they are bundled into a single action or a small number of actions. And that is the purpose: to economize material resources and civil service capacity by inflicting penalties in a single burst rather than in a wide and ambiguous campaign of persistence. In a domain in which sophisticated offensive weapons often lose their value after being used because this can reveal the weaknesses in the opponent's systems – without which customized weapons cannot function – economy of response is vital.[5]

In short, rather than constructing norms or defending forward (the essence of persistent engagement), punctuated deterrence seeks to *punish backward*. Its chief goal is conflict reduction by adjusting the opponent's calculus of strategic gains by inflicting intolerable costs, rather than by overwhelming it with a swarm of intrusive activity (although this approach could partly affect the cost calculus if it diminishes the expected efficacy of the opponent's weapons by targeting them). Punctuated deterrence and persistent engagement are not exclusive, or even competing, approaches to conflict reduction. Constant grappling with the enemy for the purpose of "denial by disorientation" does not preclude the option of preventing future attacks by punishing past ones.

If one accepts this notion, then several principles of action become clear: the necessity for punishing a series of blows rather than single actions; the expansion of the arc of deterrence to the intangible interests of information security (the nation's "virtual" integrity); the linkage of issues across domains; and, above all, clarity and firmness in signaling a willingness to strike back. The remainder of this chapter elaborates on these four principles to orient the implementation of punctuated deterrence in a manner that addresses shortcomings in prevailing cyber strategy. But before continuing, it is worth asking whether an alternative rational approach is relevant: appeasing the opponent.

CYBER APPEASEMENT: AN ALTERNATIVE APPROACH?

The question of appeasement arises from the charge that foreign political hacking is motivated by Western nations' intervention in the adversaries' domestic affairs. It is the argument of moral equivalency: by supporting opposition leaders and groups in Russia, for example, the West invokes intrusions against its own system of government. In April 2021, Vladimir Putin denounced the United States for "organizing coups and planning political assassinations of top officials," referring to public demonstrations against Venezuelan President Nicolás Maduro and the former Russophile president of Ukraine, Viktor Yanukovych.[6] During the 2011 Duma election and the 2012 presidential election, a precarious moment for Putin's regime during which large numbers of protestors flooded the streets of Moscow, the U.S. government provided financial support for opposition candidates.[7]

Putin has expressed his greatest ire for foreign support of the main opposition leader, Alexei Navalny. Two weeks before meeting President Joe Biden at a bilateral summit in Geneva in June 2021, Putin acidly remarked: "We don't have any issues with the U.S. But it has an issue with us. It wants to contain our development and publicly talks about it. Economic restrictions and attempts to influence our country's domestic politics, relying on forces they consider their allies inside Russia, stem from that."[8] Earlier in the year, EU foreign policy chief Josep Borrell visited Moscow on a mission to plead for Navalny's release from prison. "The Russian government is going down a worrisome authoritarian route," lamented Borrell, not realizing that it had already reached its destination. "There seems to be almost no room for the development of democratic alternatives . . . [the authorities] are merciless in stifling any such attempts." An outraged foreign minister Sergei Lavrov warned that if the EU proceeded to levy economic sanctions against Russia for Navalny's detention (and poisoning with the novichok nerve agent in 2020), then his country was poised to sever diplomatic ties with the union. "We don't want to isolate ourselves from global life, but we have to be ready for that," Lavrov warned. "If you want peace then prepare for war."[9]

Russian officials have not openly recognized the reciprocity of political intrusions. True to the principle that one cannot accept blame for actions one denies having carried out, the Kremlin has asserted that it was not behind the ransomware attacks that disrupted U.S. fuel supplies and meat processing earlier in the year. It has denied involvement in the DNC hacking operation in 2016. "[W]e definitely do not do this at the state level," Putin said soon after the email leak, which he described as a public good: "The important thing is that the content was given to the public."[10] Just as Americans have a gift for transparency so do the Russians have a gift for humor!

Russian officials played an intricate game of subterfuge to undermine public confidence in their responsibility for political hacking. Putin's chief Internet advisor German Klimenko slyly observed about the stolen DNC data: "Usually these kinds of leaks take place not because hackers broke in, but, as any professional will tell you, because someone simply forgot the password or set the simple password 123456. Well, it's always simpler to explain this away as the intrigues of enemies, rather than one's own incompetence." And Putin's spokesperson Dmitry Peskov commented: "I absolutely rule out the possibility that the [Russian] government or government agencies were involved in this."[11] But even the naïvest analyst in Washington would have caught the implicit allusion in Putin's and Lavrov's excoriations: by meddling in our domestic political system you will suffer similar disturbances, or worse.

Appeasement as a conflict avoidance policy is a one-sided attempt to redress the other side's grievances. British appeasers of Nazi Germany in the 1930s sought to resolve by diplomatic concession what they perceived as "the legitimate grievances of nations dissatisfied with the peace settlement of 1919,"[12] which had placed a vanquished Germany in a state of subjugation by the First World War's victors, in particular France. The interwar appeasers strived to preserve the peace of Europe by mollifying German sensitivities. Faced with the vengeful Nazi regime and its leader's ferocious temper, this policy in 1938 sacrificed a neutral and democratic Czechoslovakia to German territorial avarice.

A policy of cyber appeasement would equate to a policy of doing nothing: tolerating adversaries' hostile activity while curtailing one's own in the hope that the underlying objections which motivate them will subside – in short, a settling of scores as recorded by the other side. The policy's success would have two essential requirements: the opponent's grievances must be legitimate and accord with the customs of international relations; and the redress must be proportionate to them. Otherwise, a policy of concessions merely whets the appetite of deviant and expansionist powers such as Nazi Germany.

Do legitimate grievances motivate the autocratic nations' cyber behavior? Nothing in the empirical record suggests that a concern for their grievances should motivate Western leniency. Despite Russian officials' chastisements, whatever the scale of Western interference in Russia's domestic affairs, it has failed to achieve political change in the country. The Putin regime, now in its third decade, remains firmly in power and enjoys wide popular appeal.[13] By contrast, the political reverberations in the United States from the Russian GRU's hacking of Democratic Party officials' email records continue to this day. Thus, even if Russia's grievances were legitimate, as its leaders perceive, even if its political hacking activities were less an effort to disrupt democratic institutions, less a campaign to influence the liberal international order, and more a defense against foreign attempts to influence its own political system, the question of the proportionality of the adversary's response would remain.

As we saw in previous chapters, the record of cyber conflict is so skewed in favor of the main geopolitical adversaries that it is Western nations – not Russia or China – that express more convincing objections to the other side's intrusions. Whereas the enterprise of democratization in Russia (if such a thing can be imagined today) has long passed[14] – and in some quarters, not even the aspiration remains – the autocrat's attempts to tamper with the institutions of democracy continue apace. Appeasement, in brief, fails the test of legitimate grievances. And as a policy of doing nothing, it is inherently escalatory. Nations that pursue it will again teach opponents the lesson from 1938: further gains from aggression lie in wait.

THE ACCRETIONAL PRINCIPLE

The first principle of punctuated deterrence is its main defining tenet: nations that suffer sustained acts of unpeace should punish them as campaigns that inflict cumulative damage rather than as individual actions. Adversaries treat cyber operations against multiple targets in multiple nations as comprehensive campaigns of strategic competition.[15] The cyberattacks against Estonia's financial systems, the attacks against Georgia's central bank during the country's military invasion by Russia, the series of cyber offensives that struck the power grid in Ukraine after President Viktor Yanukovych's ousting from power in 2014, the attempt to meddle with the French presidential election in 2017 – all were elements of a broad Russian effort to undermine public confidence in the unity of the European Union and NATO or else to raise the costs of accession into them by weakening the internal cohesion of aspiring entrants. Adversaries ordinarily do not regard their actions as isolated incidents. Neither should the victims.

To say that every offensive action demands a punitive response, however, is not to prescribe punishment immediately or singly. That is the approach of classical or "total" deterrence. It makes sense in the realm of nuclear war where even a single blow can cause a cataclysmic strategic loss. It is nonsensical in the cyber domain, where the main strategic effect is achieved over a series of actions rather than in any single one. In a realm of constant conflict, immediacy of punishment for all actions has also a practical cost: it burdens a civil and military service with responding to multiple single actions while it is in the midst of assessing the purpose and extent of each one. Instead, intelligence, human, and financial resources to mount a punitive response are better reserved for later use, not least because the design of the penalties requires accurate knowledge of the attacker's identity, location, and motives as well as the scale of harm, which can take time to ascertain at a high level of confidence.

Punctuated deterrence, by contrast, seeks to regain the macro initiative of spectral cyber conflict by delivering penalties in a concentrated fashion – hence its "punctuated" nature. The victim responds at a time and location, and in a manner, that it defines, not the opponent.

Let us illustrate the accretional principle in relation to real events. Take the case of Russian cyber activities. Chapter 4 discussed their regularity and intensity against Western targets. To summarize the list of relevant incidents: against Estonia, Russian-based actors (whom Russian authorities did not investigate) disrupted the country's financial system with distributed denial-of-service attacks, while conducting influence campaigns to stir discontent among Estonia's ethnic Russian minority. Against the United States, Russian state hackers caused a political conflagration during the 2016 presidential election by releasing stolen email records of political leaders; conducted social media campaigns to fan confusion and discord among the electorate during the 2018 mid-term elections; targeted the digital records of more than two hundred political campaigners, advocacy groups, and political consultancies in the leadup to the 2020 presidential election;[16] penetrated machines to steal and reveal the private information of hundreds of officials at the U.S. Anti-Doping Agency;[17] and compromised vital Internet networking routers and switches.[18] Against Britain, Russian agents carried out social media campaigns with similarly divisive purposes during the already highly contentious Brexit referendum; hacked the email records of former trade minister Liam Fox; and conducted a kompromat operation that involved the public disclosure of sensitive trade documents in an attempt to disrupt the country's 2019 parliamentary election.[19] Against Germany, Russians exploited supply-chain vulnerabilities to infiltrate vital infrastructure in the water and energy sectors;[20] penetrated the computers of politicians and political parties;[21] provided social media support to euroskeptic and anti-immigration parties during the 2017 federal election;[22] and targeted the email records of lawmakers, defense officials, and diplomatic staff in several embassies.[23] This list may seem long; in fact, it is short next to the full record of known Russian cyber activity.

One kind of concentrated response that is imaginable in the context above is the single-nation response: the governments of the targeted nations each assembles its own package of penalties. As we saw in Chapter 6, the penalties might include, in diminishing order of impact, broad-spectrum sanctions against the adversary's economy, industry, or governmental sector; narrow-spectrum sanctions affecting the financial interests of individuals or agencies; or criminal indictments limiting the international freedom of movement of the same individuals. They might also entail cyber actions, in kind or of a more severe degree. The important point here is that the punishing nation acts alone; it signals to the offender that the punished activities are not tolerable and will elicit a unilateral a punitive response, thus narrowing the unhealthy gulf between the costs and expected gains of attack.

The power of unilateral punctuation is that it affords the responder full control over the choice of penalties, the selection of targets, and the timing of the delivery. It is best suited to states with a high capacity to inflict punitive harm: for example, the United States, with its jurisdiction over the banking system that routes global flows of the dollar, the world's largest reserve currency; or Britain, with its large store of weaponized code, whose oversight is the responsibility of a unified entity – the National Cyber Force – established in 2020 to draw together personnel and resources from GCHQ, the Ministry of

Defence, the Secret Intelligence Service (MI6), and the Defence Science and Technology Laboratory.[24]

The main limitation of the unilateral response is the reverse: because the responding nation acts alone, it does not draw from the resources – whether passive (such as intelligence) or active (effects capacity) – of friendly nations. For the same reason, the geographic arc of deterrence resulting from the punishment will likely encompass only the punishing nation's interests. It cannot teach adversaries not to target allies instead of oneself.[25]

THE PRINCIPLE OF VIRTUAL INTEGRITY

International law, as we saw in Chapter 2, privileges the physical world over the virtual world. The Western conception of cybersecurity reflects this prejudice: it gives more weight to the protection of material infrastructure and geographic territory than to the integrity of information spaces. It is an artifact of a previous era in which the cohesion of the polity relied fundamentally on the inviolability of the national soil. Spies and other foreign agents could affect internal affairs, but nowhere near the extent of influence that is possible with remote, bot-assisted, and algorithmically enhanced maneuvers within modern information spaces.

By contrast, Russian and Chinese conceptions of cybersecurity (if they even call it that) stress "information security" (their preferred term), or efforts to protect the integrity of domestic information flows via the Internet.[26] For the purposes of information security, the Russian and Chinese governments operate a vast apparatus of Internet surveillance and censorship within their borders (on which more below). The two activities go hand in hand: suppressing Internet content entails an ability to monitor it and its users. Although one can surveil without censoring, the latter requires prior surveillance.

From the distinction between Western and authoritarian notions of cybersecurity emerges a different understanding also of sovereignty. Russia and China adopt a positivist interpretation grounded in material threats and territorial sanctity – but only to an extent that serves their interests. When Russia denounces as a violation of its sovereignty the financial and other material support that foreign governments give to opposition parties and political figures, or when China protests the United States' failure to accept Chinese territorial claims over Taiwan and the East China Sea, the autocrats invoke the material dimensions of the sovereignty principle. They speak a legal language that other nations grasp. When these countries affirm cyber sovereignty as a rule of law,[27] they mean that the Internet is not a global public good; they will impose full sovereign control upon it.[28] Left conveniently unspoken are their own rampant intrusions into Western information spaces. Because such actions transpire in virtual rather than in physical space, they are harder to capture within traditional notions of sovereignty protection. As Jack Goldsmith and Alex Loomis observed, "[T]he UN Charter's prohibition on certain uses of force and the customary international-law rule of nonintervention constrains cyber operations by one state in another. The hard question" – the focus of much contention among states today – "is whether international law related to sovereignty prohibits anything more."[29]

Moscow and Beijing, in short, are quick to invoke the sovereignty principle in the case of material intrusions upon their national soil. They apply the principle to assert sovereign control over the Internet's physical infrastructure and its data. But they are silent in their own violation of other nations' virtual integrity via cyber operations, a breach of sovereignty that international law does not neatly capture and which therefore could fall within the realm of unpeace.

Democratic polities increasingly experience a particular form of contention: not over basic political values (the commitment to democracy is overall robust) but about the veracity of important information and events within political discourse. Various kinds of information integrity have come under assault from foreign influence operations: information about the views of political candidates; about the actions of officials; about the policies and activities of government agencies and departments; and perhaps most damaging of all about the reliability of a fundamental democratic institution – elections.

Against this backdrop, the Western security agenda must give greater attention to information security. It is no longer the concern mainly of authoritarian nations whose regimes strive to preserve legitimacy against the grievances of "confused" citizens (as Chinese authorities put it).[30] It is also a legitimate interest of liberal democracies with porous information frontiers. Its scope must expand beyond the normal concern of stemming illicit activity such as financial fraud and incitement of political violence. Containing malicious political and social content, especially in voting contexts, deserves the urgent attention of security planners.

Crucially, information security must not be divorced from infrastructure security; for here is where the virtual world of information and the physical world of machines intersect for political impact. What matters are not the effects on particular aspects of political discourse or specific machines, but how the two kinds of effect compound each other: for example, how the confusion arising from reports of proven compromises of vote-counting machines might interact with the disorientation caused by misinformation about malicious behavior among vote counters. Moreover, the damage to election integrity must be assessed across the entire universe of jurisdictions, parties, candidates, and elections within the polity. Let us reaffirm: punctuated deterrence calculates penalties not according to single actions but according to an estimation of their *aggregating* effects across all areas of national security interest.

For liberal democracies, however, information security is a severely conscribed practice. They are up against a double asymmetry favoring the autocrats. For one thing, on the defensive side, information control does not come naturally to societies that regard freedom of expression as a fundamental right. Russia's 2016 hacking and social media operations showed that the very openness which defines Western democratic political culture makes nations especially vulnerable to foreign information campaigns. Democratic societies struggle with a fundamental tension that autocracies are spared: how to protect the integrity of political discourse while preserving basic rights of expression.

The challenge of information governance is complicated by the fact that social media platforms are designed, owned, and operated by private companies (e.g. Facebook and Twitter) which are free from the control of government and which might even work against its interests. The need to involve them at the center of regulatory efforts is another hurdle that autocracies do not face. Yet, private sector interests will not always align with the government's, as demonstrated in the Apple–FBI contention following the San Bernardino terrorist attack in 2015, during which the company refused to obey a court order to decrypt a deceased terrorist suspect's private iPhone.[31]

On the offensive side, Western nations have fewer opportunities to operate within the autocrats' information spaces. Closed political systems enjoy levers of information control that can stamp out the expression of internal dissent but which are constitutionally unavailable in a democracy. Chinese authorities operate a vast apparatus of Internet surveillance and censorship that they routinely use to stanch the flow of ideas which the regime considers subversive.[32] Its most prominent tool is the so-called Great Firewall, which blocks access to Twitter, Facebook, Google, and Western Internet services. The censorship engine is both automatically and manually operated. For the regime in Beijing it is a powerful device to avoid their citizens becoming disoriented by encountering democratic political ideals.[33]

Vladimir Putin's government censors have not been as stringent as Xi Jinping's. Russian information control has tended to be more assimilative: it seeks to persuade citizens to use native Russian services – or as Andrei Soldatov put it, "to live in a bubble of Russian apps."[34] But the regime has devised a legal framework for Internet surveillance and acquired censoring tools that it often uses to repress political dissent. It operates the System of Operative Search Measures (SORM), now in its third generation, which, in collaboration with the national Internet service providers (ISPs), captures online data almost completely. Recent legislation supports the collection of information.[35] In 2016, the Russian Duma passed two bills – collectively known as the "Yarovaya Law" after one of its drafters – requiring ISPs to store users' metadata and content for varying periods of time.[36] Censorship tactics are robust and involve not just Internet blockages, but also disruptive cyberattacks against the websites and machines of domestic political dissidents: for example, the distributed denial-of-service attacks against the radio station Ekho Moskvy and the vote-monitoring organization Golos during the 2011 parliamentary election.[37]

The autocrats' domestic Internet is not frontierless like democratic networks. Because routers and servers occupy physical space, online communication is readily subject to the regimes' jurisdictional control. Western nations, moreover, do not have a hundred years of doctrinal understanding of information warfare as Russia does. They should develop their own concept and method that governments can employ where opportunities for strategic gain arise, or at least to counteract the effects of adversary maneuvers. Here, the double asymmetry may limit the gains while presenting new dangers. A central challenge is to figure out how to limit foreign intruders' ability to harm the polity's virtual integrity from within, while respecting basic freedoms at home and one's notion of appropriate behavior abroad.

Punctuated deterrence offers punitive options outside of the information domain that transcend the plane of contention in which autocrats enjoy a distinct advantage. Punishing to deter information operations requires exposing inconsistencies in the adversaries' stance on sovereignty, which at home asserts sovereign prerogatives of Internet governance and information control, while abroad allowing intrusions upon the information space of other nations. It is a mark of the artfulness of Russian diplomacy that it can operate decisively between these two contradictory policies and succeed at both.

Because it operates across domains, not just in the immediate plane of contention, punctuated deterrence offers punitive options in any domain the punisher wants to select. But its enactment first requires a reordering of cyber-security priorities to align the growing threat of information warfare against the integrity of democratic institutions.

THE PRINCIPLE OF ISSUE LINKAGE

Punctuated deterrence prescribes a combination of options to inflict costs in multiple domains. Existing law, as we noted in previous chapters, limits counter-measures in the cyber domain – that is, a response in kind. At any rate, to punish aggression only in kind encourages the view that adversaries can harm interests in a domain in which they enjoy advantages while avoiding costs in other realms where one is strategically and tactically superior. The linkage method addresses this imbalance. It encompasses "cross-domain" deterrence, which, for example, can involve the use of broad-spectrum financial and economic sanctions to punish a cyberattack or a malicious information campaign.

Western policy so far has made insufficient use of these punitive devices. Some U.S. officials have warned that Russia is already "pretty sanctioned out."[38] We saw in Chapter 6 that the most common forms of punishment for Russian cyber activity have been narrow-spectrum sanctions and indictments targeting individuals or organizations that were directly involved in an operation. The economic and industrial interests of the parent government have largely been spared direct effects. Rare is the use of broad-spectrum penalties for technological aggression. One exception was the Obama Administration's sanctions against North Korea for the Sony Pictures hack. By curtailing the country's arms research and procurement industries, the sanctions delivered a far more potent retaliatory punch than those targeting Russian state hackers and criminals following the DNC hack. Kim Jong Un's already heavily embargoed state was closer to being "over-sanctioned" than Russia,[39] despite the Russian actions producing greater disruption than North Korea's cyberattack. This juxtaposition reveals the absence of a calibrated punishment policy that metes out penalties in a degree that accords with the severity of the aggression and the strategic aims behind it.

When punishing with broad-spectrum sanctions, policymakers must consider blowback effects. As Henry Kissinger pointed out at the height of the Cold War, linkage is often a reality of diplomacy rather than a choice because of the interdependence of issues.[40] Issue interdependence is especially true in today's technologically entwined world. Actions in one compartment of cyberspace inevitably affect interests beyond it; possibly they influence issues and regions much further afield. The interconnectedness that links networks and machines across the globe is the vital technical skin of the deeper globalization which exists in financial and commercial affairs. Disruption of economic activity in a particular sector in China or Russia could affect global supply chains that rely on production or transit nodes within it.

If the punisher fails to evaluate correctly the scale of economic blowback, the use of broad-spectrum sanctions sets the stage for a potential climbdown in punishment. Consider the case of the Trump Administration's sanctioning of the Russian aluminum company Rusal in April 2018. The company produced 7 percent of the world's aluminum supply. The sanctions caused a 10-percent spike in the metal's price. Fearing the blowback against the U.S. economy, the U.S. government withdrew them.[41] This outcome is precisely the opposite signaling that effective deterrence requires. The use of broad-spectrum sanctions to punish cyber activity requires a clear framework of activation thresholds and a reliable model of anticipated effects (enlisting the support of economists and financial analysts).

Nations with large and diversified domestic markets will be less susceptible to the effects of economic closure abroad. The possibilities for the effective use of broad-spectrum sanctions, therefore, are diminished in relation to nations such as North Korea or Iran, whose participation in the global markets is significantly lower than larger and more open economies such as China's or Russia's, which are more susceptible to the damaging effect of economic closure.

Punitive linkage opportunities exist more broadly than in the economic sphere alone. Victims of cyberattack can also deliberately link progress and concessions in separate realms of diplomacy. For example, cyber activity can be punished by imposing costs in negotiations for a new nuclear arms limitation treaty with Russia; in the commercial relationship with China, which involves contentions over import tariffs and currency exchange rates; or in the form of stronger bilateral security guarantees for nations such as Ukraine, Taiwan, or Japan, which the main geopolitical adversaries sometimes view as residing within their own spheres of influence.

The case of nuclear diplomacy merits illustration. With the landmark Strategic Arms Reduction Treaty (START) approaching expiration in 2009, the Russians courted the Bush Administration for its replacement. Since the end of the Cold War, the treaty had reduced Washington's and Moscow's deployed nuclear forces from about 10,000 warheads each to 6,000.[42] The New START Treaty signed in 2009 set more stringent arms limitation terms. Critics argued that the treaty benefited Russia: the country would have reduced its nuclear arsenal anyway; why then bind the United States unnecessarily to the new stringent terms?[43] President Donald Trump in fact intimated that his administration would allow the treaty to lapse. Instead, he pursued a broader trilateral agreement that included China. Following the failure of this approach owing to Russian and Chinese opposition, the Biden Administration agreed with Moscow to extend the existing treaty. In the end not only did Washington propose binding itself to a potentially unfavorable treaty structure, it also failed to bind one of the main adversaries at all.

The chance to leverage the issue of the treaty's extension (or not) for the benefit of U.S. national interests in the nuclear and cyber domains will appear again in 2026. In April 2021, Assistant Secretary of State Christopher Ford illustrated the language of a linkage stick: "[W]e are giving Moscow and Beijing incentives to negotiate seriously with us by being prepared to compete ruthlessly and effectively with them – and to win the competition – if they will not talk."[44] The incentives for extension need not involve only nuclear concessions; they could also pertain to a reduction in intrusive cyber activity.

Linkage in the end entails a political choice: a deliberate move to leverage interests in one realm by affecting them in another. The reluctance of large Western nations to make greater use of economic and diplomatic punishment is ironic, for they are in a privileged position to inflict it owing to their disproportionate role in global economic governance and the diplomacy of international security. The architecture of the global economy and the toolbox of linkage diplomacy await more expansive and creative use for cyber conflict reduction.

THE PRINCIPLE OF DECLARATORY CREDIBILITY

Deterrence is, at bottom, a psychological mechanism: it relies on the attacker's firm belief that the penalty for attack is not worth assuming because it is costlier than the gains, and that the penalty will actually ensue following an attack. Thus, it puts a high price on verbalism: the adversary must understand that one's words reflect a state of will rather than an ideal.

Accordingly, two dangers exist here. One is a vague promise of penalties. The problem arises before an attack has occurred. To state that one might retaliate against cyber actions invites the attacker to consider that one might *not* retaliate. It is important to state plainly, therefore, the intent to retaliate and that one will do so for a series of actions in accordance with the accretional principle. The unfulfilled promise of penalties presents a second danger. It exists after an attack has taken place and thus affects deterrence against further attack. Nothing is more damaging to the psychological edifice of deterrence than to announce penalties that do not materialize in the presence of the triggering conditions. Although the attacker controls the conditions that invoke punishment, it is the responsibility of the victim to mete it out.

Effective signaling, therefore, is essential to the success of punctuated deterrence. Multiple signaling pathways are possible: public pronouncements (such as in a public attribution of a cyber operation),[45] diplomatic channels, trusted neutral parties, or other communications in bargaining situations. Signaling must communicate to opponents that, for punishment purposes, single actions will be decisively treated as a comprehensive set of offensive activities, not as isolated moves eliciting isolated penalties.

Current practice already punishes some offensive activity jointly – but too broadly and often confusingly. For example, the U.S. sanctions and indictments against Russian actors that we discussed in the previous chapter listed a variety of offenses ranging from the hacking of politicians' email accounts to the penetration of election infrastructure. What is wrong with this approach and how does punctuated deterrence differ?

The current bundling approach suffers a major shortcoming: it gathers together strategic-level activity (such as political hacking, e.g. election interference) and low-level criminal activity (such as financial fraud). One is a matter of international law and diplomacy, the other an issue for the domestic courts. One involves the imperatives of national security, the other the ends of criminal justice. One is a concern for security and defense doctrine, the other a matter for jurisprudence. One targets influential decisionmakers and their proxies, the other punishes unaffiliated rascals in the criminal underworld. Thus, the current bundling approach fails to communicate clear red lines of conduct. Astute interpreters in Moscow or Beijing might conclude (probably correctly) that financial fraud is tolerable but that the corruption of vote tallies is unacceptable. But the danger exists that they will misinterpret kompromat operations against prominent political figures in the midst of a hotly contested presidential election as bearable because the response bundles them alongside low-level criminal activity. The problem with the current bundling approach, therefore, is one of mixed signaling: it punishes similar means rather than similar effects, thus complicating the establishment of clear lines of acceptable and unacceptable offensive action.

Here, one can invoke Thomas Schelling's important advice: in order to succeed, a declaratory posture must communicate precisely which actions fall within its punitive ambit and which ones do not.[46] Any such limits are distinguishable only qualitatively. The deterring party will want the opponent to understand that some offensive measures are consistent with the concept of a limited rivalry while others violate it. Indiscriminate bundling gives too much symbolic content to activity that fails to meet the relevance threshold of punctuation. A more discriminating approach that bundles only strategic-level activity (punishing criminal actions elsewhere) would build mutual understanding of the limits of tolerable cyber conflict.

Another signaling dynamic to consider is the potential drawback of a response in kind. If the punitive cyber action is covert because the responder wishes to protect knowledge of vulnerabilities that it exploits in the response – that is, it does not want to burn intelligence equities – then the punishment message will have just one recipient, the original attacker. Other aspiring attackers will fail to receive and learn from it. Covert retaliation has no place in punctuated deterrence. What is deterrence if not a convincing chain of communications to influence future expectations of behavior? Here we find an important difference between punctuation and persistent engagement. Persistent engagement activities often occur below the surface of observation. Harassing the adversary in its computer terrain in order to divert its resources away from one's own terrain does not require the communication of intent if a quiet disabling action gets the job done. Clear communication, in fact, can hinder the effort if it exposes one's presence within the adversary's terrain, thereby aiding one's expulsion from it.

8
WHAT KIND OF NATO?
Punctuated Deterrence in Practice

COLLECTIVE PUNCTUATION

The prescription to punish adversarial moves cumulatively need not be applied in isolation. Military alliances and economic communities offer collective means of punctuation that can strengthen the message of deterrence and increase the chance that the other side will read it convincedly.

Among the Western world's various institutions, the North Atlantic Treaty Organization stands out. It is the world's most powerful military alliance; its thirty member states represent more than half of the global military expenditure. Among its ranks are three of the world's nine nuclear powers. A military club of liberal democracies founded to deter – or if deterrence failed, to thwart – a Soviet onslaught in Europe,[1] the alliance achieved great prestige following the Communist bloc's demise in the late 1980s. A dozen formerly captive nations, three of them former constituent republics of the Soviet Union itself,[2] have since joined the club. Three more nations formally await an accession invitation – all having experienced the dire consequences of not being in the club.[3] The alliance has intervened in foreign lands to end human rights abuses in Kosovo, to establish peace in Bosnia and Herzegovina, to combat pirates off the Horn of Africa, and to expel Al-Qaeda terrorists from their safe haven in Afghanistan.[4]

NATO in brief is the largest and most powerful collective framework for the prevention of aggression and the reduction of conflict. Its activity and record in the cyber domain are the acid test of the Western world's adaptability to the changing tides of modern conflict.

This chapter considers NATO's steps, successes, and shortcomings in addressing the challenge of cyber conflict prevention, with a special emphasis on the principles of action introduced in the preceding chapter. Can this mighty alliance deter technological aggression against its member states in the realm of unpeace? If not, can it bolster the strategy of punctuation to achieve this objective in the future?

By the standard of its founding purpose, NATO's record of achievement is perfect: no member state of the alliance has ever suffered an armed attack from another state. The only time that the famed Article 5 on collective defense was ever invoked was in 2001 in response to the attacks by Al-Qaeda against civilian and military targets in New York and Washington – a scenario that the organization's founders did not envisage. The alliance, nevertheless, adapted itself to the threat of global terrorism; a lengthy and costly campaign succeeded in eradicating the attackers' presence in their havens in Afghanistan – a country so far away that the alliance's conceivers in 1949 could not have imagined combined operations there.

Despite its impressive record in preventing armed attack, NATO has struggled to adapt its defense doctrine to the era of technological unpeace. Officials are realizing the hard way – by way of repeating and intensifying conflict – that strategic success on the traditional plane of war, political and moral achievements in the club's expansion, and tactical victories in the violent fight against unconventional enemies do not guarantee success in preventing lesser forms of conflict in the form of intangible threats burrowed deeply within the home terrain. Recall that the "demonstration shot" of strategic cyber conflict was fired in 2007 against one of the alliance's own member states, Estonia. And as we saw in preceding chapters, actions against the political and economic interests of member states continue unabated. Even if the alliance has successfully deterred armed attack, even as it continues to make strides in distant battlefields, its member states' political sovereignty and core economic interests are repeatedly assailed in cyberspace.

The recurrence of Russian territorial avarice in Ukraine is tangible proof that NATO's founding purpose remains vital. But alone it is insufficient to guarantee security in our times. Article 5 emerged in an era when the line between war and peace was sharp. Its conceivers did not have to ask how actions below it could strike at the heart of the democratic system. That era is long past. Having prevented the Iron Curtain's advance into the homelands, but now facing a growing virtual menace directly within them, the alliance must find ways to roll it back. The failure to reduce strategic cyber activity is remarkable if one considers how long NATO has strived towards this end. A review of NATO's history in the cyber domain will reveal where the alliance has gone – and not gone but could go – in addressing the problem.

NATO IN CYBERSPACE: AN ALLIANCE AWAKENS

The alliance's first foray into the cyber domain occurred before policymakers and analysts broadly recognized it as such. In an epoch of change, the swing of history does not always reveal itself readily to the scrutiny of contemporaries. What seems like foresight could, in fact, be false conjecture. Before the Estonia crisis, many observers would have dismissed the strategic significance of cyber threats; even today, some continue to deny it.[5] But, as early as 2002, prescient officials pushed for the adoption of the alliance's first cyber defense mission. The principles and even some of the technologies (such as social media) of cyber conflict did not yet exist. But a sense of a new era in security affairs was already in the offing.

At the Prague Summit that year, the alliance announced a cyber defense program, which resulted in the establishment of the NATO Computer Incident Response Capability (NCIRC). The program was a reaction to a series of cyberattacks and information warfare campaigns against the alliance as it implemented Operation Allied Force during the Kosovo War.[6] As NATO bombs fell on Serbian targets (achieving a sweeping military victory), hackers sympathetic to Slobodan Milošević's cause disrupted the alliance's websites, servers, and email services. NATO's public affairs website went offline, hindering officials' ability to shape the war's narrative. U.S. government websites also experienced a spike in attacks.[7] Although the attacks were notable for the hackers' assiduity, the consequences were not strategically significant; they paled in comparison to what awaited.

What came in the spring of 2007 was a moment of reckoning. The torrents of data requests that disrupted the financial system and government communications of one of the alliance's smallest and newest members showed that a defensive awareness program and incident response team would not suffice to resist so rapid and pervasive a form of attack. Attuned to the perils of digital dependence even before the cyberattacks that hit their country, Estonian officials in 2004 had proposed establishing a joint NATO center of excellence for cyber defense. Having rebuffed the Estonian proposal, alliance partners after 2007 could no longer defer the lessons of current affairs.

Thereafter, NATO began to address cyber conflict as a focal issue at its summits, the annual diplomatic pageantries which signal shifts in the consensus (or else expose its cracks) over evolving strategic threats. At the Bucharest Summit in 2008, the allies discussed the lessons learned from the Estonian crisis. "NATO remains committed to strengthening key Alliance information systems against cyberattacks," stated the Leaders' Declaration. "We . . . are developing the structures and authorities to carry it out. Our Policy on Cyber Defense emphasizes the need for NATO and nations to protect key information systems in accordance with their respective responsibilities; share best practices; and provide a capability to assist allied nations, upon request, to counter a cyberattack."[8] This language contains the usual banalities that flow from such summits, but the dryness of diplomacy does not conceal the significance of the new policy course. For the statement conveyed a newly cemented consensus: cyber defense was now firmly within the alliance's security agenda and area of competence.

Following the recognition of the pressing necessity for collective action, a slew of institutional reforms ensued. The Bucharest meeting resulted in the establishment of the Cyber Defense Management Authority (CDMA) in Brussels and the Cooperative Cyber Defense Center of Excellence (CCD-COE) in Tallinn in 2008. The CDMA sought to centralize operational capabilities and serve as a focal point of coordination in a crisis. The CCD-COE's purpose was to provide a research arm to bolster the development of new security thinking – a vital area of activity if we recall the point in Chapter 1 about the necessity for doctrinal refinement in times of technological revolution. Also that year, NATO adopted its first cyber defense policy, which emphasized defensive measures.[9]

These moves seem like passive defensive improvements in a quest for a "virtual" Maginot Line, which gained intensity in 2011 when NATO adopted the Cyber Defense Policy and Action Plan and started to develop a rapid reaction team for deployment in crises.[10] Within that important document one finds a failure of credible signaling: that is, haziness on the matter of punitive responses. The policy focused on "the protection of NATO networks and on cyber defense requirements related to national networks that NATO relies upon to carry out its core tasks: collective defense and crisis management." It stipulated: "Any collective defense response by NATO will be subject to political decisions of the North Atlantic Council. NATO does not pre-judge any response and therefore maintains flexibility in deciding a course of action that may or may not be taken."[11] An external observer could be excused for interpreting the cryptic language as a sign that the question of when and how to respond to a strategic cyberattack – beyond the mere coordination of resilience efforts – was a cause of great internal division, a situation likelier to produce bureaucratic inertia than to spur doctrinal ingenuity and decisive action.

The next important NATO documents emerged at the Chicago Summit in 2012 and the Wales Summit in 2014. They renewed defensive commitments while eschewing clear assertions of punishment. The latter meeting culminated in a declaration that "cyber defense is part of NATO's core task of collective defense"[12] – another banality, for it was clear that a fatal and highly destructive cyberattack would, by virtue of its warlike consequences, provide sufficient grounds for the activation of Article 5. That such a scenario would be evaluated on a "case-by-case basis" could only further showcase weak consensus by suggesting that publicly drawing out even the "red lines" of cyberwar was a topic of contention among the allies (by contrast, one does not hear about treating cruise missile attacks or an aerial strike on a case-by-case basis). Further defensive maneuvers came in the form of two major cyber defense exercises in 2014 in Estonia, "Cyber Coalition" and "Locked Shields." That same year, the alliance established the NATO Industry Cyber Partnership, which increased collaboration between government authorities and the private sector to strengthen infrastructure resilience, thereby adding yet another layer of passive defense, but one with a promising potential for impact (more on this below).

In 2016, almost a decade after the Estonian crisis, the allies reached their most substantial milestones. At the Warsaw Summit, they formally designated cyberspace as an "operational domain" of NATO alongside air, land, and sea.[13] They also made a Cyber Defense Pledge that bound them to reinforce their own national cyber defenses. As if the pledge required an institutional expression to be believable, the allies gathered for an awkwardly named "Cyber Defense Pledge Conference" in Paris in May 2018. There the vagueness about a muscular response to cyber hostilities reared its doubting head. Impeded by diplomacy from conveying anything more than the consensus, and unable to force a new one into existence, Secretary General Jens Stoltenberg remained reluctant to define the circumstances under which the alliance would activate its collective defense clause. Equivocation diluted the messaging:

> I am often asked, "under what circumstances would NATO trigger Article 5 in the case of a cyber-attack?" My answer is: we will see. The level of cyber-attack that would provoke a response must remain purposefully vague. As will the nature of our response. But it could include diplomatic and economic sanctions, cyber-responses, or even conventional forces, depending on the nature and consequences of the attack. We need a full spectrum response. So we can respond to serious cyber-attacks even if they don't cross the Article 5 threshold. But whatever the response, NATO will continue to follow the principle of restraint. And act in accordance with international law. Knowing who has carried out an attack can often be difficult – initially at least.[14]

In other words, the message to potential attackers seems to have been the following: NATO may or may not reply to your cyberattack. Even when responding, we will constrain ourselves by legal interpretations more prohibitive than yours (recall the norm-generating aspirations of cyber legalism in Chapter 2). Conceal your identity and location well enough, and we might not respond at all. Allies and partners hearing this message could not plausibly indulge in the conceit that the diplomatic bedrock of retaliation below the war line was concrete. Scheming attackers could assume that it was plastic.

Institutional steps continued apace. At the Brussels Summit in July 2018, the allies agreed to set up a Cyber Operations Center in Mons, Belgium, although it is unclear whether the Center would be able to perform its own offensive cyber operations. The Secretary General's 2019 *Annual Report* stated: "Allies will retain control of their national cyber capabilities at all times when they are used during NATO missions or operations."[15] Vanished was any firm hope of a joint response in kind.

More passive defense pledges ensued with few, or no credibly articulated, punitive measures to accompany them. Another Cyber Defense Pledge Conference held in 2019 prioritized education and training of the alliance population on the hazards of cyber threats. But at the event Stoltenberg expressed stronger language than in previous years: "[W]hen needed, we must be ready to use our cyber capabilities to fight an enemy," adding: "For deterrence to have full effect, potential attackers must know that we are not limited to respond in cyberspace when we are attacked in cyberspace. We can and will use the range of capabilities at our disposal."[16] At last a potentially decisive declaration of punishment seemed in the offing – but again there was no specificity about the triggering conditions or about the ensuing collective response. In 2020, after a number of intrusions into member states' health infrastructures during the Covid-19 pandemic, NATO issued a statement concerning malicious cyber activities, reiterating the previous undefined pledges to defend health systems and data from unnamed hackers. And in it, too, appeared the customary propitiations to international law and a "rules-based" cyberspace.[17]

At another summit in Brussels in 2021 came an important moment. The allies reaffirmed their commitment to evaluating the potential invocation of Article 5 in a stronger tone than theretofore. "We will make greater use of NATO as a platform for political consultation among Allies, sharing concerns about malicious cyber activities, and exchanging national approaches and responses, as well as considering possible collective responses," stated the summit communiqué, adding: "If necessary, we will impose costs on those who harm us. Our response need not be restricted to the cyber domain."[18] Although the tone of the punishment pledge was notably stronger, it continued to suffer vagueness about thresholds and indecision among the allies regarding the nature and extent of a joint response. And it repeated the affirmation that cyberattacks would be treated on a case-by-case basis. Many an adversary could still hope and expect that their harmful actions would not invoke the pledge.

Why does confusion run high when the matter of the alliance's response to strategic cyber activity is brought up? Beyond the fragmentation of consensus among allies, the deeper root of the problem lies in an outmoded strategic doctrine that reflects their policy dogmas – in a commitment to sustain peace and prepare for war while fumbling around in the middle of the spectrum of conflict. True to the tenets of cyber legalism, the alliance's collective defense concept privileges the physical world over the virtual world, conventional military security over cyber and information security. Especially important in this regard is the language of the foundational Article 5, which explicitly sets the threshold for collective defense at the level of armed attack.[19]

From a strictly military perspective, the emphasis on war makes sense. Nuclear attack and conventional war remain plausible threats. Look no further than Ukraine and Russia's growing nuclear shadow. Russia possesses the world's largest nuclear arsenal, which comprises not just the weapons it inherited from the Soviet Union, but also potent new arms that it is modernizing.[20] Its enormous if enfeebled conventional army regularly amasses along NATO's eastern flank for shows of force. It has unleashed this destructive power onto Ukraine, only miles away from the alliance's Polish border, while threatening the alliance with the nuclear specter. The Chinese military spook also grows larger. At the summit in June 2021, NATO leaders warned for the first time about the "systemic challenges" to international order posed by China in light of its rapidly growing and modernizing armed forces.[21] NATO's remit, clearly, does not cover events in Asia or the Pacific. But China's growing military power increasingly projects into the periphery of Europe and the North Atlantic region (e.g. the expansion of forward military bases in Djibouti and other African nations).[22]

But recall a crucial point about security in our times: the prevention of war no longer means the preservation of peace. NATO's troubles in the cyber domain are an analog of the West's difficulty in updating its strategic doctrine to address new forms of technological rivalry that are not warlike.

Legal scholars have recommended revision of the treaty's collective defense provision so that it applies to situations of national emergency less than war. The recommendation has not yet found many supporters.[23] "From a political perspective, this proposal was problematic, because the Washington Treaty was sacrosanct – nobody wanted to touch it," explained Christian-Marc Lifländer, the head of cyber defense at NATO headquarters in Brussels. Relaxation of the formal conditions in which Article 5 applies risks undermining the alliance's credibility in face of armed attack. "NATO is a military alliance," continued Lifländer. "Maneuvering below the threshold of war is difficult. Below that threshold, whatever you do is escalatory because you do not have any other tools but armed attack."[24] So goes the escalation concern: having operated for so long above the war threshold, expanding the range of responses below war could intensify the conflict into it.

And yet maneuvering within the realm of unpeace has become a central preoccupation of NATO. If relaxing the formal language of collective defense risks diluting the psychological basis of deterring armed attack, what more, then, could the alliance do to strengthen the preventive logic of penalties? The answer lies in the guiding principles of punctuated deterrence.

PRINCIPLES OF PUNCTUATION IN ACTION

The starting precept of punctuated deterrence is the accretional principle: punish a series of offensive actions and their cumulative effects rather than single actions.[25] The principle has begun to gain officials' attention. The alliance adopted it in Brussels in 2021. "Significant malicious cumulative cyber activities might, in certain circumstances, be considered as amounting to an armed attack," stated the communiqué of the meeting, noting that "cyber threats to the security of the Alliance are complex, destructive, coercive, are becoming ever more frequent." Yet, again, however, the doctrine of cyber legalism clutched the tenet of self-restraint. The ensuing sentence affirmed: "We remain committed to act in accordance with international law, including the UN Charter,"[26] which by implication boxed the consideration of cumulative effects within the rubric of armed attack and use of force. The usual solicitation for "norms of responsible state behavior in cyberspace" was also voiced (but not heard by adversaries in China, whose offensive activity against alliance targets more than doubled in the following year).[27] How persistent the liberal desire to erect a normative utopia in an anarchic jungle rife with villains can be!

Appeals to the UN Charter generally, and to standards of armed attack specifically, invite a dual problem. For one thing, the Charter contains no explicit provisions against offensive activity below the threshold of armed attack or use of force – hence the law's appeal to the enterprising strategists in Moscow and Beijing, who read it more permissively than officials in Western capitals. For another, no accumulation of non-violent effects could ever meet the legal criteria of violence and death. In the same way that no amount of economic sanctions (formally an act of peace under international law) could equate to, say, a cruise missile strike, no number of kompromat operations or infiltrations of governmental agencies or disruptions of banking systems could amount to the same. No matter how forcefully the interpretive wheel of cyber legalism turns, the existing legal system's machinery cannot print new categories of state conduct or merge them into old ones.

The sum of unpeace in short can never equate to war. The legal and doctrinal fixation with armed attack within NATO, although partly legitimate (more on this below), has led it to deprecate lesser forms of conflict that have widened the struggle for geopolitical mastery in the twenty-first century. The fixation with armed attack and the passion for law and norms that opponents interpret narrowly has meant, in reality, the limitation of the alliance's relevant scope of action.

Yet, public affirmation of the accretional principle is a vital step towards superior conflict prevention. How, then, to render it applicable?

The answer may lie in the coordination of informal action that circumvents rigid legal procedures. Collective punctuation faces the drawbacks of any joint action among sovereign actors. As a multinational response, it entails the necessity for consensus and the passion for consultation that are hallmarks of diplomacy. Possibly, not all allies will be equally willing to partake in the full package of penalties if they find it excessive or, if it seems subdued, to constrain their freedom to hit back harder. Concerting action through formal channels in the absence of consensus and in the presence of legal ambiguity risks a protracted or no collective response.

Informal action among a group of allies drawing from political relationships several decades in the making offers a bypass. "You can have a group of allies working together to put the new approach of addressing cumulative effects into good use," observed Lifländer. This approach "would rely on a 'coalition of the willing' emerging to provide that support to NATO from outside the alliance framework, something the alliance benefits from but that wouldn't be from within our framework."[28] The prescience of this statement is the recognition that NATO is more than just a formal alliance; it is also a *community*. Or in the words of Secretary General Lord Ismay in 1956: "NATO is a political as well as a military alliance."[29] Its binding force is more than mere treaty legalese; it is also common values, shared interests, and a commitment to realize them. Viewing threats through the prism of the community they imperil opens up new fields of collective endeavor in protecting them. And that is the point: to mobilize action to defend the values that the alliance embodies and the interests it serves without having to resort to formal procedures that do not clearly apply. A sustained record of informal action, moreover, could produce parallelism: the process whereby success in informal collective action sets the foundations for consensus on formal collective action.

At present, NATO does not formally allow the formation of sub-groupings in the activation of its important treaty articles. But nothing prevents an informal coalition of the willing from pursuing enhanced cooperation while benefiting from the alliance's diplomatic resources. Much as Finland and Sweden began, in April 2022, to negotiate informal security guarantees with some member states to cover the period before the Nordic countries' planned accession to the alliance – who until then cannot legally benefit from collective defense – so too a sub-coalition could draw up firmer guarantees of retaliation until the general consensus parallels theirs.

The mobilization of a sub-coalition would enjoy procedural advantages. Convening a smaller club of member states has the advantage of circumventing institutional channels that reluctant allies could use to constrain a joint response. The reluctance could involve intelligence sharing – the classical problem of intelligence equities, whereby the sharing of secrets diminishes their perceived value. Sharing intelligence among a smaller group enables cooperation on response targeting following an incident, while limiting the concern that some allies will misuse or misplace secrets. Action among a sub-coalition, therefore, could facilitate cooperation in the preparation of sterner punitive action. Possibly, too, the participating nations could marshall the institutional resources of NATO headquarters, which houses a group of capable analysts, some of them with precious experience handling the political, diplomatic, legal, and technical difficulties of cyber conflict.

Allies bound by trust and driven by common purpose have many options to break out of the institutional box. Let us recall the maxim of Secretary General Paul-Henri Spaak from 1959: *"Animus in consulendo liber"* ("in discussion a free mind"). Members of permanent delegations posted in the alliance's headquarters in Brussels encounter this statement within its halls. Call it a spur to action among a select group of them to chart a bolder course.

Another key principle is declaratory credibility. Signaling becomes even more important yet complex in scenarios of collective punctuation. As we saw, the alliance has failed to implement it effectively. Declaratory vagueness has overstepped its limits of utility in NATO practice. Although too much certainty about thresholds and mechanisms of response can hinder deterrence, not enough certainty can have a similar, or worse, effect on the incidence of conflict. And not just vagueness is the problem. In the absence of clarity about thresholds of response, repeating the "pledge" of retaliation contains within itself a paradox: the more one publicly pledges a commitment without defining it, the more opponents have reason to wonder whether it can be defined at all.

To address the shortcoming of declaratory vagueness, the verbal policies of member states, big and small, must converge. But first they must smooth out remaining internal differences among them regarding the thresholds of seriousness triggering a response – the enduring bane of consensus makers. Here, again, a sub-coalition of allies could form to present a bolder interpretation of response lines than the thin consensus allows. The communications must convince adversaries that collectively bundled punishment for, say, electoral interference in the French presidential election (which Russia attempted in 2017) and an intrusion into a major government body such as the U.S. Anti-Doping Agency (2018) will be punished if the actions are repeated against *any* of the participating nations. The larger the group of allies partaking in the coalition, the more clearly their words and actions fill in the declaratory gaps of the cyber defense pledge, the more credible its punitive elements become. The arc of deterrence could thereby be widened to encompass the interests of all parties involved for the entire range of named incidents.

Another area for policy improvement within the alliance concerns the principle of issue linkage. This is the question of collective punctuation if deterrence fails, that is, the member states combining to deliver a joint punishment in whatever domains – economic, diplomatic, arms control, etc. – are chosen for a response. The available penalties from which to choose are varied and could involve broad-spectrum sanctions by the United States, which has levers of control over the world's financial architecture; narrow-spectrum sanctions by Britain affecting foreign suspects with financial interests in London; or a collective negotiation with Russia on troop reductions along its periphery. Leaders in Moscow know that arms control and troop reductions cannot be agreed until they address fundamental issues in the relationship; greater restraint in strategic cyber activity belongs in that discussion (with two crucial caveats: in the absence of an imminent Russian threat and if the reduction does not imperil the security of frontline allies).

A fourth initiative for NATO and its member states to adopt concerns the principle of virtual integrity. The aim here is to widen the arc of deterrence not among allies but into information security – an area of national security that traditional Western doctrine has not privileged. Securing the integrity of political institutions within a modern democracy entails the necessity of the private sector's participation in the provision of public security. In every democracy, the division of the polity into private and public spheres serves to preserve individual freedoms. Inviting the private sector into the national security enterprise means also beckoning the government into the private life of business. Some companies will resist this responsibility and that presence. Or else they will oppose the diversion of private talents to the national security enterprise. Consider Google. In April 2018, more than 3,000 employees signed an open letter protesting their company's collaboration with the Pentagon "in the business of war," in particular, the so-called Project Maven, which involved the use of artificial intelligence to enhance the interpretation of video imagery in counterinsurgency and counterterrorism operations.[30]

But the evils of foreign information intrusions affect both sides. Government's challenge is to incorporate the private sector without absorbing it. Industry's challenge is to bring harmony to national security and the technological world without stifling it. Flexible and specialized partnerships are essential. NATO can help to orchestrate them. The Industry Cyber Partnership marks an important step in this direction. But industry need not step into the world of producing weapons to assist in efforts to curtail or defend against their use. Take, for example, 5G infrastructure. Alliance officials have worked actively with telecommunications providers to understand its vulnerabilities and to identify security standards that allies can disseminate and apply.[31]

Unlike autocracies, democracies cannot organize strategic technology industries by way of diktat. But democracies can benefit from the inventive energies that the political independence of industry unleashes. Like its member states, an alliance of democracies must respect the separation of public and private life. The challenge, then, is to achieve some of the results of the centralized state without its concomitants – coercion of executives and public appropriation of assets. Because the "democratic" technology company often straddles many markets and jurisdictions, because, therefore, no single government can orchestrate its contribution to civil defense, an alliance that can do both is in a strong position to lead the coordination of civil cyber defense.

An alliance that defines itself by repulsing an invading army or by avenging nuclear devastation is not in its most creative state, particularly when the nature of threats is broader. NATO was founded on the assumption that clarity about the thresholds for punishing aggression would prevent it. The behavior of opponents has evolved on the premise that by not clearly violating them aggression offers rewards. The core challenge of collective punctuation is also its necessity: to meet the changing threats of the new world by maneuvering within – and if necessary around – the institutions of the old.

9

DATA EMBASSIES AND STATE CONTINUITY
The Return of Denial?

NEW TECHNOLOGIES FOR OFFENSE DENIAL

Sterner punishment does not exhaust the methods of cyber conflict prevention and reduction. The commitment to bolster the framework of penalties does not relieve security planners of the duty to shore up defenses to reduce the efficacy of offensive actions. Just as some experts have been too quick to dismiss deterrence by punishment, one must be careful not to disparage denial prematurely. Innovations in cyberspace can enhance the security of infrastructure and data residing within it such that foreign disruptors are deprived of at least some of their expected gains.

Consider the case of "blockchain" technology: the construction of specific types of distributed ledgers comprising immutable blocks of data (hence the label). Each block contains a list of transactions that references the preceding block in a continuous data chain. Although the concept existed decades earlier, the technology's first wide application was in the bitcoin protocol, which an anonymous author (or authors) under the pseudonym "Satoshi Nakamoto" conceived in 2008.[1] The protocol offered a payment system to achieve consensus securely and effectively among untrusting parties about the veracity of data transactions between them. The protocol's distributed nature removed the need for trusted intermediaries.[2] Thus, it circumvented the conventional financial system – an elegant (if energy-intensive)[3] software substitute for banks.

From a security perspective, the power of bitcoin was to showcase the viability of distributed ledgers in wider applications. The technical difficulty of creating a distributed digital replacement of fiat currency was in some respects similar to the challenge of using cryptographic tools to secure information exchange and storage in other contexts. Although bitcoin remains the most popular use of blockchain technology, its applications have expanded far beyond private payments. Blockchain technology is also a subject of increasing attention among government officials. Central banks across the globe increasingly speak of launching digital tokens that mirror national fiat currencies.[4] According to the British government, it "could transform the conduct of public and private sector organizations."[5] It could assist security efforts by offering new ways of protecting the integrity of data in vital public infrastructure and services. For example, European Parliament researchers have explored the use of blockchains to protect the integrity of data in future "e-voting" systems.[6] Similarly, Estonian private companies have begun to develop blockchain applications in digital ID services and public health systems.[7]

These technological initiatives, still largely in a design stage, represent an attempt to redress the distinct advantages that cyber attackers ordinarily enjoy against defenders.[8] Accepting the premise that the most sophisticated adversaries will live permanently, and often secretly, within computer infrastructures, the purpose of such efforts is to diminish their ability to cause harm from *within* the home terrain.

Other defensive innovations lie in wait. Among the most ambitious and daring denial mechanisms presently under development is the Estonian "data embassies" initiative. It seeks to replicate a layer of government data and services running from computer servers located abroad, thereby ensuring the systems' redundancy during breakdowns in the domestic cyberspace.[9]

This chapter reviews the data embassies initiative and its potential enhancement of adversary denial. It presents two main arguments. The first concerns national security: data embassies can provide important, although as yet unproven, benefits to state survival following a loss of territorial integrity. Thus, the security benefits of data embassies far transcend cyberspace: they could help to ensure the continuation of the domestic political system not just during a cyber breakdown but also in a scenario of military occupation. The greatest potential benefit to state continuity is the ability to exercise at least partial state functions remotely, most importantly the monitoring of the occupied population's opinion, thus sustaining the government's moral, symbolic, and – crucially – functional legitimacy. Insofar as data embassies can enhance the legitimacy of the exiled or underground government, it will raise the costs of occupation of a potential invader; thus, it would strengthen deterrence against such an invasion. Second, the chapter argues that data embassies, if successfully deployed, have profound implications for understandings of the state and its survival in the twenty-first century. The inseparable relationship between state sovereignty and territorial integrity is established dogma in political theory.[10] The data embassies concept challenges this dogma by enabling sovereign functions that do not rely strictly on the absolute sanctity of the national soil. Even by the standard of Estonia's intrepid approach to cyberspace, the initiative shows that great progress can be made in the ability to secure state institutions without incurring impossible costs.

The remainder of this chapter has four sections. First, it discusses the concepts of the nation that data embassies strive to protect and the state whose functions they seek to preserve. Second, it describes the concept and origins of the data embassies project as it emerged in Estonia. This discussion will involve some reconceptualization of existing terms. Third, it reviews conceivable scenarios and presents success factors and obstacles to the implementation of the project during a foreign military incursion. Fourth, it examines the implications of data embassies for concepts, principles, and models of the territorial state and for established conventions of international diplomacy, such as extraterritoriality, diplomatic immunity, and data sovereignty.

THE NATION AND THE STATE: A VIRTUAL ENTANGLEMENT

The essence of the nation is intangible: it comprises political values and cultural traits that distinguish a people from all others. The essence of the state, by contrast, is tangible: it combines resources, institutions, and powers whose goal is to protect the national entity against threats to it. Not all nations are states; some are subsumed within larger states comprising multiple coexisting (or oppressed) nationalities. But the preservation of all national units relies on the existence of a benevolent state that strives to conserve them.

It follows that the gravest external threat to the nation is absorption by a hostile power – that is, a program of conquest that prescribes the liquidation of the native identity by foreign forces. State survival is necessary to national survival; state extinction opens the way for national demise.

Leaders of the small nation of Estonia in Northern Europe are familiar with this essential relationship between the state's function and the nation's preservation. In June 1940, invading Soviet forces sought to subsume the Estonian nation within a heavily Russified political entity.[11] Soon after the Soviet Union's annexation of Estonia on July 21, the Communist revolution revealed the shades of its true complexion: Sovietization meant not only one-party rule from Moscow, but also an orchestrated project of denationalization, including by means of the mass relocation of peoples – Estonians to Siberia and Russian-speaking immigrants into Estonia.

And yet the Estonian state endured the occupation legally and morally, if not in fact. In the period from 1953 to 1991, when the Republic of Estonia regained its independence, there existed five governments-in-exile, based first in Oslo, then mainly in New York.[12] All of these governments were equally powerless to affect affairs inside the borders of their captive country. The notion of state continuity, while important legally and diplomatically, meant little in practice because officials had no viable means to bring their authority to bear on the national territory. For Estonian "diplomats without a country," the absence of a territory to rule meant that state continuity was in practical terms meaningless.[13]

Today, the Estonian government is striving to sever the reliance of state continuity on territorial control by integrating core functions of the state into the cloud – Internet-based distributed computing – that could outlive a foreign occupation.[14] The data embassies initiative involves computer servers based on foreign soil that host vital information registries and which can also provide some essential public services to the Estonian population via the Internet.

The project represents an expansion of the "Estonian Government Cloud" initiative. The main purpose of data embassies is to ensure the government's "digital continuity," or the preservation of some of Estonia's vast system of "e-services" in cases where the main data servers become unavailable.[15] There are technical limitations to the project. Some state services such as, importantly, the issuance of physical eIDs, which contain the digital signatures that underpin the national identification system, might never be administered on the cloud. But because of Estonia's high degree of reliance on hundreds of e-services, ranging from e-prescriptions to incapacity work benefits and the use of data registries, digital continuity in effect amounts to partial *state* continuity.

The national security contingencies that motivate the data embassies project are varied. According to Estonian officials Mikk Lellsaar and Laura Kask, the principal motives are protection against a major cyberattack, such as occurred in the spring of 2007, or a natural disaster that disrupts the data servers on which government registries and online services rely for their proper functioning.[16] Other sources have voiced a more ambitious objective: the provision of a digital form of state continuity in the remote possibility that the nation suffers a military invasion – that is, a repeat of the 1940 scenario or a replication of Russia's invasion of Ukraine in 2014 and 2022. As Estonia's *Cyber Security Strategy, 2014–2017* put it: "Virtual embassies will ensure the functioning of the state, regardless of Estonia's territorial integrity."[17] Taavi Kotka, the Estonian government's former chief information officer and the originator of the data embassies concept (as well as other pioneering initiatives, such as Estonian "e-residency"), drew from this experimental project a transforming view of the modern state. "The concept of a country has changed," he expressed. "Land is so yesterday. It doesn't matter where you physically live or operate. That is how the game will change."[18]

Although ensuring the state's continuity amid a military invasion is not the only or even primary motive behind data embassies, there are strong reasons to consider their potential benefits in helping to secure this objective. For one, Estonia's national security strategy implies such an eventuality by alluding to the loss of territorial integrity. For another, the recent deterioration of regional security affairs makes such a scenario more conceivable than previously. In March 2014, Russia annexed the Crimean Peninsula in Ukraine. In February 2022, it sent almost 200,000 troops into the country, at one point nearly encircling its capital city, Kyiv. Ominously, Estonia's former occupier intermittently violates the country's airspace.[19] In the aftermath of the 2014 Ukrainian crisis, the Estonian Defense League (*Kaitseliit*) has accelerated the pace of its civilian armament program.[20] Following the outbreak of a wider war in Ukraine, Estonia's Internal Security Service (*Kaitsepolitseiamet*) warned of a possible Russian invasion as soon as February 2024. "Russia's military blunders in Ukraine so far make an invasion of Estonia less likely," observed former Estonian President Toomas Hendrik Ilves, who had warned his Western partners about the gravity of the Russian threat long before many of them saw it. "Russia is not in any position to invade any other country now. But that is a practical question. Politically and morally, the idea of a Russian military attack elsewhere has become more real."[21] And although NATO recently recognized the growing threat posed by China, the American chargé d'affaires at the alliance singled out Russia as "the most immediate threat to the common security of the allies"[22] – a perception that gained credence following Russia's full-scale war on Ukraine.

Estonia's current cybersecurity strategy summarizes the thinking behind the project; it merits extensive quotation. First is the relationship between data systems and modern state functions:

> The preservation of Estonian statehood means increasingly not only defending Estonian territory but also maintenance of digital assets. The digital assets that require protection the most are the basic data the state has on citizens, the territory of the state and legislative drafting – in other words, databases of critical importance. If critical data for the state are modified in unauthorized fashion or destroyed, there is a risk that the state cannot manage its principal duties . . .

And then the corollary point about the state's online preservation abroad:

> Outside Estonian territory, a network of data embassies will be developed, and from there applications and databases could be activated. Both in the case of government cloud and the data embassy solution, high availability is ensured based on the principle that the data stored there can be used and the services operated in real time. That means that if Estonian data centres become inoperable for any reason, the state can provide critical services remotely via the data embassy's technical solution.[23]

Against the backdrop of intensifying security threats in both physical space and cyberspace, especially along the periphery of a newly expansionist Russia, the remainder of this chapter asks: What possible advantages do Estonian data embassies provide for state continuity during a major security crisis, such as a large-scale military invasion, and how do these advantages compare with conventional means of state security? In answering this question, the analysis explores some of the doctrinal, institutional, legal, and diplomatic prerequisites for the success of data embassies in their core function of providing digital continuity to the Estonian state. The study also explores the broader implications of data embassies for understandings of sovereignty and state survival within political theory and international relations. Although the focus of the analysis is on a military invasion scenario, the benefits of digital continuity arising from functional data embassies also apply to other security crises, such as a major cyberattack, an inadvertent technological breakdown, or a natural disaster that disrupts the operations of government data systems. Overall, these scenarios resonate with pressing concerns about the survivability of modern state functions under conditions of deep technological dependence: for example, the U.S. Senate security chief's fear that foreign hackers could "really cripple the government's ability to function by locking down cyber communications networks."[24]

The notion of the state's continuity on a foreign cloud challenges the theoretical dogma of the state's territorial nature. Political thinkers have long conceived of sovereignty on geographic terms: they define it as the government's *indivisible* ability to control a defined physical space and to manage the activities and relations of a population residing within it.[25] "[A] divided sovereignty is logically absurd and politically unfeasible," wrote political theorist Hans Morgenthau, echoing the earlier views of Jean-Jacques Rousseau and Immanuel Kant. "[T]wo or more entities – persons, groups of persons, or agencies – cannot be sovereign within the same time and space."[26] Indeed, some political theorists believe that the attachment of the state to physical terrain is rooted in biological evolution: humans are "soft-wired" to behave territorially.[27]

The implications of the data embassies project challenge this dogma. If they function correctly, they would partly sever the traditional reliance of sovereignty on the condition of territoriality that has defined the essence of the modern state. In principle, data embassies enable a *divisible* form of sovereignty, one that does not rely strictly on the exclusive control of a physical territory, even if it is contested between a remotely located government that has the native population's broad support and the invading nation's authorities which do not. In this way, the project could enable a new form of sovereignty that is not temporally or spatially bound to land.

These arguments have two important caveats. First, only a limited number of government functions can plausibly survive in a remote cloud. The list of endurable functions is, in the case of Estonia, higher than in most other nations, owing to the country's high level of dependence on digital methods of government. But the arguments of this analysis apply to other digitally advanced states such as Denmark, South Korea, Australia, and Britain.[28] And, as the periods of national lockdown during the Covid-19 pandemic showed, the necessity for government to be able to deliver essential services to the population remotely has grown.[29]

Yet, even under optimal conditions, digital continuity via data embassies cannot completely replace the territorial state. Data embassies have the potential to prolong the life, legitimacy, and activities of the state – for example, by storing data in order to restore the pre-crisis situation – but digital continuity alone cannot last forever. And however long it lasts, it will always be partial. Virtual sovereignty does not equate to physical sovereignty. Some state functions require physical interactions between the state and its citizens – that is, they are properly indivisible. Importantly, in all nations that offer them, the issuance of eIDs requires by law a physical interaction between the issuing authorities and the citizen.[30]

Second, although data embassies promise to relax the traditional reliance of state sovereignty on territorial integrity, they also create new requirements of *virtual* integrity – the security of information spaces that we discussed in Chapter 7. The requirements of virtual integrity and territorial integrity might overlap in practice. How, for example, can officials protect citizens' interactions with data embassy services if the citizens' method of access to the Internet is restricted by, or under the supervision of, an occupying force?

DATA EMBASSIES: CONCEPTS AND ORIGINS

The data embassies idea first emerged in Estonia during the Fukushima nuclear disaster in March 2011. "We observed that Japan's public administration lost important data records as a result of the explosion at a nuclear power plant caused by the earthquake," recalled Ilves. "We realized that if you are a country located in a seismically active region, or in a bad geopolitical neighborhood, then you want to have backup servers for your vital governmental data somewhere abroad. Geographically large countries such as the United States or Russia can probably back up their systems sufficiently within their own territory. But a small country like Estonia has to look elsewhere."[31]

Two years later, the Estonian government formally introduced the data embassies initiative.[32] Until then, Estonian officials had backed up important state information in a static form on CD-ROMs stored in Estonian legations abroad. The new initiative was far more ambitious and complex: it proposed storing data dynamically so that it could be accessed and used in the live provision of public services.[33] Or in the words of Estonia's former ambassador for cyber diplomacy Heli Tiirmaa-Klaar: "Essential databases, such as e-health, population registries, ownership structures, banking data and government data are duplicated in real-time to a server in another European country."[34]

The first step in exploring the security implications of data embassies is to define their meaning and their place within the policy landscape, specifically within the Estonian Government Cloud.[35] This section proposes a conceptual framework that both captures and distinguishes the variety of existing usages of the term "government cloud."

Some confusion surrounds its meaning. The term features prominently in policy and research documents, yet its usage across them is inconsistent. Current naming conventions present three problems. First, the label applies not only to the Estonian Government Cloud – the diverse environment of cloud services hosting data registries and services – but also to one of its sub-components: the Government Cloud, which comprises computer servers under strict government control. Thus, existing policy conventions conflate a narrow and a broad conception of the government cloud under a single label.[36] Second, a Microsoft report commissioned by the Estonian government refers to the Public Cloud, which operates on private company servers, as "virtual data embassies."[37] Yet, according to other definitions, data embassies reside entirely within government-controlled servers.[38] Third, according to some observers, the term "data embassies" is itself problematic, because it is sometimes used as a "catchword" to capture "essentially what is a government cloud." This observation reveals confusion about the relationship of data embassies to the broader government cloud system.[39]

Let us therefore define and clarify Estonia's government cloud initiative, of which data embassies are a central part. An important next step in the process of conceptual clarification is to relabel the Estonian Government Cloud as the *Estonian National Cloud* (ENC). Its chief purpose is to provide e-services to Estonian citizens as well as to back up and reinforce the data and servers on which these services rely. According to Taavi Kotka and Innar Liiv, "The main reason for cloud hosting was the need for flexible server resource management and the availability of sufficient performance capacity."[40] The advantage of this proposed term relative to the official label is that it is agnostic about the question of whether data servers are run by the government or by the private sector, or whether they are domestic or foreign-based – distinctions that will matter later in this analysis. The ENC has three main components: the government cloud; public cloud; and data embassies. All entail the use of distributed Internet-based computing – but in different ways, to different extents, and for different purposes.

As the label implies, the Government Cloud consists of computer servers operated by the government. It resides entirely within Estonian soil. Its main purpose is to maintain data backups and public services within national borders. Despite its label, which suggests a primary or even exclusive government role, the Government Cloud is a partnership among the public and private sectors. The Estonian government does not have the capacity to build cloud servers itself; it relies on the private sector's hardware and technical assistance in establishing and running them. The government obtains such assistance via a public procurement procedure. In 2016, for example, it signed a contract with a consortium of private firms (Ericsson, Telia, EMC/Dell, Cybernetica, and OpenNode) to establish a pilot of the Government Cloud by the end of the year.[41] Nevertheless, the government operates the servers and owns all data within them.

Notwithstanding its label, the Public Cloud consists of data centers operated by private companies, such as Amazon, located almost entirely abroad. Or else the data are stored locally but often transit via foreign jurisdictions. At present, private sector servers do not host important state data registries or services. Rather, the Public Cloud handles non-sensitive data, such as the "smart roads" data of the Tark Tee service, which provides Estonian drivers live information about road conditions – hence the name "public" cloud, because it contains data that are already publicly available.[42] As we saw, Microsoft refers to the Public Cloud as "virtual data embassies." This analysis avoids the term, because the notion of data embassies by definition already implies a "virtual" character.

Data embassies are distinct to the preceding two components of the Estonian National Cloud. They differ from the Government Cloud because they reside on foreign soil. They are distinct to the Public Cloud because they could house sensitive information and are designed to operate important government services. What most distinguishes the project is the objective of guaranteeing the state's digital continuity "no matter what."[43] In addition to backing up official data, data embassies seek to provide assurances of data integrity ("non-repudiation")[44] and, more fundamentally, to ensure the continuity of online government services.[45]

These goals are novel and boldly ambitious. Almost no other country has pursued them.[46] True, other governments also back up data in storage centers, some of which might reside abroad. For example, the Australian and British national archives have digital continuity policies in place. The British government actively uses public cloud infrastructure.[47] But the Estonian project goes much further, because, in a fully developed scenario, "it could keep the government running without the physical state."[48] Or as the *Digital Agenda 2020* envisages, the purposes of data embassies is to create data environments "in safe third party countries to act as data embassies, offshore protection to secure public data in the event of a national emergency."[49]

Beyond this broad specification, it is not always clear how, exactly, data embassies will function or who will operate them. For the purposes of exposition, therefore, it is important to distinguish three varieties of data embassy. The first are the *Extraterritorial Data Embassies* (EDEs) – backup servers located within Estonian embassy buildings that, in a national invasion scenario, would remain the property of the exiled government in those states which did not formally recognize the *de jure* government's loss of sovereignty. The second concerns *Allied Data Embassies* (ADEs) – backup servers located within the territory of a friendly foreign country but outside of the perimeter of Estonian legations and beyond Estonian officials' physical control.[50] *Private Data Embassies* (PDEs) represent a third variety – an extension of the Public Cloud to cover the hosting of sensitive data registries and essential public services in foreign-based computer servers that are owned and operated by private firms. Microsoft, for instance, noted that the official website of the Estonian President and the State Gazette (Riigi Teataja), which officially records new laws, could be "migrated and hosted on the Microsoft Azure cloud computing platform."[51] For this reason, PDEs may also be regarded as an overlapping component of the Public Cloud, which would thereby perform fundamentally new functions. To be clear, they do not fit within the government's original data embassies concept; their inclusion here represents a stretching of the concept. But the expansion of the meaning of data embassies in this way might be important in some scenarios of national emergency.[52]

Based on interviews with Estonian officials, AEDs are the project's main original component.[53] Kotka and Liiv elaborate on this important point: "The goal is to procure resources under bilateral agreements from the Government Clouds of states that are friendly to Estonia." The countries that host data embassies must share Estonia's fundamental political values. They continue: "The Estonian state would sign a bilateral treaty, under which Estonia will rent special floor space or an enclosed room in an existing datacenter that has been constructed and operates according to necessary standards. The corresponding perimeter would be physically separated, equipped with security devices in order to ensure that the Estonian state maintains complete control over the servers within that agreed-upon perimeter. Similarly to a physical embassy, Estonian jurisdiction would be applicable within that established perimeter, and it would have all the same provisions (including immunity) as a physical embassy or an ambassadorial residence."[54]

Under current plans, data embassies would house a number of critical data registries and online services. The list of registries identified for inclusion is diverse and consists of the following:[55] State Budget Information System (Riigikassa Infosüsteem or "e-Treasury"), Registry of Taxable Persons (Maksekohuslaste register), Social Security Register (Pensionikindlustuse register), e-File Registry (e-toimik), e-Land Register (e-Kinnistusraamat), e-Business Register (e-Äriregister), State Gazette (Riigi Teataja), Population Register (Rahvastikuregister), Identity Documents Database (Isikut tõendavate dokumentide register – UUSIS), and Land Cadastre (Maakataster) – an impressive collection of vital government registries. Officials are also weighing the possibility of backing up essential public services to the cloud. The services targeted for inclusion in the project have not been identified, but they could include online voting or tax filing. The main advantage of data embassies in this regard is *scalability*: for example, if tax collection servers go down, as they sometimes do during periods of high demand such as a national lockdown, the services can switch to foreign servers to buttress capacity.[56]

Overall, the data embassies project represents a complex constellation of actors that includes mostly public, but also private, players and largely foreign, but also national, authorities. Some of the backup servers will be located within physical Estonian embassies. Others will reside on the territory of allied nations. Still others might one day (although the government did not originally plan this contingency) exist in privately owned servers located abroad. All data embassies will rely for their proper functioning on basic infrastructure and services, such as power supply and security details, provided directly or indirectly by the hosting nation.

Here, one transforming potential of data embassies appears. Their complex agent constellation radically alters the very notion of an "embassy." EDEs mean that traditional embassies would now have important data provision and direct governing functions. ADEs allow for the possibility of these functions no longer being the strict purview of accredited diplomats. And perhaps most fundamentally, the notion of PDEs implies that discharging some state functions might no longer involve the use of publicly owned buildings and resources – not even those of the parent government.

The data embassies project is presently undergoing implementation. Estonia's *Cyber Security Strategy, 2014–2017* stipulated that all essential state registers must be constantly updated and mapped as well as having mirror and backup alternatives abroad.[57] Faithful to this objective, in 2019 the government launched the world's first data embassy within a high-security data center in Luxembourg.[58] Undersecretary for Digital Development Siim Sikkut explained the choice: "Luxembourg is located in Europe, similarly to Estonia, and should a pan-European crisis situation occur, a data embassy in another country would provide additional security for the continuity of our digital services."[59] Previously, the only means of data backup in Estonian embassies was static that is, by the physical transportation of data stored in magnetic tapes. No Estonian embassy location currently has the necessary infrastructure to host data embassies. At the same time, the government is procuring space from, and negotiating arrangements with, foreign governments to situate ADEs on their soil.[60] In all, the possible network of data embassies includes locations in nations that share the values and understanding of the data embassies concept – including its legal, diplomatic, and technological requirements. Beyond Luxembourg, such locations might include London, Berlin, Ottawa, New York, São Paulo, Cape Town, Tokyo, and Sydney.[61]

DIGITAL CONTINUITY IN A NATIONAL EMERGENCY

In a nation where cyberspace permeates government functions so completely as in Estonia, the protection of data centers and services is an essential priority of national security policy. The Estonian government no longer stores much government information on paper – a trend that other governments are following.[62] This makes the security and integrity of virtual registries vital. It means that digital continuity is not merely about preserving the state's information spaces; it is also about preserving the state *itself*.

The provision of digital and therefore state continuity is different to protecting the private sector's essential computer systems – a task that falls ultimately on the private sector, although government agencies such as computer emergency response teams (CERTs) can provide guidance in the midst of cyber incidents.[63] But because it entails privately owned and operated systems, the range of activity that the government may legitimately pursue is limited. By contrast, although authorities can turn to the private sector for assistance, the scope for government action in the provision of state continuity is naturally supreme. In other words, the provision of state continuity is essentially a government function. This section examines the benefits and limitations of data embassies in providing continuity during the gravest scenario of national emergency: a foreign military occupation.

Like other countries situated along Russia's western perimeter, Estonia's security situation is in the midst of disruption. During much of the thirty years since the country's return to independence in 1991, its geopolitical position seemed secure. In the 1990s, the nation rebuilt its military almost from scratch. It has trained 60,000 reserve troops, 21,000 of them at a high level of readiness.[64] In 2004, it acceded into both NATO and the European Union; the one organization provides a blanket guarantee of protection against armed attack, the other an institutional expression of its place in the Western political firmament. Alliance partners have reinforced their collective defense pledge by deploying, on a rotational basis, troops and equipment on Estonian soil.[65]

Recent developments have seriously eroded this sense of security. As noted above, in February 2014, Russia, the former occupier – with which Estonia shares about three hundred kilometers of border – invaded and annexed Ukraine's Crimean Peninsula, an action that the International Criminal Court in The Hague formally recognized as military occupation.[66] And eight years later, Russia expanded its war in Ukraine, reigning terror (literally from rocket attacks) on the civilian population throughout the country. Russia's aggression was not an isolated event. It represented the intensification of a pattern of interventionist and expansionist activity that began, in fact, in Estonia, with the cyberattacks of 2007 and which continued in the land invasion of Georgia the following year. "We experienced this conflict in 2008 and at the time the world did not pay enough attention," remarked Georgian Prime Minister Irakli Garibashvili about the Ukrainian invasion.[67] At the time, Estonian President Toomas Hendrik Ilves regarded a similar invasion of Estonia as "inconceivable" – after all, Estonia enjoyed NATO's protection, whereas Georgia did not.[68] Yet, the alliance's continuous troop deployments signal that leaders are less sanguine about the firmness of Estonia's territorial integrity than their public statements aver.

Therein lies a paradox of deterrence logic: a move to bolster defenses seeks to increase the deterrent factor even as it signals a recognition of its past weakness. Some observers, indeed, have questioned whether NATO's troop deployment – a small force against Russia's million-strong army – is sufficient to deter the adversary. Estonian and Baltic leaders have consistently sought a greater allied troop presence in their countries. "Russia's military planners are well aware that even a brigade-sized allied unit in every Baltic country would be insufficient for any attack against Russia," opined Mikk Marran of Estonia's Information Board, even as he described such a scenario as "very unlikely."[69] The 2016 election as president of the United States of Donald Trump, who depicted NATO as "obsolete," further undermined confidence in his country's commitment to collective defense.[70] Joe Biden's arrival in the White House in January 2021 has not fully restored European confidence in America's defense commitment.[71] Concerns have also grown about the reliability in a crisis of some European allies whose leaders (such as Hungary's Viktor Orbán) have hewed a softer line towards Putin. Formal activation of the alliance's Article 5 collective defense provision requires unanimity among the allies; it takes but one of them quavering at Putin's retaliations or seeking his inducements to veto the action.

The analysis in this chapter accepts the premise that a Russian seizure of Estonian territory is in the present circumstances unlikely (even if the risk has notably grown). At the same time, it recognizes such a scenario as sufficiently plausible to merit serious analytical attention.

But a seizure of what kind and to what extent? The answer to this question affects the potential of data embassies to provide state continuity. This study uses as a baseline scenario a "wargaming" analysis conducted by the RAND Corporation in 2014 and 2015. According to this report, a combined NATO and local force could not currently repel a Russian military invasion. Military geography and the short distances of the theater both favor the invader. Across multiple test scenarios, the invading forces reached the capital city Tallinn in no more than sixty hours. The report found that a force of seven brigades could forestall the Russian advance; but as we saw, such a large NATO deployment is not in prospect. Having thus eliminated the majority of the defending military forces and taken the capital city, occupation of the remainder of the country would not present serious challenges, especially if the invader combined the use of motorized and mechanized units (the main thrust of attack from the northeast) with airborne insertions and naval landings along Estonia's flat western coast.[72]

The invasion and occupation scenario presupposes, moreover, the existence of a legitimate government in exile which, after a brief period of relocation to a friendly or neutral territory willing to receive it, retains access to essential data registries and some public services remotely via data embassy cloud systems.

In such invasion circumstances, data embassies could provide three main advantages to the defenders. The first advantage is an ability to lessen the financial impact of the invasion on the native population in the occupied territory. International law imposes restrictions on the scope of action of occupying forces. As Adam Roberts has explained, international humanitarian law (traditionally known as *jus in bello*) stipulates that the occupying power should respect the prevailing legal and economic arrangements within the occupied territory. This "conservationist principle," however, "stands in potential conflict with the transformative goals of certain occupations"[73] – such as an annexationist land grab that alters the constitutional status of the territory in question. Regardless of the occupiers' intentions, any population under foreign military occupation will suffer some form of economic and social hardship: for example, severe limitations on cash withdrawals at banks and market dislocations arising from the introduction of a new currency (e.g. a change of legal tender from the euro to the Russian ruble).[74] Data embassies could avoid or defray these costs by preserving the local population's ability to transact business and other payments. A functional Social Security Register would enable pensioners to continue to receive retirement benefits. The e-File Registry (e-to-imik) would enable procedural parties and their representatives to submit electronic documents and evidence to the courts, some of which might continue to function in exile or in enclaves of resistance. The parties might even be able to observe the progress of the proceedings related to them by remote video link.[75]

The maintenance of the most important economic activity, namely, personal and commercial payments, would rely on the operations of PDEs run by financial institutions. The government's original data embassies project, however, does not envisage such a system. The four largest banks in Estonia, which together hold 85 percent of the market share,[76] might strenuously resist its creation, because the invading nation – a major global power – would probably impose costs on both the parent company and the parent government of the banking PDE. Among the large banks, only one, Danske Bank, is headquartered in a NATO member state (others are based in neutral Sweden and Finland, which might soon join the alliance) and thus could be open to the concept of operating a PDE under occupation. But the company represents only 8 percent of banking activity in Estonia. Were a banking PDE to function, however, it could significantly reduce the economic and commercial impact of the occupation among the local population, which already relies on online banking services for the vast majority of financial transactions.[77] Coupled with the Social Security, Land, and Business Registers, a functional banking PDE would enable the native population to circumvent many of the economic controls and rent-seeking activities of the foreign powers. Furthermore, if the tax-filing system – which collects 95 percent of tax declarations in Estonia – were to continue to operate through an Allied or an Extraterritorial Data Embassy, then the government in exile would be able to levy taxes, thereby acquiring financial resources for itself while simultaneously depriving them to the adversary.

A second possible advantage of data embassies involves the native population's sentiments. In what will be a hostile popular environment, the invading power will seek to sever communications links between the native population and the government in exile as well as the outside world. The invader will not want information about the occupation's perceived illegitimacy or about war crimes or human-rights abuses of their system of political control to reach the outside world. The government, by contrast, will have much to gain by demonstrating to the world that it continues to command political legitimacy at home.

The preservation of political legitimacy will depend on the government's ability to construct a credible narrative of popular support by the means of plebiscitary democracy. In this regard, data embassies could enable the government to tally the votes of the population on important questions such as a referendum on the transference of powers to the exiled government or on the illegitimacy of the occupation itself – whose officials, enlisting the support of local satraps, could seek to fake in a sham vote. Estonia's Referendum Act stipulates that referendums must be "free, general, uniform, and direct."[78] Paper balloting would not likely be available in an extreme military situation. But the law provides for the vote to be achieved electronically among voters who request an e-voting card. The processing of this request requires access to the Population Register, one of the vital registries that the government is backing up abroad.[79] The vote to be sure would face numerous practical obstacles. Questions might arise about its fairness, about the ability of all citizens to participate, about restrictions on campaigning, or about the ability of the parliament (Riigikogu) to convoke the vote in the first place – all of which would require amendments in extant law to allow for special exclusions during a declared emergency.

Data embassies, in short, could be a powerful instrument to counter intense information warfare in the midst of foreign subjugation. Beyond the satisfaction of a legally binding mandate to continue its operations abroad, the result of a referendum – which independent observers could verify by accessing voting records stored in servers abroad – would enable the exiled government to counter the fabrication of alternative perceptions seeking to legitimize the occupation.

A third benefit concerns the more practical aspects of state continuity: the ability to achieve a sovereign restoration at lower cost than would be the case only with paper records. During the nationalization process of Soviet rule that began in July 1940, the occupying power transferred nearly 90 percent of Estonian industrial and transportation assets to centralized Soviet ownership. The industrial sector came under the oversight of the People's Commissariats of Light Industry and Local Industry. Commercial nationalization occurred more gradually, but the state captured some large enterprises outright. That same summer, the real estate market, too, fell under state control. By October, all buildings larger than 220 m² in the cities (170 m² elsewhere) were nationalized without compensation[80] – for that was the purpose: to dispossess the bourgeoisie rascals of their illegitimate property! The occupiers implemented a wholesale transfer of private property on paper.

Data embassies offer a foundation on which to restore occupation economic ownership. The Business and Land Registers in particular would play an important role in this function. True, some property transfers conducted during the occupation could be the subject of legitimate business; life, after all, must continue even in instances where business cannot be transacted via data embassies. But these registries would provide a basis to challenge illegal seizures of property by the occupying power or by irregular troops – a common problem during a military incursion that produces a temporary breakdown in local law and order.

Attainment of the above advantages specifically, and the viability of the state's digital continuity generally, would depend on a number of technical conditions being met but which can be difficult to satisfy in case of an extreme national emergency. One condition is the security of the foreign-based data servers on which registries and public services reside. Take, for example, the Land Registry. Its essential information exists in a database server that records facts about property sales and uses, and in a file server that logs these transactions in the form of a static, verifiable record. These servers are housed in a physical layer of machines that are themselves susceptible to hacking and data-integrity attacks.

Another technical requirement is security of the remote communications between Estonian citizens and the data embassy servers. The use of cyberattacks to block Internet traffic in the data embassies' hosting nation would be technically difficult.[81] It might also impose political and diplomatic costs on the attacker, provided that attribution of the attacker's identity and location – not always an easy task – is possible to a strong degree of certainty.[82] Blocking traffic in the occupied territories would be far easier to achieve. For the native population, Internet connections in the presence of the enemy might not be available or secure. The adversary, moreover, could attack the application layer that connects end users to the data embassy file and database servers. If this layer is compromised, then the information traveling between data embassies and users could be blocked or, worse, corrupted, thereby defeating the project's very purpose. This application layer might reside in personal computing and other devices. It is located in the occupied territory; that is, beyond the ability of the data embassy providers to control it directly. A further complication is that access to the servers relies fundamentally on the eID card, the system of digital and mobile identification used by more than 90 percent of the population.[83] Estonia's banking laws allow citizens to open bank accounts via online interviews.[84] But as we saw, the government does not plan to issue ID cards online. Thus, under current plans, data embassies would become inaccessible to citizens if the occupier forced them to relinquish their physical ID cards, or if the cards simply ceased to function once their in-built period of validity expired.[85] In these cases, exiled authorities would have little or no means to reissue eIDs to citizens. At most, the data embassies project would have a maximum lifespan of five years, that is, the period of validity of the cards and their digital certificates.[86]

Assuming that the Estonian authorities succeeded in overcoming these obstacles, the data embassies project could positively affect national security, not just by mitigating the political and legal disruption of invasion but also by deterring one. The intense media attention that the data embassies project has attracted might already have raised the deterrence value against attack in the eyes of an adversary that believes in their functional viability. (For this same reason, if the adversary accepts the viability of data embassies but still invades, then it will proactively seek to target their underlying infrastructure during the incursion.) More concretely, data embassies have the effect of altering the cost structure of classical deterrence logic. They reduce the harm that the invader imposes on the defender, while raising the costs of the attacker in mounting the invasion and the costs that the defender imposes on the invader following the attack. The overall effect is to increase the deterrence value against a military occupation.

CHALLENGES FOR LAW AND DIPLOMACY

The data embassies project has potentially profound implications for the theory and principles of the territorial state as well as for established conventions of interstate relations. This section reviews these implications, drawing broader insights for statecraft, and scrutinizes some of the project's main legal and institutional challenges.

Let us begin with the notion of the territorial state: it is established dogma within the theory and practice of modern statecraft. Seventeenth-century English philosopher John Locke gave credence to the notion by basing state sovereignty on citizen ownership rights. Individuals acquire rights to the "common property" of the Earth by laboring it, argued Locke.[87] These property claims are "pre-political": they precede and legitimize the rights of the state, whose authority over a specific terrain is conditional on the state's ability to protect citizens' property – a duty that citizens themselves must consent to place under the state's jurisdiction. Logically and morally, then, the land precedes the state for the same reason that humans precede citizens: it is conditional on natural law, the body of eternal moral principles that apply universally across time and place.

Other political thinkers, notably Immanuel Kant, disagreed with Locke's notion of natural ownership rights, yet they upheld his view that the state played an essential role in protecting and adjudicating citizens' claims to the land.[88] Thus, in both the Lockean and the Kantian theory of the state, the state's existence is inconceivable without a firm attachment to some defined territory. It is by virtue of their habitation within a defined geographic space that citizens belong to a state and fall under its legitimate political authority.

The Estonian data embassies project challenges this dogma: it raises the prospect of continued sovereign rights, authority, and practical functions even in the total absence of territoriality. The project gives rise to the prospect of *divisible sovereignty*, a form of state existence that is not conditional on territorial control. Sovereignty in this sense would be divisible in two ways: it would rely on the competing sovereignty claims of the occupying force that has seized national territory and on the acquiescence of the host nation's government. The necessity for such acquiescence would apply to all three varieties of data embassies. EDEs and ADEs require the consent of the single allied government that hosts the cloud servers. PDEs are more complicated because they would require the consent of the governments of the nation in which the private cloud provider is headquartered, of the nation where its servers are physically located, and of the nations whose jurisdiction the data crosses in traveling between end users in the home nation (or elsewhere) and the servers (more on this below). In principle and in practice, therefore, the data embassies concept represents a partial and temporary transference of indivisible, territorial sovereignty from the home state to the hosting state. On this basis, the divisibility of digital sovereignty would rely on the continued indivisibility of the host's territorially based sovereignty. In judging the viability of the data embassies project, the continuity of the host's own territorial integrity becomes a matter not only of legal but also practical necessity.

Legal and diplomatic challenges also exist. Negotiating the bilateral partnerships that are required to bind the home nation's divisible digital continuity to another nation's indivisible territorial sovereignty has proven complicated. Here, a number of potential problems arise that apply differently to the three types of data embassies explored in this study.

ADEs raise the question of the diplomatic status of data. Can the home nation claim sovereignty rights over packets traveling between end users and foreign-based cloud servers located beyond legations and enjoy the same protections as conventional diplomatic post? The relevant treaty here is the Vienna Convention on Diplomatic Relations. Its provisions apply to official communications between diplomats, or their legations, and their parent governments. It excludes data traffic flowing into non-embassy cloud servers. Nevertheless, the home government might appeal to property rights in claiming "data sovereignty" over ADEs.[89]

The concept of data sovereignty is largely unestablished and untested, however. Property rights ordinarily apply to the physical objects onto which information is written – not the information itself, which is intangible. In some cases, intellectual property rights and data protection laws can provide some basis for data ownership, but the claim will not be failsafe. "Information 'ownership' is a nonlegalistic term commonly used to mean that information 'belongs' to an individual user or organization who administers this information on their own behalf," explained Kristina Irion. "Thus, data sovereignty cannot be derived from property rights."[90] For this reason, ownership rights – and national data sovereignty – would depend on the existence of a bilateral treaty among the home nation and the hosting nation expressly establishing such rights.

A treaty on data sovereignty would represent a major development in the principle's consolidation within the legal and diplomatic firmament of international relations. It may also, however, give impetus to the broader fragmentation of the Internet along traditional lines of sovereignty arising from new "data localization" laws in Europe and Russia following Edward Snowden's revelation in 2013 of mass surveillance programs in the United States.[91]

The Preamble of the bilateral agreement between Estonia and its data embassy host Luxembourg recognizes these legal complications. "[T]his agreement is in the spirit of the Vienna Convention on Diplomatic Relations," it states, but notes that "the Vienna Convention . . . is not sufficient to set a legal framework for the hosting of data and information systems" because the convention does not offer "provisions on the hosting of data."[92] The data's territorial entanglement to another state creates complications for an aspiring attacker. It would have to consider the retaliatory costs not only of capturing or destroying the Estonian data, but also of violating Luxembourg's virtual integrity.

EDEs also face legal obstacles involving the Vienna Convention, but of a smaller nature. Written in the 1950s and 60s, the Convention pre-dates the creation of the ARPANET – the precursor to the modern Internet – by almost a decade and the "social" Internet by about four decades. Its framers did not have digital data in mind; its articles might nevertheless apply. "It is a new precedent in international law, since previously, the Vienna Convention . . . did not include server rooms, data, or intangible assets," explained Tiirmaa-Klaar. "It is something completely new under international law."[93] Article 24 asserts the diplomatic inviolability of "archives and documents of the mission at any time and wherever they may be." Article 1 further specifies that these "archives" include "all the papers, documents, correspondence, books, films, tapes and registers of the consular post, together with the ciphers and codes, the card indexes and any article of furniture intended for their protection and safekeeping." According to Laura Kask, "Taken together, the Vienna Conventions therefore explain that any relevant information is to be protected."[94] But these articles protect data traffic among diplomatic and consular officials and officials in their home governments. They exclude traffic among the diplomatic corps or the parent government and home citizens. Thus, the customary protections of diplomatic pouches might not automatically apply to EDEs. Conceivably, the legations could tag the metadata of outgoing packets as diplomatic mail, but this designation would be difficult to apply to incoming traffic from citizens. Here, too, the way around the problem could be a bilateral treaty ascribing diplomatic protections to all incoming data packets.

The concept of PDEs raises its own set of legal and diplomatic challenges. The most obvious obstacle is the Estonian government's refusal (at the time of writing) to accept the notion of PDEs. The reasons for this resistance are not hard to fathom. Most important, PDEs raise concerns about the ability of the government to impose its sovereignty over data transiting through or residing in private clouds based in foreign jurisdictions. The Microsoft report addressed this concern. It contended that governments should "respect the integrity and sovereignty of another country's data in the cloud as it would its physical territory."[95] Interestingly, this observation equates the security of data centers to the security of physical territory – an "equivalence" doctrine that prevailing legal and diplomatic conventions do not recognize. A customized private contract between the parties could specify rights and obligations of equivalence. But data sovereignty could never rest entirely on a commercial treaty, because its applicability would rely on specific conditions (e.g. service-level agreements) and would be at all times subject to the jurisdiction of the hosting nation's courts. The tendency of data in some private cloud systems (think of the "Amazon Drive" or "Microsoft Azure" clouds) to migrate across multiple jurisdictions compounds this problem. According to whose laws and by which technical standards will data protection be ensured? Even if clear jurisdictional lines can be agreed, data protection standards might vary – at times significantly – across them. Overall, the PDE framework presents a complex agent setup involving at least four sets of relevant players: (a) the home nation authorities (in our scenario, in exile); (b) the private cloud service provider (a foreign-based company); (c) the government(s) of the nation(s) in which the cloud servers physically reside; and (d) the government of the nation (if different from c) in which the cloud provider is legally headquartered.

Despite these legal complexities, the PDE concept has its attractions. The private cloud providers are likely to enjoy ample experience in securing data clouds. Because the providers typically work with diverse clients, they face commercial incentives to take data integrity and security very seriously indeed. By contrast, governments are newer to the cloud environment; they have relatively less time, experience, resources, and expertise to secure it.

Yet, it is not clear where one should legitimately draw the line of government control over the cloud. If the government cannot trust private cloud servers to store potentially sensitive data, why should it trust private ISPs to transfer them? Should the government develop its own physical infrastructure of cables and routers, as authoritarian countries such as China do?[96] Possibly, advances in cryptography enabling greater security at the application and data layers will convince the Estonian government to entertain the notion of "Software as a Service" in the operation of PDEs.[97] (By relinquishing government control of the application, data, and other layers to the private sector, the implementation of PDEs would represent a shift from the left to the right of Table 2 below.) For the time being, however, the government's present reluctance to consider this notion dictates that Tallinn will have to keep its most sensitive data and functions backed up in less technologically capable, and possibly less secure, ADEs and EDEs.

Another problem – the threat of espionage – affects all data embassy variants. International law does not prohibit intelligence collection by electronic or other means. Thus, although some legal protections could apply to data embassy information *in situ*, these protections would cease when the information was in

Table 2. Cloud Service Models

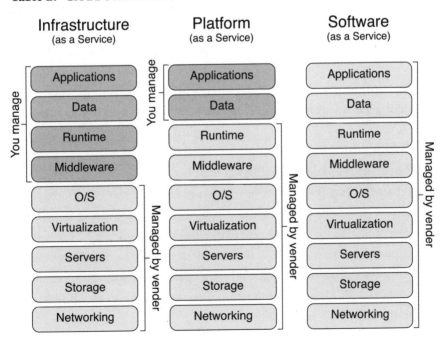

transit outside of the host nation's jurisdiction – and even then the host could decide to intercept, inspect, or impede data traffic on the grounds of national security or local law enforcement. The U.S. government, for instance, routinely issues subpoenas ("National Security Letters") under the Patriot Act to compel private cloud providers to relinquish the data of foreign clients.[98] Often, the clients of the private cloud providers do not know of the investigation and the existence of subpoenas targeting their data.

THE SURVIVAL OF THE TECHNOLOGICAL STATE

Perhaps in no other nation do the functions of state and society depend so intimately on computer technology as in Estonia – the frontrunner of the current cyber revolution. The advanced state of the Estonian e-society means that the preservation of government cloud systems on which essential registries and public services depend is a matter of national security importance. On this basis, the Estonian government is implementing a data embassies project whose purpose is to back up the functions of the Government Cloud in the event that they become unserviceable, such as during a major cyberattack or a technological breakdown. Scholars and analysts have begun to explore the potential benefits of data embassies in achieving this purpose. This chapter has pursued a related but more expansive line of thinking, one that ascribes to data embassies a mission more ambitious than their adherents perhaps imputed: the continuity of the state itself during a foreign occupation. The chief motive in considering this question is the growing geopolitical threat against Estonia and other formerly captive nations of Russia against the backdrop of its invasion and occupation of parts of Ukraine.

What conclusions do the findings of this chapter allow? Two are important. One is that the data embassies project offers notable benefits to national security against the threat of foreign occupation. Data embassies can enable a government in exile (or of resistance) to diminish the invading force's economic impact on the native population, to demonstrate the government's continued support among the native population while challenging the occupation government's legitimacy, and to lessen the costs of state restoration following the resumption of full sovereignty.

Insofar as data embassies provide the government new means of sustaining moral and functional legitimacy, while raising the enemy's costs of aggression, they increase the deterrence value against such aggression in the first place. Thus, the successful implementation of data embassies lowers the chances that the government will ever have to activate them. While the focus of this analysis has been on a military occupation scenario, the benefits of digital continuity also apply to other security crises involving a disruption of government cloud systems.

The second conclusion concerns the very meaning of the modern state: data embassies enable new forms of sovereignty that are not strictly reliant on territoriality as conceived by classical political thinkers such as Locke and Kant. If, in the Estonian context, digital continuity equates to state continuity, then digital continuity provides grounds for a divisible form of sovereign existence on the cloud – one that could survive, for a time at least, under extreme conditions of foreign military repression.

These findings have implications for our understanding of the relationship between technological dependence and national security. Many analysts rightly regard the expansion of cyberspace into the core functions of government and society as a growing source of risk to national security. They warn of serious, possibly unknown, threats to intelligence assets, commercial interests, industrial infrastructures, and even the functionality of military weapons systems.[99] An old remark by former U.S. Director of Central Intelligence George Tenet conveys the anguish of defense planners: "We have built our future upon a capability we have not learned how to protect."[100]

Data embassies suggest the possibility of a reverse relationship: the potential for innovations in cyberspace to bolster deterrence by denial against both a crippling cyberattack and a military invasion, thereby augmenting national security. Ordinarily, the main motives behind the integration of state functions into the cloud are efficiency and convenience in public administration, imperatives which sometimes trump security concerns. Data embassies, by contrast, seek to enhance national security and defense. Herein lies another splendid paradox: data embassies can give impetus to the territorial state's gradual demise (about which political thinkers have long warned)[101] but in a way that strengthens rather than weakens the state.

The above benefits and implications of data embassies for national security and state survival are as yet untested. The project's implementation continues to face legal, diplomatic, and institutional challenges. The concept of ADEs raises unresolved questions about the diplomatic status of data. EDEs invoke legal conundrums about "digital" diplomatic pouches that officials struggle to fit into existing conventions. PDEs, which the Estonian government does not support but which offer unique security benefits, involve a complex arrangement of public and private actors that raises jurisdictional complications.

New concepts and research are required to make sense of these challenges. Political theorists must adjust their notions of sovereignty to grasp the meaning of the state in the era of cyberspace. Legal scholars are in need of new instruments to support the doctrine of data sovereignty in a world in which data intangibles are increasingly more important than physical assets. Students of international relations require new frameworks of diplomacy to adapt statecraft to the peculiarities of a world in which states and citizens increasingly conduct their affairs, domestic and foreign, through a medium that shatters geographical and jurisdictional constraints. These conundrums are no longer abstract: data embassies are already functional. And not just Estonia's. Borrowing from Tallinn's experiment, in July 2021 the government of Monaco established an "e-embassy" on Luxembourg soil, which holds a twin copy of Monaco's government cloud system.[102] The expansion of the technological state into the realm of "cloud diplomacy" will continue to prove the tendency of modern technology to move faster than the ability of law and theory to adapt to it.

10
CONCLUSION
A Partial Restoration of Peace

Some readers may misinterpret the purpose of this book. It does not provide a manual on the principles of rivalry and conflict in cyberspace. Nor is it a playbook to guide decisionmakers on how to seize strategic gains. True, some elements of the work provide a basis for such investigations. Its main aim, however, is to study problems in the prevention and reduction of conflict – not its prosecution. It is to correct flaws in the organization of the strategic defense rather than to embolden impatient hawks spoiling for the strategic offense. The value system of Western democratic societies and their model of open information spaces dictate a mainly defensive posture. Whether to widen the strategic horizon into offensive action, and how to implement it without relinquishing basic values, are questions for other works to explore.

The implications of cyber space for the nature of force and conflict was a central theme of the book. Many a strategist has looked for them in the transformation of warfare; others in interstate conquest or coercion. Not finding substantial implications there, skeptics have declared the cyber revolution stillborn. But they look in the wrong places: they give the right answers to the wrong questions. If one reduces the cyber revolution to traditionalists' cherished criteria of war fighting, conquest and coercion then one will fail to see it.

The flaw of this perception calls forth what has been written long ago and repeated in these pages. The effects of virtual weapons on military affairs is not their main contribution; rather, their true potential is in expanding the range of strategic competition *between* the conditions of war and peace.[1] The cyber revolution plays out not in the battlefield but in the battle over the functions of machines and the minds of humans.

Virtual weapons can coerce state behavior only with difficulty. And they cannot seize or retain territory. Yet because some challenger states still crave it, war continues to mar international politics. Flashes of raw power are especially relevant in the relations among, on the one side, powerful nations such as Russia and, on the other, smaller nations on their periphery, such as Ukraine, which rejected subservience to the former masters. In the direct relations among the large (and especially nuclear) powers themselves, war remains – so far – where it was during the last seven decades: absent.

What is truly distinctive about the current era, then, is not the silencing of guns among large nations but the end of peace in a growing number of neighborhoods that have long been free from war.

Life in the cyber domain spares its inhabitants the horrors of war but exposes them to a growing problem: disruption and weakening from within by intruders acting from afar. Penetrated by malicious code, pierced by pernicious information fanning division, open societies are having to learn that there are aspects of security which are not taught in the military academies and forms of conflict that are not won on the battlefield. What has emerged instead is a new version of political debilitation: it primarily works not by altering state behavior but by weakening it. The central idea is that the weakening of policy can deliver some of the effects of changing it, while avoiding the repercussions of armed force and the costs of coercion. And even if cyber activity does not achieve strategic effect, it can still harm vital security and economic interests on a scale that political leaders will pay a price for not reducing.

Behind all of the difficult questions of how to secure cyberspace against intensifying conflict is the adaptation of strategy to its new modes. Nations that fail to master the technological revolution of their times will suffer the consequences of competitors' superior maneuvers. Scratch the surface of the major military blunders in history and you are likely to find a bad theory of what was then an emerging technology.

We saw in Chapter 1 how ruinous the consequences of obsolete policy dogmas in conditions of technological transformation can be. Because of their inability to grasp the strategic implications of submarine warfare, the Royal Navy suffered stunning defeats at the start of the First World War. A single invention rendered obsolescent a magnificent fighting force that, for centuries, had ruled the world's sea lanes. In the next World War, an invention in the skies – the strategic bomber – nearly caused Britain's capitulation to Nazi Germany. The integration of a countervailing invention – radar – into a sophisticated air defense system turned the tide of the conflict against the mighty aggressor. In the same war, having failed for a period of two decades to interpret correctly the military implications of the tank, French security planners paid the ultimate penalty: their country's rapid conquest by a foe armed with superior doctrine to guide the use of an emergent weapon. In just six weeks, a supposedly preeminent France succumbed to mechanized invaders whose country a generation earlier the defenders had vanquished. How quickly technological and doctrinal developments can combine to reshuffle the table of international power! Perhaps nowhere else was the divorce between the perception and the reality of martial greatness so wide as in Paris in the spring of 1940.

These and other failures in strategic adaptation to technological revolution reveal a recurrent pattern. The perhaps inevitable temptation of security planners facing urgent pressures for action in a crisis is to escape the uncertainties of new threats by imposing upon them familiar concepts. The urge for decisive action combined with technological intricacies condemn officials to substitute creativity with mental reflex. Arsenals expand beyond the limits of theory to clarify their implications. Reality moves faster than the ability to grasp it. The science of certainty overtakes the art of interpretation. Conditions arise for a shock strategic reversal. Outcomes happen that no one would believe possible had they not occurred.

The current epoch of technological change presents such a danger to Western and democratic nations. It is an irony that defines our times: the nations most adept at harnessing cyberspace for economic gain, the ones who invented the related technologies and continue to perfect them, are also the societies most exposed by its vulnerabilities.

Chapter 2 reviewed a central manifestation of this problem: the limitations of Western nations' commitment to operate within the confines of their liberal view of international order. The Western approach to cyber conflict prevention – cyber legalism – prioritizes law and norms of restraint in interstate relations. The effect of norm construction so far has not been to compel large adversaries to renounce attacks, however. How could it if they reject the liberal interpretation of law and no higher authority exists to force it upon them? Instead, the legalistic approach has allowed adversaries to continue pushing against the edges of a moral universe that lacks clear boundaries and which they do not wish to inhabit because doing so contravenes their interests. Visions of new global norms binding the transgressors by force of persuasion are an optical illusion. Cyber legalism suffers not from what it can one day become – that is its main strength – but from a conflation of aspiration with reality. This picture is not pretty but it is accurate.

Consequently, the race to develop new principles of unpeace in cyberspace is being won in Eastern capitals. The implications of the doctrinal race are profound for international order: the nations that are ahead challenge it. Accordingly, Chapter 3 examined the phenomenon of revisionism in the international system and presented a framework to orient its study. It illustrated the framework by exploring Russia's activist foreign policy in historical context. Chapter 4 pushed this analysis further by analyzing the Putin regime's adaptation of cyberspace to divisive political ends. Uninhibited by legalistic dogmas that focus on interstate war while constraining behavior below it, more attuned to the ideological aspects of the global struggle for information supremacy, Moscow is more aware of the strategic opportunities of cyberspace and less absorbed by its risks; in fact, it views risks as opportunities. Chapter 5 expanded the study to China – another challenger state but with greater technological capacities. The expansion of geopolitics into cyberspace offers China new means to challenge the regional and international order while avoiding a ruinous war of displacement. Technological events alone will not define the struggle for power among China and the United States. But they increasingly influence the extent and character of a China-centric order.

As these two chapters showed, virtual weapons are at the center of Russia's and China's doctrinal redevelopment. They offer the challenger states a powerful alternative to a military clash that their leaders wish to avoid because they know they cannot win (if anyone can win at all). A strategic doctrine that eschews rigid notions of war and peace has made it possible to devise intermediary means of rivalry that Western doctrine largely excludes. Western nations act as if international rivalry were binary, not fully realizing that the contest for security and political influence unfolding within their own borders is spectral.

They are learning the hard way that having the most potent arsenals does not guarantee victory and that preventing war does not secure peace.

Democratic nations are in the midst of a turning point in the evolution of conflict. They cannot afford to extend the relative decline in the refinement of strategic doctrine that has defined the last decade. Decisionmakers will be judged not by the potency – indeed, majesty – of the fine weapons that they add to their virtual stockpiles but by the superiority of the principles that guide their use. At the precise historical moment when the assertion of Western power and influence is most required to secure national interests and uphold the international order, at a moment of historical transition in the arrangement of power within the states system, whose basic institutions the rising nations challenge, the attitude of boldness is absent.

What is to be done about this situation? Western policy of cyber conflict reduction requires new approaches that affect adversaries' calculations of material interests rather than invoking ideals for a world which they do not want to inhabit. It must fill the gap of law and norms by operating, much like the other side, in spaces whose activity the legal system does not recognizably constrain. Perhaps what the success of security strategy requires is a moratorium on the quest for a liberal utopia. And perhaps in a world with few heroes and many villains that is not a bad thing.

The case for an interest-based solution began, in Chapter 6, with a review of the flaws in what is currently being done. The analysis examined the quest for a stable deterrent against cyberattack, the main thrust of U.S. efforts to prevent technological aggression in the last decade. The quest has largely failed. The approach ran into trouble, first because of the gaping holes in denial: in a domain where the offense roams freely, it is difficult to deprive attackers of their advantage. Second, and more importantly, because of cracks in the machinery of punishment: indecision and weakness in penalizing intrusions have failed to convince opponents to cease exploitative moves that readily align with their interests and value systems.

For adherents of persistent engagement, a recent U.S. policy innovation, the problem of the old policy of classical deterrence was one of mindset. Why expend precious resources on rescuing the morbid patient of deterrence? Persistent engagement represents a positive development in U.S. and Western cyber strategy.

For once, strategists view the plane of action mainly from the perspective of opportunities rather than of risks. But despite the new policy's defensive mantra, we saw that persistent engagement exhibits potential for offense. As a policy to achieve offensive gains, it is promising; it can help to redress the strategic balance by adding points to one's side rather than by preventing their being knocked off the ledger. But as a concept of defense, it offers few clear advantages. To deny the adversary by absorbing him in one's own maneuvers risks self-absorption. To engage persistently is to expend resources persistently. What if the end result is an attritional contest of wills? An unhappy metaphor comes to mind: two large wrestlers, grappling ceaselessly, with no umpire to take the score and define limits, and with no exit off the mat – and where even does the mat end?

Chapter 7 discussed what policy changes should follow in light of what preceded. It presented an alternative rational approach to the problem of cyber conflict reduction – punctuated deterrence. A more robust and adaptive punitive strategy, it represents a plea to consider the pragmatic benchmark of conflict reduction, rather than a preachment for liberal ideals that events have ruled out. It is not enough to seek to pin down the opponent in a persistent fight. When so much is at stake, when the very integrity of democratic processes is in peril, security strategy requires an option to strike back to convince the opponent that rules must be followed even if they are still being written. The grudging – even forced – acceptance of new rules is the first step in the long road to their internalization by adversaries who contest them.

The essence of punctuated deterrence is not defending forward but *punishing backward* – credibly, forcefully, and intently, including with forward operations within enemy networks. The approach is an attempt to inhibit boldness with boldness. If one accepts this notion, then several principles of action become clear: the necessity for punishing an accretion of blows and their effects rather than single actions; the expansion of the arc of deterrence to the intangible interests of information security; the linkage of issues across domains to widen the punitive toolbox into areas of diplomacy where one enjoys relative advantages; and, above all, clarity and firmness in signaling a willingness to respond forcefully. Western strategic doctrine must escape the confines of an outmoded legal system that prioritizes the binary construct of war and peace and which offers few constraints within the spectrum of action between them.

CONCLUSION

As argued in Chapter 8, the NATO alliance – a community of values more than just an institutionalization of interests – can support this essential task. But collective punctuation faces its own challenges. Overcoming them requires NATO's political masters to decide whether they want an alliance equipped to address the new tides of conflict. In the twenty-first century, serving the purpose of an alliance of democracies requires more than repelling an invading army. Until NATO adopts nimbler procedures of cyber crisis management, unless it clears up the legal clutter of collective defense below the war line, the allies should draw more creatively from its informal political toolkit when addressing strategic cyber activity. One cannot be angry at diplomacy for not acting out its threats when it is not ready to translate them into clear policy. In the absence of a consensus for decisive action, the allies should explore options to implement the principles of punctuation in smaller informal coalitions among themselves. Perhaps an effective motor of a bolder consensus is the successful example of a smaller harmony.

Striking back more effectively does not entail striking first or persistently. What it demands is a degree of sincerity that existing strategy does not supply: a commitment to defend national interests and values with decisive punishment until future generations of lawyers and diplomats have created the conditions for lasting stability. The protection of national security cannot function in the future perfect tense. It calls for solutions (even temporary ones) in the present – including innovative uses of the very technology that causes vulnerability, such as the Estonian government's development of data embassies to enhance deterrence by denial – the topic of Chapter 9. This initiative by the nation that suffered the "demonstration shot" of cyber conflict in 2007 shows that cyberspace can be turned, at least partly, from a source of national vulnerability to a channel of national survival.

Arguments have been made against striking back harder or at all. The concern is that counterblows risk accelerating conflicts – a real prospect in a realm of competition with so few clear guideposts. But there is a larger countervailing danger. Those who seek to contain a conflict by withdrawal risk precipitating it by their irresolution. We can ask with irony how it came to be that a country such as Russia which has invaded and absorbed the territory of neighboring democratic states and which has erupted onto the election landscape at home has in the past qualified for the prize of being a security partner. A more plausible case can be made that a sterner response will embolden, not the hawks in Moscow who perceive opportunity in weakness, but the moderate factions who are attuned to the risks of offensive adventures.

Future historians can decide whether a new policy course that exacts greater penalties risks more conflict than it prevents. But analysts today can already conclude that the current policy of inaction and weak response has produced unacceptable results. In the current era of technological conflict, officials cannot afford to indulge in the conceit that old policy dogmas apply where events negate them. The organization of Western cybersecurity requires new departures in thinking.

Nothing in the history of cyberspace suggests that peace can be fully restored to it. The search for a total cyber peace would fare no better than the centuries-old quest for eternal peace among nations. The problem is partly one of political will. No state can ever be so dissatisfied with the threats that propagate through computers that it would relinquish all the opportunities for action that they offer; that it would give up the benefits which machines have provided to society and the economy. But the problem is also technological. Even if nations agreed to halt the intrusions of code, the vulnerabilities that inhere in computer software and hardware would mean that the consensus could be broken at any time and without notice. Politics negates a practical peace; technology does not allow even a theoretical peace.

Officials striving to reduce conflict, therefore, can aspire only to outcomes far short of total success in their task. Even the finest strategy and the most ingenious doctrine could not deliver a perfection that science rules out. But a mirage and a mistake are not the same thing. The correction of doctrinal deficiencies can bring better outcomes than hitherto: a partial, and perhaps temporary, restoration of peace in the quarters of cyberspace that are most important to the protection of national interests and democratic values. That the total success of deterrence and universal peace are not possible does not mean that policy refinements cannot deliver a stabler future. It is false to expect that a better policy approach could eradicate threats completely. It is falser to believe that one is not needed.

NOTES

INTRODUCTION: THE EVOLVING MENACE OF TECHNOLOGICAL AGGRESSION

1. The Americans viewed *Ostpolitik* cautiously. U.S. Secretary of State Henry Kissinger feared that it would drive a wedge into Western relations. "The deeper motivation of Soviet overtures . . . was to ease tension with some allies while maintaining an intransigent position toward us." Henry A. Kissinger, *The White House Years* (New York: Simon and Schuster, 1979). On *Ostpolitik*, see Richard W. Stevenson, *The Rise and Fall of Détente: Relaxations of Tension in US–Soviet Relations 1953–84* (London: Macmillan, 1985); and Bernd Schaefer and Carole Fink, eds, *Ostpolitik, 1969–1974: European and Global Responses* (Cambridge: Cambridge University Press, 2011).
2. "CSU-Spion enttarnt," *Der Spiegel*, November 26, 2000, www.spiegel.de/politik/csu-spion-enttarnt-a-88479d7f-0002-0001-0000-000017925474.
3. Ibid.
4. For first-hand accounts of East German intrusions into West Germany by former Stasi agents, see Gotthold Schramm, ed, *Der Botschaftsflüchtling und andere Agentengeschichten* (Berlin: Edition Ost, 2006); Peter Pfütze, *Besuchszeit: Westdiplomaten in besonderer Mission* (Berlin: Edition Ost, 2007); and David Shimer, *Rigged: America, Russia, and One Hundred Years of Covert Electoral Interference* (New York: Knopf, 2020), which contains rich details of the events of 1972. Schramm's book features a foreword by former Stasi chief Markus Wolf. How quickly the Communist agents turned capitalist in pursuit of commercial spoils! Detractors have contested important claims in published studies. For example, one former captive personally and vehemently decried Pfütze's assertion that all Stasi prisoners had confessed to their political crimes. See "Books by Former GDR Secret Police Officers Spark Outrage," *Deutsche Welle*, April 13, 2006, www.dw.com/en/books-by-former-gdr-secret-police-officers-spark-outrage/a-1968907.
5. Some analysts have questioned the effectiveness of the Stasi's methods in Operation INFEKTION. See, for instance, Erhard Geissler and Robert Hunt Sprinkle, "Disinformation Squared: Was the HIV-from-Fort-Detrick Myth a Stasi Success?" *Politics and the Life Sciences* 32, no. 2 (2013), pp. 2–99.
6. See Vann R. Newkirk II, "What Went Wrong With All the Polls?" *The Atlantic*, November 9, 2016, www.theatlantic.com/politics/archive/2016/11/what-went-wrong-polling-clinton-trump/507188/. For an account of the 2016 hacking operation and its political effects, see Lucas Kello, *The Virtual Weapon and International Order* (New Haven, CT: Yale University Press, 2017), Chapter 8.
7. In relation to the punishment problem analyzed in this book, the term "Western" denotes the liberal democratic states of Europe and North America as well as politically and culturally related countries such as Australia. Although cyber threats affect many other nations (including democratic ones), the book focuses on Western states because of their shared

political values, common strategic traditions, and a history of close cooperation in political, economic, and security affairs within institutions such as NATO, the European Union, and the Five Eyes community, which together envelop the family of Western nations. On the commonalities of Western strategic thinking and practice, see Alastair Iain Johnston, "Thinking About Strategic Culture," *International Security* 19, no. 4 (1995), pp. 32–64.

8. Ellen Nakashima, "White House Says Sony Hack Is a Serious National Security Matter," *Washington Post*, December 18, 2014, www.washingtonpost.com/world/national-security/white-house-says-sony-hack-is-a-serious-national-security-matter/2014/12/18/01eb8324-86ea-11e4-b9b7-b8632ae73d25_story.html.

9. John Bolton, *The Room Where It Happened* (New York: Simon and Schuster, 2020), p. 174.

10. Ewen MacAskill, "Hostile States Pose 'Fundamental Threat' to Europe, Says MI6 Chief," *The Guardian*, December 8, 2016, https://www.theguardian.com/uk-news/2016/dec/08/hostile-states-pose-fundamental-threat-to-europe-says-mi6-chief.

11. James McAuley, "France Starts Probing 'Massive' Hack of Emails and Documents Reported by Macron Campaign," *Washington Post*, May 6, 2017, www.washingtonpost.com/world/macrons-campaign-says-it-has-been-hit-by-massive-hack-of-emails-and-documents/2017/05/05/fc638f18-3020-11e7-a335-fa0ae1940305_story.html.

12. Laurens Cerulus, "Von Der Leyen Calls Out China for Hitting Hospitals with Cyberattacks," *Politico*, June 22, 2020, https://www.politico.eu/article/eu-calls-out-china-for-hitting-hospitals-with-cyberattacks/.

13. Greg Miller, Ellen Nakashima, and Adam Entous, "Obama's Secret Struggle to Punish Russia for Putin's Election Assault," *Washington Post*, June 23, 2017, www.washingtonpost.com/graphics/2017/world/national-security/obama-putin-election-hacking/.

14. Aaron Blake, " 'I Feel Like We Sort of Choked': Obama's No-Drama Approach to Russian Hacking Isn't Sitting Well," *Washington Post*, June 23, 2017, https://www.washingtonpost.com/news/the-fix/wp/2017/06/23/the-russia-2016-blame-game-finds-obama/.

15. Matt Tait, "The Macron Leaks: Are They Real, and Is It Russia?" *Lawfare* (blog), May 8, 2017.

16. See Florian J. Egloff, "Public Attribution of Cyber Intrusions," *Journal of Cybersecurity* 6, issue 1 (2020).

17. See Stefan Soesanto, "Europe's Incertitude in Cyberspace," *Lawfare* (blog), August 3, 2020; and Jeff Stone, "EU Cyber Sanctions ID Russian Intel, Chinese Nationals and a North Korean Front Company for Alleged Hacks," *CyberScoop*, July 30, 2020.

18. See Matina Stevis-Gridneff, "E.U. Recommends Limiting, but Not Banning, Huawei in 5G Rollout," *The New York Times*, January 29, 2020, www.nytimes.com/2020/01/29/world/europe/eu-huawei-5g.html.

19. The unsophisticated but disruptive attacks against Estonia's financial and governmental computer systems in 2007 were "a virtual demonstration shot" that elevated cyber threats to the top of many countries' national security agendas. See Kello, *The Virtual Weapon and International Order*, p. 212.

20. Author interview with former senior British government official.

21. Daniel R. Coats, "Worldwide Threat Assessment of the US Intelligence Community" (Office of the Director of National Intelligence, February 13, 2018).

22. See Ellen Nakashima, "U.S. Cyber Command Operation Disrupted Internet Access of Russian Troll Factory on Day of 2018 Midterms," *Washington Post*, February 27, 2019, https://www.washingtonpost.com/world/national-security/us-cyber-command-operation-disrupted-internet-access-of-russian-troll-factory-on-day-of-2018-midterms/2019/02/26/1827fc9e-36d6-11e9-af5b-b51b7ff322e9_story.html.

23. Quoted in David Mardiste, "Show Putin Strength, Not Weakness, Says Estonian Defense Minister," *Atlantic Council* (blog), November 10, 2014.

24. Matthew Impelli, "Colorado Representative Says SolarWinds Hack Could Be 'Cyber Equivalent of Pearl Harbor,' " *Newsweek*, December 18, 2020, www.newsweek.com/colorado-representative-says-solarwinds-hack-could-be-cyber-equivalent-pearl-harbor-1555994.

25. See Nicole Perlroth and David E. Sanger, "Iranian Hackers Target Trump Campaign as Threats to 2020 Mount," *The New York Times*, October 4, 2019, https://www.nytimes.com/2019/10/04/technology/iranian-campaign-hackers-microsoft.html.

26. "SolarWinds Hack Was 'Largest and Most Sophisticated Attack' Ever: Microsoft President," *Reuters*, February 15, 2021, https://www.reuters.com/business/media-telecom/solarwinds-hack-was-largest-most-sophisticated-attack-ever-microsoft-president-2021-02-16/.

27. See Helen Warrell, "SolarWinds and Microsoft Hacks Spark Debate over Western Retaliation," *Financial Times*, March 12, 2021, www.ft.com/content/0548b0fb-4dce-4b9e-ab4b-4fac2f5ec111.

28. See "Fact Sheet: Imposing Costs for Harmful Foreign Activities by the Russian Government," The White House, April 15, 2021.

29. See Luke Jenkins, Sarah Hawley, Parnian Najafi, and Doug Bienstock, "Suspected Russian Activity Targeting Government and Business Entities around the Globe," *Mandiant* (blog), December 6, 2021. As Jack Goldsmith noted, the United States' own persistent intrusions in foreign government networks deprives the country of "principled basis" for a sterner response. See Jack Goldsmith, "Self-Delusion on the Russia Hack," *The Dispatch*, December 18, 2022, https://thedispatch.com/p/self-delusion-on-the-russia-hack?s=r.

30. On the role of risk reduction in U.S. cyber policy, see Monica Kaminska, "Restraint under Conditions of Uncertainty: Why the United States Tolerates Cyberattacks," *Journal of Cybersecurity* 7, no. 1 (March 9, 2022).

31. On cyber legalism, see Lucas Kello, "Cyber Legalism: Why It Fails and What to Do about It," *Journal of Cybersecurity* 7, issue 1 (2021).

32. See, for example, Mette Eilstrup-Sangiovanni, "Why the World Needs an International Cyberwar Convention," *Philosophy and Technology* 31, no. 3 (July 21, 2017), pp. 379–407; Harriet Moynihan, "The Application of International Law to State Cyberattacks," Chatham House (December 2019); and Michael N. Schmitt, "Taming the Lawless Void: Tracking the Evolution of International Law Rules for Cyberspace," *Texas National Security Review* 3, no. 3 (Summer 2020), pp. 32–47.

33. See Michael N. Schmitt, *Tallinn Manual on the International Law Applicable to Cyber Warfare* (Cambridge: Cambridge University Press, 2013); Michael N. Schmitt, *Tallinn Manual 2.0 on the International Law Applicable to Cyber Operations* (Cambridge: Cambridge University Press, 2017); Martha Finnemore and Duncan B. Hollis, "Constructing Norms for Global Cybersecurity," *American Journal of International Law* 110, no. 3 (2016), pp. 425–79; Przemysław Roguski, "Application of International Law to Cyber Operations: A Comparative Analysis of States' Views" (The Hague Program for Cyber Norms Policy Brief, 2020); and François Delerue, *Cyber Operations and International Law* (Cambridge: Cambridge University Press, 2020).

34. On the role of war as a force of change in history, especially European history, see Michael Howard, *War in European History*, updated edition (Oxford and New York: Oxford University Press, 2009).

35. See James D. Fearon and David D. Laitin, "Ethnicity, Insurgency, and Civil War," *American Political Science Review* 97, no. 1 (2003), pp. 75–90; Francisco Gutiérrez Sanín and Elisabeth Jean Wood, "Ideology in Civil War: Instrumental Adoption and Beyond," *Journal of Peace Research* 51, no. 2 (March 1, 2014), pp. 213–26; Dominic D.P. Johnson and Monica Duffy Toft, "Grounds for War: The Evolution of Territorial Conflict," *International Security* 38, no. 3 (January 1, 2014), pp. 7–38; Lars-Erik Cederman and Manuel Vogt, "Dynamics and Logics of Civil War," *Journal of Conflict Resolution* 61, no. 9 (2017); and Barbara F. Walter, "The New New Civil Wars," *Annual Review of Political Science* 20, no. 1 (2017), pp. 469–86.

36. See Maria Tsvetkova, "Putin Puts Nuclear Deterrent on Alert; West Squeezes Russian Economy," *Reuters*, February 28, 2022, www.reuters.com/world/india/war-with-ukraine-putin-puts-nuclear-deterrence-forces-alert-2022-02-27/.

37. See Brandon Valeriano and Ryan C. Maness, "The Coming Cyberpeace," *Foreign Affairs,* October 1, 2015; Scott J. Shackelford, "Toward Cyberpeace: Managing Cyberattacks through Polycentric Governance," *American University Law Review* 62, no. 5 (2013), pp. 1273–364.

38. On the widening of the spectrum of conflict between the extremes of war and peace in cyberspace, see Lucas Kello, "The Meaning of the Cyber Revolution: Perils to Theory and Statecraft," *International Security* (Fall 2013), pp. 7–40. To label this phenomenon, I introduced the term "unpeace" in Kello, *The Virtual Weapon and International Order.* See especially Part I on "Theory and Concepts."

39. See Steven Pinker, *The Better Angels of Our Nature: Why Violence Has Declined* (New York: Viking Books, 2011), Chapters 5 and 6.

40. On strategic behavior in cyberspace below the war threshold, see Kello, *The Virtual Weapon and International Order*; and Richard J. Harknett and Max Smeets, "Cyber Campaigns and Strategic Outcomes," *Journal of Strategic Studies* (2020), pp. 1–34.

41. Joshua Rovner, "Cyber War as an Intelligence Contest," *War on the Rocks*, September 16, 2019; Jon R. Lindsay, "Cyber Conflict vs. Cyber Command: Hidden Dangers in the American Military Solution to a Large-Scale Intelligence Problem," *Intelligence and National Security* 36, no. 2 (February 23, 2021), pp. 260–78.

42. Warwick Ashford, "NotPetya Offers Industry-Wide Lessons, Says Maersk's Tech Chief," ComputerWeekly.com, June 7, 2019, https://www.computerweekly.com/news/252464773/NotPetya-offers-industry-wide-lessons-says-Maersks-tech-chief.

43. Although the two operations shared a similar strategic aim of intelligence gathering, their methods were different. The Russian operation targeted select agencies and organizations; the Chinese campaign was broadly indiscriminate. See Dmitri Alperovitch and Ian Ward, "How Should the U.S. Respond to the SolarWinds and Microsoft Exchange Hacks?" *Lawfare* (blog), March 12, 2021; and Brian Krebs, "At Least 30,000 U.S. Organizations Newly Hacked Via Holes in Microsoft's Email Software," *Krebs on Security* (blog), March 5, 2021.

44. See James Shires, "The Simulation of Scandal: Hack-and-Leak Operations, the Gulf States, and U.S. Politics," *Texas National Security Review* 3, no. 4 (Fall 2020), pp. 10–29.

45. See Juan Andres Guerrero-Saade, Costin Raiu, Daniel Moore, and Thomas Rid, "Penquin's Moonlit Maze: The Dawn of Nation-State Digital Espionage" (Kaspersky Lab. 2018).

46. "Achieve and Maintain Cyberspace Superiority: Command Vision for US Cyber Command" (U.S. Cyber Command, 2018), p. 3.

47. See Erik Reichborn-Kjennerud and Patrick Cullen, "What Is Hybrid Warfare?" (Norwegian Institute of International Affairs, 2016); Christopher S. Chivvis, "Hybrid War: Russian Contemporary Political Warfare," *Bulletin of the Atomic Scientists* 73, no. 5 (August 21, 2017), pp. 316–21; and Dmitri Trenin, "Avoiding U.S.–Russia Military Escalation during the Hybrid War," Carnegie Endowment for International Peace, January 2018, p. 8.

48. John Barroso, Mary Fallin, and Virginia Foxx, "Republican Platform 2016" (CreateSpace Independent Publishing Platform, July 21, 2016).

49. This analysis, it is important to realize, does not focus on scenarios in which cyber actions occur in conjunction with conventional or unconventional acts of war or uses of force: for example, Russian actors' cyberattacks against Georgia in 2008, or hypothetically, a situation involving attacks that disable a nation's command and control infrastructure at the same time as deploying ground forces within that nation's territory. Such a scenario would clearly implicate traditional laws governing uses of force and territorial violations of sovereignty. Thus it would not invoke the legal and strategic conundrums of unpeace that this book addresses. The question of how to respond to cyberwar or the use of cyberspace in war is almost too easy to consider because violent cyberattacks would involve the familiar legal machinery of war.

50. Ben Jacobs, "John McCain Says US Has no Strategy to Deal with Russian Cyber Warfare," *The Guardian*, January 27, 2017, https://www.theguardian.com/us-news/2017/jan/27/john-mccain-says-us-has-no-strategy-to-deal-with-russian-cyber-warfare.

51. For a conceptual framework categorizing degrees of technological revolution and their implications for international relations, see Kello, *The Virtual Weapon and International Order*, Chapter 3.

1. TECHNOLOGICAL REVOLUTION IN HISTORICAL PERSPECTIVE: LESSONS FOR OUR TIMES

1. See Johnston, "Thinking about Strategic Culture."

2. J. David Singer, "Man and World Politics: The Psycho-Cultural Interface," *Journal of Social Issues* 24, no. 3 (1968), pp. 127–56.

3. See Daniel Diermeier, "Rational Choice and the Role of Theory in Political Science," *Critical Review* 9, no. 1–2 (1995), pp. 59–70; and Duncan B. Snidal, "Rational Choice and International Relations," in *Handbook of International Relations*, ed. Walter Carlsnaes, Thomas Risse, and Beth A. Simmons (London: SAGE Publications, 2012).

4. Alan Turing first proposed the concept of the modern computer – or "Turing machine," as it became known – in the seminal paper, Alan M. Turing, "On Computable Numbers, with an Application to the Entscheidungsproblem," *Proceedings of the London Mathematical Society* 2, no. 42 (1937 [delivered to the Society in 1936]), pp. 230–65.

5. See Sara J. Schechner, "The Mark I Computer at Harvard," Harvard School of Engineering and Applied Sciences, 2014, www.scholar.harvard.edu/saraschechner/presentations/mark-i-computer-harvard-2014.

6. Although China has made large investments in the development of AI technology, it still lags behind the United States in research output and skills. See Sarah O'Meara, "Will China Lead the World in AI by 2030?" *Nature* (August 21, 2019); and Richard Waters, "The Billion-Dollar Bet to Reach Human-Level AI," *Financial Times*, August 3, 2019, www.ft.com/content/c96e43be-b4df-11e9-8cb2-799a3a8cf37b.

7. See Cade Metz, "Yale Professors Race Google and IBM to the First Quantum Computer," *The New York Times*, November 13, 2017, https://www.nytimes.com/2017/11/13/technology/quantum-computing-research.html; and Michael Bradley, "Google Claims to Have Invented a Quantum Computer, But IBM Begs to Differ," *The Conversation*, January 20, 2020, https://theconversation.com/google-claims-to-have-invented-a-quantum-computer-but-ibm-begs-to-differ-127309.

8. In 2013, the Snowden leaks revealed the existence of the NSA's elite hacking unit, the Tailored Access Operations (TAO), tasked with – in its own words – "getting the ungettable." "Documents Reveal Top NSA Hacking Unit," *Der Spiegel*, December 29, 2013, www.spiegel.de/international/world/the-nsa-uses-powerful-toolbox-in-effort-to-spy-on-global-networks-a-940969.html.

9. See Craig Young, "Shining Light on The Shadow Brokers," *Tripwire*, May 18, 2017, www.tripwire.com/state-of-security/security-data-protection/shining-light-shadow-brokers/; and Ellen Nakashima and Craig Timberg, "NSA Officials Worried about the Day Its Potent Hacking Tool Would Get Loose. Then It Did," *Washington Post*, May 16, 2017, www.washingtonpost.com/business/technology/nsa-officials-worried-about-the-day-its-potent-hacking-tool-would-get-loose-then-it-did/2017/05/16/50670b16-3978-11e7-a058-ddbb23c75d82_story.html.

10. Today's GCHQ was originally known as the Government Code and Cypher School. For an excellent history of the agency, see Richard J. Aldrich, *GCHQ: The Uncensored Story of Britain's Most Secret Intelligence Agency* (London: HarperCollins UK, 2011).

11. See Lucy Fisher, "New Cyberweapons Take Fight to Isis," *The Times*, September 20, 2018, www.thetimes.co.uk/article/new-cyber-weapons-take-fight-to-isis-mr3zlf7hv.

12. Quoted in David Bond, "Inside GCHQ: The Art of Spying in the Digital Age," *Financial Times*, May 23, 2019, www.ft.com/content/ccc68ffc-7c1e-11e9-81d2-f785092ab560.

13. See Julia Voo et al., "National Cyber Power Index 2020" (Belfer Center for Science and International Affairs, Harvard Kennedy School, 2020), p. 8. The report's category of "objectives" omits information warfare, or the use of digital information spaces – often in conjunction with disruptive cyberattacks and hacking operations – to create political disorder and weaken adversaries from within their home polity. Few nations have developed doctrinal understandings and capacities in this area, or used them to such notable strategic effect, as Russia.

14. See *Global Cybersecurity Index (GCI) 2018* (Geneva: International Telecommunication Union, 2019).

15. See "Cyber Power Index," Economist Intelligence Unit (2011), pp. 4–6.

16. New Zealand, the fifth member of the Five Eyes alliance, does not feature in top cyber power rankings, probably because of the country's small size.

17. See Scott Shane, "No Morsel Too Minuscule for All-Consuming N.S.A.," *The New York Times*, November 2, 2013, www.nytimes.com/2013/11/03/world/no-morsel-too-minuscule-for-all-consuming-nsa.html; "The NSA's Secret Spy Hub in Berlin," *Der Spiegel*, October 27, 2013, www.spiegel.de/international/germany/cover-story-how-nsa-spied-on-merkel-cell-phone-from-berlin-embassy-a-930205.html.

18. See Adam Segal, "The Code Not Taken: China, the United States, and the Future of Cyber Espionage," *Bulletin of the Atomic Scientists* 69, no. 5 (September 1, 2013), pp. 38–45.

19. One of China's most notable hacking achievements, for example, was breaching the Pentagon's computer systems to gain access to the designs and blueprints of U.S. stealth fighter jets. See Andrea Gilli and Mauro Gilli, "Why China Has Not Caught Up Yet: Military-Technological Superiority and the Limits of Imitation, Reverse Engineering, and Cyber Espionage," *International Security*, 43, no. 3 (February 1, 2019), pp. 141–89.

20. See "Active Social Network Penetration in Selected Countries and Territories as of January 2022," *Statista*, www.statista.com/statistics/282846/regular-social-networking-usage-penetration-worldwide-by-country/, accessed June 15, 2020. China and Russia occupy the thirteenth and fourteenth positions in the overall cyber power ranking referenced above.

21. See BBC Staff, "North Korea 'Hacked Crypto-Currency Exchange in South,'" *BBC News*, December 16, 2017, www.bbc.co.uk/news/world-asia-42378638.

22. See Venkatesh Narayanamurti and Toluwalogo Odumosu, *Cycles of Invention and Discovery: Rethinking the Endless Frontier* (Cambridge, MA: Harvard University Press, 2016). The separation of basic and applied research is not universally true of U.S. industry research. One notable exception was Bell Labs, which in the 1980s and 90s fostered an integrative research culture that produced major advances in both the development and use of telecommunications technology.

23. Albert Einstein, "Letter to F.D. Roosevelt" (Franklin D. Roosevelt Presidential Library and Museum, August 2, 1939). In his letter, Einstein warned Roosevelt about Nazi Germany's quest for nuclear bombs, prompting FDR to order immediate action establishing the Manhattan Project.

24. Neil deGrasse Tyson and Avis Lang, *Accessory to War: The Unspoken Alliance Between Astrophysics and the Military* (New York: W.W. Norton, 2018).

25. Quoted in Alexander Chancellor, "Michael Gove Wants to Add Me to His Professional Network," *The Spectator*, September 22, 2016, www.spectator.co.uk/article/michael-gove-wants-to-add-me-to-his-professional-network.

26. Kissinger, *The White House Years*, p. 99.

27. In the 1930s, German defense planners integrated radar into some military systems. For example, the Kriegsmarine used microwave transmitters to measure the distance between naval objects. But because radar was primarily a defensive technology, Hitler, who favored offensive weapons, did not prioritize its development. Conseqeuntly, German defense planners failed to grasp how to integrate radar into air defenses. See Harry von Kroge, *GEMA: Birthplace of German Radar and Sonar*, transl. and ed. Louis Brown (Philadelphia, PA: Institute of Physics Publishing, 2000).

28. Richard Hough, *Dreadnought: A History of the Modern Battleship* (Penzance: Periscope Publishing, 2003), p. 11.
29. Quoted in Giles Edwards, "How the Dreadnought Sparked the 20th Century's First Arms Race," *BBC News*, June 2, 2014, www.bbc.co.uk/news/magazine-27641717.
30. See Shawn T. Grimes, *Strategy and War Planning in the British Navy, 1887–1918* (Woodbridge: Boydell Press, 2012); Arthur Jacob Marder, *From the Dreadnought to Scapa Flow: The Royal Navy in the Fisher Era, 1904–1919* (Oxford: Oxford University Press, 1978); Nicholas A. Lambert, *Planning Armageddon* (Cambridge, MA: Harvard University Press, 2012).
31. On the Royal Navy's difficulties defending against German U-boats, see Jan S. Breemer, *Defeating the U-boat: Inventing Antisubmarine Warfare* (Newport: Naval War College Press, 2010).
32. For a gripping account of this episode, see Robert K. Massie, *Castles of Steel: Britain, Germany, and the Winning of the Great War at Sea* (New York: Random House, 1991), Chapter 7.
33. For example, the sinking of HMS *Pathfinder* by U-21 on September 5, 1914.
34. See Karl Lautenschlager, "The Submarine in Naval Warfare, 1901–2001," *International Security* 11, no. 3 (1986), p. 95.
35. At the start of the First World War, Britain controlled about half of the world's merchant tonnage. See John Rushworth Jellicoe, *The Crisis of the Naval War* (Frankfurt am Main: Outlook Verlag, 2018).
36. Lautenschlager, "The Submarine in Naval Warfare," pp. 111–12.
37. Jellicoe, *The Crisis of the Naval War*.
38. Ibid.
39. See Lautenschlager, "The Submarine in Naval Warfare," p. 113.
40. Jellicoe, *The Crisis of the Naval War*.
41. On the anti-submarine strategy, see Lautenschlager, "The Submarine in Naval Warfare."
42. See Anthony Beevor, *The Battle for Spain: The Spanish Civil War 1936–1939* (London: Weidenfeld & Nicolson, 2006), pp. 217–18.
43. Later, between 1938 and 1943, Germany's Japanese allies unleashed their own campaign of aerial barbarity upon the Chinese city of Chongqing.
44. See Beevor, *The Battle for Spain*; Ángel Viñas, *Guerra, Dinero y Dictadura* (Barcelona: Editorial Crítica, 1984); James S. Corum, *Wolfram von Richthofen: Master of the German Air War* (Lawrence: University Press of Kansas, 2008).
45. See Beevor, *The Battle for Spain*, p. 219.
46. George L. Steer, "The Tragedy of Guernica, Town Destroyed in Air Attack," *The Times*, April 27, 1937.
47. Quoted in Jörg Diehl, "Practicing Blitzkrieg in Basque Country," *Der Spiegel*, April 26, 2007, www.spiegel.de/international/europe/hitler-s-destruction-of-guernica-practicing-blitzkrieg-in-basque-country-a-479675.html.
48. The speech was reproduced in Stanley Baldwin, "The Bomber Will Always Get Through," *The Times of London*, November 11, 1932.
49. Ibid.
50. See Giulio Douhet, *The Command of the Air*, transl. Dino Ferrari (Maxwell Air Force Base, AL: Air University Press, 2019).
51. See Guy Hartcup, *The Effect of Science on the Second World War* (Basingstoke: Palgrave Macmillan, 2000), pp. 18–38.
52. "The Battle of Britain, August–October 1940" (The Ministry of Information, 1941).
53. Germany's future superiority worried French military planners so much that, by the end of the 1930s, they accepted that France alone could not defeat the former foe. The help of allies and of Britain especially would be indispensable. See Norrin M. Ripsman and Jack S. Levy, "The Preventive War that Never Happened: Britain, France, and the Rise of Germany in the 1930s," *Security Studies* 16, no. 1 (January–March 2007), p. 38.

54. René Tournès, "The French Army, 1936," *Foreign Affairs* 14, no. 3 (April 1936).
55. George Fielding Eliot, "The Offensive Still Gives Victory," *Foreign Affairs* 17, no. 1 (October 1938).
56. Tournès, "The French Army, 1936," p. 494.
57. David P. Deeter and Joel C. Gaydos, eds, *Occupational Health: The Soldier and the Industrial Base* (Office of the Surgeon General, U.S. Department of the Army, 1993), p. 171.
58. Tournès, "The French Army, 1936," p. 490.
59. Jean Lacouture, *De Gaulle: The Rebel, 1890–1944* (New York: Random House, 1991).
60. See Hamilton Fish Armstrong, "The Downfall of France," *Foreign Affairs* 19, no. 1 (October 1940), pp. 55–144.
61. Max Hastings, "Botch on the Rhine," *The New York Review of Books*, May 28, 2020, www.nybooks.com/articles/2020/05/28/battle-arnhem-botch-rhine/. Swift adaptation to tactical circumstances was a hallmark not just of offensive but also of defensive German action. For example, German panzer units reacted quickly and effectively to the surprising appearance of Allied paratroopers outside of the Dutch town of Arnhem in September 1944.
62. See Armstrong, "The Downfall of France."
63. André Beaufre, *1940: The Fall of France* (London: Cassell, 1967), p. 179.

2. CYBER LEGALISM: THE LIMITS OF LAW AND NORMS

1. The topic of law and norms of interstate cyber conduct has received growing attention within political science and international relations. See, for example, Finnemore and Hollis, "Constructing Norms for Global Cybersecurity," pp. 425–79; Mark Raymond, "Managing Decentralized Cyber Governance: The Responsibility to Troubleshoot," *Strategic Studies Quarterly* 10 (2016), pp. 123–49; Mark Raymond, "Engaging Security and Intelligence Practitioners in the Emerging Cyber Regime Complex," *The Cyber Defense Review* 1, no. 2 (2016), pp. 81–94; Aaron F. Brantly, "The Most Governed Ungoverned Space: Legal and Policy Constraints on Military Operations in Cyberspace," *SAIS Review of International Affairs* 26, no. 2 (2016), pp. 29–39; Alex Grigsby, "The End of Cyber Norms," *Survival* 59, no. 6 (2017), pp. 109–22. On cyber legalism and its challenges, see Lucas Kello, "Cyber Legalism."
2. Author interview with Gary Corn.
3. Interview with Gary Corn. It is important to realize that unpeace and the "gray zone," as analysts commonly use the term, are not the same. Although both notions denote offensive action that falls between the extremes of war and peace, unpeace is narrower because its consequences are not directly violent or fatal (while not all forms of violence are necessarily acts of war).
4. See Valentin Weber, "The Worldwide Web of Chinese and Russian Information Controls" (Oxford University Centre for Technology and Global Affairs, 2019).
5. On problems of Internet and cyber governance, see, for example, Laura DeNardis, *Protocol Politics* (Cambridge, MA: MIT Press, 2009); Laura DeNardis and Mark Raymond, "Thinking Clearly about Multistakeholder Internet Governance" (GigaNet: Global Internet Governance Academic Network, Annual Symposium 2013, July 2016); and Lucas Kello, "Cyber Security: Gridlock and Innovation," in *Beyond Gridlock*, ed. Thomas Hale and David Held (Cambridge: Polity Press, 2017).
6. "Advance Questions for Lieutenant General Keith Alexander, USA Nominee for Commander, United States Cyber Command" (United States Senate, April 15, 2010). See also "Operational Law Handbook, Chapter 5, Standing Rules of Engagement (Instr. 3121.01B)" (Chairman of the Joint Chiefs of Staff, June 13, 2015); Michael N. Schmitt, "International Law in Cyberspace: The Koh Speech and Tallinn Manual Juxtaposed," *Harvard International Law Journal* 54 (December 2012), p. 25.
7. Jim Michaels, "Hagel Encourages 'Restraint' in Cyber Warfare," *USA Today*, March 28, 2014, https://eu.usatoday.com/story/nation/2014/03/28/hagel-nsa-snowden-cyber-command/7020127/.

8. Paul M. Nakasone and Michael Sulmeyer, "How to Compete in Cyberspace," *Foreign Affairs*, 2020.
9. "Pillars of the International Strategy for Cyberspace" (U.S. Office of the Coordinator for Cyber Issues, 2009).
10. Painter's biography at Stanford University states: "His efforts helped create a new area of foreign policy focus that included promoting norms of responsible state behavior and cyber stability . . . He and his team also spearheaded the promotion of an international framework of cyber stability that includes building a consensus around norms of acceptable behavior" ("Christopher Painter," Stanford University web profile, accessed April 1, 2021, https://cisac.fsi.stanford.edu/people/christopher-painter).
11. "Christopher Painter: Coordinator for Cyber Issues," U.S. Department of State, 2017, https://2009-2017.state.gov/r/pa/ei/biog/161848.htm; Dennis Broeders and Fabio Cristiano, "Cyber Norms and the United Nations: Between Strategic Ambiguity and Rules of the Road," Italian Institute for International Political Studies, April 2, 2020; Dennis Broeders, "Mutually Assured Diplomacy: Governance, 'Unpeace' and Diplomacy in Cyberspace," Observer Research Foundation, October 19, 2019; Dennis Broeders and Sergei Boeke, "The Demilitarisation of Cyber Conflict," *Survival* 60, no. 6 (November 2018), pp. 73–90.
12. Lucas Kello, "Private Sector Cyber Weapons: An Adequate Response to the Sovereignty Gap?" in *Bytes, Bombs, and Spies: The Strategic Dimensions of Offensive Cyber Operations*, ed. Amy Zegart and Herb Lin (Washington, D.C.: Brookings Institution, 2019).
13. See Jason Healey, "The Implications of Persistent (and Permanent) Engagement in Cyberspace," *Journal of Cybersecurity* 5, no. 1 (January 1, 2019); and Richard J. Harknett, "Persistent Engagement and Cost Imposition: Distinguishing Between Cause and Effect," *Lawfare* (blog), February 6, 2020. On the theory and practice of persistent engagement, see Michael P. Fischerkeller, Emily O. Goldman, and Richard J. Harkett, *Cyber Persistence Theory: Redefining National Security in Cyberspace (Bridging the Gap)* (Oxford: Oxford University Press, 2022).
14. "Paris Call for Trust and Security in Cyberspace," French Ministry for Europe and International Affairs, November 12, 2018, https://pariscall.international/en/call, accessed April 14, 2022.
15. Alexander Evans, "Our Shared Commitment to Law, Norms and Confidence Building in Cyberspace" (Foreign and Commonwealth Office, September 9, 2019).
16. *A Strong Britain in an Age of Uncertainty: The National Security Strategy* (UK Government Cabinet Office, 2010).
17. See Ian Manners, "Normative Power Europe: A Contradiction in Terms?" *JCMS: Journal of Common Market Studies* 40, no. 2 (2002), pp. 235–58.
18. "EU Cyber Diplomacy Toolbox" (European Union External Action Service, 2019).
19. "Statement by the North Atlantic Council Concerning Malicious Cyber Activities" (NATO, June 3, 2020).
20. Russell Buchan, "Cyber Attacks: Unlawful Uses of Force or Prohibited Interventions?" *Journal of Conflict and Security Law* 17, no. 2 (2012), pp. 211–27.
21. Dennis Broeders, Liisi Adamson, and Rogier Creemers, "A Coalition of the Unwilling? Chinese and Russian Perspectives on Cyberspace," The Hague Program for Cyber Norms Policy Brief, November 2019.
22. Jack L. Goldsmith and Eric A. Posner, *The Limits of International Law* (Oxford and New York: Oxford University Press, 2007), pp. 178–9.
23. The Bush Administration did not begin to emphasize the goal of democracy promotion in Iraq and the Middle East until after the invasion was underway. On the goals of the Iraq War, see David Lake, "Two Cheers for Bargaining Theory: Assessing Rationalist Explanations of the Iraq War," *International Security* 35, no. 3 (Winter 2010/11), pp. 7–52; Jane Cramer and Eric Duggan, "In Pursuit of Primacy," in *Why Did the United States Invade Iraq?* ed. Jane Cramer and Trevor Thrall (New York: Routledge, 2012), pp. 210–20; Alexandre Debs

and Nuno P. Monteiro, "Known Unknowns: Power Shifts, Uncertainty, and War," *International Organization* 68, no. 1 (January 2014), pp. 1–31; and Ahsan I. Butt, "Why Did the United States Invade Iraq in 2003?" *Security Studies* 28, no. 2 (2019), pp. 250–85.

24. Shaun Waterman, "Clapper: U.S. Shelved 'Hack Backs' Due to Counterattack Fears," *CyberScoop*, October 2, 2017, www.cyberscoop.com/hack-back-james-clapper-iran-north-korea/.

25. Interview with Gary Corn.

26. John Markoff and Thom Shanker, "Halted '03 Iraq Plan Illustrates U.S. Fear of Cyberwar Risk," *The New York Times*, August 1, 2009, www.nytimes.com/2009/08/02/us/politics/02cyber.html.

27. Eric Schmitt and Thom Shanker, "U.S. Debated Cyberwarfare in Attack Plan on Libya," *The New York Times*, October 17, 2011, www.nytimes.com/2011/10/18/world/africa/cyber-warfare-against-libya-was-debated-by-us.html.

28. Cory Bennett, "Pentagon Hits ISIS with 'Cyber Bombs' in Full-Scale Online Campaign," *The Hill*, April 25, 2016, https://thehill.com/policy/cybersecurity/277493-pentagon-targets-isis-with-first-full-scale-cyber-campaign/.

29. See Adam P. Liff, "Cyberwar: A New 'Absolute Weapon'? The Proliferation of Cyberwarfare Capabilities and Interstate War," *Journal of Strategic Studies* 35, no. 3 (June 1, 2012), pp. 401–28; David E. Sanger, *Confront and Conceal: Obama's Secret Wars and Surprising Use of American Power* (New York: Penguin Random House, 2013).

30. On the notion of "extreme emergency" in just war theory, see Michael Walzer, *Just and Unjust Wars: A Moral Argument with Historical Illustrations* (New York: Basic Books, 1977).

31. Samuel P. Huntington, *The Common Defense: Strategic Programs in National Politics* (New York: Columbia University Press, 1961).

32. Nakasone and Sulmeyer, "How to Compete in Cyberspace."

33. See Catherine Lotrionte, "Reconsidering the Consequences for State-Sponsored Hostile Cyber Operations under International Law," *The Cyber Defense Review* 3, no. 2 (2018), pp. 73–114.

34. "Advance Questions for Lieutenant General Keith Alexander."

35. The universality of liberal democratic values is a precept not only of American foreign policy but also of European approaches to international affairs. See Francis Fukuyama, *The End of History and the Last Man* (New York: Simon and Schuster, 2006); Andrew Gamble, "The Western Ideology 1," *Government and Opposition* 44, no. 1 (2009), pp. 1–19; Samuel P. Huntington, *The Clash of Civilizations and the Remaking of World Order* (New York: Simon and Schuster, 2011); G. John Ikenberry, "The End of Liberal International Order?" *International Affairs* 94, no. 1 (January 1, 2018), pp. 7–23; and Jörg Faust, "Liberal Democracy as Universal Value" (Deutsches Institut für Entwicklungspolitik, 2013).

36. Harold Hongju Koh, "International Law in Cyberspace," *Harvard International Law Journal* 54 (December 2012), p. 12.

37. Federica Mogherini, "Declaration by the High Representative on Behalf of the EU on Respect for the Rules-Based Order in Cyberspace" (Council of the European Union, April 12, 2019); "Open-Ended Working Group on Developments in the Field of Information and Telecommunications in the Context of International Security – Final Substantive Report" (United Nations General Assembly, March 20, 2021).

38. Barack Obama, "Statement by the North Atlantic Council Concerning Malicious Cyber Activities," NATO, June 3, 2020.

39. Corn expressed a similar point: "I don't anticipate that at the GRU or in PLA hacking units there is an analogue of Gary Corn telling the commander that international law says this or that about what we can do. I don't see Russia or China particularly constrained by international law." (Interview with Gary Corn.)

40. Obama, "Statement by the North Atlantic Council Concerning Malicious Cyber Activities," NATO, June 3, 2020.

41. Jens Stoltenberg, "Statement by NATO Secretary General Jens Stoltenberg on Russian Cyber Attacks," NATO, October 4, 2018.

42. Broeders, Adamson, and Creemers, "A Coalition of the Unwilling?" For a discussion of national perspectives on international law and cybersecurity, see Roguski, "Application of International Law to Cyber Operations."

43. Vladimir Putin, "Основы государственной политики Российской Федерации в области международной информационной безопасности на период до 2020 года" (Security Council of the Russian Federation, July 24, 2013).

44. "Statement by the Representative of the Russian Federation at the Online Discussion of the Second 'Pre-Draft' of the Final Report of the UN Open-Ended Working Group on Developments in the Field of Information and Telecommunications in the Context of International Security (Unofficial Translation)" (Russian Federation, June 15, 2020).

45. Jeffrey T. Biller and Michael N. Schmitt, "Classification of Cyber Capabilities and Operations as Weapons, Means, or Methods of Warfare," *International Law Studies* 95 (2019), pp. 179–225.

46. Quoted in Mark Clayton, "Stuxnet: Ahmadinejad Admits Cyberweapon Hit Iran Nuclear Program," *Christian Science Monitor*, November 30, 2010, www.csmonitor.com/USA/2010/1130/Stuxnet-Ahmadinejad-admits-cyberweapon-hit-Iran-nuclear-program.

47. "Peace and Security" (United Nations, August 30, 2016).

48. "Resolution 1645 (2005)" (UN Security Council, December 20, 2005).

49. See Hans Morgenthau, *Politics Among Nations* (Boston: Knopf, 1948) and Stanley Hoffmann, *The State of War: Essays on the Theory and Practice of International Politics* (London: Praeger, 1965). See also Mark A. Heller, "The Use & Abuse of Hobbes: The State of Nature in International Relations," *Polity* 13, no. 1 (September 1, 1980), pp. 21–32; Hedley Bull, "Hobbes and the International Anarchy," *Social Research* 48, no. 4 (1981), pp. 717–38; Michael C. Williams, "Hobbes and International Relations: A Reconsideration," *International Organization* 50, no. 2 (1996), pp. 213–36; and Jack Donnelly, *Realism and International Relations* (Cambridge: Cambridge University Press, 2000).

50. Hedley Bull, *The Anarchical Society: A Study of Order in World Politics* (London: Macmillan, 1977), pp. 17–18.

51. Hamadoun I. Touré, "The Quest for Cyber Peace" (International Telecommunication Union, January 2011).

52. Thomas Brewster, "North Korean Hackers Accused of 'Biggest Cryptocurrency Theft of 2020' – Their Heists Are Now Worth $1.75 Billion," *Forbes*, February 9, 2021, www.forbes.com/sites/thomasbrewster/2021/02/09/north-korean-hackers-accused-of-biggest-cryptocurrency-theft-of-2020-their-heists-are-now-worth-175-billion/?sh=b80c5fd5b0bb.

53. "Resilient Military Systems and the Advanced Cyber Threat" (U.S. Department of Defense Science Board, January 2013); Jack L. Goldsmith, "How Cyber Changes the Laws of War," *European Journal of International Law* 24, no. 1 (2013), pp. 133–4.

54. Goldsmith and Posner, *The Limits of International Law*, pp. 133–4.

55. "Achieve and Maintain Cyberspace Superiority," p. 3.

56. Michael Cieply and Brooks Barnes, "Sony Cyberattack, First a Nuisance, Swiftly Grew Into a Firestorm," *The New York Times*, December 30, 2014, www.nytimes.com/2014/12/31/business/media/sony-attack-first-a-nuisance-swiftly-grew-into-a-firestorm-.html.

57. Gary Corn and Eric Talbot Jensen, "The Use of Force and Cyber Countermeasures," SSRN Scholarly Paper (Rochester: Social Science Research Network, December 2, 2018); Ashley Deeks, "Defend Forward and Cyber Countermeasures," *Lawfare* (blog), August 12, 2020.

58. The legal doctrine of *clausula rebus sic stantibus* allows the violation of legal obligations when the circumstances underlying an agreement change.

59. See Lucas Kello, "The Virtual Weapon: Dilemmas and Future Scenarios," *Politique Étrangère* 79, no. 4 (2015); and Kello, "Cyber Security."

3. CHALLENGER STATES: REVISIONISM IN THE INTERNATIONAL SYSTEM

1. See Ivan Krastev, "Russian Revisionism: Putin's Plan for Overturning the European Order," *Foreign Affairs*, March 3, 2014; Roy Allison, "Russia and the Post-2014 International Legal Order: Revisionism and Realpolitik," *International Affairs* 93, no. 3 (May 2017), pp. 519–43; and Keir Giles, *Moscow Rules: What Drives Russia to Confront the West* (Washington, D.C.: Brookings Institution, 2018).
2. Recall Francis Fukuyama's famous description of the triumph of political and economic liberalism at the end of the Cold War as "the end of history." See Fukuyama, *The End of History and the Last Man*.
3. On the prospect of war between China and Taiwan, see Mike Gallagher, "Taiwan Can't Wait: What America Must Do to Prevent a Successful Chinese Invasion," *Foreign Affairs*, February 1, 2022; Helen Davidson and Julian Borger, "China Could Mount Full-Scale Invasion by 2025, Taiwan Defence Minister Says," *The Guardian*, October 6, 2021, www.theguardian.com/world/2021/oct/06/biden-says-he-and-chinas-xi-have-agreed-to-abide-by-taiwan-agreement; and Michael Shuman, "Is Taiwan Vulnerable After Putin's Ukraine Invasion?" *The Atlantic*, February 24, 2022, www.theatlantic.com/international/archive/2022/02/vladimir-putin-ukraine-taiwan/622907/.
4. On the notion of the "international society" in international relations theory, the seminal work is Bull, *The Anarchical Society*.
5. Whereas Russia varyingly held the status of a great power from at least the reign of Peter I during the seventeenth century, China's decisive entry into geopolitics occurred only during the last five decades. True, during the Qing dynasty (1636–1912), the country acquired a large empire by conquest, but it was never able to exert significant influence beyond East Asia; it was mainly a regional, rather than a global, power. In fact, by the early nineteenth century, the Qing empire itself succumbed to inglorious colonial intrusions as the European empires, greatly empowered by the Industrial Revolution, sent their navies and armies to Chinese shores. See Rana Mitter, *A Bitter Revolution: China's Struggle with the Modern World* (Oxford: Oxford University Press, 2005); David Scott, *China and the International System, 1840–1949: Power, Presence, and Perceptions in a Century of Humiliation* (Albany: State University of New York Press, 2008); Julia Lovell, *The Opium War: Drugs, Dreams and the Making of China* (London: Picador, 2011); and Chapter 5 of this book.
6. Much of international relations thinking about international society originates in the "English School" theoretical tradition, a seminal work of which is Bull, *The Anarchical Society*. For a full treatment of the "conventional model" of the international system and categories of revolutionary change within it, see Kello, *The Virtual Weapon and International Order*, Chapter 3. On international revolution more generally, see Martin Wight, *International Theory: The Three Traditions* (Leicester: Leicester University Press, 1991); David Armstrong, *Revolution and World Order: The Revolutionary State in International Society* (Oxford: Clarendon Press, 1993); and Barry Buzan, *From International to World Society? English School Theory and the Social Structure of Globalisation* (Cambridge: Cambridge University Press, 2004).
7. For this reason, some political thinkers describe international politics as comprising not only a mechanical system of rational interactions – the world conceived by John Stuart Mill, in which "economic man" pursues defined ends according to their numerical value – but also a "society of states" – the world of Immanuel Kant or Woodrow Wilson, whose actors' behavior is also shaped by values, ideas, and sometimes passions, which displace selfish conveniences. See John Stuart Mill, *Essays on Some Unsettled Questions of Political Economy* (London: Longmans, Green, Reader, and Dyer, 1874).
8. See Kenneth N. Waltz, *Theory of International Politics*; and Bull, *The Anarchical Society*, pp. 67–8.

9. On the "balance of players," see Kello, *The Virtual Weapon and International Order*, p. 264. If successful, the two types of foreign policy revisionism described in this work would equate to, respectively, "first-order" and "second-order" revolution in the international system. On the categories of international revolution, see Kello, *The Virtual Weapon and International Order*, Chapters 4–6.

10. Theorists have long debated the influence (or not) of international institutions on state conduct. A good point of entry into this literature is Andreas Hasenclever, Peter Mayer, and Volker Rittberger, *Theories of International Regimes*, Cambridge Studies in International Relations (Cambridge: Cambridge University Press, 1997).

11. Archival research on the foreign policy of the Tsars is recent compared to the study of other nations of the same period because, until the Soviet Union's dissolution in 1991, the archives were largely closed to foreign researchers. The field of study burgeoned thereafter. See Hugh Ragsdale, V.N. Ponomarev, and Lee H. Hamilton, *Imperial Russian Foreign Policy* (Cambridge: Cambridge University Press, 1993).

12. Howard, *War in European History*.

13. Ibid., pp. 54–75.

14. The campaigns played out in two stages over land and sea. They failed owing largely to the Ottoman Navy's superiority, which forced the Russians to relinquish their land grabs. See Charles W. Ingrao, Nikola Samardžić, and Jovan Pesalj, *The Peace of Passarowitz, 1718* (West Lafayette, IN: Purdue University Press, 2011).

15. Evgenii V. Anisimov and J.T. Alexander, *The Reforms of Peter the Great: Progress Through Violence in Russia* (Abingdon: Routledge, 2015).

16. See Mikheil Saakashvili, "Russia's Next Land Grab Won't Be in an Ex-Soviet State. It Will Be in Europe," *Foreign Policy*, March 15, 2019.

17. The slowness of Russian industrialization prevented Peter I and later tsars from grabbing territories further afield.

18. See Karl Marx and Friedrich Engels, *The Russian Menace to Europe: A Collection of Articles, Speeches, Letters, and News Despatches*, ed. Paul W. Blackstock and Bert F. Hoselitz (London: Allen and Unwin, 1953).

19. See Emanuel Sarkisyanz, "Russian Imperialism Reconsidered," in *Russian Imperialism from Ivan the Great to the Revolution*, ed. Taras Hunczak (New Brunswick, NJ: Rutgers University Press, 1974), pp. 45–6.

20. See Friedrich Engels and Karl Marx, *The German Ideology*, 2nd edn (London: Laurence and Wishart, 1974); and Vladimir I. Lenin, *The State and Revolution: The Marxist Theory of the State and the Tasks of the Proletariat in the Revolution* (London: Union Books, 2013).

21. As Jeronim Perović argued, the split between Tito and Stalin did not involve different views of the correct path to Socialism; rather, they disagreed about the necessity for Soviet hegemony along that path. See Jeronim Perović, "The Tito–Stalin Split: A Reassessment in Light of New Evidence," *Journal of Cold War Studies* 9, no. 2 (April 2007), pp. 32–63.

22. Adam B. Ulam, *The Communists: The Story of Power and Lost Illusions, 1948–1991* (New York: Macmillan, 1992), p. 174.

23. Ibid., pp. 176–80.

24. "Ogarkov on Implications of Military Technology (Interview)," *Krasnaya Zvezda*, May 9, 1984.

25. Andrei A. Grechko and Nikolai V. Ogarkov, "A New Conception of War." *Military Thought* 6, no. 3 (1997), pp. 50–3.

26. In 1915, Lenin defined war, borrowing from Clausewitz, as "simply the continuation of politics by other (i.e. violent) means." But contra Clausewitz, he attributed its causes not to state purposes but to the struggles of particular social sectors. See Vladimir I. Lenin, "The Collapse of the Soviet International," in *Collected Works* 21 (Moscow: Progress Publishers), pp. 205–59; Lenin, "Address to the Second All-Russian Congress of Communist Organizations of the Peoples of the East," in *Collected Works* 30 (Moscow: Progress

Publishers, 1919), pp. 151–61; and Oscar Jonsson, *The Russian Understanding of War: Blurring the Lines Between War and Peace* (Washington, D.C.: Georgetown University Press, 2018), Chapter 1.

27. Quoted in Joseph S. Nye, Jr., "Nuclear Learning and U.S.–Soviet Security Regimes," *International Security* 41, no. 3 (Summer 1987), p. 400.

28. Slava Gerovitch, "InterNyet: Why the Soviet Union Did Not Build a Nationwide Computer Network," *History and Technology* 24, no. 4 (December 1, 2008), p. 347.

29. "Viktor Gregor'yevich Afanas'yev, Chief Editor, Pravda," U.S. Central Intelligence Agency, reproduced by Wikimedia Commons, https://upload.wikimedia.org/wikipedia/commons/5/56/Espionage_den04_33.png, accessed May 7, 2021. The tinge of ideology aside, the CIA regarded Afanasyev's enthusiastic advocacy of the use of computers in management as progressive.

30. Quoted in Slava Gerovitch, "How the Computer Got Its Revenge on the Soviet Union," *Nautilus*, April 9, 2015.

4. RUSSIA AND NEW TECHNOLOGICAL THREATS TO DEMOCRACY

1. The question of the role of the USSR's defense spending on the Union's collapse is hotly contested. See, for example, Fred Chernoff, "Ending the Cold War: The Soviet Retreat and the US Military Buildup," *International Affairs* 67, no. 1 (1991), pp. 111–26; Richard Ned Lebow and Janice Gross Stein, "Reagan and the Russians," *The Atlantic Monthly*, 273, no. 2 (1994), pp. 35–7; and Celeste A. Wallander, "Western Policy and the Demise of the Soviet Union," *Journal of Cold War Studies* 5, no. 4 (2003), pp. 137–77.

2. Quoted in Andrew Osborn and Andrey Ostroukh "Putin Rues Soviet Collapse as Demise of 'Historical Russia,'" *Reuters*, December 12, 2021, www.reuters.com/world/europe/putin-rues-soviet-collapse-demise-historical-russia-2021-12-12/.

3. A 2010 presidential decree on military doctrine reads: "In the event of a military conflict involving conventional means of destruction . . . which threatens the very existence of the state, the possession of nuclear weapons can lead to the escalation of such a military conflict into a nuclear military conflict." Военная доктрина Российской Федерации (Moscow: Security Council of the Russian Federation, June 25, 2010) [translation mine]. A later document, from 2020, states that Russia can use nuclear weapons "for the prevention of an escalation of military actions and their termination on terms that are acceptable. . ." "Указ Президента Российской Федерации от 02.06.2020 № 355 'Об Основах государственной политики Российской Федерации в области ядерного сдерживания'" (Moscow: Kremlin, June 2, 2020) [translation mine].

4. See Jay Ross, "Time to Terminate Escalate to De-Escalate – It's Escalation Control," *War on the Rocks*, April 24, 2018, https://warontherocks.com/2018/04/time-to-terminate-escalate-to-de-escalateits-escalation-control/.

5. See Henry Foy, Max Seddon, and Demetri Sevastopulo, "West Takes Putin's Nuclear Weapons Threat Seriously," *Financial Times*, February 27, 2022, www.ft.com/content/e12976cf-59be-414e-b90f-56875df79753?shareType=nongift.

6. In the midst of Russia's attempt to conquer Ukraine in 2022, the Finnish and Swedish governments began to take steps towards NATO accession, which has enjoyed a spike in popular support in both countries. See Robbie Gramer, " 'Thanks, Putin': Finnish and Swedish Lawmakers Aim for NATO Membership," *Foreign Policy*, April 22, 2022.

7. Author interview with Toomas Hendrik Ilves.

8. Aaron Blake, "Why Biden and the White House Keep Talking about World War III," *Washington Post*, March 17, 2022, www.washingtonpost.com/politics/2022/03/17/why-biden-white-house-keep-talking-about-world-war-iii/.

9. Mark Trevelyan, "Russia Tests Nuclear-Capable Missile that Putin Calls World's Best," *Reuters*, April 21, 2022, www.reuters.com/world/europe/russia-tests-new-intercontinental-ballistic-missile-2022-04-20/.

10. See Svyatoslav N. Kozlov, Mikhail V. Smirnov, Ivan S. Baz, and Petr A. Sidorov, О советской военной наукой (Moscow: Voyenizdat, 1964). Dmitri A. Volkagonov and Stepan A. Tiushkcvich, Война: Советская военная энциклопедия (Moscow: Voenizdat, 1976), p. 301. For an analysis of the Soviet theory of war, see Jonsson, *The Russian Understanding of War*, Chapter 1.

11. "Episode 65: Katarzyna Zysk: Russian Creativity and Risk-Taking," Western Way of War Podcasts, Royal United Services Institute, September 23, 2021, https://rusi.org/podcasts/western-way-of-war/episode-65-katarzyna-zysk-russian-creativity-and-risk-taking.

12. As Kimberley Thachuk noted, corruption in the Russian military after the Soviet Union's demise became "almost legendary and reflects the corruption that pervades Russian society." Thachuk, "Corruption and International Security," *The SAIS Review of International Affairs* 25, no. 1 (Winter–Spring 2005), pp. 143–52.

13. For an excellent analysis of this point, see Mark Galeotti, *Putin's Hydra: Inside Russia's Intelligence Services*, European Council and Foreign Relations Policy Brief, 2016.

14. This analysis does not make the common mistake of labeling information operations as "attacks."

15. Kello, *The Virtual Weapon and International Order*, Chapter 8; Mason Richey, "Contemporary Russian Revisionism: Understanding the Kremlin's Hybrid Warfare and the Strategic and Tactical Deployment of Disinformation," *Asia Europe Journal* 16, no. 1 (March 1, 2018), pp. 101–13.

16. Roy Allison labels the first view "legal revisionism." See Allison, "Russia and the Post-2014 International Legal Order," p. 519.

17. Joseph Biden, "Remarks by President Biden on Russia," The White House, April 15, 2021.

18. Sam Fleming et al., "Berlin and Paris Propose Reset for EU Relations with Moscow," *Financial Times*, June 23, 2021, www.ft.com/content/03528026-8fa1-4910-ab26-41cd26404439.

19. Laurenz Gehrke, "Germany's Scholz Calls For EU Ostpolitik," *Politico*, August 12, 2021, www.politico.eu/article/youre-so-vague-germanys-scholz-calls-for-new-russia-policy/.

20. See Sarah Ann Aarup, "Le Pen Vows to Keep Russia Close to Prevent an Alliance with China," *Politico*, April 18, 2022, www.politico.eu/article/le-pen-vows-to-keep-russia-close-to-prevent-an-alliance-with-china/.

21. See Péter Krekó, "Viktor Orban Is the West's Pro-Putin Outlier," *Foreign Policy*, March 20, 2022.

22. James D. Melville, Jr., "I Stepped Down as U.S. Ambassador to Estonia. Here's Why," *Washington Post*, October 3, 2018, www.washingtonpost.com/opinions/i-stepped-down-as-us-ambassador-to-estonia-heres-why/2018/10/03/f579c7a4-c5c4-11e8-9b1c-a90f1daae309_story.html.

23. See Thomas D. Grant, *Aggression Against Ukraine: Territory, Responsibility, and International Law* (New York: Palgrave Macmillan, 2015).

24. See Allison, "Russia and the Post-2014 International Legal Order."

25. Quoted in Dave Majumdar, "Newly Declassified Documents: Gorbachev Told NATO Wouldn't Move Past East German Border," *The National Interest*, December 12, 2017. Although scholars have questioned the veracity of these declarations, CIA Director Robert Gates himself criticized Western policy "at a time of a special humiliation and difficulty for Russia, [of] pressing ahead with expansion of NATO eastward, when Gorbachev and others were led to believe that wouldn't happen, at least in no time soon. . ." (Quoted in "Robert M. Gates Oral History," Transcript, Miller Center, University of Virginia, July 23–24, 2000, https://millercenter.org/the-presidency/presidential-oral-histories/robert-m-gates-deputy-director-central. See also Svetlana Savranskaya and Tom Blanton, "NATO Expansion: What Gorbachev Heard," National Security Archive, Briefing Book No. 613, December 12, 2017, https://nsarchive.gwu.edu/briefing-book/russia-programs/2017-12-12/nato-expansion-what-gorbachev-heard-western-leaders-early. For a contrasting view, see

Mark Kramer, "The Myth of a No-NATO-Enlargement Pledge to Russia," *Washington Quarterly* 32, no. 2 (April 2009), pp. 39–61.

26. For example, Jeffrey Sachs, a senior economic advisor to Clinton, vehemently argued in favor of a "Marshall Plan" for Russia. See Jeffrey D. Sachs, *A New Foreign Policy: Beyond American Exceptionalism* (New York: Columbia University Press, 2018), Chapter 5.

27. Vladimir Putin, "Speech and the Following Discussion at the Munich Conference on Security Policy," President of Russia, February 10, 2007.

28. Krishnadev Calamur, "Why Ukraine Is Such a Big Deal for Russia," NPR.org, February 21, 2014, www.npr.org/sections/parallels/2014/02/21/280684831/why-ukraine-is-such-a-big-deal-for-russia.

29. On Kievan Rus and the origins of modern Russia, see for instance Serhii Plokhy, *The Origins of the Slavic Nations: Premodern Identities in Russia, Ukraine, and Belarus* (Cambridge: Cambridge University Press, 2006); and Iver B. Neumann, "Russia in International Society over the Longue Durée: *Lessons from Early Rus' and Early Post-Soviet State Formation,*" in *Russia's Identity in International Relations: Images, Perceptions, Misperceptions,* ed. Raymond Taras (Abingdon: Routledge, 2014).

30. Quoted in "Russian Operation in Ukraine Contributes to Freeing the World from Western Oppression – Lavrov," *Tass,* April 30, 2022, https://tass.com/politics/1445755.

31. Huntington, *The Clash of Civilizations.* For a similar critique, see John J. Mearsheimer, *Great Delusion: Liberal Dreams and International Relations* (New Haven, CT: Yale University Press, 2018).

32. For a discussion of this topic, see Stephen M. Walt, "The End of Hubris and the New Age of American Restraint," *Foreign Affairs,* May/June 2019; and Mearsheimer, *The Great Delusion.*

33. Allison, "Russia and the Post-2014 International Legal Order," p. 520.

34. The full text of the speech is available in "Putin's Prepared Remarks at 43rd Munich Conference on Security Policy," *Washington Post,* February 12, 2007, www.washingtonpost.com/wp-dyn/content/article/2007/02/12/AR2007021200555.html.

35. *The Military Doctrine of the Russian Federation,* No. Pr.-2976, Russian Embassy in the United Kingdom, December 25, 2014, https://rusemb.org.uk/press/2029.

36. A report by the Estonian Internal Security Service (Kaitsepolitseiamet) – a country long at the forefront of the cyber revolution and Russian maneuvers within it – encapsulated Moscow's strategic doctrine as follows: "Since the first presidency period of Vladimir Putin the long-term strategic aim of the administration of the Russian Federation has been restoring the sphere of influence in the so-called near-foreign countries, and securing Russia's status as a superpower on the international level. As there is insufficient economic and military power to fulfill this dream at the moment, Russia has contributed in the creation of supporting myths, in order to make people in their native land and abroad believe in this wishful belief. Myth creation of Russia is characterized by focusing on the so-called soft power and psychological warfare." Annual Review 2009 (Tallinn: Security Police of the Republic of Estonia, 2009), p. 18, https://kapo.ee/sites/default/files/content_page_attachments/Annual%20Review%202009.pdf.

37. See Edward Lucas, *The New Cold War: Putin's Threat to Russia and the West* (London: Bloomsbury, 2014).

38. Pierre Vaux, "Ukraine Presents Russian Sniper Rifle Taken from Captured Soldiers, Will Charge Them with 'Terrorism,'" Pressimus, 2007. On Russia's recent military modernization efforts, see Richard Connolly and Mathieu Boulègue, "Russia's New State Armament Programme: Implications for the Russian Armed Forces and Military Capabilities to 2027," Research Paper, Chatham House.

39. See Christopher A. Wray and Richard Haas, "A Conversation with Christopher Wray," Council on Foreign Relations, April 26, 2019, https://www.cfr.org/event/conversation-christopher-wray-0.

40. Kello, *The Virtual Weapon and International Order*, Chapter 8. For an excellent discussion of SORM, see Andrei Soldatov and Irina Borogan, *The Red Web: The Struggle between Russia's Digital Dictators and the New Online Revolutionaries* (New York: PublicAffairs, 2015).
41. See Adam B. Ulam, *Stalin: The Man and His Era* (Boston, MA: Beacon, 1989); and Aleksandr Orlov, *The Secret History of Stalin's Crimes* (New York: Jarrolds, 1953).
42. An example includes the dissemination of an offensive government document "proving" that U.S. President Jimmy Carter supported South Africa's apartheid regime in order to foment uprisings in Africa. The false U.S. National Security Council document was disseminated by KGB agents at Soviet embassies around the world. See Fletcher Schoen and Christopher J. Lamb, *Deception, Disinformation, and Strategic Communications: How One Interagency Group Made a Major Difference* (Washington, D.C.: National Defense University Press, June 2012), p. 24; and J. Michael Waller, *Strategic Influence: Public Diplomacy, Counterpropaganda, and Political Warfare* (Washington, D.C.: Institute of World Politics Press, 2009), pp. 159–61.
43. See Mark Galeotti, "I'm Sorry for Creating the 'Gerasimov Doctrine,'" *Foreign Policy*, March 5, 2018.
44. Valeriy Gerasimov, "Ценность науки в предвидении," ["The Value of Science is in Foresight"], Военно-промышленный курьер (February 27, 2013). For an English translation and commentary, see Mark Galeotti, "The 'Gerasimov Doctrine' and Russian Non-Linear War," *In Moscow's Shadows* (blog), July 6, 2014, https://inmoscowsshadows.wordpress.com/2014/07/06/the-gerasimov-doctrine-and-russian-non-linear-war/. See also Sergei Chekinov and Sergei A. Bogdanov, "The Nature and Content of a New-Generation War," *Military Thought* 4 (2013); and Keir Giles, "Russia's 'New' Tools for Confronting the West: Continuity and Innovation in Moscow's Exercise of Power," Research Paper, Russia and Eurasia Programme, Chatham House (March 2016).
45. Giles, "Russia's 'New' Tools for Confronting the West," p. 10.
46. For more on Russian information warfare doctrine, see Kello, *The Virtual Weapon and International Order*, Chapter 8.
47. Sergei G. Chekinov and Sergei A. Bogdanov, "Прогнозирование характера и содержания войн будущего: проблемы и суждения," Военная мысль 10 (2015) [translation mine].
48. Sergei G. Chekinov and Sergei A. Bogdanov, "Военная стратегия: взгляд в будущее," Военная мысль 11 (2016) [translation mine].
49. See "Background to 'Assessing Russian Activities and Intentions in Recent US Elections': The Analytic Process and Cyber Incident Attribution," Report of the Director of National Intelligence (January 6, 2017). See also Adam Meyers, "Danger Close: Fancy Bear Tracking of Ukrainian Field Artillery Units," *Crowdstrike* (blog), December 22, 2016, www.crowdstrike.com/blog/danger-close-fancy-bear-tracking-ukrainian-field-artillery-units/; and Matt Flegenheimer, "Countering Trump, Bipartisan Voices Strongly Affirm Findings on Russian Hacking," *The New York Times*, January 5, 2017, www.nytimes.com/2017/01/05/us/politics/taking-aim-at-trump-leaders-strongly-affirm-findings-on-russian-hacking.html.
50. Rovner, "Cyber War as an Intelligence Contest."
51. By contrast, the United States' cyber posture has traditionally been more risk averse. See Kaminska, "Restraint under Conditions of Uncertainty."
52. "A Review of the FBI's Performance in Deterring, Detecting, and Investigating the Espionage Activities of Robert Philip Hanssen" (Office of the Inspector General, August 14, 2002). Among the many ironies of the Hanssen episode is the fact that the culprit was at one point tasked by the FBI to uncover the identity of the mole who had betrayed the two Soviet double agents (Valery Martynov and Sergei Motorin). In other words, Hanssen's task was to search for himself.
53. The development of quantum computing has introduced a nuance in the physical state of computer code. A quantum bit, or a "qubit," can exist either as a 0, a 1, or a superposition of both states at once. When it is read, however, a qubit always appears to the observer as a 0 or a 1.

54. Kello, *The Virtual Weapon and International Order*, p. 5.

55. For a gripping account of the incident, see Kim Zetter, "Inside the Cunning, Unprecedented Hack of Ukraine's Power Grid," *Wired*, March 3, 2016, www.wired.com/2016/03/inside-cunning-unprecedented-hack-ukraines-power-grid/.

56. Brian Barrett, "Squirrels Menace the Power Grid, But a Cyberattack Would Still Be Worse," *Wired*, October 1, 2017, www.wired.com/2017/01/squirrels-may-beat-power-grid-glad-not-russia/.

57. "Міністерство енергетики та вугільної промисловості україни: міненерговугілля має намір утворити групу за участю представників усіх енергетичних компаній, що входять до сфери управління міністерства, для вивчення можливостей щодо запобігання несанкціонованому втручанню в роботу енергомереж" (Ukrainian Ministry of Energy, February 12, 2016); Dustin Volz, "U.S. Government Concludes Cyber Attack Caused Ukraine Power Outage," *Reuters*, February 25, 2016, www.reuters.com/article/us-ukraine-cybersecurity-idUSKCN0VY30K.

58. "Міністерство енергетики та вугільної промисловості України."

59. For a gripping account of Sandworm's origins and activities, see Andy Greenberg, *Sandworm: A New Era of Cyberwar and the Hunt for the Kremlin's Most Dangerous Hackers* (New York: Penguin Random House, 2019).

60. On the use of cyberspace for subversive purposes, see Lennart Maschmeyer, "The Subversive Trilemma: Why Cyber Operations Fall Short of Expectations," *International Security* 46, no. 2 (October 25, 2021), pp. 51–90. The analysis views subversion through the lens of interstate conquest and coercion; hence its discussion of the stratetic limitations of cyberspace is itself limited.

61. Select Committee on Intelligence, "Report of the Select Committee on Intelligence, United States Senate, on Russian Active Measures Campaigns and Interference in the 2016 U.S. Election" (U.S. Senate, 116th Congress, July 2019), p. 22.

62. "Report of the Select Committee on Intelligence," p. 38. The first public attribution of the election system intrusions to Russian state hackers appeared in a joint report of the FBI and Department of Homeland Security on December 29, 2016. See FBI and Department of Homeland Security, "Joint Analysis Report, JAR-16-20296A, GRIZZLY STEPPE – Russian Malicious Cyber Activity," December 29, 2016.

63. See "Report of the Select Committee on Intelligence."

64. U.S. District Court for the District of Columbia, "Mueller Indictment of 12 Russian Military Officers," July 2018; National Security Agency, "Russia/Cybersecurity: Main Intelligence Directorate Cyber Actors [Redacted] Target U.S. Companies and Local U.S. Government Officials," 2017.

65. *Russian Targeting of Election Infrastructure During the 2016 Election: Summary of Initial Findings and Recommendations*, U.S. Senate Intelligence Committee, May 8, 2018, www.intelligence.senate.gov/publications/russia-inquiry.

66. Quoted in Teresa Lawlor, "Relying on Electronic Voting Machines Puts Us at Risk, Security Expert Says," The World from PRX, August 17, 2020, www.pri.org/stories/2020-08-17/relying-electronic-voting-machines-puts-us-risk-security-expert-says. Among the most assiduous analysts of election system vulnerabilities is Kim Zetter. See, for example, Kim Zetter, "The Myth of the Hacker-Proof Voting Machine," *The New York Times*, February 21, 2018, www.nytimes.com/2018/02/21/magazine/the-myth-of-the-hacker-proof-voting-machine.html; Zetter, "How Close Did Russia Really Come to Hacking the 2016 Election?" *Politico*, December 26, 2019, www.politico.com/news/magazine/2019/12/26/did-russia-really-hack-2016-election-088171; Zetter, "Fixing Democracy: The Election Security Crisis and Solutions for Mending It," *Texas National Security Review*, Fall 2020.

67. "Report of the Select Committee on Intelligence," p. 10.

68. "Partisanship and Political Animosity in 2016," *Pew Research Center* (blog), June 22, 2016, www.pewresearch.org/politics/2016/06/22/partisanship-and-political-animosity-in-2016/.

69. Patrick Healy and Jonathan Martin, "Donald Trump Won't Say If He'll Accept Result of Election," *The New York Times*, October 19, 2016, www.nytimes.com/2016/10/20/us/politics/presidential-debate.html.
70. "Homeland Security Intelligence Assessment: Cyber Actors Continue to Engage in Influence Activities and Targeting of Election Infrastructure," U.S. Department of Homeland Security, October 11, 2018.
71. See Linda Qiu, "How Sidney Powell Inaccurately Cited Venezuela's Elections as Evidence of U.S. Fraud," *The New York Times*, November 19, 2020, www.nytimes.com/2020/11/19/technology/sidney-powell-venezuela.html; and Ali Swenson, "AP FACT CHECK: Trump Legal Team's Batch of False Vote Claims," AP News, November 19, 2020, https://apnews.com/article/fact-check-trump-legal-team-false-claims-5abd64917ef8be9e9e2078180973e8b3. On Russian-Venezuelan ties, see Alison Brown, "An Enduring Relationship – From Russia, With Love," Center for Strategic and International Studies (blog), September 24, 2020, www.csis.org/blogs/post-soviet-post/enduring-relationship-russia-love.
72. Gohmert's unsubstantiated claims gained wide traction on social media among Trump sympathizers. See "Fact Check: The U.S. Military Has Not Seized Election Servers in Germany," *Reuters*, November 16, 2020, www.reuters.com/article/uk-factcheck-election-syctl-military-idUSKBN27W1UW.
73. See Alia Shoaib and Yelena Dzhanova, "Jeffrey Clark, Trump-Appointed DOJ Official, Claimed Chinese Thermostats Changed Votes in 2020 Election, Reports Say," *Business Insider*, August 8, 2021, www.businessinsider.com/trump-appointed-doj-official-claimed-chinese-thermostats-changed-votes-2021-8?r=US&IR=T.
74. Russian security services also use kompromat systematically to coerce domestic opponents of the Kremlin. See Daniel Hoffmann, "Blackmail Culture Goes Digital in Putin's Russia," The Cipher Brief, November 8, 2017, www.thecipherbrief.com/column_article/blackmail-culture-goes-digital-putins-russia.
75. "Homeland Threat Assessment" (U.S. Department of Homeland Security, October 2020).
76. *Report of the U.S. Senate Intelligence Committee on Russian Active Measures Campaigns and Interference in the 2016 U.S. Election*, U.S. Senate Intelligence Committee, 2020, p. 3, www.intelligence.senate.gov/sites/default/files/documents/Report_Volume2.pdf.
77. Zetter, "Fixing Democracy."
78. Alexa Corse, "Voting Machine Supplier Criticized by Trump in Spotlight on Election Integrity," *Wall Street Journal*, November 17, 2020, www.wsj.com/articles/voting-machine-supplier-criticized-by-trump-in-spotlight-on-election-integrity-11605624361.
79. See Gloria Gonzalez, Ben Lefebvre, and Eric Geller, "'Jugula' of the U.S. Fuel Pipeline System Shuts Down After Cyberattack," *Politico*, May 8, 2021, www.politico.com/news/2021/05/08/colonial-pipeline-cyber-attack-485984.
80. See A.J. Vicens, "Political Fallout in Cybercrime Circles Upping the Threat to Western Targets," *Cyberscoop*, May 14, 2022, www.cyberscoop.com/russia-ukraine-cybercrime-ransomware-threat/.
81. See "Russia Cyber Threat Overview and Advisories," Cybersecurity and Infrastructure Security Agency, www.cisa.gov/uscert/russia, accessed on April 24, 2022.
82. See "Annual Threat Assessment of the U.S. Intelligence Community" (Washington, D.C.: Office of the Director of National Intelligence, February 22, 2022), https://docs.house.gov/meetings/IG/IG00/20220308/114469/HHRG-117-IG00-Wstate-HainesA-20220308.pdf.
83. Quoted in "Four Russian Government Employees Charged in Two Historical Hacking Campaigns Targeting Critical Infrastructure Worldwide," U.S. Department of Justice, March 24, 2022, www.justice.gov/opa/pr/four-russian-government-employees-charged-two-historical-hacking-campaigns-targeting-critical.
84. See Zolan Kanno-Youngs, "Biden Warns the Private Sector that Russia is Exploring Options for Cyberattacks," The New York Times, March 21, 2022, https://www.nytimes.com/2022/03/21/world/europe/biden-russia-cyberattack.html. For an analysis of this

danger, see Lucas Kello and Monica Kaminska, "Cyberspace and War in Ukraine: Prepare for Worse," *Lawfare* (blog), April 14, 2022, www.lawfareblog.com/cyberspace-and-war-ukraine-prepare-worse.

85. On covert Russian agents operating abroad, see, for example, Gordon Corera, *Russians Among Us: Sleeper Cells, Ghost Stories and the Hunt for Putin's Agents* (London: HarperCollins, 2020).

86. See Andrew Rettman, "Illicit Russian Billions Pose Threat to EU Democracy," *EU Observer*, April 21, 2017, https://euobserver.com/world/137631.

87. Michael Schwirtz, "As West Warns of Russian Attack, Ukraine Sends Different Message," *The New York Times*, January 25, 2022, www.nytimes.com/2022/01/25/world/europe/ukraine-russia-invasion.html.

88. "The Impacts of NotPetya Ransomware: What You Need to Know," *InfoTransec* (blog), March 5, 2019, https://infotransec.com/news/the-impacts-of-notpetya-ransomware-what-you-need-to-know/.

89. Morgan Chalfant, "Trump Admin Blames Russia for Massive Global Cyberattack," *The Hill*, February 15, 2018, https://thehill.com/policy/cybersecurity/374104-trump-admin-blames-russia-for-global-cyberattack-warns-of-international.

90. See "Press Release: Treasury Sanctions Russian Federal Security Service Enablers," U.S. Department of the Treasury, June 11, 2018, https://home.treasury.gov/news/press-releases/sm0410. Another indictment in 2020 indicted six GRU officers for a range of actions, including NotPetya. See "Six Russian GRU Officers Charged in Connection with Worldwide Deployment of Destructive Malware and Other Disruptive Actions in Cyberspace," U.S. Department of Justice, October 19, 2020, www.justice.gov/opa/pr/six-russian-gru-officers-charged-connection-worldwide-deployment-destructive-malware-and.

91. In 2014, Russia tested its own system for financial payments, the SPFS (Система передачи финансовых сообщений). Its viability as an alternative payments system is limited by the absence of foreign banks (only twelve use it) in the system. See Harley Balzer, "Cutting off Russia from SWIFT Will Really Sting," *Atlantic Council* (blog), January 12, 2022.

92. See Nick Wadhams, "Russia Is Now the World's Most-Sanctioned Nation," *Bloomberg*, March 7, 2022, www.bloomberg.com/news/articles/2022-03-07/russia-surges-past-iran-to-become-world-s-most-sanctioned-nation.

93. See "Russia: Gross Domestic Product (GDP) in Current Prices from 1996 to 2026," Statista. com, www.statista.com/statistics/263772/gross-domestic-product-gdp-in-russia/, accessed on April 20, 2022.

94. Russia's security elites have broadly supported Putin's policy towards Ukraine. A burning question for Kremlin watchers is whether the support will crack from the follies of the larger invasion. See Denis Volkov, "Russian Elite Opinion after Crimea," Carnegie Endowment for International Peace (March 23, 2016).

95. See Lucas Kello, "Keynote Speech at the U.S. Cyber Command Legal Conference," March 10, 2022, https://www.dvidshub.net/video/834249/cyber-policy-expert-professor-lucas-kello-gives-keynote-remarks-2022-uscybercom-legal-conference.

5. CHINA AND CYBERSPACE: THE RISING TECHNOLOGICAL HEGEMON

1. I am grateful to Greg Austin for his extremely valuable insights on Chinese history and culture, which aided the writing of this chapter.

2. On China's international aspirations, see, for example, Jeffrey W. Legro, "What China Will Want: The Future Intentions of a Rising Power," *Perspectives on Politics* 5, no. 3 (2007), pp. 515–34; and Graham Allison, *Destined for War: Can America and China Escape Thucydides's Trap?* (Boston, MA: Houghton Mifflin, 2017).

3. Eyre Crowe, "Memorandum on the Present State of British Relations with France and Germany," January 1, 1907.

4. Thucydides, *History of the Peloponnesian War* (Harmondsworth: Penguin Books, 1972). In the context of China's rise, see Allison, *Destined for War*.

5. Melanie Hart, Jabin Jacob, Nadège Rolland, and Angela Stanzel, "Grand Designs: Does China Have a 'Grand Strategy'?" *ECFR* (blog), October 18, 2017.

6. Quoted in Robert Sutter, *Chinese Foreign Relations: Power and Policy Since the End of the Cold War*, 3rd edn (Lanham, MD: Rowman and Littlefield, 2012), pp. 9–10. Wang Jisi also stated in 2011: "Whether China has any such strategy today is open to debate" and ". . . the Chinese government has yet to disclose any document that comprehensively expounds the country's strategic goals and the ways to achieve them." Wang Jisi, "China's Search for a Grand Strategy: A Rising Great Power Finds Its Way," *Foreign Affairs* 90, no. 2 (2011), pp. 68–79. See also Rush Doshi, *The Long Game: China's Grand Strategy to Displace American Order* (Oxford: Oxford University Press, 2021), pp. 7–8.

7. Recent scholarship has illuminated the objectives and organizing tenets of Chinese foreign policy. See, for example, Doshi, *The Long Game* – an expertly researched work that cuts deeply into the available archival evidence.

8. See, for example, Alastair Iain Johnston, *Cultural Realism: Strategic Culture and Grand Strategy in Chinese History* (Princeton, NJ: Princeton University Press, 1995); Johnston, "Cultural Realism and Strategy in Maoist China," in *The Culture of National Security: Norms and Identity in World Politics*, ed. Peter J. Katzenstein (New York: Columbia University Press, 1996); Andrew Scobell, *China and Strategic Culture* (U.S. Army War College, 2002); Andrew Scobell, "China's Real Strategic Culture: A Great Wall of the Imagination," *Contemporary Security Policy* 35, no. 2 (June 2014); Huiyun Feng, *Chinese Strategic Culture and Foreign Policy Decision-Making: Confucianism, Leadership and War* (New York: Routledge, 2007); Tiewa Liu, "Chinese Strategic Culture and the Use of Force: Moral and Political Perspectives," *Journal of Contemporary China* 23 (January 2014); Andrea Ghiselli, "Revising China's Strategic Culture: Contemporary Cherry-Picking of Ancient Strategic Thought," *The China Quarterly* 233 (2018), pp. 166–85; and Rosita Dellios, "Chinese Strategic Culture – Part 2: Virtue and Power," *Culture Mandala* 13, Special Issue 3 (February 2020). Johnston's work is a pivotal reference point in the study of Chinese strategic culture. Although dated, it has aged well.

9. Until the mid-nineteenth century, only Russia had a foreign representation in the country – a small cultural office.

10. It is debatable, whether the invasions first by the Mongols and then by the Manchus were an internal "Chinese" phenomenon. Contemporary Chinese propaganda has settled the debate for its hapless consumers. About the Mongol emperor Kublai Khan, a government website states: "[He] ended the centuries-long situation in which many independent regimes existed alongside each other, by forming one united state. . ." "Song, Yuan, Ming and Qing Dynasties (960–1911)," China.org.cn, http://www.china.org.cn/archive/2006-12/27/content_1192271.htm, accessed April 15, 2022.

11. Before the early nineteenth century, Chinese elites were largely unaware of the flourishing of human civilization in places like the West and the Islamic world.

12. Quoted in Ulam, *The Communists*, p. 77.

13. Mao's Communist forces, however, did not fully defeat the pre-civil war elite, whose leadership fled to the island of Taiwan.

14. Evidently, the Central Committee's instruction in August 1966 to take "special care" of scientific experts went largely unheeded. See Jonathan D. Spence, *The Search for Modern China* (London: Hutchinson, 1990), p. 605.

15. David Shambaugh, *China's Communist Party: Atrophy and Adaptation* (Berkeley: University of California Press, 2008).

16. Quoted in Yinghong Cheng, "Fidel Castro and 'China's Lesson for Cuba': A Chinese Perspective," *The China Quarterly* 189 (2007), p. 26.

17. Ibid., p. 30.

18. Quoted in Chris Buckley, "China's History Is Revised, to the Glory of Xi Jinping," *The New York Times*, November 16, 2021, www.nytimes.com/2021/11/16/world/asia/china-history-xi-jinping.html.

19. The behavior is criminalized under Article 293 of the 1997 revision of the Penal Code of the People's Republic of China. It carries a maximum penalty of five years' imprisonment.

20. And not just in China. To European thinkers such as Voltaire who were swept by the fads of *chinoiserie* in the eighteenth century, the Qing emperor seemed like a close approximation of the ideal "Philosopher King." Voltaire's *Essai sur les mœurs et l'esprit des nations* opened with a detailed discussion of China and its emperor, in whose honor the French philosopher wrote poems. See Spence, *The Search for Modern China*, Chapter 7.

21. Quoted in Doshi, *The Long Game*, p. 28.

22. See Ngaire Woods, "The United States and the International Financial Institutions: Power and Influence within the World Bank and the International Monetary Fund," in *U.S. Hegemony and International Organizations* ed. Rosemary Foot, Neil MacFarlane, and Michael Mastanduno, (Oxford: Oxford University Press, 2003).

23. Quoted in Ananth Kirshnan, "Xi's 'Global Security Initiative' Looks to Counter Quad," *The Hindu*, April 28, 2022, www.thehindu.com/news/international/xis-global-security-initiative-looks-to-counter-quad/article65363978.ece.

24. See Shannon Tiezzi, "China's Bid to Write the Global Rules on Data Security," *The Diplomat*, September 10, 2020, https://thediplomat.com/2020/09/chinas-bid-to-write-the-global-rules-on-data-security/.

25. Ibid., p. 28.

26. Quoted ibid., p. 271.

27. Hui Lu, "Commentary: Milestone Congress Points to New Era for China, The World" (Xinhua, October 24, 2017).

28. For an informative review of the "Community of Common Destiny," see Doshi, *The Long Game*, pp. 168–75.

29. Ibid., pp. 248–9.

30. Ibid., pp. 72–3.

31. Sujian Guo, *China's "Peaceful Rise" in the 21st Century: Domestic and International Conditions* (Farnham: Ashgate, 2006), p. 2.

32. "China Warns Taiwan Independence 'Means War' as US Pledges Support," *BBC News*, January 29, 2021, www.bbc.co.uk/news/world-asia-55851052.

33. As in the security relationship with Russia, an accelerating war (even a nuclear one) with China could inadvertently occur. On this danger, see Fionna S. Cunningham and M. Taylor Fravel, "Dangerous Confidence? Chinese Views on Nuclear Escalation," *International Security* 44, no. 2 (Fall 2019), pp. 61–109.

34. Peter Layton, "China's Enduring Grey-Zone Challenge" (Air and Space Power Centre, 2021), p. 45; Kevin Bilms, "Beyond War and Peace: The PLA's 'Non-War Military Activities' Concept," Modern War Institute, January 26, 2022.

35. As Alastair Iain Johnston aptly observed: "China has historically exhibited a relatively consistent hard realpolitik or parabellum strategic culture that has persisted across different structural contexts into the Maoist period (and beyond). Chinese decision makers have internalized this strategic culture such that China's strategic behavior exhibits a preference for offensive uses of force, mediated by a keen sensitivity to relative capabilities." Johnston, "Cultural Realism and Strategy in Maoist China."

36. "2021 Annual Threat Assessment of the U.S. Intelligence Community" (Washington, D.C.: Office of the Director of National Intelligence, April 13, 2021).

37. On the Thucydides Trap of international anarchy, see Allison, *Destined for War*.

38. On China's information security priorities and practices, see, for instance, Greg Austin, *Cyber Policy in China* (Cambridge: Polity Press, 2014); and Greg Austin, *Cybersecurity in China: The Next Wave* (New York: Springer, 2018).

39. Adam Segal, "When China Rules the Web: Technology in Service of the State," *Foreign Affairs*, September/October 2018.

40. See Joseph S. Nye, Jr., "The Regime Complex for Managing Global Cyber Activities," Global Commission on Internet Governance Paper Series No. 1 (May 2014).

41. Indrani Bagchi, "Doklam Standoff: China Playing Out Its 'Three Warfares' Strategy against India," *The Times of India*, August 8, 2017, https://timesofindia.indiatimes.com/india/china-playing-out-its-three-warfares-strategy-against-india/articleshow/60036197.cms.

42. Kathrin Hille, "Taiwan's Unity Cracks under Chinese Disinformation Onslaught," *Financial Times*, June 29, 2021, www.ft.com/content/f22f1011-0630-462a-a21e-83bae4523da7.

43. Gregory Winger, "China's Disinformation Campaign in the Philippines," *The Diplomat*, October 6, 2020, https://thediplomat.com/2020/10/chinas-disinformation-campaign-in-the-philippines/.

44. See Yan Zhuang and John Liu, "How Australia's Leader Lost Control of His Chinese Social Media Account," *The New York Times*, January 24, 2022, www.nytimes.com/2022/01/25/world/australia/scott-morrison-wechat-account.html.

45. Pau Karp and Donna Lu, "Josh Frydenberg Ads Appear on WeChat Despite Liberal MPs Calling for Boycott," *The Guardian*, February 21, 2022, www.theguardian.com/australia-news/2022/feb/21/josh-frydenberg-ads-appear-on-wechat-despite-liberal-mps-calling-for-boycott.

46. Scott W. Harold, "The U.S.–China Cyber Agreement: A Good First Step," The Rand (blog), August 1, 2016.

47. Jeff Jones, "Confronting China's Efforts to Steal Defense Information," Belfer Center for Science and International Affairs, Harvard Kennedy School, May 2020. On the strategic effects of Chinese cyber theft, see Joe Devanny, Ciaran Martin, and Tim Stevens, "On the Strategic Consequences of Digital Espionage," *Journal of Cyber Policy* 6, no. 3 (September 2, 2021), pp. 429–50. For a more skeptical view on this topic, see Gilli and Gilli, "Why China Has Not Caught Up Yet."

48. See Kim Zetter, " 'Google' Hackers Had Ability to Alter Source Code," *Wired*, March 3, 2010, www.wired.com/2010/03/source-code-hacks/.

49. See Harriet Sherwood, "Vatican Enlists Bots to Protect Library from Onslaught of Hackers," *The Guardian*, November 8, 2020, www.theguardian.com/world/2020/nov/08/vatican-enlists-bots-to-protect-library-from-onslaught-of-hackers.

50. Daniel Hurst, "Hackers Linked to China Allegedly Stole Data from Australian Defence Contractor," *The Guardian*, July 22, 2020, www.theguardian.com/australia-news/2020/jul/22/hackers-linked-to-china-allegedly-stole-data-from-australian-defence-contractor.

51. See Matt Burgess, "Chinese Hackers Targeted Major UK Companies as Coronavirus Raged," *Wired*, July 23, 2020, www.wired.co.uk/article/china-coronavirus-hacking-uk-us; and Christopher Bing and Marisa Taylor, "China-backed Hackers 'Targeted Covid-19 Vaccine from Moderna'," *Reuters*, July 30, 2020, www.reuters.com/article/us-health-coronavirus-moderna-cyber-excl-idUSKCN24V38M.

52. Nicholas Weaver, "The Microsoft Exchange Hack and the Great Email Robbery," *Lawfare* (blog), March 9, 2021, www.lawfareblog.com/microsoft-exchange-hack-and-great-email-robbery. Alperovitch described it as "an exceptionally reckless and dangerous tactic that has weakened the security of tens of thousands of networks around the globe". Alperovitch and Ward, "How Should the U.S. Respond to the SolarWinds and Microsoft Exchange Hacks?"

53. See Daitian Li, Tony W. Tong, and Yangao Xiao, "Is China Emerging as the Global Leader in AI?" *Harvard Business Review* (February 18, 2021); and Christina Larson, "China's Massive Investment in Artificial Intelligence Has an Insidious Downside," *Science*, February 8, 2018, www.science.org/content/article/china-s-massive-investment-artificial-intelligence-has-insidious-downside.

54. "Military and Security Developments Involving the People's Republic of China 2021 – Annual Report to Congress" (Office of the Secretary of Defense, 2021), p. 88.

55. Brad D. Williams, "CYBERCOM Has Conducted 'Hunt-Forward' Ops in 14 Countries, Deputy Says," BreakingDefense.com, November 10, 2021, https://breakingdefense.com/2021/11/cybercoms-no-2-discusses-hunt-forward-space-cybersecurity-china/.

56. Scott W. Harold, Nathan Beauchamp-Mustafaga, and Jeffrey W. Hornung, "Chinese Disinformation Efforts on Social Media," *Combating Foreign Disinformation on Social Media Series* (Rand Corporation, 2021), Chapter 5.

57. "Democracy Facing Global Challenges: V-Dem Annual Democracy Report 2019" (V-Dem Institute, University of Gothenburg, May 2019). The report names Taiwan as one of "the strongest holds for democracy in the world" (p. 10).

58. Quoted in Edward White, "Taiwan Braced for Chinese Meddling Ahead of Election," *Financial Times*, July 8, 2018, www.ft.com/content/cbb0f12e-7ff4-11e8-bc55-50daf11b720d. See also Joshua Kurlantzick, "How China Is Interfering in Taiwan's Election," Council on Foreign Relations, November 7, 2019; Yuki Tatsumi, Pamela Kennedy, and Jason Li, "Taiwan Security Brief – Cybersecurity as a Sine Qua Non of Digital Economy: Turning Taiwan into a Reliable Digital Nation?" (Stimson Center, September 2019); and Sean P. Quirk, "Lawfare in the Disinformation Age: Chinese Interference in Taiwan's 2020 Elections," *Harvard International Law Journal* 62, no. 2 (2021).

59. Daniel Hurst, "Australia Accuses China of Spreading 'Fear and Division' as Diplomatic Tensions Escalate," *The Guardian*, June 16, 2020, www.theguardian.com/australia-news/2020/jun/16/australia-accuses-china-of-spreading-fear-and-division-as-diplomatic-tensions-escalate.

60. NATO, "Brussels Summit Communiqué Issued by the Heads of State and Government Participating in the Meeting of the North Atlantic Council in Brussels 14 June 2021," NATO, June 14, 2021.

61. For a detailed study of China's information warfare outfits and activities, see Paul Charon and Jean-Baptiste Jeangène Vilmer, *Chinese Influence Operations: A Machiavellian Moment* (Paris: Ministry of Armed Forces, October 2021).

62. Quoted in Ralph Jennings, "How China Could Cyberattack Taiwan," VOA, December 10, 2021, www.voanews.com/a/how-china-could-cyberattack-taiwan/6349594.html.

63. Linda Zhang, "How to Counter China's Disinformation Campaign in Taiwan," Army University Press, U.S. Army, October 2020.

64. Mark Sweney, "Global Shortage in Computer Chips 'Reaches Crisis Point,'" *The Guardian*, March 21, 2021, www.theguardian.com/business/2021/mar/21/global-shortage-in-computer-chips-reaches-crisis-point.

65. Tzu-ti Huang, "Output Value of Taiwan's Semiconductor Sector Logged US$115 Billion in 2020," *Taiwan News*, February 22, 2021, www.taiwannews.com.tw/en/news/4133393.

66. The United States, however, has fallen behind as a geographic location for the manufacturing of semiconductors. See *2021 State of the U.S. Semiconductor Industry*, Semiconductor Industry Association, 2021, www.semiconductors.org/wp-content/uploads/2021/09/2021-SIA-State-of-the-Industry-Report.pdf.

67. James A. Lewis, "Risks in the Semiconductor Manufacturing and Advanced Packaging Supply Chain," Center for Strategic and International Studies, April 16, 2021.

68. Alarmed by China's rise, Taiwan and Japan recently tightened their bilateral relations in the technology field – for example, by agreeing a major bilateral manufacturing deal. See Ryosuke Eguchi, "Japan's Wooing of TSMC Pays Off with $7bn Chip Plant," *Nikkei Asia*, October 12, 2021, https://asia.nikkei.com/Business/Tech/Semiconductors/Japan-s-wooing-of-TSMC-pays-off-with-7bn-chip-plant.

69. Jordan Robertson and Michael Riley, "The Long Hack: How China Exploited a U.S. Tech Supplier," *Bloomberg*, February 12, 2021.

70. "UK and Allies Hold Chinese State Responsible for a Pervasive Pattern of Hacking," GOV.UK, July 19, 2021.

71. "Hearing before the U.S.–China Economic and Security Review Commission, One-Hundred Fourteenth Congress, Second Session" (United States Congress, June 9, 2016).

72. "Huawei Denies German Report It Colluded with Chinese Intelligence," *Reuters*, January 29, 2020, www.reuters.com/article/uk-germany-usa-huawei-idUKKBN1ZS194.
73. Insikt Group "China-Linked Group RedEcho Targets the Indian Power Sector Amid Heightened Border Tensions," *Recorded Future*, February 28, 2021.
74. As Charon and Vilmer put it, this evolution (which began in 2017) represents a " 'Russification' of Chinese influence operations"; *Chinese Influence Operations*, p. 18.

6. THE DIMENSIONS OF CURRENT STRATEGY: TO DETER OR NOT TO DETER?

1. Valeriano and Maness, "The Coming Cyberpeace." This article is unfortunately timed. It claimed that "Moscow is willing to use cyberwarfare for disruption and propaganda, but not to inflict injuries or lasting infrastructural damage" – an obvious point considering that no cyber-attack had sought to kill people, and only few at the time, such as Stuxnet, in which Russia did not participate, had destroyed physical infrastructure. Nevertheless, one year after this bold assertion, the Russian military divulged the email records of Democratic Party leaders which it had hacked in the leadup to the U.S. presidential election, miring the country in a situation of enduring political controversy that President Trump's National Security Advisor John Bolton misguidedly but alarmingly described as "an 'act of war' against our constitutional structures" (Bolton, *The Room Where It Happened*, p. 174). This is hardly a picture of cyber "peace."
2. Brandon Valeriano and Ryan C. Maness, "How We Stopped Worrying about Cyber Doom and Started Collecting Data," *Politics and Governance* 6, no. 2 (June 11, 2018), pp. 49–60.
3. Consider, for instance, Russia's annexation of Crimea in February 2014. Russian unconventional ground forces invaded the peninsula. They sequestered Ukrainian naval assets in Sevastopol but caused little damage to physical infrastructure. Loss of life was implied but did not occur. And yet observers widely condemned the action as a use of force and even an act of war. See Veronika Bilková, "The Use of Force by the Russian Federation in Crimea," *Heidelberg Journal of International Law* 75, no. 1 (2015), pp. 27–50; and Kersti Kaljulaid, "President of Estonia Kersti Kaljulaid: We Cannot Silently Consent to Russia's Aggression in the Sea of Azov," Office of the President, November 27, 2018, https://president.ee/en/official-duties/statements/3525-president-estonia-kersti-kaljulaid-we-cannot-silently-consent-to-russias-aggression-sea-azovm, accessed August 30, 2020.
4. Ben Hubbard et al., "Pompeo Calls Attacks on Saudi Arabia 'Act of War' and Seeks Coalition to Counter Iran," *The New York Times*, September 18, 2019, www.nytimes.com/2019/09/18/world/middleeast/us-iran-saudi-arabia.html.
5. The relationship between the state and private hackers in Iran is murky. The country's preeminent cyber force resides within the Islamic Revolutionary Guard Corps, but the group routinely outsources its foreign operations to contractors and other private actors. One report identified as many as fifty private actors with which the Corps coordinates attacks via intermediaries. Levi Gundert, Sanil Chohan, and Greg Lesnewich, "Iran's Hacker Hierarchy Exposed: How the Islamic Republic of Iran Uses Contractors and Universities to Conduct Cyber Operations," *Recorded Future* (blog), May 9, 2018.
6. Perlroth and Sanger, "Iranian Hackers Target Trump Campaign."
7. Ellen Nakashima, "U.S. Undertook Cyber Operation Against Iran as Part of Effort to Secure the 2020 Election," *Washington Post*, November 3, 2020, www.washingtonpost.com/national-security/cybercom-targets-iran-election-interference/2020/11/03/aa0c9790-1e11-11eb-ba21-f2f001f0554b_story.html.
8. Jon R. Lindsay, "Tipping the Scales: The Attribution Problem and the Feasibility of Deterrence against Cyberattack," *Journal of Cybersecurity* 1, no. 1 (2015), pp. 53–67.
9. William J. Lynn III, "Defending a New Domain," *Foreign Affairs*, September/October, 2010.
10. Author interview with senior British civil servant.
11. *International Strategy for Cyberspace: Prosperity, Security, and Openness in a Networked World*, White House, May 2011, p. 14.

12. Executive Office of the President, "Report on Cyber Deterrence Policy" (White House, 2015).
13. Lynn, "Defending a New Domain."
14. "Department of Defense Cyberspace Policy Report: A Report to Congress Pursuant to the National Defense Authorization Act for Fiscal Year 2011, Section 934" (U.S. Department of Defense, November 2011), p. 2.
15. "Advance Questions for Vice Admiral Michael S. Rogers, USN: Nominee for Commander, United States Cyber Command" (U.S. Senate Armed Services Committee, March 11, 2014).
16. "National Cyber Strategy of the United States of America" (The White House, September 2018).
17. "Summary: Department of Defense Cyber Strategy" (U.S. Department of Defense, 2018), p. 4.
18. See Joseph S. Nye, Jr., "Nuclear Lessons for Cyber Security?" *Strategic Studies Quarterly* 5, no. 4 (2011); and Robert Jervis, "Some Thoughts on Deterrence in the Cyber Era," *Journal of Information Warfare* 15, no. 2 (2016), pp. 66–73.
19. For a discussion of the affinities between nuclear and cyber strategy, see, for instance, Stephen J. Cimbala, "Nuclear Deterrence and Cyber Warfare: Coexistence or Competition?" *Defense & Security Analysis* 33, no. 3 (2017), pp. 193–208.
20. Sean Lyngaas, "NSA's Rob Joyce Outlines How U.S. Can Disrupt and Deter Foreign Hacking," *CyberScoop*, February 28, 2019.
21. Quoted in Andrew Tillen, "Punish Countries That Launch Cyber Attacks, Global Expert Chris Painter Says," *Australian Financial Review*, February 28, 2018, www.afr.com/politics/punish-countries-that-launch-cyber-attacks-global-expert-chris-painter-says-20180228-h0ws23.
22. "Cyberspace Solarium Commission – Report" (U.S. Cyberspace Solarium Commission, co-chaired by Angus King, Jr., and Mike Gallagher, March 11, 2020).
23. Henry Farrell and Abraham L. Newman, "Weaponized Interdependence: How Global Economic Networks Shape State Coercion," *International Security* 44, no. 1 (2019), pp. 42–79.
24. Devlin Barrett, "Obama Says Sony 'Made a Mistake' Canceling Film," *Wall Street Journal*, December 19, 2014, www.wsj.com/articles/obama-says-sony-made-a-mistake-canceling-film-1419017168.
25. "Treasury Imposes Sanctions Against the Government of the Democratic People's Republic of Korea" (U.S. Department of the Treasury, January 2, 2015).
26. Ibid.
27. "Fact Sheet: Actions in Response to Russian Malicious Cyber Activity and Harassment," Office of the Press Secretary, The White House, December 29, 2016.
28. "Grand Jury Indicts Thirteen Russian Individuals and Three Russian Companies for Scheme to Interfere in the United States Political System" (U.S. Department of Justice, February 16, 2018); "Grand Jury Indicts 12 Russian Intelligence Officers for Hacking Offenses Related to the 2016 Election" (U.S. Department of Justice, July 13, 2018); "Treasury Sanctions Russian Cyber Actors for Interference with the 2016 U.S. Elections and Malicious Cyber-Attacks" (U.S. Department of the Treasury).
29. "Treasury Sanctions Russian Cyber Actors for Interference with the 2016 U.S. Elections and Malicious Cyber-Attacks."
30. "Treasury Sanctions Russian Federal Security Service Enablers" (U.S. Department of the Treasury, June 11, 2018).
31. Kello, *The Virtual Weapon and International Order*, pp. 214–15.
32. For an excellent account of the NotPetya incident, see Greenberg, *Sandworm*.
33. "Treasury Targets Russian Operatives over Election Interference, World Anti-Doping Agency Hacking, and Other Malign Activities" (U.S. Department of the Treasury, December 19, 2018).
34. "Treasury Targets Assets of Russian Financier Who Attempted to Influence 2018 U.S. Elections" (U.S. Department of the Treasury, September 30, 2019).

35. "Treasury Sanctions Evil Corp, the Russia-Based Cybercriminal Group Behind Dridex Malware" (U.S. Department of the Treasury, December 5, 2019).
36. "Treasury Sanctions Russian Cyber Actors for Virtual Currency Theft" (U.S. Department of the Treasury, September 16, 2020).
37. "Treasury Sanctions Russian Government Research Institution Connected to the Triton Malware" (U.S. Department of the Treasury, October 23, 2020).
38. "Treasury Sanctions North Korean State-Sponsored Malicious Cyber Groups" (U.S. Department of the Treasury, September 13, 2019).
39. "Treasury Sanctions Iranian Entities for Attempted Election Interference" (U.S. Department of the Treasury, October 22, 2020).
40. "Treasury Sanctions Individuals Laundering Cryptocurrency for Lazarus Group" (U.S. Department of the Treasury, March 2, 2020).
41. Garrett Hinck and Tim Maurer, "Persistent Enforcement: Criminal Charges as a Response to Nation-State Malicious Cyber Activity," *Journal of National Security Law and Policy* 10 (2020), pp. 530–34.
42. "U.S. Charges Five Chinese Military Hackers for Cyber Espionage Against U.S. Corporations and a Labor Organization for Commercial Advantage" (U.S. Department of Justice, May 19, 2014).
43. Hinck and Maurer, "Persistent Enforcement."
44. Quoted in Josh Rogin, "NSA Chief: Cybercrime Constitutes the 'Greatest Transfer of Wealth in History," Foreign Policy, July 9, 2012.
45. Jacquelyn Schneider, "Deterrence in and through Cyberspace," in *Cross-Domain Deterrence: Strategy in an Era of Complexity*, ed. Eric Gartzke and Jon R. Lindsay (Oxford and New York: Oxford University Press, 2019).
46. For a discussion of the stability–instability paradox in the cyber domain, see Kello, "The Virtual Weapon"; and Kello, *The Virtual Weapon and International Order*, Chapter 7.
47. James R. Clapper, *Facts and Fears: Hard Truths from a Life in Intelligence* (New York: Penguin Random House, 2018), pp. 534–35.
48. "Achieve and Maintain Cyberspace Superiority."
49. "Hearing to Receive Testimony on Foreign Cyber Threats to the United States" (U.S. Senate Armed Services Committee, January 5, 2017).
50. Michael P. Fischerkeller and Richard J. Harknett, "Deterrence Is Not a Credible Strategy for Cyberspace," *Orbis* 61, no. 3 (January 1, 2017), pp. 381–93; Emily O. Goldman, "From Reaction to Action: Adopting a Competitive Posture in Cyber Diplomacy," *Texas National Security Review*, Fall 2020.
51. Nakasone and Sulmeyer, "How to Compete in Cyberspace."
52. "Achieve and Maintain Cyberspace Superiority."
53. "Department of Defense Strategy for Operating in Cyberspace" (U.S. Department of Defense, July 2011), p. 7.
54. Healey, "The Implications of Persistent (and Permanent) Engagement in Cyberspace"; Nakasone and Sulmeyer, "How to Compete in Cyberspace."
55. Lyngaas, "NSA's Rob Joyce Outlines How U.S. Can Disrupt and Deter Foreign Hacking."
56. Nakasone and Sulmeyer, "How to Compete in Cyberspace."
57. Ibid.
58. Fischerkeller and Harknett, "Deterrence Is Not a Credible Strategy for Cyberspace"; Michael P. Fischerkeller and Richard J. Harknett, "Persistent Engagement, Agreed Competition, and Cyberspace Interaction Dynamics and Escalation," *Cyber Defense Review*, Special edition (2019), pp. 267–87.

7. PUNCTUATED DETERRENCE: HOW TO STRIKE BACK

1. Legal scholars often distinguish between *lex lata*, or existing international law, and *lex ferenda*, future law. As discussed in Chapter 2, because much of cyber activity does not fall neatly

within existing legal categories of interstate war and peaceful rivalry, new laws and norms may have to be developed to categorize it – a lengthy and laborious process of institutional construction. On *lex lata* and *lex ferenda*, see, for instance, Antonio Cassese et al., *Change and Stability in International Law-Making* (Berlin: Walter de Gruyter, 1988), Chapter 1.

2. James G. March and Johan P. Olsen, "The Logic of Appropriateness," *ARENA Working Papers* 4, no. 9 (2004), p. 28; Finnemore and Hollis, "Constructing Norms for Global Cybersecurity," pp. 425–79.

3. Martin C. Libicki, *Cyberdeterrence and Cyberwar* (Santa Monica, CA: RAND Corporation, 2009); Will Goodman, "Cyber Deterrence: Tougher in Theory than in Practice?" *Strategic Studies Quarterly* 4, no. 3 (2010), pp. 102–35; Joseph S. Nye, "Deterrence and Dissuasion in Cyberspace," *International Security* 41, no. 3 (January 2017), pp. 44–71; Kello, *The Virtual Weapon and International Order*, Chapter 7.

4. Kello, *The Virtual Weapon and International Order*, Chapter 7.

5. See Max Smeets, "A Matter of Time: On the Transitory Nature of Cyberweapons," *Journal of Strategic Studies* 41, no. 1 (February 2017).

6. "Putin Warns of 'Quick and Tough' Response to Any Provocation by the West," France 24, April 21, 2021, www.france24.com/en/europe/20210421-putin-warns-of-quick-and-tough-response-to-any-provocation-by-the-west; and Max Smeets, *No Shortcuts: Why States Struggle to Develop a Military Cyber-Force* (London: Hurst, 2022).

7. Fiona Hill, "Three Reasons Russia's Vladimir Putin Might Want to Interfere in the U.S. Presidential Elections," *Brookings* (blog), August 3, 2016.

8. Quoted in "Ahead of Putin Summit, Biden Says U.S. Must Lead from 'Position of Strength,'" Radio Free Europe/Radio Liberty, June 6, 2021, www.rferl.org/a/putin-summit-biden/31292663.html.

9. Quoted in Scott Neuman, "Russia Threatens to Cut Ties with EU if Sanctions Are Imposed over Jailing of Navalny," NPR.org, February 12, 2021, www.npr.org/2021/02/12/967344804/russia-warns-eu-against-imposing-sanctions-over-jailing-of-opposition-leader.

10. Andrew Roth, "Putin Denies That Russia Hacked the DNC But Says It Was for the Public Good," *Washington Post*, September 2, 2016, www.washingtonpost.com/world/putin-denies-that-russia-hacked-the-dnc-but-says-it-was-for-the-public-good/2016/09/02/d507a335-baa8-40e1-9805-dfda5d354692_story.html.

11. Quoted in Andrew Roth, "Russia Denies DNC Hack and Says Maybe Someone 'Forgot the Password,'" *Washington Post*, June 15, 2016, www.washingtonpost.com/news/worldviews/wp/2016/06/15/russias-unusual-response-to-charges-it-hacked-research-on-trump/.

12. Frank McDonough, *Neville Chamberlain, Appeasement and the British Road to War* (Manchester: Manchester University Press, 1998), p. 1.

13. Daniel Treisman, "Putin's Popularity since 2010: Why Did Support for the Kremlin Plunge, Then Stabilize?" *Post-Soviet Affairs* 30, no. 5 (September 3, 2014), pp. 370–88; Timothy Frye et al., "Is Putin's Popularity Real?" *Post-Soviet Affairs* 33, no. 1 (January 2, 2017), pp. 1–15. Military setbacks in Ukraine might eat into Putin's popular support, which, however, is difficult to measure owing to the Kremlin's tightening censorship of political views. See Joshua Yaffa, "Why Do So Many Russians Say They Support the War in Ukraine?" *The New Yorker*, March 29, 2022, www.newyorker.com/news/news-desk/why-do-so-many-russians-say-they-support-the-war-in-ukraine.

14. Kathy Lally and Will Englund, "Russia, Once Almost a Democracy," *Washington Post*, August 18, 2011, www.washingtonpost.com/world/russia-once-almost-a-democracy/2011/08/12/gIQAMriNOJ_story.html.

15. See Kello, *The Virtual Weapon and International Order*, pp. 205–11; and Harknett and Smeets, "Cyber Campaigns and Strategic Outcomes."

16. Tom Burt, "New Cyberattacks Targeting U.S. Elections," *Microsoft on the Issues* (blog), September 10, 2020.

17. "U.S. Charges Russian GRU Officers with International Hacking and Related Influence and Disinformation Operations" (U.S. Department of Justice, October 4, 2018).

18. "Russian State-Sponsored Cyber Actors Targeting Network Infrastructure Devices" (Cybersecurity and Infrastructure Security Agency, August 16, 2018).
19. Jack Stubbs and Guy Faulconbridge, "Papers Leaked before UK Election in Suspected Russian Operation Were Hacked from Ex-Trade Minister," *Reuters*, August 3, 2020, www.reuters.com/article/us-britain-russia-hack-exclusive-idUSKCN24Z1V4.
20. Quoted in Sean Lyngaas, "German Intelligence Agencies Warn of Russian Hacking Threats to Critical Infrastructure," *CyberScoop*, May 26, 2020.
21. Delcker, Janosch, "Germany Fears that Russia Stole Information to Disrupt Election," Politico, March 20, 2017, https://www.politico.eu/article/hacked-information-bomb-under-germanys-election/.
22. Andrea Shalal, "Europe Erects Defenses to Counter Russia's Information War," *Reuters*, January 12, 2017, www.reuters.com/article/us-usa-cyber-russia-europe-idUSKBN14W2BY.
23. "Germany Detects New Cyber Attack by Russian Hacker Group," *Reuters*, November 29, 2018, www.reuters.com/article/germany-cyber-russia-idUSL8N1Y47J5.
24. "National Cyber Force Transforms Country's Cyber Capabilities to Protect the UK," GCHQ, November 19, 2020.
25. See Chapter 8 for a discussion of collective punctuation within NATO.
26. Adam Segal, "When China Rules the Web: Technology in Service of the State," *Foreign Affairs*, September/October, 2018.
27. Broeders, Adamson, and Creemers, "A Coalition of the Unwilling?"
28. Roguski, "Application of International Law to Cyber Operations."
29. Jack L. Goldsmith and Alex Loomis, " 'Defend Forward' and Sovereignty," *Lawfare* (blog), April 30, 2021.
30. Jane Li, "China Wants Regular Citizens to Monitor Online Comments for 'Harmful' History," Quartz, April 13, 2021, https://qz.com/1995362/china-asks-citizens-to-monitor-harmful-history-comments-online/.
31. Leander Kahney, "The FBI Wanted a Back Door to the iPhone. Tim Cook Said No," *Wired*, April 16, 2019, www.wired.com/story/the-time-tim-cook-stood-his-ground-against-fbi/.
32. Segal, "When China Rules the Web."
33. Weber, "The Worldwide Web of Chinese and Russian Information Controls."
34. Quoted in Anton Troianovski, "China Censors the Internet. So Why Doesn't Russia?" *The New York Times*, February 21, 2021, www.nytimes.com/2021/02/21/world/europe/russia-internet-censorship.html.
35. Zack Whittaker, "Documents Reveal How Russia Wiretaps Phone Companies," *TechCrunch* (blog), September 18, 2019.
36. Ivan Nechepurenko, "Russia Moves to Tighten Counterterror Law, Rights Activists See Threat to Freedoms," *The New York Times*, June 24, 2016, www.nytimes.com/2016/06/25/world/europe/russia-counterterrorism-yarovaya-law.html.
37. Andrei Soldatov, "The Kremlin and the Hackers: Partners in Crime?" openDemocracy, April 25, 2012, www.opendemocracy.net/en/odr/kremlin-and-hackers-partners-in-crime/. For an excellent account of Internet suppression in Russia, see Soldatov and Borogan, *The Red Web*.
38. David E. Sanger, "Declaring Democracy Won't Be Subverted, Biden Demands Russia and Myanmar Reverse Course," *The New York Times*, February 3, 2021, www.nytimes.com/2021/02/03/us/politics/biden-myanmar-russia.html.
39. The European Union, United States, South Korea, and other nations began to impose heavy sanctions on North Korea following its first nuclear weapons test in 2006. Even its traditionally close partners such as China have penalized the North for its breach of non-proliferation rules. See Eleanor Albert, "What to Know About Sanctions on North Korea," Council on Foreign Relations, July 16, 2019.
40. Kissinger, *The White House Years*, pp. 125–26.
41. Edward Fishman, "How to Fix America's Failing Sanctions Policy," *Lawfare* (blog), June 4, 2020.
42. Wade Boese, "Russia Seeks New Nuclear Accord," Arms Control Association, September 2006.

43. Amy F. Woolf, "The New START Treaty: Central Limits and Key Provisions" (Congressional Research Service, February 3, 2021).
44. Ibid., p. 53.
45. Egloff, "Public Attribution of Cyber Intrusions."
46. On Thomas Schelling's theory of conflict prevention, see, for example, Thomas C. Schelling, *The Strategy of Conflict* (Cambridge, MA: Harvard University Press, 1981); and Schelling, *Arms and Influence* (New Haven, CT: Yale University Press, 2008).

8. WHAT KIND OF NATO? PUNCTUATED DETERRENCE IN PRACTICE

1. Respect for democratic institutions was not always a requirement of NATO membership. One founding member, Portugal, under the rule of António de Oliveira Salazar, was a right-wing dictatorship.
2. NATO had a role in the Soviet Union's collapse. In his famous "Evil Empire" speech on March 8, 1983, U.S. President Ronald Reagan advocated for NATO's deployment of nuclear-tipped intermediate-range ballistic warheads in Western Europe. According to John Lewis Gaddis, this hardening of rhetoric and policy marked the end of the tradition of relaxed East–West tensions, or *détente*, paving the way for the Communist bloc's demise. See John Lewis Gaddis, *The Cold War: A New History* (New York and London: Penguin Random House, 2006).
3. The alliance has formally recognized Ukraine, Georgia, and Bosnia and Herzegovina as aspiring members.
4. NATO's larger effort to defeat the Taliban and democratize Afghanistan failed. In 2021, the alliance began the process of withdrawing its troops from the country. For a discussion of the implications of NATO's failure in the country, see, for example, Robin Niblett, "Failure in Afghanistan Won't Weaken America's Alliances," *Foreign Affairs*, August 19, 2021.
5. Skeptics such as Bruce Schneier have long argued, for example, that governments inflate cyber threats to justify their control over the Internet, that nations are unlikely to attack civilian infrastructure because doing so would constitute a war crime, and that they would not want to risk escalation into real war. Only the last point seems persuasive, however, and it does not hold true in situations of military crisis (think of the war in Ukraine). For a classic debate on this question, see, for example, "The Cyber War Threat Has Been Grossly Exaggerated," Intelligence2 Debates (June 8, 2010), www.intelligencesquaredus.org/debate/cyber-war-threat-has-been-grossly-exaggerated/. See also Kello, *The Virtual Weapon and International Order*, Chapter 2.
6. Jason Healey and Leendert Van Bocjoven, "NATO's Cyber Capabilities: Yesterday, Today, and Tomorrow," Issue Brief (Atlantic Council, 2011), www.atlanticcouncil.org/in-depth-research-reports/issue-brief/natos-cyber-capabilities-yesterday-today-and-tomorrow/.
7. Dan Verton, "Serbs Launch Cyberattack on NATO," FCW, April 4, 1999, fcw.com/articles/1999/04/04/serbs-launch-cyberattack-on-nato.aspx; Jason Healey, "Cyber Attacks Against NATO, Then and Now," *Atlantic Council* (blog), September 6, 2011.
8. Quoted in Rex B. Hughes, "NATO and Cyber Defence: Mission Accomplished?" *Atlantisch Perspectief*, no. 8 (2008).
9. Laura Brent, "NATO's Role in Cyberspace," NATO Review, February 12, 2019. It's also in 2008 that the Estonian government published the world's first national cyber defense strategy paper. See "National Cyber Security Strategy" (Estonian Ministry of Economic Affairs and Communications, 2008).
10. See NATO, "NATO Rapid Reaction Team to Fight Cyber Attack," NATO, March 13, 2012, http://www.nato.int/cps/en/natohq/news_85161.htm. The policy was approved amid NATO's air campaign in Libya, during which the alliance suffered cyber incidents by hacker collectives, including Anonymous and LulzSec. The incidents' impact was small, but they gave proof to the growing salience of cyber issues.

11. "Defending the Networks: The NATO Policy on Cyber Defence," NATO, 2011.
12. "Wales Summit Declaration," NATO, September 5, 2014.
13. In 2019, the alliance also added space. See "NATO's Approach to Space," NATO, December 2, 2021, www.nato.int/cps/en/natohq/topics_175419.htm#:~:text=In%202019%2C%20Allies%20adopted%20NATO's,as%20communications%2C%20navigation%20and%20intelligence.
14. Jens Stoltenberg, "Speech by NATO Secretary General Jens Stoltenberg at the Cyber Defence Pledge Conference (Ecole Militaire, Paris)," NATO, May 15, 2018, http://www.nato.int/cps/en/natohq/opinions_154462.htm.
15. NATO, "Secretary General's Annual Report 2019," NATO, April 21, 2020, www.nato.int/cps/en/natohq/topics_174399.htm.
16. Jens Stoltenberg, "Remarks by NATO Secretary General Jens Stoltenberg at the Cyber Defence Pledge Conference, London," NATO, May 23, 2019, http://www.nato.int/cps/en/natohq/opinions_166039.htm.
17. See "Statement by the North Atlantic Council Concerning Malicious Cyber Activities," NATO, June 3, 2020, www.nato.int/cps/en/natohq/official_texts_176136.htm.
18. NATO, "Brussels Summit Communiqué."
19. The Treaty text reads: "The Parties agree that an armed attack against one or more of them in Europe or North America shall be considered an attack against them all."
20. The new weapons include the Kalibr cruise missiles fitted into the Yasen nuclear submarines and the Admiral Gorshkov class of frigates.
21. Helen Warrell and Michael Peel, "Senior Nato Officer Warns of China's 'Shocking' Military Advances," *Financial Times*, June 25, 2021, www.ft.com/content/8a0b3975-1938-4815-af3b-22b5d3e6aca4.
22. See Michaël Tanchum, "China's New Military Base in Africa: What It Means for Europe and America," European Council on Foreign Relations Commentary, December 14, 2021, https://ecfr.eu/article/chinas-new-military-base-in-africa-what-it-means-for-europe-and-america/.
23. Michael N. Schmitt, "The North Atlantic Alliance and Collective Defense at 70: Confession and Response Revisited," *Emory International Law Review* 34 (2019), p. 36.
24. Author interview with Christian-Marc Lifländer. Having served as Director of Policy Planning in the Estonian Ministry of Defense during the cyberattacks that affected his country in 2007, Lifländer was a leading figure in the "genesis" cohort of cyber-defense policymakers.
25. For my original proposal (more conceptual than applied) of the accretional principle, see Kello, *The Virtual Weapon and International Order*, pp. 205–11.
26. NATO, "Brussels Summit Communiqué."
27. "Cyber Attacks from Chinese IPs on NATO Countries Surge by 116%," Check Point Blog, March 21, 2022, https://blog.checkpoint.com/2022/03/21/cyber-attacks-from-chinese-ips-on-nato-countries-surge-by-116/.
28. Author interview with Lifländer.
29. Quoted in "The Consultation Process and Article 4," NATO, February 24, 2022, www.nato.int/cps/en/natohq/topics_49187.htm.
30. Quoted in Scott Shane and Daisuke Wakabayashi, "'The Business of War': Google Employees Protest Work for the Pentagon," *The New York Times*, April 4, 2018, www.nytimes.com/2018/04/04/technology/google-letter-ceo-pentagon-project.html.
31. Author interview with Lifländer.

9. DATA EMBASSIES AND STATE CONTINUITY: THE RETURN OF DENIAL?

1. Satoshi Nakamoto, "Bitcoin: A Peer-to-Peer Electronic Cash System" (Bitcoin.org, 2008).
2. For a study on the use of blockchains in governmental systems, see Ivan Martinovic, Lucas Kello, and Ivo Sluganovic, "Blockchains for Governmental Services: Design Principles,

Applications, and Case Studies" (Oxford University Centre for Technology and Global Affairs, 2017).

3. James Vincent, "Bitcoin Consumes More Energy than Switzerland, According to New Estimate," *The Verge*, July 4, 2019, www.theverge.com/2019/7/4/20682109/bitcoin-energy-consumption-annual-calculation-cambridge-index-cbeci-country-comparison.

4. "Central Bank Digital Currencies" (Bank of International Settlements, Committee on Payments and Market Infrastructures, March 2018).

5. "Distributed Ledger Technology: Beyond Blockchain" (UK Government Office for Science, 2016).

6. Philip Boucher, "What if Blockchain Technology Revolutionised Voting?" (Scientific Foresight Unit [STOA], European Parliament Research Service, September 2016).

7. "Estonia – The Digital Republic Secured by Blockchain" (PricewaterhouseCoopers, 2019).

8. Kello, "The Meaning of the Cyber Revolution"; and Lynn, "Defending a New Domain."

9. See *Transforming Digital Continuity: Enhancing IT Resilience Through Cloud Computing* (Tallinn: Estonian Ministry of Economic Affairs & Communications and Microsoft, May 2016).

10. The conventional understanding of sovereignty appears, for example, in Stuart Elden's point that "political independence requires both exclusive internal and equal external sovereignty." Stuart Elden, "Contingent Sovereignty, Territorial Integrity and the Sanctity of Borders," *The SAIS Review of International Affairs* 26, no. 1 (Winter–Spring 2006), p. 11.

11. Nazi forces then occupied Estonia between 1941 and 1944, when Soviet forces returned. See Toivo U. Raun, *Estonia and the Estonians*, 2nd edn (Stanford, CA: Hoover Institution Press, 2002), p. 182; and Lucas Kello, "The Advantages of Latitude: Estonia's Post-Communist Success Story," in *Democratization and Security in Central and Eastern Europe and the Post-Soviet States*, ed. David Bosold et al. (Baden-Baden: Nomos, 2012), pp. 28–9.

12. Oslo was selected as a seat of government because Norwegian authorities, unlike the Swedes, permitted political exile activities. The United States and other Western governments never recognized the Soviet Union's annexation of Estonia (or of Latvia and Lithuania). On October 8, 1992, prime minister-in-exile Heinrich Mark relinquished his credentials to President Lennart Meri, thus concluding a legally seamless transition of power that stretched from the last democratically elected government of Jüri Uluots prior to the Soviet invasion. See Lauri Mälksoo, "Professor Uluots, the Estonian Government in Exile and the Continuity of the Republic of Estonia in International Law," *Nordic Journal of International Law* 69, no. 3 (2000), pp. 289–316.

13. On the activities of Estonian diplomats in exile and their status under international law, see James T. McHugh and James S. Pacy, *Diplomats Without a Country: Baltic Diplomacy, International Law, and the Cold War* (Santa Barbara, CA: Greenwood Press, 2001).

14. On the history of the Estonian "e-state," see, for example, Mart Laar, *Estonia: Little Country That Could* (London: Centre for Research into Post-Communist Economies, 2002); and Kello, "The Advantages of Latitude."

15. Author interview with Mikk Lellsaar and Laura Kask.

16. Author interview with Lellsaar and Kask.

17. *Cyber Security Strategy, 2014–2017* (Tallinn: Ministry of Economic Affairs and Communications, 2014), p. 9. According to a report by Microsoft, virtual embassies are different to data embassies, but for the purposes of exposition, this chapter treats the former as a category of the latter. See *Implementation of the Virtual Data Embassy Solution: Summary Report of the Research Project on Public Cloud Usage for Government* (Tallinn: Ministry of Economic Affairs and Communications and Microsoft Corporation, February 2015).

18. See Matthew Reynolds, " 'Land Is So Yesterday': e-Residents and 'Digital Embassies' Could Replace Country Borders," *Wired*, October 17, 2016.

19. Russian war planes have violated Estonian airspace multiple times. Russia routinely violates the airspace and seas of other NATO or Northern European nations, such as Norway,

Sweden, and Britain. See Mark Piggott, "Nato: Estonian Ministry of Defense Accuses Russian Military Plane of Airspace Incursion," *International Business Times*, September 6, 2016.

20. Andrew E. Kramer, "Spooked by Russia, Tiny Estonia Trains a Nation of Insurgents," *The New York Times*, October 31, 2016.

21. Author interview with Ilves. According to Ilves, the failure to grasp the reality of the Russian threat was evident in President Obama's diplomatic "reset" with Moscow in the year after it invaded Georgia.

22. "NATO Needs to Confront China, but Russia Remains 'Most Immediate Threat,' Says US Official," Euronews, June 13, 2021.

23. "CyberSecurity Strategy, 2019–2022," Estonian Ministry of Economic Affairs and Communications, 2019.

24. Jacob Knutson, "Senate Sergeant-at-Arms Says a Cyber Attack against Congress 'Keeps Me Up at Night,'" Axios, June 5, 2021.

25. See Daniel Philpott, *Revolutions in Sovereignty: How Ideas Shaped Modern International Relations* (Princeton, NJ: Princeton University Press, 2001), p. 17.

26. Hans J. Morgenthau, "The Problem of Sovereignty Reconsidered," *Columbia Law Review* 48, no. 3 (1948), pp. 360–61. For a general discussion of the notion of sovereignty within political science, see Jack Donnelly, "Sovereignty," in *The Oxford Companion to International Relations*, ed. Joel Krieger, 3rd edn (Oxford: Oxford University Press, 2014).

27. Johnson and Toft, "Grounds for War," pp. 7–38. Johnson and Toft argue that, although not all actors seek to expand their territory, they universally seek to preserve it.

28. According to a United Nations study, these nations (along with Estonia) are at the top of e-government rankings. "2020 United Nations E-Government Survey" (United Nations Department of Economic and Social Affairs, July 20, 2020).

29. "COVID-19: Embracing Digital Government During the Pandemic and Beyond" (United Nations Department of Economic and Social Affairs, April 14, 2020).

30. See Regulation (EU) No. 910/2014 of the European Parliament and of the Council, July 23, 2014, http://eur-lex.europa.eu/legal-content/EN/TXT/HTML/?uri=CELEX:32014R0910&from=EN.

31. Author interview with Ilves.

32. See *Implementation of the Virtual Data Embassy Solution*, p. 8.

33. Author interview with Ilves.

34. Author interview with Heli Tiirmaa-Klaar.

35. See Taavi Kotka and Innar Liiv, "Concept of Estonian Government Cloud and Data Embassies," in *Electronic Government and the Information Systems Perspective: Proceedings of the 4th International Conference, EGOVIS 2015 in Valencia, Spain, September 1–3, 2015*, ed. Andrea Kő and Enrico Francesconi (Cham: Springer, 2015), pp. 149–62.

36. See *Estonian Government Cloud* (Tallinn: Estonian Ministry of Economic Affairs and Communications, September 22, 2016).

37. See, for example, *Implementation of the Virtual Data Embassy Solution*.

38. Ibid.

39. Instead, Pernik suggested the term "digital monuments." Piret Pernik, "E-Residency and Data Embassies: A Country Without Borders," *European Cybersecurity Journal* 2, no. 1 (2016), p. 59

40. Kotka and Liiv, "Concept of Estonian Government Cloud and Data Embassies," p. 150.

41. See "Ericsson Leads Cloud Transformation of Public Sector in Estonia," Ericsson (press Release), August 26, 2016.

42. Some publicly available data may be important to the state despite their open nature. An example of such data are the records of the State Gazette. Author interview with Lellsaar and Kask.

43. Ibid., p. 1.

44. Ibid., p. 7. "Non-repudiation" refers to the assurance that a user or person has performed an action that was undeniably theirs. For example, if the NSA database system had ensured non-repudiation, then Edward Snowden would not have been able to download and leak sensitive government files and then claim someone else must have downloaded them, because evidence would exist (typically via authentication) that it was he, and not someone else, who performed the action.
45. Ibid.
46. In July 2021, the government of Monaco opened a data embassy in Luxembourg, becoming the second country to operate one. See "Monaco Opens Data Embassy in Luxembourg" Government of the Grand-Duchy of Luxembourg, September 14, 2021, www.tradeandinvest.lu/news/monaco-opens-data-embassy-in-luxembourg/, accessed on April 23, 2022.
47. See *Government Cloud Strategy: A Sub Strategy of the Government ICT Strategy*, HM Government, March 2011.
48. Author interview with Lellsaar and Kask.
49. Anna-Maria Osula, "National Cyber Security Organisations: Estonia" (Tallinn: NATO Cooperative Cyber Defence Centre of Excellence, March 24, 2015).
50. See Kevin Townsend, "Estonia's 'Data Embassy' Could Be UK's First Brexit Cyber Casualty," *Security Week*, August 20, 2016, http://www.securityweek.com/estonias-data-embassy-could-be-uks-first-brexit-cyber-casualty.
51. *Implementation of the Virtual Data Embassy Solution*, p. 5.
52. While the Estonian government has not recognized the PDE concept, the notion is potentially important, because it opens up the possibility that a privately held backup server could host sensitive government data or support vital state functions. In this regard, it is conceptually distinct from the Public Cloud. As Kask explained, because the PDE would be privately operated, the Vienna Convention might confer diplomatic protections and immunities on the hosting government, not the Estonian government. Author interview with Lellsaar and Kask.
53. Author interview with Lellsaar and Kask.
54. Kotka and Liiv, "Concept of Estonian Government Cloud and Data Embassies."
55. See "Suur arhitektuurinõukogu," Estonian State Information Systems Authority (RIA), September 14, 2016.
56. Author interview with Lellsaar and Kask.
57. Pernik, "E-Residency and Data Embassies," p. 54, although this source cites Ministry of Economic Affairs and Communications, *Cyber Security Strategy, 2014–2017*.
58. Haley Samsel, "Estonia Creates World's First-Ever 'Data Embassy' to Improve Information Security," Security Today, July 3, 2019.
59. Quoted in Helen Wright, "Estonia Mulling New Data Embassy Outside of Europe," *ERR*, September 14, 2021. In October 2017, Estonia and Luxembourg signed a five-year agreement enabling Estonia to store backups of national data on servers located in Luxembourg. The server setup was completed the following year and the first data were transferred in early 2019. The Estonian government reportedly paid a lease of €2.2 million. The European Regional Development Fund covers 85 percent of the costs. National co-financing covers the remainder.
60. See Pernik, "E-Residency and Data Embassies," p. 54. See also "CyberSecurity Strategy, 2014–2017," Estonian Ministry of Economic Affairs and Communications, 2014.
61. Kotka and Liiv, "Concept of Estonian Government Cloud and Data Embassies."
62. For example, the Land Register (Kinnistusraamat) has an exclusively digital existence. See Registrite ja Infosüsteemide Keskus, "e-kinnistusraamat," http://www.rik.ee/en/e-land-register.
63. Author interview with Lellsaar and Kask.
64. See "Estonian Defence Forces," Ministry of Defence, Tallinn, http://www.mil.ee/en/defence-forces.

65. In 2022, following Russia's renewed invasion of Ukraine, Britain, which presently leads NATO forces in Estonia, doubled its troop commitment in the country. See Ben Riley-Smith, "Britain Commits 650 Troops to Nato's Baltic Forces to Counter Vladimir Putin," *The Telegraph*, July 8, 2016. These measures are part of the Readiness Action Plan that was agreed at the NATO Warsaw Summit in 2014. See "Securing the Nordic-Baltic Region," *NATO Review* (2016), http://www.nato.int/docu/Review/2016/Also-in-2016/security-baltic-defense-nato/EN/index.htm.

66. See *Report on Preliminary Examination Activities 2016*, International Criminal Court, November 14, 2016, https://www.icc-cpi.int/news/report-preliminary-examination-activities-2016; and Paul Roderick Gregory, "International Criminal Court: Russia's Invasion of Ukraine Is a 'Crime,' Not a Civil War," *Forbes*, November 20, 2016, https://www.forbes.com/sites/paulroderickgregory/2016/11/20/international-criminal-court-russias-invasion-of-ukraine-is-a-crime-not-a-civil-war/.

67. Dhara Ranasinghe, "How Much Should Russia's Neighbors Fear Moscow?" *CNBC*, January 23, 2015, https://www.cnbc.com/2015/01/23/how-much-should-russias-neighbors-fear-moscow.html.

68. Ibid.

69. Ott Ummelas, "NATO Troop Boost Too Small to Stoke Russian Fears, Estonia Says," *Bloomberg*, March 21, 2016, https://www.bloomberg.com/news/articles/2016-03-21/nato-troop-boost-too-small-to-stoke-russian-fears-estonia-says#xj4y7vzkg. See also "The Decline of Deterrence," *The Economist*, May 1, 2014.

70. William A. Galston, "Memo to Trump: NATO Is Not 'Obsolete'," *Wall Street Journal*, November 29, 2016.

71. "Why the EU Is Still Wary of America," *The Economist*, March 27, 2021, www.economist.com/europe/2021/03/27/why-the-eu-is-still-wary-of-america.

72. See David A. Shlapak and Michael Johnson, *Reinforcing Deterrence on NATO's Eastern Flank: Wargaming the Defense of the Baltics* (Santa Monica, CA: RAND Corporation, 2016).

73. Adam Roberts, "Transformative Military Occupation: Applying the Laws of War and Human Rights," in *International Law and Armed Conflict: Exploring the Faultlines* [Essays in Honor of Yoram Dinstein], ed. Michael N. Schmitt and Jelena Pejic (Leiden: Brill, 2006), p. 580.

74. This is true even in cases where the invader enjoys a high degree of support among the local population. In March 2014, almost 97 percent of Crimean residents opted to join the Russian Federation (on a turnout of 83 percent). Since then, however, the peninsular economy has suffered significant hardship. See Tadeusz A. Olszański and Agata Wierzbowska-Miazga, "The Consequences of the Annexation of Crimea," Centre for Eastern Studies (OSW), March 19, 2016, www.osw.waw.pl/en/publikacje/analyses/2014-03-19/consequences-annexation-crimea.

75. See "e-File," Centre of Registers and Information Systems, http://www.rik.ee/en/e-file.

76. Swedbank AS (39.7 percent), AS SEB Pank (21.9 percent), Nordea Bank AB (15.2 percent), and Danske Bank (8.2 percent). See "Banks in Estonia," *TheBanks.eu*, May 11, 2016, https://thebanks.eu/articles/banks-in-Estonia.

77. Estonian residents carry out less than 1 percent of bank transfers in person. See "Financial Services," *e-Estonia.com*, https://e-estonia.com/solutions/ease_of_doing_business/e-banking/.

78. Referendum Act, Riigi Teataja, www.riigiteataja.ee/en/eli/514112013007/consolide/current.

79. In Estonia, registries that hold citizen data are interdependent, in the sense implied by the "once-only" principle, which bans the collection of the same data in more than one registry. All citizen information (e.g. name, birth date, ID code) is accessed from the Population Register via the "X-road" – Estonia's information super highway. See Public Sector Information Act, Article 433 (3), www.riigiteataja.ee/en/eli/518012016001/consolide.

80. See Raun, *Estonia and the Estonians*, p. 151.

81. See Regina Sirendi, "Could Estonia Survive in the Cloud?" *Estonian World*, March 6, 2014.

82. See Thomas Rid and Benjamin Buchanan, "Attributing Cyber Attacks," *Journal of Strategic Studies* (2015), pp. 4–37.

83. See eGovernance Academy, *e-Estonia: eGovernance in Practice*, http://ega.ee/wp-content/uploads/2016/06/e-Estonia-e-Governance-in-Practice.pdf, p. 15.
84. See Money Laundering and Terrorism Financing Prevention Act, December 19, 2007, http://www.ebrd.com/downloads/legal/securities/estaml.pdf.
85. Renewal of ID cards entails a physical presence test. Estonian citizens abroad can satisfy this requirement by visiting Estonian *physical* embassies.
86. Although digital certificates can be suspended, the ID card would continue to function as an identification document where the use of the certificates was not required. See "ID-kaardi sertifikaatide peatamine," www.sk.ee/kontakt/id-kaardi-sertifikaatide-peatamine.
87. See John Locke, *Two Treatises of Government* (Cambridge: Cambridge University Press, 1967); James Tully, *A Discourse on Property* (Cambridge: Cambridge University Press, 1980); Gerald A. Cohen, *Self-Ownership, Freedom, and Equality* (Cambridge: Cambridge University Press, 1995); and Anna Stilz, "Why Do States Have Territorial Rights?" *International Theory* 1, no. 2 (2009), p. 190.
88. See Stilz, "Why Do States Have Territorial Rights?" p. 198.
89. For a discussion of the implications of cloud data storage for the Vienna Convention, see Eileen Denza, *Diplomatic Law Commentary on the Vienna Convention on Diplomatic Relations*, 4th edn (Oxford: Oxford University Press, 2016); Bartłomiej Sierzputowski, "The Data Embassy under Public International Law," *International & Comparative Law Quarterly* (January 2019), pp. 242–55; and Nick Robinson, Laura Kask, and Robert Krimmer, "The Estonian Data Embassy and the Applicability of the Vienna Convention: An Exploratory Analysis," *ICEGOV2019: Proceedings of the 12th International Conference on Theory and Practice of Electronic Governance* (Melbourne, April 2019), pp. 391–96.
90. Kristina Irion, "Government Cloud Computing and National Data Sovereignty," *Policy and Internet* 4, nos. 3–4 (2012), p. 50. See also Gartner Research, "Data Sovereignty Can Be a Hurdle for the Adoption of Cloud Computing," July 11, 2011; and David Vaile, Kevin Kalinich, Patrick Fair, and Adrian Lawrence, *Data Sovereignty and the Cloud: A Board and Executive Officer's Guide*, Version 1.0, Cyberspace Law and Policy Centre, University of New South Wales Faculty of Law (July 2013).
91. See Anupam Chander and Uyên P. Lê, "Data Nationalism," *Emory Law Journal* 64 (2015); and Iva Mihaylova, "Could the Recently Enacted Data Localization Requirements in Russia Backfire?" *Journal of World Trade* 50, no. 2 (2016).
92. "Agreement Between the Republic of Estonia and the Grand Duchy of Luxembourg on the Hosting of Data and Information Systems," *Riigi Teataja*, June 20, 2017. For a discussion of legal aspects of data embassies, see Bartłomiej Sierzputowski, "The Data Embassy under Public International Law," *International & Comparative Law Quarterly* 68, no. 1 (January 2019), pp. 225–42.
93. Author interview with Tiirmaa-Klaar.
94. Laura Kask, "The Concept of Data Embassies – Safeguarding Digital Continuity" (unpublished paper).
95. *Implementation of the Virtual Data Embassy Solution.*
96. See Zixian Tan, William Foster, and Seymour Goodman, "China's State-Coordinated Internet Infrastructure," *Communications of the ACM* 42, no. 6 (June 1999); and Jonathan L. Zittrain and Benjamin G. Edleman, "Internet Filtering in China," *IEEE Internet Computing* (March–April 2003).
97. I am grateful to Innar Liiv for this insight.
98. See, for instance, Amitai Etzioni, *How Patriotic Is the Patriot Act? Freedom Versus Security in the Age of Terrorism* (New York: Routledge, 2005). An interesting case in this context is the one between Microsoft and the U.S. courts regarding the company's customer emails held in servers in Ireland. The courts ordered Microsoft to relinquish customer email records to U.S. authorities. The company appealed and won, validating the views of Microsoft's deputy general counsel David Howard: "A US prosecutor cannot obtain a US warrant to search

someone's home located in another country, just as another country's prosecutor cannot obtain a court order in her home country to conduct a search in the United States. We think the same rules should apply in the online world, but the government disagrees." See "Microsoft 'Must Release' Data Held on Dublin Server," *BBC News*, April 29, 2014, https://www.bbc.com/news/technology-27191500.

99. See Joel Brenner, *America the Vulnerable: Inside the New Threat Matrix of Digital Espionage, Crime, and Warfare* (New York: Penguin Press, 2011), Introduction; Josh Rogin, "NSA Chief: Cybercrime Constitutes the 'Greatest Transfer of Wealth in History'," *Foreign Policy*, July 9, 2012; Kenneth Geers, "The Cyber Threat to National Critical Infrastructures: Beyond Theory," *Information Security Journal: A Global Perspective* 18, no. 1 (2009); and Martin Rudner, "Cyber-Threats to Critical National Infrastructure: An Intelligence Challenge," *International Journal of Intelligence and Counterintelligence* 26, no. 3 (2013).

100. Robert O'Harrow, Jr., "Understanding Cyberspace Is Key to Defending against Digital Attacks," *Washington Post*, June 2, 2012, https://www.washingtonpost.com/investigations/understanding-cyberspace-is-key-to-defending-againstdigital-attacks/2013/06/03/d46860f8-ad58-11e4-9c91-e9d2f9fde644_story.html.

101. See, for instance, John H. Herz, "Rise and Demise of the Territorial State," *World Politics* 9, no. 4 (July 1957), pp. 473–93.

102. "E-Embassies in Luxembourg," The Government of Luxembourg.

10. CONCLUSION: A PARTIAL RESTORATION OF PEACE

1. See Kello, "The Meaning of the Cyber Revolution," p. 22.

BIBLIOGRAPHY

"2020 United Nations E-Government Survey." United Nations Department of Economic and Social Affairs, July 20, 2020. www.un.org/development/desa/publications/publication/2020-united-nations-e-government-survey.

"2021 Annual Threat Assessment of the U.S. Intelligence Community." Office of the Director of National Intelligence, April 13, 2021. www.dni.gov/index.php/newsroom/reports-publications/reports-publications-2021/item/2204-2021-annual-threat-assessment-of-the-u-s-intelligence-community.

"Achieve and Maintain Cyberspace Superiority: Command Vision for US Cyber Command." U.S. Cyber Command, 2018. https://assets.documentcloud.org/documents/4419681/Command-Vision-for-USCYBERCOM-23-Mar-18.pdf.

"Advance Questions for Lieutenant General Keith Alexander, USA Nominee for Commander, United States Cyber Command." United States Senate, April 15, 2010. https://fas.org/irp/congress/2010_hr/041510alexander-qfr.pdf.

"Advance Questions for Vice Admiral Michael S. Rogers, USN: Nominee for Commander, United States Cyber Command." U.S. Senate Armed Services Committee, March 11, 2014. www.armed-services.senate.gov/imo/media/doc/Rogers_03-11-14.pdf.

"Agreement Between the Republic of Estonia and the Grand Duchy of Luxembourg on the Hosting of Data and Information Systems." *Riigi Teataja*, June 20, 2017. www.riigiteataja.ee/aktilisa/2280/3201/8002/Lux_Info_Agreement.pdf.

Albert, Eleanor. "What to Know About Sanctions on North Korea." Council on Foreign Relations, July 16, 2019. www.cfr.org/backgrounder/what-know-about-sanctions-north-korea.

Aldrich, Richard J. *GCHQ: The Uncensored Story of Britain's Most Secret Intelligence Agency.* London: HarperCollins UK, 2011.

Allison, Graham. *Destined for War: Can America and China Escape Thucydides's Trap?* Boston, MA: Houghton Mifflin, 2017.

Allison, Roy. "Russia and the Post-2014 International Legal Order: Revisionism and Realpolitik." *International Affairs* 93, no. 3 (May 2017): 519–43.

Alperovitch, Dmitri and Ian Ward. "How Should the U.S. Respond to the SolarWinds and Microsoft Exchange Hacks?" *Lawfare* (blog), March 12, 2021. www.lawfareblog.com/how-should-us-respond-solarwinds-and-microsoft-exchange-hacks.

Anisimov, Evgenii V. and J. T. Alexander. *The Reforms of Peter the Great: Progress Through Violence in Russia.* Abingdon: Routledge, 2015.

Armstrong, David. *Revolution and World Order: The Revolutionary State in International Society.* Oxford: Clarendon Press, 1993.

Armstrong, Hamilton Fish. "The Downfall of France," *Foreign Affairs* 19, no. 1 (October 1940): 55–144.

Austin, Greg. *Cyber Policy in China.* Cambridge: Polity Press, 2014.

———. *Cybersecurity in China: The Next Wave.* New York: Springer, 2018.

Balzer, Harley. "Cutting off Russia from SWIFT Will Really Sting." *Atlantic Council* (blog), January 12, 2022. www.atlanticcouncil.org/blogs/ukrainealert/cutting-off-russia-from-swift-will-really-sting/.

Barroso, John, Mary Fallin, and Virginia Foxx. "Republican Platform 2016." CreateSpace Independent Publishing Platform, July 21, 2016. https://prod-static-ngop-pbl.s3.amazonaws.com/media/documents/DRAFT_12_FINAL%5B1%5D-ben_1468872234.pdf.

"The Battle of Britain, August–October 1940." The Ministry of Information, 1941.

Beaufre, André. *1940: The Fall of France.* London: Cassell, 1967.

Beevor, Anthony. *The Battle for Spain: The Spanish Civil War 1936–1939.* London: Weidenfeld & Nicolson, 2006.

Beliakova, Polina. "Russian Military's Corruption Quagmire." *Politico*, March 8, 2022, www.politico.eu/article/russia-military-corruption-quagmire/.

Biden, Joseph. "Remarks by President Biden on Russia." The White House, April 15, 2021. www.whitehouse.gov/briefing-room/speeches-remarks/2021/04/15/remarks-by-president-biden-on-russia/.

Bilková, Veronika. "The Use of Force by the Russian Federation in Crimea." *Heidelberg Journal of International Law* 75, no. 1 (2015): 27–50.

Biller, Jeffrey T. and Michael N. Schmitt. "Classification of Cyber Capabilities and Operations as Weapons, Means, or Methods of Warfare." *International Law Studies* 95 (2019): 179–225.

Bilms, Kevin. "Beyond War and Peace: The PLA's 'Non-War Military Activities' Concept." Modern War Institute, January 26, 2022. https://mwi.usma.edu/beyond-war-and-peace-the-plas-non-war-military-activities-concept/.

"Военная доктрина Российской Федерации." Moscow: Security Council of the Russian Federation, June 25, 2010. https://web.archive.org/web/20110504070127/http://www.scrf.gov.ru/documents/33.html, accessed April 17, 2022.

Boese, Wade. "Russia Seeks New Nuclear Accord." Arms Control Association, September 2006. www.armscontrol.org/act/2006-09/russia-seeks-new-nuclear-accord.

Bolton, John. *The Room Where It Happened.* New York: Simon and Schuster, 2020.

Boucher, Philip. "What If Blockchain Technology Revolutionised Voting?" Scientific Foresight Unit (STOA), European Parliament Research Service, September 2016.

Brantly, Aaron F. "The Most Governed Ungoverned Space: Legal and Policy Constraints on Military Operations in Cyberspace." *SAIS Review of International Affairs* 26, no. 2 (2016): 29–39.

Breemer, Jan S. *Defeating the U-boat: Inventing Antisubmarine Warfare.* Newport: Naval War College Press, 2010.

Brenner, Joel. *America the Vulnerable: Inside the New Threat Matrix of Digital Espionage, Crime, and Warfare.* New York: Penguin Press, 2011.

Brent, Laura. "NATO's Role in Cyberspace." NATO Review, February 12, 2019. www.nato.int/docu/review/articles/2019/02/12/natos-role-in-cyberspace/index.html.

Broeders, Dennis. "Mutually Assured Diplomacy: Governance, 'Unpeace' and Diplomacy in Cyberspace." Observer Research Foundation, October 19, 2019. www.orfonline.org/expert-speak/mutually-assured-diplomacy-governance-unpeace-diplomacy-cyberspace-56800/.

Broeders, Dennis, Liisi Adamson, and Rogier Creemers. "A Coalition of the Unwilling? Chinese and Russian Perspectives on Cyberspace." The Hague Program for Cyber Norms Policy Brief, November 2019.

Broeders, Dennis and Sergei Boeke. "The Demilitarisation of Cyber Conflict." *Survival* 60, no. 6 (November 2018): 73–90.

Broeders, Dennis and Fabio Cristiano. "Cyber Norms and the United Nations: Between Strategic Ambiguity and Rules of the Road." Italian Institute for International Political Studies, April 2, 2020. www.ispionline.it/en/pubblicazione/cyber-norms-and-united-nations-between-strategic-ambiguity-and-rules-road-25417.

"Brussels Summit Communiqué Issued by the Heads of State and Government Participating in the Meeting of the North Atlantic Council in Brussels 14 June 2021." North Atlantic Treaty Organization, June 14, 2021. www.nato.int/cps/en/natohq/news_185000.htm.

Buchan, Russell. "Cyber Attacks: Unlawful Uses of Force or Prohibited Interventions?" *Journal of Conflict and Security Law* 17, no. 2 (2012): 211–27.

Bull, Hedley. "Hobbes and the International Anarchy." *Social Research* 48, no. 4 (1981): 717–38.

———. *The Anarchical Society: A Study of Order in World Politics*. London: Macmillan, 1977.

Burt, Tom. "New Cyberattacks Targeting U.S. Elections." *Microsoft On the Issues* (blog), September 10, 2020. https://blogs.microsoft.com/on-the-issues/2020/09/10/cyberattacks-us-elections-trump-biden/.

Butt, Ahsan I. "Why Did the United States Invade Iraq in 2003?" *Security Studies* 28, no. 2 (2019): 250–85.

Buzan, Barry. *From International to World Society? English School Theory and the Social Structure of Globalisation*. Cambridge: Cambridge University Press, 2004.

Cassese, Antonio, Joseph Weiler, and European University Institute. *Change and Stability in International Law-Making*. Berlin: Walter de Gruyter, 1988.

Cederman, Lars-Erik and Manuel Vogt. "Dynamics and Logics of Civil War." *Journal of Conflict Resolution* 61, no. 9 (2017).

"Central Bank Digital Currencies." Bank of International Settlements, Committee on Payments and Market Infrastructures, March 2018. www.bis.org/cpmi/publ/d174.pdf.

Chander, Anupam and Uyen P. Le. "Data Nationalism." *Emory Law Journal* 64, no. 3 (2015).

Charon, Paul and Jean-Baptiste Jeangène Vilmer. *Chinese Influence Operations: A Machiavellian Moment*. Paris: Ministry of Armed Forces, October 2021.

Chekinov, Sergei and Sergei A. Bogdanov. "The Nature and Content of a New-Generation War." *Military Thought* 4 (2013).

———. "Прогнозирование характера и содержания войн будущего: проблемы и суждения." Военная мысль 10 (2015).

———. "Военная стратегия: взгляд в будущее." Военная мысль 11 (2016).

Cheng, Yinghong. "Fidel Castro and 'China's Lesson for Cuba': A Chinese Perspective." *The China Quarterly* 189 (2007): 24–42.

Chernoff, Fred. "Ending the Cold War: The Soviet Retreat and the US Military Buildup." *International Affairs* 67, no. 1 (1991): 111–26.

Chivvis, Christopher S. "Hybrid War: Russian Contemporary Political Warfare." *Bulletin of the Atomic Scientists* 73, no. 5 (August 21, 2017): 316–21.

Cimbala, Stephen J. "Nuclear Deterrence and Cyber Warfare: Coexistence or Competition?" *Defense & Security Analysis* 33, no. 3 (2017): 193–208.

Clapper, James R. *Facts and Fears: Hard Truths from a Life in Intelligence*. New York: Penguin Random House, 2018.

Coats, Daniel R. "Worldwide Threat Assessment of the US Intelligence Community." Office of the Director of National Intelligence, February 13, 2018. www.dni.gov/files/documents/Newsroom/Testimonies/2018-ATA---Unclassified-SSCI.pdf.

Cohen, Gerald A. *Self-Ownership, Freedom, and Equality*. Cambridge: Cambridge University Press, 1995.

Connolly, Richard and Mathieu Boulègue. "Russia's New State Armament Programme: Implications for the Russian Armed Forces and Military Capabilities to 2027." Research Paper, Chatham House.

Corn, Gary and Eric Talbot Jensen. "The Use of Force and Cyber Countermeasures." *Temple International & Comparative Law Journal* 127 (2018).

Corum, James S. *Wolfram von Richthofen: Master of the German Air War*. Lawrence: University Press of Kansas, 2008.

BIBLIOGRAPHY

"COVID-19: Embracing Digital Government During the Pandemic and Beyond." United Nations Department of Economic and Social Affairs, April 14, 2020. www.un.org/develop ment/desa/dpad/publication/un-desa-policy-brief-61-covid-19-embracing-digital-government-during-the-pandemic-and-beyond/.

Cramer, Jane and Eric Duggan. "In Pursuit of Primacy," in Jane Cramer and Trevor Thrall, eds, *Why Did the United States Invade Iraq?* (New York: Routledge, 2012): 210–20.

Crowe, Eyre. "Memorandum on the Present State of British Relations with France and Germany," January 1, 1907.

Cunningham, Fionna S. and M. Taylor Fravel. "Dangerous Confidence? Chinese Views on Nuclear Escalation." *International Security* 44, no. 2 (Fall 2019): 61–109.

"Cyber Power Index." Economist Intelligence Unit, 2011.

"Cybersecurity Strategy, 2014–2017." Ministry of Economic Affairs and Communications, Republic of Estonia, 2014.

"Cybersecurity Strategy, 2019–2022." Ministry of Economic Affairs and Communications, Republic of Estonia, 2019.

"Cyberspace Solarium Commission – Report." U.S. Cyberspace Solarium Commission, co-chaired by Angus King, Jr. and Mike Gallagher, March 11, 2020. www.solarium.gov/report.

Debs, Alexandre and Nuno P. Monteiro. "Known Unknowns: Power Shifts, Uncertainty, and War." *International Organization* 68, no. 1 (January 2014): 1–31.

Deeks, Ashley. "Defend Forward and Cyber Countermeasures." *Lawfare* (blog), August 12, 2020. www.lawfareblog.com/defend-forward-and-cyber-countermeasures.

Deeter, David P. and Joel C. Gaydos, eds. *Occupational Health: The Soldier and the Industrial Base.* Office of the Surgeon General, U.S. Department of the Army, 1993.

"Defending the Networks: The NATO Policy on Cyber Defence." NATO, 2011. www.nato.int/nato_static/assets/pdf/pdf_2011_08/20110819_110819-policy-cyberdefence.pdf.

Delerue, François. *Cyber Operations and International Law.* Cambridge: Cambridge University Press, 2020.

Dellios, Rosita. "Chinese Strategic Culture – Part 2: Virtue and Power." *Culture Mandala* 13, Special Issue 3 (February 2020).

"Democracy Facing Global Challenges: V-Dem Annual Democracy Report 2019." V-Dem Institute, University of Gothenburg, May 2019.

DeNardis, Laura. *Protocol Politics.* Cambridge, MA: MIT Press, 2009.

DeNardis, Laura and Mark Raymond. "Thinking Clearly about Multistakeholder Internet Governance." GigaNet: Global Internet Governance Academic Network, Annual Symposium 2013, July 2016.

Denza, Eileen. *Diplomatic Law Commentary on the Vienna Convention on Diplomatic Relations,* 4th edn. Oxford: Oxford University Press, 2016.

"Department of Defense Cyberspace Policy Report: A Report to Congress Pursuant to the National Defense Authorization Act for Fiscal Year 2011, Section 934." U.S. Department of Defense, November 2011.

"Department of Defense Strategy for Operating in Cyberspace." U.S. Department of Defense, July 2011.

Devanny, Joe, Ciaran Martin, and Tim Stevens. "On the Strategic Consequences of Digital Espionage." *Journal of Cyber Policy* 6, no. 3 (September 2, 2021): 429–50.

Diermeier, Daniel. "Rational Choice and the Role of Theory in Political Science." *Critical Review* 9, no. 1–2 (1995): 59–70.

"Distributed Ledger Technology: Beyond Blockchain." UK Government Office for Science, 2016. https://assets.publishing.service.gov.uk/government/uploads/system/uploads/attachment_data/file/492972/gs-16-1-distributed-ledger-technology.pdf

Donnelly, Jack. *Realism and International Relations.* Cambridge: Cambridge University Press, 2000.

BIBLIOGRAPHY

————. "Sovereignty," in Joel Krieger, ed., *The Oxford Companion to International Relations*, 3rd edn. Oxford: Oxford University Press, 2014.

Doshi, Rush. *The Long Game: China's Grand Strategy to Displace American Order*. Oxford: Oxford University Press, 2021.

Douhet, Giulio. *The Command of the Air*. Translated by Dino Ferrari. Maxwell Air Force Base, AL: Air University Press, 2019.

"E-Embassies in Luxembourg." The Government of Luxembourg. http://luxembourg.public.lu/en/invest/innovation/e-embassies-in-luxembourg.html.

Egloff, Florian J. "Public Attribution of Cyber Intrusions." *Journal of Cybersecurity* 6 (January 1, 2020).

Eilstrup-Sangiovanni, Mette. "Why the World Needs an International Cyberwar Convention." *Philosophy and Technology* 31, no. 3 (July 21, 2017): 379–407.

Einstein, Albert. "Letter to F.D. Roosevelt." Franklin D. Roosevelt Presidential Library and Museum, August 2, 1949.

Elden, Stuart. "Contingent Sovereignty, Territorial Integrity and the Sanctity of Borders." *The SAIS Review of International Affairs*, 26, no. 1 (Winter–Spring 2006): 11–24.

Eliot, George Fielding. "The Offensive Still Gives Victory." *Foreign Affairs* 17, no. 1 (October 1938): 51–64.

Engels, Friedrich and Karl Marx. *The German Ideology*, 2nd edn. London: Laurence and Wishart, 1974.

"Estonia - The Digital Republic Secured by Blockchain." PricewaterhouseCoopers, 2019. www.pwc.com/gx/en/services/legal/tech/assets/estonia-the-digital-republic-secured-by-blockchain.pdf.

Etzioni, Amitai. *How Patriotic Is the Patriot Act? Freedom Versus Security in the Age of Terrorism* New York: Routledge, 2005.

"EU Cyber Diplomacy Toolbox." European Union External Action Service, 2019. www.enisa.europa.eu/events/artificial-intelligence-an-opportunity-for-the-eu-cyber-crisis-management/workshop-presentations/20190603-eeas-eu-cyber-diplomacy-toolbox.pdf.

Evans, Alexander. "Our Shared Commitment to Law, Norms and Confidence Building in Cyberspace." Foreign and Commonwealth Office, September 9, 2019. www.gov.uk/government/speeches/our-shared-commitment-to-law-norms-and-confidence-building-in-cyberspace.

"Fact Sheet: Actions in Response to Russian Malicious Cyber Activity and Harassment," Office of the Press Secretary, The White House, December 29, 2016. https://obamawhitehouse.archives.gov/the-press-office/2016/12/29/fact-sheet-actions-response-russian-malicious-cyber-activity-and.

"Fact Sheet: Imposing Costs for Harmful Foreign Activities by the Russian Government," The White House, April 15, 2021. www.whitehouse.gov/briefing-room/statements-releases/2021/04/15/fact-sheet-imposing-costs-for-harmful-foreign-activities-by-the-russian-government/.

Farrell, Henry and Abraham L. Newman. "Weaponized Interdependence: How Global Economic Networks Shape State Coercion." *International Security* 44, no. 1 (2019): 42–79.

Faust, Jörg. "Liberal Democracy as Universal Value." Deutsches Institut für Entwicklungspolitik, 2013.

Fearon, James D. and David D. Laitin. "Ethnicity, Insurgency, and Civil War." *American Political Science Review* 97, no. 1 (2003): 75–90.

Feng, Huiyun. *Chinese Strategic Culture and Foreign Policy Decision-Making: Confucianism, Leadership and War*. New York: Routledge, 2007.

Fink, Carole. *Ostpolitik, 1969–1974: European and Global Responses*. Cambridge: Cambridge University Press, 2009.

Finnemore, Martha and Duncan B. Hollis. "Constructing Norms for Global Cybersecurity." *American Journal of International Law* 110, no. 3 (2016): 425–79.

BIBLIOGRAPHY

Fischerkeller, Michael P., Emily O. Goldman, and Richard J. Harknett. *Cyber Persistence Theory: Redefining National Security in Cyberspace (Bridging the Gap)*. Oxford: Oxford University Press, 2022.

Fischerkeller, Michael P. and Richard J. Harknett. "Deterrence Is Not a Credible Strategy for Cyberspace." *Orbis* 61, no. 3 (January 1, 2017): 381–93.

———. "Persistent Engagement, Agreed Competition, and Cyberspace Interaction Dynamics and Escalation." *Cyber Defense Review*. Special edition (2019): 267–87.

Fishman, Edward. "How to Fix America's Failing Sanctions Policy," *Lawfare* (blog), June 4, 2020. www.lawfareblog.com/how-fix-americas-failing-sanctions-policy.

Frye, Timothy, Scott Gehlbach, Kyle L. Marquardt, and Ora John Reuter. "Is Putin's Popularity Real?" *Post-Soviet Affairs* 33, no. 1 (January 2, 2017): 1–15.

Fukuyama, Francis. *The End of History and the Last Man*. New York: Simon and Schuster, 2006.

Gaddis, John Lewis. *The Cold War: A New History*. New York and London: Penguin Random House, 2006.

Galeotti, Mark. *Putin's Hydra: Inside Russia's Intelligence Services*. European Council and Foreign Relations Policy Brief, 2016.

———. "I'm Sorry for Creating the 'Gerasimov Doctrine'." *Foreign Policy*, March 5, 2018.

Gallagher, Mike. "Taiwan Can't Wait: What America Must Do To Prevent a Successful Chinese Invasion." *Foreign Affairs,* February 1, 2022. https://www.foreignaffairs.com/articles/china/2022-02-01/taiwan-cant-wait?utm_medium=social.

Gamble, Andrew. "The Western Ideology 1." *Government and Opposition* 44, no. 1 (2009): 1–19.

Geers, Kenneth. "The Cyber Threat to National Critical Infrastructures: Beyond Theory." *Information Security Journal: A Global Perspective* 18, no. 1 (2009).

Geissler, Erhard and Robert Hunt Sprinkle. "Disinformation Squared: Was the HIV-from-Fort-Detrick Myth a Stasi Success?" *Politics and the Life Sciences* 32, no. 2 (2013): 2–99.

Gerasimov, Valeriy. "Ценность науки в предвидении" ["The Value of Science is in Foresight"]. Военно-промышленный курьер (February 27, 2013).

Gerovitch, Slava. "How the Computer Got Its Revenge on the Soviet Union." *Nautilus*, April 9, 2015.

———. "InterNyet: Why the Soviet Union Did Not Build a Nationwide Computer Network." *History and Technology* 24, no. 4 (December 1, 2008): 335–50.

Ghiselli, Andrea. "Revising China's Strategic Culture: Contemporary Cherry-Picking of Ancient Strategic Thought." *China Quarterly* 233 (2018): 166–85.

Giles, Keir. "Russia's 'New' Tools for Confronting the West: Continuity and Innovation in Moscow's Exercise of Power." Research Paper, Russia and Eurasia Programme, Chatham House (March 2016).

———. *Moscow Rules: What Drives Russia to Confront the West*. Washington, D.C.: Brookings Institution, 2018.

Gilli, Andrea and Mauro Gilli. "Why China Has Not Caught Up Yet: Military-Technological Superiority and the Limits of Imitation, Reverse Engineering, and Cyber Espionage." *International Security* 43, no. 3 (February 1, 2019): 141–89.

Goldman, Emily O. "From Reaction to Action: Adopting a Competitive Posture in Cyber Diplomacy." *Texas National Security Review* (Fall 2020).

Goldsmith, Jack L. "How Cyber Changes the Laws of War." *European Journal of International Law* 24, no. 1 (2013): 129–38.

Goldsmith, Jack L. and Alex Loomis. "'Defend Forward' and Sovereignty." *Lawfare* (blog), April 30, 2021. www.lawfareblog.com/defend-forward-and-sovereignty.

Goldsmith, Jack L. and Eric A. Posner. *The Limits of International Law*. Oxford and New York: Oxford University Press, 2007.

Goodman, Will. "Cyber Deterrence: Tougher in Theory than in Practice?" *Strategic Studies Quarterly* 4, no. 3 (2010): 102–35.

Gramer, Robbie. "'Thanks, Putin': Finnish and Swedish Lawmakers Aim for NATO Membership." *Foreign Policy*, April 22, 2022.

"Grand Jury Indicts 12 Russian Intelligence Officers for Hacking Offenses Related to the 2016 Election." U.S. Department of Justice, July 13, 2018. www.justice.gov/opa/pr/grand-jury-indicts-12-russian-intelligence-officers-hacking-offenses-related-2016-election.

"Grand Jury Indicts Thirteen Russian Individuals and Three Russian Companies for Scheme to Interfere in the United States Political System." U.S. Department of Justice, February 16, 2018. www.justice.gov/opa/pr/grand-jury-indicts-thirteen-russian-individuals-and-three-russian-companies-scheme-interfere.

Grant, Thomas D. *Aggression Against Ukraine: Territory, Responsibility, and International Law.* New York: Palgrave Macmillan, 2015.

Grechko, Andrei A. and Nikolai V. Ogarkov. "A New Conception of War." *Military Thought* 6, no. 3 (1997): 50–53.

Greenberg, Andy. *Sandworm: A New Era of Cyberwar and the Hunt for the Kremlin's Most Dangerous Hackers.* New York: Penguin Random House, 2019.

Grigsby, Alex. "The End of Cyber Norms." *Survival* 59, no. 6 (2017): 109–22.

Grimes, Shawn T. *Strategy and War Planning in the British Navy, 1887–1918.* Woodbridge: Boydell Press, 2012.

Gundert, Levi, Sanil Chohan, and Greg Lesnewich. "Iran's Hacker Hierarchy Exposed: How the Islamic Republic of Iran Uses Contractors and Universities to Conduct Cyber Operations." *Recorded Future* (blog), May 9, 2018.

Guo, Sujian. *China's "Peaceful Rise" in the 21st Century: Domestic and International Conditions.* Farnham: Ashgate, 2006.

Harknett, Richard J. "Persistent Engagement and Cost Imposition: Distinguishing Between Cause and Effect." *Lawfare* (blog), February 6, 2020. www.lawfareblog.com/persistent-engagement-and-cost-imposition-distinguishing-between-cause-and-effect.

Harknett, Richard J. and Max Smeets. "Cyber Campaigns and Strategic Outcomes." *Journal of Strategic Studies* (2020), 1–34.

Harold, Scott W. "The U.S.–China Cyber Agreement: A Good First Step." The Rand (blog), August 1, 2016. www.rand.org/blog/2016/08/the-us-china-cyber-agreement-a-good-first-step.html.

Harold, Scott W., Nathan Beauchamp-Mustafaga, and Jeffrey W. Hornung. "Chinese Disinformation Efforts on Social Media." Combatting Foreign Disinformation on Social Media Series. Rand Corporation, 2021.

Hartcup, Guy. *The Effect of Science on the Second World War.* Basingstoke: Palgrave Macmillan, 2000.

Hasenclever, Andreas, Peter Mayer, and Volker Rittberger. *Theories of International Regimes.* Cambridge Studies in International Relations. Cambridge: Cambridge University Press, 1997.

Healey, Jason. "Cyber Attacks Against NATO, Then and Now." *Atlantic Council* (blog), September 6, 2011. www.atlanticcouncil.org/blogs/new-atlanticist/cyber-attacks-against-nato-then-and-now/.

———. "The Implications of Persistent (and Permanent) Engagement in Cyberspace." *Journal of Cybersecurity* 5, no. 1 (January 1, 2019).

Healey, Jason, and Leendert Van Bocjoven. "NATO's Cyber Capabilities: Yesterday, Today, and Tomorrow." Issue Brief. Atlantic Council, 2011.

"Hearing before the U.S.–China Economic and Security Review Commission, One-Hundred Fourteenth Congress, Second Session." United States Congress, June 9, 2016.

"Hearing to Receive Testimony on Foreign Cyber Threats to the United States." U.S. Senate Armed Services Committee, January 5, 2017.

Heller, Mark A. "The Use and Abuse of Hobbes: The State of Nature in International Relations." *Polity* 13, no. 1 (September 1, 1980): 21–32.

Herz, John H. "Rise and Demise of the Territorial State." *World Politics* 9, no. 4 (July 1957): 473–93.

Hill, Fiona. "Three Reasons Russia's Vladimir Putin Might Want to Interfere in the U.S. Presidential Elections." *Brookings* (blog), August 3, 2016. www.brookings.edu/blog/order-from-chaos/2016/08/03/3-reasons-russias-vladimir-putin-might-want-to-interfere-in-the-u-s-presidential-elections/.

Hinck, Garrett and Tim Maurer. "Persistent Enforcement: Criminal Charges as a Response to Nation-State Malicious Cyber Activity." *Journal of National Security Law and Policy* 10 (2020): 525–61.

Hoffmann, Stanley. *The State of War: Essays on the Theory and Practice of International Politics.* London: Praeger, 1965.

"Homeland Security Intelligence Assessment: Cyber Actors Continue to Engage in Influence Activities and Targeting of Election Infrastructure." U.S. Department of Homeland Security, October 11, 2018.

"Homeland Threat Assessment." U.S. Department of Homeland Security, October 2020.

Hough, Richard. *Dreadnought: A History of the Modern Battleship.* Penzance: Periscope Publishing, 2003.

Howard, Michael. *War in European History.* Updated edition: Oxford University Press, 2009.

Hughes, Rex B. "NATO and Cyber Defence: Mission Accomplished?" *Atlantisch Perspectief,* no. 8 (2008). https://csl.armywarcollege.edu/SLET/mccd/CyberSpacePubs/NATO%20and%20Cyber%20Defence%20-%20Mission%20Accomplished.pdf.

Huntington, Samuel P. *The Clash of Civilizations and the Remaking of World Order.* New York: Simon and Schuster, 2011.

———. *The Common Defense: Strategic Programs in National Politics.* New York: Columbia University Press, 1961.

Ikenberry, G. John. "The End of Liberal International Order?" *International Affairs* 94, no. 1 (January 1, 2018): 7–23.

Implementation of the Virtual Data Embassy Solution: Summary Report of the Research Project on Public Cloud Usage for Government. Tallinn: Ministry of Economic Affairs and Communications and Microsoft Corporation, February 2015.

InfoTransec. "The Impacts of NotPetya Ransomware: What You Need to Know," March 5, 2019. https://infotransec.com/news/the-impacts-of-notpetya-ransomware-what-you-need-to-know/.

Ingrao, Charles W., Nikola Samardžić, and Jovan Pesalj. *The Peace of Passarowitz, 1718.* West Lafayette, IN: Purdue University Press, 2011.

Insikt Group. "China-Linked Group RedEcho Targets the Indian Power Sector Amid Heightened Border Tensions." Recorded Future, February 28, 2021. www.recordedfuture.com/redecho-targeting-indian-powersector/.

Irion, Kristina. "Government Cloud Computing and National Data Sovereignty." *Policy and Internet* 4, nos. 3–4 (2012): 40–71.

Jellicoe, John Rushworth. *The Crisis of the Naval War.* Frankfurt am Main: Outlook Verlag, 2018.

Jenkins, Luke, Sarah Hawley, Parnian Najafi, and Doug Bienstock. "Suspected Russian Activity Targeting Government and Business Entities around the Globe." *Mandiant* (blog), December 6, 2021. www.mandiant.com/resources/russian-targeting-gov-business.

Jervis, Robert. "Some Thoughts on Deterrence in the Cyber Era." *Journal of Information Warfare* 15, no. 2 (2016): 66–73.

Jisi, Wang. "China's Search for a Grand Strategy: A Rising Great Power Finds Its Way." *Foreign Affairs* 90, no. 2 (2011): 68–79.

Johnson, Dominic D.P., and Monica Duffy Toft. "Grounds for War: The Evolution of Territorial Conflict." *International Security* 38, no. 3 (January 1, 2014): 7–38.

Johnston, Alastair Iain. *Cultural Realism: Strategic Culture and Grand Strategy in Chinese History*. Princeton, NJ: Princeton University Press, 1995.

———. "Thinking About Strategic Culture." *International Security* 19, no. 4 (1995): 32–64.

———. "Cultural Realism and Strategy in Maoist China," in Peter J. Katzenstein, ed, *The Culture of National Security: Norms and Identity in World Politics*, edited by Peter J. Katzenstein. New York: Columbia University Press, 1996.

"Joint Analysis Report, JAR-16-20296A, GRIZZLY STEPPE – Russian Malicious Cyber Activity." FBI and Department of Homeland Security. December 29, 2016.

Jones, Jeff. "Confronting China's Efforts to Steal Defense Information." Paper, Belfer Center for Science and International Affairs, May 2020.

Jonsson, Oscar. *The Russian Understanding of War: Blurring the Lines Between War and Peace*. Washington, D.C.: Georgetown University Press, 2018.

Kaljulaid, Kersti. "President of Estonia Kersti Kaljulaid: We Cannot Silently Consent to Russia's Aggression in the Sea of Azov." Office of the President, November 11, 2018.

Kaminska, Monica. "Restraint under Conditions of Uncertainty: Why the United States Tolerates Cyberattacks." *Journal of Cybersecurity* 7, no. 1 (March 9, 2021).

Kask, Laura. "The Concept of Data Embassies – Safeguarding Digital Continuity" (unpublished paper).

Kello, Lucas. "The Advantages of Latitude: Estonia's Post-Communist Success Story." In David Bosold et al., eds, *Democratization and Security in Central and Eastern Europe and the Post-Soviet States*. Baden-Baden: Nomos, 2012.

———. "The Meaning of the Cyber Revolution: Perils to Theory and Statecraft." *International Security* 38, no. 2 (Fall 2013): 7–40.

———. "The Virtual Weapon: Dilemmas and Future Scenarios." *Politique Étrangère* 79, no. 4 (2015).

———. "Cyber Security: Gridlock and Innovation," in Thomas Hale and David Held, eds, *Beyond Gridlock*. Cambridge: Polity Press, 2017.

———. *The Virtual Weapon and International Order*. New Haven, CT: Yale University Press, 2017.

———. "Private Sector Cyber Weapons: An Adequate Response to the Sovereignty Gap?" in Amy Zegart and Herb Lin, eds, *Bytes, Bombs, and Spies: The Strategic Dimensions of Offensive Cyber Operations*. Washington, D.C.: Brookings Institution, 2019.

Kissinger, Henry A. *The White House Years*, New York: Simon and Schuster, 1979.

Koh, Harold Hongju. "International Law in Cyberspace." *Harvard International Law Journal* 54 (December 2012): 12.

Kotka, Taavi and Innar Liiv. "Concept of Estonian Government Cloud and Data Embassies," in Andrea Kő and Enrico Francesconi, eds, *Electronic Government and the Information Systems Perspective: Proceedings of the 4th International Conference EGOVIS 2015 in Valencia, Spain, September 1–3 2015*. Cham: Springer, 2015: 149–62.

Kozlov, Svyatoslav N., Mikhail V. Smirnov, Ivan S. Baz, and Petr A. Sidorov. О советской военной наукой. Moscow: Voyenizdat, 1964.

Kramer, Mark. "The Myth of a No-NATO-Enlargement Pledge to Russia." *Washington Quarterly* 32, no. 2 (April 2009): 39–61.

Krastev, Ivan. "Russian Revisionism: Putin's Plan For Overturning the European Order." *Foreign Affairs*, March 3, 2014.

Krebs, Brian. "At Least 30,000 U.S. Organizations Newly Hacked Via Holes in Microsoft's Email Software." *Krebs on Security* (blog), March 5, 2021. https://krebsonsecurity.com/2021/03/at-least-30000-u-s-organizations-newly-hacked-via-holes-in-microsofts-email-software/.

Krekó, Péter. "Viktor Orban Is the West's Pro-Putin Outlier." *Foreign Policy*, March 20, 2022.

Kroge, Harry von. *GEMA: Birthplace of German Radar and Sonar*. Transl. and ed. Louis Brown. Philadelphia, PA: Institute of Physics Publishing, 2000.

BIBLIOGRAPHY

Kurlantzick, Joshua. "How China Is Interfering in Taiwan's Election." Council on Foreign Relations, November 7, 2019. www.cfr.org/in-brief/how-china-interfering-taiwans-election.

Laar, Mart. *Estonia: Little Country That Could.* London: Centre for Research into Post-Communist Economies, 2002.

Lacouture, Jean. *De Gaulle: The Rebel, 1890–1944.* New York: Random House, 1991.

Lake, David. "Two Cheers for Bargaining Theory: Assessing Rationalist Explanations of the Iraq War." *International Security* 35, no. 3 (Winter 2010/11): 7–52.

Lambert, Nicholas A. *Planning Armageddon.* Cambridge, MA: Harvard University Press, 2012.

Lautenschlager, Karl. "The Submarine in Naval Warfare, 1901–2001." *International Security* 11, no. 3 (1986): 94–140.

Layton, Peter. "China's Enduring Grey-Zone Challenge." Air and Space Power Centre, 2021.

Lebow, Richard Ned and Janice Gross Stein. "Reagan and the Russians." *The Atlantic Monthly,* 273, no. 2 (1994): 35–7.

Legro, Jeffrey W. Legro. "What China Will Want: The Future Intentions of a Rising Power." *Perspectives on Politics* 5, no. 3 (2007): 515–34.

Lenin, Vladimir I. "The Collapse of the Soviet International." In *Collected Works* 21 (Moscow: Progress Publishers): 205–59.

———. "Address to the Second All-Russian Congress of Communist Organizations of the Peoples of the East." In *Collected Works* 30 (Moscow: Progress Publishers, 1919): 151–61.

———. *The State and Revolution: The Marxist Theory of the State and the Tasks of the Proletariat in the Revolution.* London: Union Books, 2013.

Lewis, James. A. "Risks in the Semiconductor Manufacturing and Advanced Packaging Supply Chain." Center for Strategic and International Studies, April 16, 2021. https://www.csis.org/analysis/risks-semiconductor-manufacturing-and-advanced-packaging-supply-chain.

Li, Daitian, Tony W. Tong, and Yangao Xiao. "Is China Emerging as the Global Leader in AI?" *Harvard Business Review* (February 18, 2021).

Libicki, Martin C. *Cyberdeterrence and Cyberwar.* Rand Corporation, 2009.

Liff, Adam P. "Cyberwar: A New 'Absolute Weapon'? The Proliferation of Cyberwarfare Capabilities and Interstate War." *Journal of Strategic Studies* 35, no. 3 (June 1, 2012): 401–28.

Lindsay, Jon R. "Tipping the Scales: The Attribution Problem and the Feasibility of Deterrence against Cyberattack." *Journal of Cybersecurity* 1, no. 1 (2015): 53–67.

———. "Cyber Conflict vs. Cyber Command: Hidden Dangers in the American Military Solution to a Large-Scale Intelligence Problem." *Intelligence and National Security* 36, no. 2 (February 23, 2021): 260–78.

Liu, Tiewa. "Chinese Strategic Culture and the Use of Force: Moral and Political Perspectives." *Journal of Contemporary China* 23 (January 2014).

Locke, John. *Two Treatises of Government.* Cambridge: Cambridge University Press, 1967.

Lotrionte, Catherine. "Reconsidering the Consequences for State-Sponsored Hostile Cyber Operations under International Law." *The Cyber Defense Review* 3, no. 2 (2018): 73–114.

Lovell, Julia. *The Opium War: Drugs, Dreams and the Making of China.* London: Picador, 2011.

Lu, Hui. "Commentary: Milestone Congress Points to New Era for China, The World." Xinhua, October 24, 2017.

Lucas, Edward. *The New Cold War: Putin's Threat to Russia and the West.* London: Bloomsbury, 2014.

Lynn III, William J. "Defending a New Domain." *Foreign Affairs,* September/October 2010.

Majumdar, Dave. "Newly Declassified Documents: Gorbachev Told NATO Wouldn't Move Past East German Border." *The National Interest,* December 12, 2017.

BIBLIOGRAPHY

Mälksoo, Lauri. "Professor Uluots, the Estonian Government in Exile and the Continuity of the Republic of Estonia in International Law." *Nordic Journal of International Law* 69, no. 3 (2000): 289–316.

Manners, Ian. "Normative Power Europe: A Contradiction in Terms?" *JCMS: Journal of Common Market Studies* 40, no. 2 (2002): 235–58.

March, James G. and Johan P. Olsen. "The Logic of Appropriateness." *ARENA Working Papers* 4, no. 9 (2004): 28.

Marder, Arthur Jacob. *From the Dreadnought to Scapa Flow: The Royal Navy in the Fisher Era, 1904–1919.* Oxford and New York: Oxford University Press, 1978.

Mardiste, David. "Show Putin Strength, Not Weakness, Says Estonian Defense Minister." *Atlantic Council* (blog), November 10, 2014. www.atlanticcouncil.org/blogs/natosource/show-putin-strength-not-weakness-says-estonian-defense-minister/.

"The Mark I Computer at Harvard." Accessed September 28, 2020. http://sites.harvard.edu/~chsi/markone/about.html.

Martinovic, Ivan, Lucas Kello, and Ivo Sluganovic. "Blockchains for Governmental Services: Design Principles, Applications, and Case Studies." Oxford University Centre for Technology and Global Affairs, 2017.

Marx, Karl and Friedrich Engels. *The Russian Menace to Europe: A Collection of Articles, Speeches, Letters, and News Despatches.* Ed. Paul W. Blackstock and Bert F. Hoselitz. London: Allen and Unwin, 1953.

Maschmeyer, Lennart. "The Subversive Trilemma: Why Cyber Operations Fall Short of Expectations." *International Security* 46, no. 2 (October 25, 2021): 51–90.

Massie, Robert K. *Castles of Steel: Britain, Germany, and the Winning of the Great War at Sea.* New York: Random House, 1991.

McDonough, Frank. *Neville Chamberlain, Appeasement, and the British Road to War.* Manchester: Manchester University Press, 1998.

McHugh, James T. and James S. Pacy. *Diplomats Without a Country: Baltic Diplomacy, International Law, and the Cold War.* Santa Barbara, CA: Greenwood Press, 2001.

Mearsheimer, John J. *The Great Delusion: Liberal Dreams and International Realities.* New Haven, CT: Yale University Press, 2018.

Mihaylova, Iva. "Could the Recently Enacted Data Localization Requirements in Russia Backfire?" *Journal of World Trade* 50, no. 2 (2016).

"Міненерговугілля має намір утворити групу за участю представників усіх енергетичних компаній, що входять д." Ukrainian Ministry of Energy, February 12, 2016.

"Military and Security Developments Involving the People's Republic of China 2021 – Annual Report to Congress." Office of the Secretary of Defense, 2021.

Mill, John Stuart Mill. *Essays on Some Unsettled Questions of Political Economy.* London: Longmans, Green, Reader, and Dyer, 1874.

Mitter, Rana. *A Bitter Revolution: China's Struggle with the Modern World.* Oxford: Oxford University Press, 2005.

Mogherini, Federica. "Declaration by the High Representative on Behalf of the EU on Respect for the Rules-Based Order in Cyberspace." Council of the European Union, April 12, 2019. http://www.consilium.europa.eu/en/press/press-releases/2019/04/12/declaration-by-the-high-representative-on-behalf-of-the-eu-on-respect-for-the-rules-based-order-in-cyberspace/.

Morgenthau, Hans J. *Politics Among Nations.* Boston, MA: Knopf, 1948.

———. "The Problem of Sovereignty Reconsidered." *Columbia Law Review* 48, no. 3 (1948): 360–61.

Moynihan, Harriet. "The Application of International Law to State Cyberattacks." Chatham House, December 2019.

Nakamoto, Satoshi. "Bitcoin: A Peer-to-Peer Electronic Cash System." Bitcoin.org, 2008. https://bitcoin.org/bitcoin.pdf.

BIBLIOGRAPHY

Nakasone, Paul M. and Michael Sulmeyer. "How to Compete in Cyberspace." *Foreign Affairs*, 2020.

Narayanamurti, Venkatesh and Toluwalogo Odumosu. *Cycles of Invention and Discovery: Rethinking the Endless Frontier.* Cambridge, MA: Harvard University Press, 2016.

"National Cyber Force Transforms Country's Cyber Capabilities to Protect the UK." GCHQ, November 19, 2020. www.gchq.gov.uk/news/national-cyber-force.

"National Cyber Security Strategy." Estonian Ministry of Economic Affairs and Communications, 2008.

National Security Agency. "Russia/Cybersecurity: Main Intelligence Directorate Cyber Actors [Redacted] Target U.S. Companies and Local U.S. Government Officials." 2017. www.docu mentcloud.org/documents/3766950-NSA-Report-on-Russia-Spearphishing.html# document/p1.

"NATO Rapid Reaction Team to Fight Cyber Attack." NATO, March 13, 2012. http://www. nato.int/cps/en/natohq/news_85161.htm.

"NATO – Secretary General's Annual Report 2019." North Atlantic Treaty Organization, April 21, 2020. www.nato.int/cps/en/natohq/topics_174399.htm.

Neumann, Iver B. "Russia in International Society over the Longue Durée: Lessons from Early Rus' and Early Post-Soviet State Formation." In Raymond Taras, ed., *Russia's Identity in International Relations: Images, Perceptions, Misperceptions* (Abingdon: Routledge, 2014).

Niblett, Robin. "Failure in Afghanistan Won't Weaken America's Alliances." *Foreign Affairs* August 19, 2021. https://www.foreignaffairs.com/articles/united-states/2021-08-19/failure-afghanistan-wont-weaken-americas-alliances.

Nye, Joseph S, Jr. "Deterrence and Dissuasion in Cyberspace." *International Security* 41, no. 3 (January 2017): 44–71.

———. "Nuclear Learning and U.S.–Soviet Security Regimes." *International Security* 41, no. 3 (Summer 1987): 371–402.

———. "Nuclear Lessons for Cyber Security?" *Strategic Studies Quarterly* 5, no. 4 (2011).

———. "The Regime Complex for Managing Global Cyber Activities." Global Commission on Internet Governance Paper Series No. 1 (May 2014).

Obama, Barack H. "Statement by the President on Actions in Response to Russian Malicious Cyber Activity and Harassment." The White House, whitehouse.gov, December 29, 2016. https://obamawhitehouse.archives.gov/the-press-office/2016/12/29/statement-president-actions-response-russian-malicious-cyber-activity.

"Ogarkov on Implications of Military Technology (Interview)." *Krasnaya Zvezda*, May 9, 1984.

"Open-Ended Working Group on Developments in the Field of Information and Telecommunications in the Context of International Security - Final Substantive Report." United Nations General Assembly, March 20, 2021. https://front.un-arm.org/wp-content/uploads/2021/03/Final-report-A-AC.290-2021-CRP.2.pdf.

"Operational Law Handbook, Chapter 5, Standing Rules of Engagement (Instr. 3121.01B)." Chairman of the Joint Chiefs of Staff, June 13, 2015.

Orlov, Aleksandr. *The Secret History of Stalin's Crimes.* New York: Jarrolds, 1953.

Osula, Anna-Maria. "National Cyber Security Organisations: Estonia." Tallinn: NATO Cooperative Cyber Defence Centre of Excellence, March 24, 2015.

Pernik, Piret. "E-Residency and Data Embassies: A Country Without Borders." *European Cybersecurity Journal* 2, no. 1 (2016): 54–61.

Perović, Jeronim. "The Tito–Stalin Split: A Reassessment in Light of New Evidence." *Journal of Cold War Studies* 9, no. 2 (April 2007): 32–63.

Pew Research Center. "Partisanship and Political Animosity in 2016." June 22, 2016. www. pewresearch.org/politics/2016/06/22/partisanship-and-political-animosity-in-2016/.

Pfütze, Peter. *Besuchszeit.* Berlin: Edition Ost, 2007.

Philpott, Daniel. *Revolutions in Sovereignty: How Ideas Shaped Modern International Relations.* Princeton, NJ: Princeton University Press, 2001.

BIBLIOGRAPHY

"Pillars of the International Strategy for Cyberspace." U.S. Office of the Coordinator for Cyber Issues, 2009. https://2009-2017.state.gov/s/cyberissues/strategy/index.htm.

Pinker, Steven. *The Better Angels of Our Nature: Why Violence Has Declined.* New York: Viking Books, 2011.

Plokhy, Serhii. *The Origins of the Slavic Nations: Premodern Identities in Russia, Ukraine, and Belarus.* Cambridge: Cambridge University Press, 2006.

Putin, Vladimir. "Speech and the Following Discussion at the Munich Conference on Security Policy." President of Russia, February 10, 2007. http://en.kremlin.ru/events/president/transcripts/24034.

———. "Основы государственной политики Российской Федерации в области международной информационной безопасности период до 2020 года." Security Council of the Russian Federation, July 24, 2013. http://www.scrf.gov.ru/security/information/document114/.

Quirk, Sean P. "Lawfare in the Disinformation Age: Chinese Interference in Taiwan's 2020 Elections." *Harvard International Law Journal* 62, no. 2 (2021).

Ragsdale, Hugh, V.N. Ponomarev, and Lee H. Hamilton. *Imperial Russian Foreign Policy.* Cambridge: Cambridge University Press, 1993.

Raun, Toivo U. *Estonia and the Estonians*, 2nd edn. Stanford, CA: Hoover Institution Press, 2002.

Raymond, Mark. "Engaging Security and Intelligence Practitioners in the Emerging Cyber Regime Complex." *The Cyber Defense Review* 1, no. 2 (2016): 81–94.

———. "Managing Decentralized Cyber Governance: The Responsibility to Troubleshoot." *Strategic Studies Quarterly* 10 (2016): 123–49.

Reichborn-Kjennerud, Erik and Patrick Cullen. "What Is Hybrid Warfare?" Norwegian Institute of International Affairs, 2016.

"Report on Cyber Deterrence Policy." Executive Office of the President, The White House, 2015.

"Report of the Select Committee on Intelligence United States Senate on Russian Active Measures Campaigns and Interference in the 2016 U.S. Election." U.S. Senate, 116th Congress, July 2019. https://apps.npr.org/documents/document.html?id=6214170-Senate-Intel-Report-On-Election-Interference.

"Resilient Military Systems and the Advanced Cyber Threat." U.S. Department of Defense Science Board, January 2013.

"Resolution 1645 (2005)." UN Security Council, December 20, 2005. www.un.org/en/ga/search/view_doc.asp?symbol=s/res/1645(2005).

"A Review of the FBI's Performance in Deterring, Detecting, and Investigating the Espionage Activities of Robert Philip Hanssen." Office of the Inspector General, August 14, 2002. https://oig.justice.gov/sites/default/files/archive/special/0308/index.htm.

Richey, Mason. "Contemporary Russian Revisionism: Understanding the Kremlin's Hybrid Warfare and the Strategic and Tactical Deployment of Disinformation." *Asia Europe Journal* 16, no. 1 (March 1, 2018): 101–13.

Rid, Thomas and Benjamin Buchanan. "Attributing Cyber Attacks." *Journal of Strategic Studies* 38, no. 1 (2015): 4–37.

Ripsman, Norrin M. and Jack S. Levy. "The Preventive War that Never Happened: Britain, France, and the Rise of Germany in the 1930s." *Security Studies* 16, no. 1 (January–March 2007): 32–67.

Roberts, Adam. "Transformative Military Occupation: Applying the Laws of War and Human Rights." In Michael N. Schmitt and Jelena Pejic, eds, *International Law and Armed Conflict: Exploring the Faultlines* [Essays in Honor of Yoram Dinstein]. Leiden: Brill, 2006.

Robinson, Nick, Laura Kask, and Robert Krimmer. "The Estonian Data Embassy and the Applicability of the Vienna Convention: An Exploratory Analysis." *ICEGOV2019: Proceedings of the 12th International Conference on Theory and Practice of Electronic Governance* (April 2019): 391–96.

Rogin, Josh. "NSA Chief: Cybercrime Constitutes the 'Greatest Transfer of Wealth in History.'" *Foreign Policy*, July 9, 2012.

Roguski, Przemysław. "Application of International Law to Cyber Operations: A Comparative Analysis of States' Views." The Hague Program for Cyber Norms Policy Brief, 2020.

Rovner, Joshua. "Cyber War as an Intelligence Contest." *War on the Rocks*, September 16, 2019. https://warontherocks.com/2019/09/cyber-war-as-an-intelligence-contest/.

Rudner, Martin. "Cyber-Threats to Critical National Infrastructure: An Intelligence Challenge." *International Journal of Intelligence and Counterintelligence* 26, no. 3 (2013).

"Russian State-Sponsored Cyber Actors Targeting Network Infrastructure Devices." Cybersecurity and Infrastructure Security Agency, August 16, 2018. https://us-cert.cisa.gov/ncas/alerts/TA18-106A.

Saakashvili, Mikheil. "Russia's Next Land Grab Won't Be in an Ex-Soviet State. It Will Be in Europe." *Foreign Policy*, March 15, 2019. https://foreignpolicy.com/2019/03/15/russias-next-land-grab-wont-be-in-an-ex-soviet-state-it-will-be-in-europe-putin-saakashvilisweden-finland-arctic-northern-sea-route-baltics-nato/.

Sachs, Jeffrey D. *A New Foreign Policy: Beyond American Exceptionalism*. New York: Columbia University Press, 2018.

Samsel, Haley. "Estonia Creates World's First-Ever 'Data Embassy' to Improve Information Security." Security Today, July 3, 2019. https://securitytoday.com/articles/2019/07/03/estonia-creates-worlds-firstever-data-embassy-to-improve-information-security.aspx.

Sanger, David E. *Confront and Conceal: Obama's Secret Wars and Surprising Use of American Power*. New York: Penguin Random House, 2013.

Sanín, Francisco Gutiérrez and Elisabeth Jean Wood. "Ideology in Civil War: Instrumental Adoption and Beyond." *Journal of Peace Research* 51, no. 2 (March 1, 2014): 213–26.

Sarkisyanz, Emanuel. "Russian Imperialism Reconsidered." In Taras Hunczak, ed. *Russian Imperialism from Ivan the Great to the Revolution*. New Brunswick, NJ: Rutgers University Press, 1974.

Schmitt, Michael N. "International Law in Cyberspace: The Koh Speech and Tallinn Manual Juxtaposed." *Harvard International Law Journal* 54 (December 2012): 25.

———. *Tallinn Manual on the International Law Applicable to Cyber Warfare*. Cambridge: Cambridge University Press, 2013.

———. *Tallinn Manual 2.0 on the International Law Applicable to Cyber Operations*. Cambridge: Cambridge University Press, 2017.

———. "The North Atlantic Alliance and Collective Defense at 70: Confession and Response Revisited." *Emory International Law Review* 34 (2019): 36.

———. "Taming the Lawless Void: Tracking the Evolution of International Law Rules for Cyberspace." *Texas National Security Review* 3, no. 3 (Summer 2020): 32–47.

Schneider, Jacquelyn. "Deterrence in and through Cyberspace." In Eric Gartzke and Jon R. Lindsay, eds. *Cross-Domain Deterrence: Strategy in an Era of Complexity*. Oxford, New York: Oxford University Press, 2019.

Schoen, Fletcher and Christopher J. Lamb. *Deception, Disinformation, and Strategic Communications: How One Interagency Group Made a Major Difference*. Washington, D.C.: National Defense University Press, June 2012.

Schramm, Gotthold. *Der Botschaftsflüchtling*. Berlin: Edition Ost, 2006.

Scobell, Andrew. *China and Strategic Culture*. U.S. Army War College, 2002.

———. "China's Real Strategic Culture: A Great Wall of the Imagination." *Contemporary Security Policy* 35, no. 2 (June 2014).

Scott, David. *China and the International System, 1840–1949: Power, Presence, and Perceptions in a Century of Humiliation*. Albany: State University of New York Press, 2008.

Segal, Adam. "The Code Not Taken: China, the United States, and the Future of Cyber Espionage." *Bulletin of the Atomic Scientists* 69, no. 5 (September 1, 2013): 38–45.

————. "When China Rules the Web," December 2, 2019.

————. "When China Rules the Web: Technology in Service of the State." *Foreign Affairs*, September/October 2018.

Shackelford, Scott J. "Toward Cyberpeace: Managing Cyberattacks through Polycentric Governance." *American University Law Review* 62, no. 5 (2013): 1273–364.

Shalal, Andrea. "Europe Erects Defenses to Counter Russia's Information War." *Reuters*, January 12, 2017. www.reuters.com/article/us-usa-cyber-russia-europe-idUSKBN14W2BY.

Shambaugh, David. *China's Communist Party: Atrophy and Adaptation*. Berkeley: University of California Press, 2008.

Shimer, David. *Rigged: America, Russia, and One Hundred Years of Covert Electoral Interference*. New York: Knopf, 2020.

Shires, James. "The Simulation of Scandal: Hack-and-Leak Operations, the Gulf States, and U.S. Politics." *Texas National Security Review* 3, no. 4 (Fall 2020): 10–29.

Shlapak, David A. and Michael Johnson. *Reinforcing Deterrence on NATO's Eastern Flank: Wargaming the Defense of the Baltics*. Santa Monica, CA: RAND Corporation, 2016.

Shuman, Michael. "Is Taiwan Vulnerable After Putin's Ukraine Invasion?" *The Atlantic*, February 24, 2022, www.theatlantic.com/international/archive/2022/02/vladimir-putin-ukraine-taiwan/622907/.

Sierzputowski, Bartłomiej. "The Data Embassy under Public International Law." *International & Comparative Law Quarterly* 68, no. 1 (January 2019): 225–42.

Singer, J. David. "Man and World Politics: The Psycho-Cultural Interface." *Journal of Social Issues* 24, no. 3 (1968): 127–56.

Smeets, Max. "A Matter of Time: On the Transitory Nature of Cyberweapons." *Journal of Strategic Studies* 41, no. 1 (February 2017).

Smeets, Max. *No Shortcuts: Why States Struggle to Develop a Military Cyber-Force* (London: Hurst, 2022).

Snidal, Duncan B. "Rational Choice and International Relations." In Walter Carlsnaes, Thomas Risse, and Beth A. Simmons, eds. *Handbook of International Relations*. London: SAGE Publications, 2006.

Soesanto, Stefan. "Europe's Incertitude in Cyberspace." *Lawfare* (blog), August 3, 2020. www.lawfareblog.com/europes-incertitude-cyberspace.

Soldatov, Andrei. "The Kremlin and the Hackers: Partners in Crime?" openDemocracy, April 25, 2012. www.opendemocracy.net/en/odr/kremlin-and-hackers-partners-in-crime/.

Soldatov, Andrei and Irina Borogan. *The Red Web*. New York: Public Affairs, 2015.

Spence, Jonathan D. *The Search for Modern China*. London: Hutchinson, 1990.

Stanzel, Melanie Hart, Jabin Jacob, Nadège Rolland, Angela. "Grand Designs: Does China Have a 'Grand Strategy'? *ECFR* (blog), October 18, 2017. https://ecfr.eu/publication/grands_designs_does_china_have_a_grand_strategy/.

"Statement by the North Atlantic Council Concerning Malicious Cyber Activities." NATO, June 3, 2020. http://www.nato.int/cps/en/natohq/official_texts_176136.htm.

"Statement by the Representative of the Russian Federation at the Online Discussion of the Second 'Pre-Draft' of the Final Report of the UN Open-Ended Working Group on Developments in the Field of Information and Telecommunications in the Context of International Security (Unofficial Translation)." Russian Federation, June 15, 2020. https://front.un-arm.org/wp-content/uploads/2020/09/oewg-informal-virtual-meetings-statement-by-the-russian-federation-15-june-2020.pdf.

Stevenson, Richard W. *The Rise and Fall of Détente: Relaxations of Tension in US–Soviet Relations 1953–84*. Chicago: University of Illinois Press, 1985.

Stilz, Anna. "Why Do States Have Territorial Rights?" *International Theory* 1, no. 2 (2009): 185–213.

Stoltenberg, Jens. "Remarks by NATO Secretary General Jens Stoltenberg at the Cyber Defence Pledge Conference, London." NATO, May 23, 2019. www.nato.int/cps/en/natohq/opinions_166039.htm.

BIBLIOGRAPHY

———. "Speech by NATO Secretary General Jens Stoltenberg at the Cyber Defence Pledge Conference (Ecole Militaire, Paris)." NATO, May 15, 2018. www.nato.int/cps/en/natohq/opinions_154462.htm.

———. "Statement by NATO Secretary General Jens Stoltenberg on Russian Cyber Attacks." NATO, October 4, 2018. www.nato.int/cps/en/natohq/news_158911.htm.

A Strong Britain in an Age of Uncertainty: The National Security Strategy. UK Government Cabinet Office, 2010. https://webarchive.nationalarchives.gov.uk/20121018134855/; http://www.direct.gov.uk/prod_consum_dg/groups/dg_digitalassets/@dg/@en/documents/digitalasset/dg_191639.pdf.

"Summary: Department of Defense Cyber Strategy." U.S. Department of Defense, 2018. https://media.defense.gov/2018/Sep/18/2002041658/-1/-1/1/CYBER_STRATEGY_SUMMARY_FINAL.PDF.

Sutter, Robert. *Chinese Foreign Relations: Power and Policy Since the End of the Cold War.* 3rd edition. Lanham, MD: Rowman and Littlefield, 2012.

Tait, Matt. "The Macron Leaks: Are They Real, and Is It Russia?" *Lawfare* (blog), May 8, 2017. www.lawfareblog.com/macron-leaks-are-they-real-and-it-russia.

Tan, Zixian, William Foster, and Seymour Goodman. "China's State-Coordinated Internet Infrastructure." *Communications of the ACM* 42, no. 6 (June 1999).

Tatsumi, Yuki, Pamela Kennedy, and Jason Li. "Taiwan Security Brief – Cybersecurity as a Sine Qua Non of Digital Economy: Turning Taiwan into a Reliable Digital Nation?" Stimson Center, September 2019.

Thachuk, Kimberley. "Corruption and International Security." *The SAIS Review of International Affairs* 25, no. 1 (Winter–Spring 2005): 143–52.

Thucydides. *History of the Peloponnesian War.* Harmondsworth: Penguin Books, 1972.

Touré, Hamadoun I. "The Quest for Cyber Peace." International Telecommunication Union, January 2011.

Tournès, René. "The French Army, 1936," *Foreign Affairs* 14, no. 3 (April 1936): 487–98.

"Treasury Imposes Sanctions Against the Government of The Democratic People's Republic of Korea." U.S. Department of the Treasury, January 2, 2015. www.treasury.gov/press-center/press-releases/Pages/jl9733.aspx.

"Treasury Sanctions Evil Corp, the Russia-Based Cybercriminal Group Behind Dridex Malware." U.S. Department of the Treasury, December 5, 2019. https://home.treasury.gov/news/press-releases/sm845.

"Treasury Sanctions Individuals Laundering Cryptocurrency for Lazarus Group," March 2, 2020. https://home.treasury.gov/news/press-releases/sm924.

"Treasury Sanctions Iranian Entities for Attempted Election Interference." U.S. Department of the Treasury, October 22, 2020. https://home.treasury.gov/news/press-releases/sm1158.

"Treasury Sanctions Russian Cyber Actors for Interference with the 2016 U.S. Elections and Malicious Cyber-Attacks." U.S. Department of the Treasury. Accessed November 19, 2020. https://home.treasury.gov/news/press-releases/sm0312.

"Treasury Sanctions Russian Cyber Actors for Virtual Currency Theft." U.S. Department of the Treasury, September 16, 2020. https://home.treasury.gov/news/press-releases/sm1123.

"Treasury Sanctions Russian Federal Security Service Enablers." U.S. Department of the Treasury, June 11, 2018. https://home.treasury.gov/news/press-releases/sm0410.

"Treasury Sanctions Russian Government Research Institution Connected to the Triton Malware." U.S. Department of the Treasury, October 23, 2020. https://home.treasury.gov/news/press-releases/sm1162.

"Treasury Targets Assets of Russian Financier Who Attempted to Influence 2018 U.S. Elections." U.S. Department of the Treasury, September 30, 2019. https://home.treasury.gov/news/press-releases/sm787.

"Treasury Targets Russian Operatives over Election Interference, World Anti-Doping Agency Hacking, and Other Malign Activities." U.S. Department of the Treasury, December 19, 2018. https://home.treasury.gov/news/press-releases/sm577.

Treisman, Daniel. "Putin's Popularity since 2010: Why Did Support for the Kremlin Plunge, Then Stabilize?" *Post-Soviet Affairs* 30, no. 5 (September 3, 2014): 370–88.

Trenin, Dmitri. "Avoiding U.S.–Russia Military Escalation During the Hybrid War." *Carnegie Endowment for International Peace*, January 2018.

Tully, James. *A Discourse on Property*. Cambridge: Cambridge University Press, 1980.

Turing, Alan M. "On Computable Numbers, with an Application to the Entscheidungsproblem." *Proceedings of the London Mathematical Society* 2, no. 42 (1937 [delivered to the Society in 1936]): 230–6.

Tyson, Neil deGrasse and Avis Lang. *Accessory to War: The Unspoken Alliance Between Astrophysics and the Military*. New York: W.W. Norton, 2018.

"UK and Allies Hold Chinese State Responsible for a Pervasive Pattern of Hacking," July 19, 2021. UK Government, www.gov.uk/government/news/uk-and-allies-hold-chinese-state-responsible-for-a-pervasive-pattern-of-hacking.

Ulam, Adam B. *Stalin: The Man and His Era* (Boston, MA: Beacon, 1989).

———. *The Communists: The Story of Power and Lost Illusions, 1948–1991*. New York: Macmillan, 1992.

"U.S. Charges Five Chinese Military Hackers for Cyber Espionage Against U.S. Corporations and a Labor Organization for Commercial Advantage." U.S. Department of Justice, May 19, 2014. www.justice.gov/opa/pr/us-charges-five-chinese-military-hackers-cyber-espionage-against-us-corporations-and-labor.

"U.S. Charges Russian GRU Officers with International Hacking and Related Influence and Disinformation Operations." U.S. Department of Justice, October 4, 2018. www.justice.gov/opa/pr/us-charges-russian-gru-officers-international-hacking-and-related-influence-and.

Vaile, David, Kevin Kalinich, Patrick Fair, and Adrian Lawrence. *Data Sovereignty and the Cloud: A Board and Executive Officer's Guide*, Version 1.0, Cyberspace Law and Policy Centre, University of New South Wales Faculty of Law (July 2013).

Valeriano, Brandon, and Ryan C. Maness. "How We Stopped Worrying about Cyber Doom and Started Collecting Data." *Politics and Governance* 6, no. 2 (June 11, 2018): 49–60.

———. "The Coming Cyberpeace." *Foreign Affairs*, October 1, 2015.

Volkagonov, Dmitri A. and Stepan A. Tiushkcvich. Война: Советская военная энциклопедия. Moscow: Voenizdat, 1976.

Volkov, Denis. "Russian Elite Opinion after Crimea." Carnegie Endowment for International Peace, March 23, 2016.

Voo, Julia, Irfan Hemani, Simon Jones, Winnona DeSombre, Daniel Cassidy, and Anina Schwarzenbach. "National Cyber Power Index 2020." Belfer Center for Science and International Affairs, Harvard Kennedy School, 2020.

"Wales Summit Declaration," September 5, 2014. NATO. www.nato.int/cps/en/natohq/official_texts_112964.htm.

Wallander, Celeste A. "Western Policy and the Demise of the Soviet Union." *Journal of Cold War Studies* 5, no. 4 (2003): 137–77.

Waller, J. Michael. *Strategic Influence: Public Diplomacy, Counterpropaganda, and Political Warfare*. Washington, D.C.: Institute of World Politics Press, 2009.

Walt, Stephen M. "The End of Hubris and the New Age of American Restraint." *Foreign Affairs*, May/June 2019.

Walter, Barbara F. "The New New Civil Wars." *Annual Review of Political Science* 20, no. 1 (2017): 469–86.

Walzer, Michael. *Just and Unjust Wars: A Moral Argument with Historical Illustrations*. New York: Basic Books, 1977.

Weber, Valentin. "The Worldwide Web of Chinese and Russian Information Controls." Oxford University Centre for Technology and Global Affairs, 2019.

Whittaker, Zack. "Documents Reveal How Russia Wiretaps Phone Companies." *TechCrunch* (blog), September 18, 2019. https://social.techcrunch.com/2019/09/18/russia-sorm-nokia-.

BIBLIOGRAPHY

Wight, Martin. *International Theory: The Three Traditions*. Leicester: Leicester University Press, 1991.

Williams, Michael C. "Hobbes and International Relations: A Reconsideration on JSTOR." *International Organization* 50, no. 2 (1996): 213–36.

Woods, Ngaire. "The United States and the International Financial Institutions: Power and Influence within the World Bank and the International Monetary Fund," in Rosemary Foot, Neil MacFarlane, and Michael Mastanduno, eds, *U.S. Hegemony and International Organizations*. Oxford: Oxford University Press, 2003.

Woolf, Amy F. "The New START Treaty: Central Limits and Key Provisions." Congressional Research Service, February 3, 2021.

Zetter, Kim. "Fixing Democracy: The Election Security Crisis and Solutions for Mending It." *Texas National Security Review*, Fall 2020.

Zhang, Linda. "How to Counter China's Disinformation Campaign in Taiwan." Army University Press, U.S. Army, October 2020.

Zittrain, Jonathan L. and Benjamin G. Edleman. "Internet Filtering in China." *IEEE Internet Computing* (March–April 2003).

INDEX

INDEX

INDEX